THE BULGARIANS

BOOKS BY CHRIST ANASTASOFF

The Bulgarians
A Visit to Yugoslavia
The Case for an Autonomous Macedonia
A Century of Balkan Turmoil
The Tragic Peninsula

Father Paissy (1722-1798) of the Khilandar Monastery at Mount Athos was by far the greatest awakener of the long-forgotten Bulgarian people. In 1762 he wrote the first Slaveno-Bulgarian history which set the spark of the national revival of the Bulgarian people.

THE BULGARIANS

FROM THEIR ARRIVAL IN THE BALKANS TO MODERN TIMES: THIRTEEN CENTURIES OF HISTORY

With Seventeen Maps, a Comprehensive Bibliography on the Balkans, and a Bulgarian Chronology

Christ Anastasoff, M.A.

An Exposition-University Book
Exposition Press   Hicksville, New York

CONTENTS

Chapter V

Byzantium and the Emergence of the Second Bulgarian State (1187-1393)

Chapter VI

Precursors of Bulgarian Self-Preservation and Awakening

MAPS

ILLUSTRATIONS

PREFACE

A comprehensive history of a Slav nation, Bulgaria, is presently especially important. Bulgaria is currently under the direct influence of the Slav-controlled Union of Soviet Socialist Republics, a leading world power. In the light of contemporary history, this is understandable. Any Slav nation, then, constitutes a subject of serious historical study, mainly because of immense probabilities affecting future events.

The author's interest in Bulgarian history dates back to his undergraduate work at Washington University in St. Louis, Missouri. Assigned to write a paper on "The Annexation of Bosnia-Herzegovina by Austria-Hungary in 1908," the author turned from premedical studies to history. Majoring in the latter, he wrote his first work, of 369 pages, *The Tragic Peninsula*, which was published in 1938. To write the history of a people with thirteen centuries of background is, indeed, a difficult task. By undertaking this project, the author in no way claims that it covers the complete story of the Bulgarian people.

The present work is the result of six years of independent research efforts. After thirty years as history teacher of the St. Louis Public School System and as founder and editor in chief of *Balkania* quarterly international magazine (1967-1973), the author had an opportunity to visit Bulgaria for the first time in 1970. Traveling throughout the country and visiting places of historical interest, he had the idea of writing the history of the Bulgarians from their inception on the Balkans to the present time.

Thirteen centuries of history! Leaving the years of their past glory and those of their decline, it is enough to remind ourselves of the fact that Bulgaria was one of the oldest states in Europe and the first Slavic state in the world!

Our emphasis in this work is on the Bulgarian Renaissance of the eighteenth century and the emergence of modern Bulgaria and the fate of its people. Many European and American scholars have written excellent works dealing with one phase or another of the Bulgarians.

For the most part, however, these scholars have failed to incorporate in their works the contribution of the Bulgarian Slavs to world culture and civilization. Realizing that Slavic scholars know little or nothing about Bulgarian liberation leaders and Bulgarian men of art and literature, the author of this work has made an effort to incorporate biographical sketches of such Bulgarians and also the development of Bulgarian literature at different epochs and especially of modern times.

From its scanty origins in the eighteenth century, Bulgarian literature has developed an individuality that differentiates it from the cultures of the other Slavic nations and corresponds to the Bulgarian national character and to the unfortunate fate of the Bulgarian nation. Many Bulgarian literary works, however, are being translated into English, French, German, and Russian.

Because of recent orthographic changes in the termination of Bulgarian personal names, one will encounter in this work two forms of spelling of names. The traditional ending of Bulgarian names is *off*, but since 1923, most Bulgarian personal names have ended with *v*. Thus, the name of the Bulgarian poet and novelist Ivan Vazoff is now written as Ivan Vazov. Either ending of personal names is correct, and both are used in this work.

The author's knowledge of the Bulgarian language has made it possible to consult voluminous documentary works of internationally recognized Bulgarian scholars. Readers will note the comprehensive bibliography, listing sources from which the author has obtained substantial information contained in this work.

In checking the original drafts in the preparation of the manuscript, the author owes a debt of gratitude to his wife, Eva, and also to his professional colleague, Edward I. Glass, M.A., St. Louis University graduate, for valuable suggestions. The frequent quotations throughout the book indicate the author's indebtedness to the various publications dealing with Balkan events and political problems. It is hoped that this work will constitute a contribution toward a more comprehensive understanding of the epochs in the centuries of Bulgarian history and its modern tragic events. For a wider scope of readings, a select bibliography has been added at the end of each chapter. The author, however, is solely responsible for any errors occurring in this work.

Christ Anastasoff

St. Louis, Missouri
April 1977

THE BULGARIANS

PRONUNCIATION OF BULGARIAN SLAV NAMES

The letter *o*, for instance, gives only one sound, not several as in English *no, not, none*. There are no diphthongs as in the English *cow, wise, void*. Each vowel in the Bulgarian language is pronounced separately.

a is always to be pronounced like *a* in *father*
e is always to be pronounced like *e* in *bell*
i is always to be pronounced like *i* in *kill*
o is always to be pronounced like *o* in *dole*
u is always to be pronounced like *u* in *full*

CHAPTER I

SOUTH AND SOUTHEASTERN EUROPE: A GEOGRAPHIC-ETHNOGRAPHIC SETTING

1. *THE IBERIAN PENINSULA*

Europe has three main peninsulas jutting into the Mediterranean. Their inhabitants, at various periods of time, have played a significant part in history. These are the Iberian, the Italian or Apennine, and the Balkan Peninsulas.

The Iberian Peninsula is made up of Spain and Portugal. It joins the European countries to the continent of Africa, which can be seen clearly across the narrow Straits of Gibraltar. Africa has played a large part in the history of the Iberian Peninsula. In 711, the Moors of North Africa invaded the peninsula, thereby spreading the Moslem faith. By 732, they had pushed all the way to Tours, France. There they were defeated and, afterward, settled back to rule the Iberian Peninsula for the next several centuries. Thus, while Christian Europe was going through its "dark ages," the Iberian Peninsula shared in the brilliant Islamic civilization, which had inherited the cultural achievements of ancient Greece, Egypt, and other Middle Eastern peoples.

The Moors, however, were not able to hold northern Spain for long. From their northern stronghold, Christian warriors were gradually able to work south and recover both Spain and Portugal. Granada, the last stronghold of the Moors, fell in 1492. This was the same year that Christopher Columbus made his first voyage to the New World.

Then, for about a hundred years, Spain and Portugal enjoyed a prosperous Golden Age. Columbus and the great Portuguese explorers were followed by others who sailed into uncharted waters to discover new trade routes and virgin continents. In the sixteenth century, income from the New World filled Spanish and Portuguese coffers. Art, architecture, and literature flourished on the Iberian Peninsula. But after the defeat of the Spanish Armada by England in 1588, Spain's influence rapidly declined and that of England rose.

Portugal fared somewhat better because of her alliance with England but, during the next three hundred years, Spain and Portugal both lost many of their colonial possessions, and their world prestige waned. Today, Portugal and Spain have fallen behind the other nations of Western Europe in national power and in the standard of living of their people. Spain and Portugal, however, continue to be important because of their strategic location at the western approach of the Mediterranean Sea.

Yet, at the same time, Spain and Portugal are the most isolated countries of Western Europe. Geographically, the Iberian Peninsula is almost surrounded by water and, on land, is walled off from the rest of Europe by the Pyrenees Mountains. Politically, Spain and Portugal differ from the other Western European countries in that they were, until 1976, both ruled by dictatorships.[1]

2. THE ITALIAN OR APENNINE PENINSULA

Italy has made a rich contribution to the Western world. In ancient times, the great Etruscan civilization flourished in central Italy. Later, the Roman Empire unified the Mediterranean area and carried law and other forms of civilization to much of the known world. Beset by invading armies of barbarians from the north and corruption at home, the Roman Empire declined and fell in 476.

About a thousand years later, however, Italy again became important as the home of the Renaissance, the great revival of learning that swept all Europe in the fourteenth, fifteenth, and sixteenth centuries. In art, architecture, literature, science, and other cultural and intellectual pursuits the other countries of Europe looked to Italy for their inspiration. It was during this period that powerful city-states, such as Florence, Genoa, and Venice, developed in Italy. In part because of their rivalries, Italy did not become united until late in the nineteenth century (1870).

The long Italian Peninsula has a unique shape and topography, often referred to as the Italian "boot," which measures 760 miles from north to south. But, it is only about a hundred miles wide on the average. In the north, the Alps guard Italy's frontiers with France, Switzerland, Austria, and Yugoslavia. The Apennine Mountains curve off the Alps in the west near the coast and stretch south to form the spine of the peninsula. The islands of Sicily and Sardinia lie off the west coast of the "boot."

A great plain between the Alps and the Apennine covers most of northern Italy. Watered by the Po River and its tributaries, the plain contains the most fertile agricultural land as well as the largest industries of Italy. The chief seaport of the region, and of the country, is Genoa.

The Apennine Mountains curve eastward to within a few miles of the Adriatic coast. These mountains have prevented any major cities from being settled between Venice and Bari on the Italian east coast. The Apennines reach all the way south to the toe of the boot, in the southern province of Calabria, and even have peaks on the island of Sicily.

3. THE BALKAN PENINSULA

The Balkan Peninsula has a triangular shape of land jutting into the Mediterranean. Most of its area is covered over by extremely rugged mountains. Pocketed between them is a jigsaw puzzle of separate nationalities and ethnic groups—Albanians, Bulgarians, Greeks, Romanians, Serbs, Turks, and others. Isolated by the mountains, these groups have a long history of warfare, both among themselves and against the many invaders who have swept across the peninsula, such as Persians, Romans, Turks, Russians, and Nazis.

The first two Mediterranean peninsulas—the Iberian and the Italian —are, as we have noted above, surrounded in the north by high, inaccessible, and easy-to-defend mountains, while the Balkan Peninsula is wide open for invasion throughout its northern border, from the estuary of the Danube in Dobrudja all through Romania to Orsava and the valley of Moldava River.

The Balkan Peninsula is bounded by the Adriatic, Aegean, and Black Seas; included therein are Romania, Bulgaria, Greece, Albania, Turkey in Europe, and Yugoslavia. The latter, augmented around Serbia in 1918, extends northwest to Austria and Italy, and may be considered both a Balkan and a central European country. Romania also has had that character since she acquired Transylvania in 1918.

Topographically, Yugoslavia can be divided roughly into four regions:

1. a narrow coastal lowland along the Adriatic Sea;
2. the rock and barren Dinaric Alps;
3. a passage through the mountains, formed by the Morava and Vardar rivers and extending from the Danube to the Aegean Sea;
4. northeastern Yugoslavia, which is part of the plains of the Danube.

The Balkan Mountain range, which crosses Bulgaria from east to west, divides the peninsula into a wider northern region and smaller southern half, starting near the Black Sea south of Varna and extending westward to Vratsa, northeastern Bulgaria; it turns northward across the Danube at Orsava, where it merges with the Transylvanian Alps and Carpathian Mountains, which envelop southeastern Romania from west and north. Another range of high mountains, Rila and Rhodope, branch out south of Sofia and extend southeast almost to Odrin (Adrianople). Between the two above mountains and the Balkan Mountains in the north is the rich Maritsa Valley, while in the south is a narrow but fertile coastline along the Aegean Sea, with the seaports of Kavala, Porto-Lagos, and Dedeagach.

In the western, Serbo-Albanian, and the southern or Greek part of the peninsula, high mountains branch out in different directions. Shar Mountain, which rises west of Skopie, south of Prizdren, and north of Tetovo, is a huge massif extending north along the length of the Adriatic Sea, the Montenegrin and Bosnian chain of mountains, while to the south begin the inaccessible Albanian peaks of the Pindus Mountains and narrow valleys, which continue southeastward into central Greece. Mount Olympus (home of the Greek gods) constitutes the easternmost peak in northern Thessaly and extends along the coast of the Aegean Sea near the entrance to the bay of Salonika (Thessaloniki).

Following the Vardar River from Salonika to Krivolak, Vélés, and Skopie, there extends the famous Vardar basin, which ends at Vrania, from whence begins a far more significant valley, that of Morava, which stretches several hundred miles north to the Danube River. It was through this valley that the old roads from west to east passed to Nish, Sofia, the Maritsa Valley, and on to Constantinople. The roads from east to west and north to south and vice versa are the same ones used in ancient times and by modern European peoples to keep contact with those of the Balkan Peninsula.

A military road from west to east ran through Belgrade, the Morava Valley, Nish, Sofia, Tatar-Pazardjik, Plovdiv, Adrianople, and on to Constantinople. The Romans, and later the Genoese, Venetians, and Ragusans used a shorter road from the Adriatic Sea to Thrace called *Via Egnatia*. The latter passed through Durazzo, Elbasan, the Albanian Mountains, Ohrid, Monastir (Bitolia) and terminated at the Salonika plain. Another road also led to Sofia and through the basins of Struma and Vardar rivers and on to Salonika and Serres.

The Thraco-Illyrians

Scholars believe that one of the oldest settlements of the Balkan Peninsula was by the Thraco-Illyrian tribe. The Illyrians occupied the western part of the peninsula to the Adriatic (Illiricum), while the Thracians occupied the area south of the Balkan Mountains to the Aegean and east to the Black Sea (now referred to as Eastern Rumelia and Thrace). To the Illyrian group belonged the ancient Macedons and Epirots, remnants of whom are noticeable in the present-day Albanians. The Thracians were also divided into a number of tribes. The most important of these tribes were the Moesians, the Tribali, and the Goths. A group of the Goths crossed the Danube during the fourth century B.C. and settled on the northern bank and beyond the river. There they were known as Dacians. The others settled north and south of the Balkan Mountains and made their living as herdsmen and farmers.

In constant contact with the Thraco-Illyrian tribe were the ancient Greeks. They founded many cities along the coastline of the Adriatic, Aegean, and Black Seas but never settled in the hinterland of these cities. The Persian King Darius I (521-486) and later Alexander of Macedonia extended their rule over the Thraco-Illyrians. To keep the Thracians under control, Alexander's father, Philip II, established the city of Philopopolis (the present Bulgarian city of Plovdiv) under his own rule. In the third century B.C., the Celts invaded the Balkan Peninsula. They were called Galathi by the Greeks (hence St. Paul's Epistle to the Galatians).

But the greatest imprint on the Balkan Peninsula was that of the Romans. During the period of the second Punic War (218-201 B.C.), when the Roman Republic was in its heyday, they appeared victoriously in Panonia and Illyria. From that time on to the beginning of the Christian Era, they conquered one after another Greece, Macedonia, Thrace, Moesia, and the entire Balkan territory to the Danube, the Adriatic, the Black, and the Aegean Seas. The conquest of the Balkan Peninsula, however, did not bring settlement of new peoples. The Thraco-Illyrian and Celtic population were thinned out by Roman garrisons and by some colonists and civil servants who brought the Latin language and the Roman civil law and jurisprudence, which characterized the Roman state prior to and after the time of the Emperors.

Rome gained the empire in the East almost without trying. Even before the first Punic War (149-146 B.C.), Alexander's empire had broken up into quarreling fragments. The divided East could not threaten Rome, and Rome did not take much interest in it. Her sole concern was to keep any single power from becoming strong enough to threaten her. When an eastern ruler showed signs of aggression, Rome sent forces to defeat him, but, as soon as the fighting ended, the army and navy returned to the West. This left the people of the East weak and disunited, with little protection against pirates or invaders. Discontent grew when Rome began to send haughty orders, as if to subject peoples. Roman interference finally brought revolt throughout Greece and Macedonia.

This time, Roman armies stayed in the East. Macedonia became a Roman province and Greece practically so (146 B.C.). The king who ruled Asia Minor died in 133 B.C., after having made a will leaving his kingdom to Rome. His lands became another Roman province—the province of Asia. Thus, to Rome had fallen the heritage of Carthage in the West and the heritage of Alexander the Great in the East.

Prior to the Christian Era and ever since, the Balkan Peninsula has been the scene of conflicts and wars. Because the main roads of western, central, and eastern Europe to the continents of Asia and Africa pass through the Balkans, the latter has become the most strategic and most coveted area in southeastern Europe. Hence comes the rivalry for domination not only by the Great European powers but also by the Balkan peoples themselves. And this is the reason we have called the area "The Tragic Peninsula."

SELECT BIBLIOGRAPHY

Gibbon, Edward, *The Decline and Fall of the Roman Empire*, Philadelphia, 1887, Vol. I, pp. 32-33; 186-218.

Professors Kosev, D., Hristo, H., and Angelov D., *Kratka Istoria na Bulgaria* (A Brief History of Bulgaria), Sofia, 1969, pp. 5-16.

McKinley, Howland A. C., and Dann, M. L., *World History in the Making*, New York, 1931, Chapters IV, IX and X.

Robinson, James H., *Medieval and Modern Times*, New York, 1919, Chapters 2 and 3.

Sakuzoff, Yanko, *Bulgarite v Svoyata Istoria*, (The Bulgarians in Their History), Sofia, 1922, pp. 16-19.

West, Willis M., *The Modern World*, Chicago, 1915, Chapters I and II.

NOTE

1. From 1932 to 1968, Dr. Antonio de Oliveria Salazar ruled Portugal with an iron hand. Salazar died on July 27, 1970. Similarly, Generalissimo Francisco Franco held a grip on Spain from 1939 until his death on November 20, 1975. Following Franco's death, the Spanish monarchy was restored with Prince Juan Carlos de Borbon as King of Spain.

CHAPTER II

THE ERA OF
PHILIP AND ALEXANDER
OF MACEDONIA

1. PHILIP II OF MACEDONIA

North of Greece and Thessaly is a mountainous land called Macedonia. In ancient times, it was inhabited by a hardy, warlike people. They lived in small villages, each under a powerful noble. Macedonia had a number of kings, but their power depended on their own ability and the help of the nobles. Most of the people were free peasant shepherds. They lived a herdsman's life, tending their flocks of sheep and goats. Fighting and hunting were really their occupations.

In 359 B.C., a very remarkable young man came to the Macedonian throne. He is known in history as Philip II of Macedon (382-336). Philip was determined to be a real king and to control the unruly Macedonian nobles and people. Instead of depending on the nobles to supply men for an army, he built up the first regular army in Macedonian history. It was the finest fighting unit between the time of the Assyrians and the development of the Roman legions.

After unifying his own kingdom, Philip extended his power by conquering the surrounding tribes. He increased his control of the Aegean coast by taking some Greek towns that Athens claimed as colonies. Then he turned south and began the task of conquering the Greek city-states and putting them under his rule.

Philip's invasion of Greece was strongly opposed by Demosthenes (384-322 B.C.), an outstanding leader of Athens. In stirring speeches, this Athenian urged his fellow citizens to lead Greece against Philip. These orations are referred to as *Philippics*, meaning a spirited speech against some person.

The appeals of Demosthenes had little effect until Philip entered

9

central Greece. Then a hastily formed alliance made a stand against the invading Macedonians, but it was too late. At Chaeronea, in Boetia, the well-drilled and disciplined Macedonian troops overcame the city-state soldiers of Greece. Philip now became the master of all the Greek states except Sparta, which managed to preserve its independence.

But Greek unity was still not accomplished. Philip planned to make himself king of Greece, and to allow some local self-government. He wanted, perhaps, Greek soldiers to join Macedonian troops in an invasion of Persia. Before these ideas could be put in effect, Philip died (336 B.C.). His son and successor, Alexander, was twenty years old.

It did not seem likely that the young Alexander (356-323) would be able to carry out Philip's plans. But those who thought so were wrong. The son proved to be even more remarkable than the father. History knows him as Alexander the Great. Philip did everything to give Alexander the best training and education possible. His military education was in the Macedonian army. He was trained in gymnastics until he was a splendid athlete with a vigorous body. To train Alexander's mind, Philip sent for the great Aristotle himself to be his tutor. Aristotle (384-322 B.C.), was a Macedonian-born philosopher.

When the time came for Alexander to command the army, he proved to be an even greater general than his father. His campaigns are considered among the greatest in history. Some of his battles were such masterpieces of tactics that they are even now studied as models by army officers. He was strong and brave to the point of rashness. His dramatic acts in battle so captured the imagination of his troops that they were willing to die for him

Alexander began his military career by easily putting down rebellions in the Greek city-states and making himself master of Greece. Then he marched into Asia Minor and defeated a Persian army, conquering all Asia Minor and Syria. Next, he invaded Egypt, meeting almost no resistance. From Egypt, he moved into Mesopotamia, defeated another Persian army, and took control of the entire Fertile Crescent.[1]

Alexander's plan was nothing less than a world empire with himself as the head. He wanted to unite all peoples into one, combining the best of the cultures of Greece, Egypt, the Fertile Crescent, and India. Even in his short lifetime, he was able to change the world. It is difficult to imagine what he might have done had he lived a normal time.

Alexander planned to accomplish his united world in two ways. The first was by founding new cities and rebuilding old cities to be the cultural centers of the empire. More than seventy cities were built. Colonies of Greeks and Macedonians were established in each city. Alexandria, in Egypt, is one of the cities that Alexander founded more than two thousand years ago.

The second method aimed at creating a united people. Alexander did everything he could to encourage intermarriages among Macedonians, Greeks, Egyptians, and the people of the Near East. He himself married the daughter of the Persian king and at times wore the robes of a Persian ruler. He took men of all religions into his army or used them as officials in his government. He established a uniform money system for the whole empire to promote prosperity and expand trade, thus bringing the parts closer together economically.

When Alexander died, his plans for a world empire had not been completed. He left no successor and the empire soon fell into three parts: (1) Egypt; (2) Syria, Mesopotamia, and Macedonia; and (3) Greece.

Although Alexander's work was unfinished when he died and his empire fell soon after, his influence was very great. The new cities he founded continued to spread Greek and Near Eastern civilization and culture long after his death. The Mediterranean world had more unity of ideas, trade, and people than ever before. So great was his influence that the period for two centuries after his death is known as the "Hellenistic Age" or the Age of Alexander.

2. THE NAME OF MACEDONIA

The name of Macedonia as a geographic province in the southwestern Balkan Peninsula originates from the name of the Illyrian tribe Macedoni, which had settled there toward the end of the thirteenth century B.C.

This tribe had given the name to the ancient Macedonian state, which had existed until 146 B.C., when it was conquered by the Romans. Its population was heterogeneous but it consisted mainly of Illyrian and Thracian tribes. Except for the name, nothing else connects the present geographic province of Macedonia with the state of Philip II and Alexander the Great. The Macedoni tribe, which had given its name to Macedonia as the Thracian and Moesian tribes had given their names to Thrace and Moesia, was assimilated in the Thraco-Illyrian mass long before the beginning of the Christian era.

With the fall of Macedonia under Roman rule, the use of its name was forbidden, and the province was renamed Pelagonia. Gradually, the Thraco-Illyrian tribes were either destroyed or assimilated. Only an insignificant number of them remained over the mountainous region along the Adriatic Sea.

During the sixth century A.D., the Byzantines began to call Macedonia a province south of Plovdiv (Philopopolis), while present Macedonia, as a geographic region, continued to be called Pelagonia.

Toward the seventh century A.D., when the Slavs had taken over almost the entire Balkan Peninsula and had reached the Peloponnesus, Macedonia was also taken by the Slavs. The following tribes settled there: the Smolyani, Stroumliani, Rinhiti, Sagondati, Dragoviti, and Braiti; they were closely related to the tribes occupying the geographic provinces of Moesia (northern Bulgaria) and Thrace, on which ethnic basis began the creation of the Bulgarian state.

The Slavic tribes that had settled in the ancient provinces of Moesia, Thrace, and Macedonia spoke the same language and had the same customs and beliefs. Gradually, they were bound together into one national community—the Bulgarian. In the ninth century, during the reign of Tsar Boris, the Slavic tribes living in the present geographic province of Macedonia were included in the composition of the Bulgarian state. And it was the dialect of one of these tribes, probably the Dragoviti dwelling on the outskirts of Soloun (Salonika), that the brothers Sts. Cyril and Methodius used as a basis for the construction of the Old Bulgarian literary language.

After the conquest of Bulgaria by the Byzantines during the eleventh century, the country was divided into several provinces. The province south of Plovidiv continued to be called Macedonia. The name of Thrace was applied to the region northwest from Constantinople, while the present geographic province of Macedonia was named Bulgaria.

The name of Macedonia became permanent as the name of the present geographic province only since the fourteenth century. With the westward broadening of the province of Thrace, the name of Macedonia was given to the lands southwest of Thrace.

Macedonia as a geographic province, in the present meaning of the term, was finally defined under the Turkish regime. When the Turks conquered Macedonia in 1371, they found there a compact Bulgarian population that strongly held on to its language, culture, and national traditions. Gradually, there settled in the country other ethnic groups, such as Turks, Albanians, and Greeks, but they were in no position to affect the assimilation of the Bulgarian population. For centuries, the latter felt its identical blood relationship and identity with the inhabitants of Moesia and Thrace (Old Bulgaria). And for many writers and authorities on the Balkans, the geographic expressions *Macedonia* and *Bulgaria* are interchangeable.

From what has been said above, it follows that Macedonia as a geographic province in the southwestern part of the Balkan Peninsula has nothing in common with the ancient Macedonian state, which at various times had embraced different territories on the peninsula, and which, during the period of Alexander of Macedonia, had spread beyond its limits.

The population of contemporary Macedonia has nothing in common with the inhabitants of the ancient Macedonian state. It settled in the limits of the country centuries after the disappearance of the ancient Thraco-Illyrian population and it was of purely Slavic origin. Macedonia's geographical denomination became permanent after the conquest of the Balkan Peninsula by the Turks.

3. HELLENISM AND THE ANCIENT MACEDONIANS

Today, however, there seems to be a widespread confusion about the relationship between the ancient Macedonians and the Greeks. Invariably when one speaks of Macedonia, it seems to many people synonymous with Greece or that the Macedonians are "Greeks." Even many scholars of history entertain this idea. Might we ask the question: Were Philip II and his son, Alexander the Great, Greek? Are the Macedonians really of ancient Hellenic descent? Has modern Greece a moral and ethnic claim to Macedonia? Does the acceptance of Hellenistic culture make one a Greek? Similarly, does the acceptance of the Roman culture in the West make the Latin countries Italian?

We shall briefly consider here the question of the nationality and the national consciousness of the ancient Macedonians, because upon its determination depends, in general, the understanding of Macedonian history. There are authorities on antiquity and ancient Hellenism who deny the theory of the Hellenistic descent of the Macedonians. Professor Gavril E. Katsarov has recently made an excellent study on the epoch of Philip II of Macedonia. Other historians, such as G. Busolt, Edward Meyer, A. Schafer, and J. Kaerst, have also made tremendous contributions on ancient Hellenism. In these works, one finds information perhaps unacceptable to Greek propagandists.

The theory of the Hellenistic descent of the Macedonians is mainly championed tendentiously by Greek scholars only, thus laying the foundation for Greece's pretentions to dominate Macedonian provinces totally inhabited by alien ethnic elements. But these are hopeless efforts, because even if it could be proven beyond any doubt that the ancient Macedonians were related to the Greeks, that in itself would not give contemporary Greece the right to claim or dominate Macedonia. The Greeks of today are delighted to claim descent from the ancient Greeks, and they deafen the world with their propaganda on behalf of Hellenism. But they forget that the ancient Greeks and Romans have long ago disappeared as nations, in the melting pot of the various tribal elements that have invaded Hellas and Italy; there have sprung up new nations that have laid the foundation for the organization of modern political states.

As far as the Hellenistic culture is concerned, it has broken off from its national basis ever since Alexander the Great. His conquests did not necessarily represent expanding Hellenic political rule, but only its culture, which at that time was influenced by the oriental cultures and was unable to preserve its peculiarity intact. In exchange, it had attained a cosmopolitan character that made it easier for foreign nations to accept it. The Hellenistic culture had also been accepted by the Romans, who even spread it in the western parts of their Empire. During the Roman period, Hellas found itself in complete political, economic, and intellectual decline; its creative power was already extinguished and it was living only with its glorious past.

The Hellenistic culture continued to flourish in the provinces of what was once Alexander's Empire, especially in Egypt, Syria, and Asia Minor; but the culture of the eastern elements, which have not been suffocated by Hellenism, in course of time began to develop and began more and more to project itself to the detriment of the Greeks. That is the reason why the Byzantine culture of the oriental and Christian elements played an even more important role than that of the Helleno-Romans. Today, it has positively been established that the Byzantine culture cannot be considered a continuation of that of the ancient Greeks; on the contrary, all the nations that were incorporated into the Byzantine Empire have contributed to its growth and development. In view of these historical facts, one can readily see how unfounded the Greek pretensions of inheriting the Byzantine Empire are. Italy could just as well lay claim over the lands once included in the former Roman Empire. This is, of course, absurd. On the basis of this, the modern Greeks ought to stop talking about antiquated Hellenistic rights, but they cannot fool any thoughtful person who has the historical development in view.

Fortunate were the Macedonian people to have such a powerful and creative leader as Philip II, who was able to organize a state in opposition to the then existing Greek city-states. In Macedonia there were no city-states such as those in Greece; there were no slaves in such number and servitude as in Greece. While an absolute democracy prevailed in ancient Greece, Macedonia presented a national democratic monarchy in which political and social conditions were entirely different from those in Greece. The Macedonian people had their own religion and were conscious of their own national political state. The Greeks, on the other hand, were organized in city-states, and thus lacked national political unity. The Macedonians were basically different from the Hellenic people, and perhaps that is why the fate and the role that these two nations have played in world history are also completely different. For the first time in history, the Macedonian people were able to create a powerful state, something that the Greeks, despite their high culture, were not able to accomplish.

Ancient Macedonia maintained its independence until 146 B.C., when the country was included in the Roman Empire. In the sixth century A.D., Macedonia was invaded by the Slavic-Bulgarian people. In the course of time, the Macedonians were assimilated by the Slavs and lost their language, but fragments of their physical and spiritual qualities continue to exist among their descendants even to the present. Some of the ancient Macedonian anthropological and spiritual features preserved by the Macedonian Slavs today are bravery, endurance, indestructible energy, statesmanship, a highly developed national feeling, and patriotism. These are, indeed, some of the inherited qualities from the ancient Macdonians. Must one enumerate examples to illustrate these qualities? Was not Macedonia the fatherland of the two brothers, Cyril and Methodius, who created conditions for the origin and development of the Slavic literature and culture? Was not Father Paissy, the precursor of the Bulgarian Renaissance, born in Macedonia?

The feeling of nationalism was so deeply embedded in the hearts of the Macedonians that there was no force strong enough to extinguish it. Notwithstanding the darkness that befell the Bulgarian Slavs after the Turkish conquest of the Balkans, the national feeling in Macedonia did not disappear; it remained dormant, waiting only for an opportune moment to rise again. It has been proven beyond any doubt that the Bulgarian Renaissance in the early part of the nineteenth century began in Macedonia; it was there that the struggle for national Bulgarian church rights began and later turned into a struggle for Bulgarian freedom and independence. The political and revolutionary movement in Macedonia in the last seven decades undoubtedly constitute an epic; there are numerous examples of valor, persistence, and limitless self-abnegation for the cause of ideals such as are seldom found in the history of other nations.

It is because of this spirit that the Macedonians of today are hoping that someday the sun of freedom will rise over the horizon of their country. Then, too, the Macedonian people will have the opportunity to develop their talents fully and thus contribute to mankind's culture.

SELECT BIBLIOGRAPHY

Davis, W. S., *Readings in Ancient History—Greece*, Chapters 9 and 10 (Selections on Alexander and the Hellenistic Period).

Ferguson, William S., *Greek Imperialism*, New York, 1913, pp. 116-148.

Ginn, Edwin (Editor), *Plutarch's Lives*, New York, 1902, Chapter 3 (Life of Alexander).

Gunther, John, *Alexander the Great*, New York, 1953. The author recounts the young Macedonian's brief and glorious years as king, giving us a sense of the interaction of Alexander's personality and the historical events of his day.

Haaren and Poland, *Famous Men of Greece*, New York, 1904, Chapter 24, Philip of Macedon; Chapter 25, Story of Alexander; Chapter 26, Demosthenes, The Great Orator of Athens.

Katsaroff, Dr. Gavnil I., *Tsar Philip II Makedonski—Istoria na Makedonia do 386 godiny Predy Hrista* (King Philip II of Macedon, History of Macedonia until 336 B.C.), Sofia, 1922, Part II, pp. 159-275; pp. 294-304.

Lamb, Harold, *Alexander of Macedon*, New York, 1946. A stirring account of a most interesting man.

Sakuzoff, Yanko, *Bulgarite v Svuyata Istoria* (The Bulgarians in Their History), Sofia, 1922, pp. 22-25.

Wells, H. G., *The Outline of History*, New York, 1921, pp. 310-341.

Wheeler, B. I., *Alexander the Great*, New York, 1900, Chapters 10 and 31.

NOTE

1. The term "Fertile Crescent" is given to that region which runs up along the eastern end of the Mediterranean Sea and swings over in a half-circle south of the highlands of Armenia and Anatolia. Then it goes down the valley of the Tigris-Euphrates rivers to the Persian Gulf. Because its shape is something like the new moon, it is called a crescent.

CHAPTER III

THE ROMAN-BYZANTINE WORLD

I. *ITS GEOGRAPHIC AND POLITICAL EXTENT*

The area of the Roman Empire embraced the Mediterranean fringe of the three continents—Europe, Africa, and Asia; it was a broad belt stretching from the Euphrates in the east to England in the west and between southern deserts to the northern waters of the Rhine, the Danube, and the Black Sea. Its territory was about as large as that of the United States of America.

In language, and somewhat in culture, the western part of the Empire remained Latin and the eastern part Greek, but trade, travel, and the mild and just Roman law made the world one in feeling. Britons, Africans, and Asians knew one another only as Romans.

To attain these vast territories, Rome had launched a policy of expansion. As a result of the Punic Wars (264-146 B.C.), North Africa became a Roman province. The Romans were then undisputed rulers of the central and western Mediterranean Sea.

To the east lay the former empire of Alexander the Great, with its predominant Hellenistic (Greek) civilization. It was, of course, divided into several kingdoms, none of which was strong enough to resist Roman power. Macedonia and some of the Greek city-states had joined Carthage, Rome's rival, against the Romans several times during the first two Punic Wars. Each time Rome defeated them but did not take territory. When Macedonia broke her treaty again and attacked Rome during the third Punic War, Rome conquered both Macedonia and the Greek city-states, making them Roman provinces in 146 B.C.

Between 264 and 146 B.C., the Roman state developed from a federation of Italian cities into a great Mediterranean empire. The consequences were far-reaching. The growth of the empire changed Roman culture and altered the course of European history.

The Roman Empire would undoubtedly have collapsed from inner

17

weakness except for two able emperors who ruled during the end of the third century and the first part of the fourth century A.D. By then it was too late to save the empire entirely. The reforms and reorganization of Diocletian and Constantine, however, postponed the collapse of the western empire for a hundred years and that of the east for more than a thousand years.

Diocletian (A.D. 284-305) was the son of a humble peasant from the eastern shore of the Adriatic Sea. He had risen through the ranks of the army to become a general. The army made him emperor but he proved to be very different from the other "barracks" emperors. He was an able organizer and administrator.

But with two emperors—Constantine and Diocletian—it was necessary to divide the territory of the empire. The most natural division was that of separating the country into the Latin and Greek halves. Latin was the official language of Italy, France, Spain, Britain, and North Africa. This became the territory of the western emperor, whose capital naturally was Rome. Greek was spoken and was the official language of Greece and the Near East. These became the territory of Diocletian as eastern emperor.

Constantine, known in history as the Great (A.D. 312-337), came to power in the western half of the empire seven years after Diocletian surprisingly resigned. Constantine's reign is known for two great events. The first was the legal recognition of the Christian religion. He became ruler in the east as well as the west in 324. The second great event of his reign was the moving of the eastern capital to a new and stronger city, which he built on the site of Byzantium, founded by the Greeks about one thousand years before. This new city was named Constantinople. Today it is the Turkish city of Istanbul.

Under Diocletian and Constantine, then, the entire empire was reorganized and in some ways strengthened. Power had shifted away from Rome to the east, where wealth was. The fact that both Diocletian and Constantine wanted to rule the eastern empire tells its own story.

At first the empire was called the Eastern Roman Empire in distinction from the Western Roman Empire, whose capital was Rome. Later on, it assumed the name of its capital, Byzantium, or Byzantine Empire. During the Middle Ages, it was the greatest, most powerful, and most civilized country in Europe. Its boundaries stretched beyond the Danube and the Euphrates. They often included all of the Caucasus, the whole of Armenia, and sometimes all of Dalmatia in Europe. But as long as it retained Constantinople, the Byzantine Empire was able to maintain its existence. Constantinople once lost, the empire was lost also. That happened twice: first when the Crusaders captured the Byzantine capital (1204) and when Mohammed II entered the city (1453) and occupied the throne of the Byzantine emperors.

2. APPEARANCE OF AND INVASION
BY NOMADIC TRIBES

From the fourth to the tenth century, however, the Empire was continually harassed and her territory encroached upon by Goths, Huns, Vandals, Slavs, Persians, Anti, Bulgarians, Avars, Serbians, Hungarians, Russians, Arabs, and others of meaningful but lesser significance. The Empire had received the most serious wounds, leaving the deepest scars, from the Slavs, and particularly from the Bulgarians.

Some of the invading nations only passed through the Empire, devastated and plundered its cities and provinces, and left. Such were the Goths, Huns, Russians, and others. Some of them occupied some of the Empire's provinces, settled and remained in them. Such were the Slavs, who began to immigrate into the Balkan Peninsula during the sixth century, and, later on, the Bulgarians, who came from the Ural region in the seventh century. During the sixth century, Slavic tribes had seized one by one Moesia (northern Bulgar, south of the Danube River), Thrace, Macedonia, Dardania, a large part of Epirus, Thessaly, and the Peloponnesus. The entire region from the Danube River to the Aegean Sea and the Peloponnesus, according to Dr. Constantine Jireček, the Czech historian, was called Slavonia.

The Slavic tribes that settled in Moesia, Thrace, Macedonia, and Dardania were more fortunate than their kinsmen in the Peloponnesus, Thessaly, and Epirus. Here they succeeded in preserving their individuality and soon created in the Balkan Peninsula a state of their own, church, literature, and culture.

In the tenth century, the invasion into the Empire had ceased, and the peoples who had settled in it established themselves first as vassals to Byzantium and, subsequently, as independent states. The first free country within the boundaries of the Byzantine Empire was Bulgaria. With its appearance, the vassalage of the Slavic states gradually vanished. The other nations to emerge as free states within the Empire were the Serbians, the Crotians, the Hungarians, and, later, in the eighth century, the Romanians. Thus Bulgarians, Serbians, and Romanians, after centuries of struggle against Byzantium as well as against each other, finally settled and delineated their ethnic boundary lines. During the Middle Ages, although the political confines of these states fluctuated, their ethnic settlements remained the same. These ethnic boundaries remained as they were during the tenth century and as they are today. The Turkish invasion of the Balkan Peninsula resulted only in the changing of the Byzantine *Basileus* (Emperor) to the Turkish *Sultan* and in the colonization of Turks in Thrace and other Balkan provinces.

The Byzantine Empire at the period of its foundation was a motley of nations and languages. From the fourth to the tenth centuries, that racial mosaic became still more variegated. The Empire was called Roman, but ethnologically it was neither Roman nor Greek. During its existence, it was able to impose its name upon the Greeks only. But from the very beginning, the Greeks, though possessing a higher culture, preferred to call themselves *Romani* or *Romaioi,* instead of *Hellenes* or *Greeks.* When the Turks captured Constantinople, they found the Greeks calling themselves with their new name. Thus, they applied it to the entire Greek people and church, that is, *Roum-mileti* (Roman people), *Roum-klissesi* (Roman church). The Greek historian Professor Paparrhigopoulo of the University of Athens says that the Hellenes had sacrificed their name in order to become masters of the Empire.

No real Romans existed in the Byzantine Empire, or, if there were any, they were very few. The Emperor, the Church, and the government officials used the Greek language. Nevertheless, the Empire was by no means Greek, neither were its emperors and public men. The patriarchs and men of letters were often persons of alien descent. The Empire was a cosmopolitan country where the opportunities for advancement to the hierarchical ranks in the clerical, civil, and military administration and even to the very throne itself were open to all talented persons irrespective of their ethnic character. That was due to the fact that Roman citizens were scarce, while the Greek element was far too insignificant in point of number to be able to satisfy the great need for government and church officials. For that reason, the Empire was compelled to avail itself of the services of able and qualified men found among the other races of which the Empire was composed. It drew its armies, war chiefs, magistrates, even its patriarchs and emperors from the Slavs, Armenians, Goths, Hosars, Arabs, Albanians, and other racial groups.

During the Middle Ages, however, a radical change took place both in the spirit and in the aims of the Empire. At that time, when Bulgaria, Serbia, and Romania, on the Balkan Peninsula, began to assert themselves as independent states, the Byzantine Empire found itself pushed toward the Aegean Sea and left only with the Greek and part of the Slavic element, the latter driven there by a wave of historical necessity. The Greek emperors and patriarchs occupying the thrones of Constantinople during that period had encroached upon the historical documents and records of Byzantium, changing and counterfeiting them, with the result that the Roman or Byzantine Empire was thus converted into a purely Greek entity. They had set themselves a new task: to subjugate, with arms and culture, the Slavic and other states by assimilating all foreign elements and converting them to Greek. The struggle began with Bulgaria, the strongest Slavic state and the one nearest to Byzantium.

The struggle between Greeks and Bulgarians continued incessantly from the reign of Anastasius II (713-715) to the invasion of the Balkans by the Turks. It was carried on not only on the field of battle but also in the school and church. During the Turkish domination of the Peninsula, the conflict was narrowed down to a struggle principally between the Bulgarian and the Greek Patriarchy, the latter no longer championing the aims and ideals of the Byzantine Empire but those of the Greeks.

Next to the Greeks, the Slavs and the Armenians supplied the Byzantine Empire with the greatest number of talented men, and all other races helped to enhance the glory and grandeur of the Byzantine rulers. Which one of the two races was more conducive to absorption is still an open question. One thing, however, is certain, and that is that both the Slavs and the Armenians gave the Empire a large number of chief magistrates, patricians, and writers, and even patriarchs, emperors, and empresses. This fact is not only not denied by Greek historians but frankly admitted by them. The Greek Professor Paparrhigopoulo writes: "Another means of attracting foreigners to the Empire was opening to them wide the doors for civil and military posts. Being fascinated by such privileges, the Slavs seem more easily than the other races to have conformed with the existing order of things. The emperors Justin and Justinian are a splendid example of this. A great many Goths and Alants were thus tamed. The Bulgarians alone remained obdurate. Indeed they studied in Constantinople, but even as conquered and slaves they imbibed as much knowledge as was expedient under the circumstances, always looking for an opportunity of escaping into their own country in order to resume their desperate struggle against Hellenism."[1]

Rambaud, Drinoff, Jireček, Paparrhigopoulo, and other Byzantine and Balkan authorities generally agree that the dynasty of Justinus I (518-527), from which Justinian (527-565) descended, and the dynasty of Basilius I (867-886) were not Greek; neither were those of Leo V (813-820) and Romanus I (920-944).

SELECT BIBLIOGRAPHY

Arnold, W. T., *Roman System of Principal Administration to the Accession of Constantine the Great*, New York, 1914 (Book for Library-Reprint).

Bury, John B., *History of the Eastern Roman Empire*, London, 1912, pp. 395-399.

Mishew, D., *The Bulgarians in the Past*, Lausanne, 1919, pp. 1-19; 100-169.

Paparrhigopoulo, M., *Histoire de la Civilisation Hellénique*, Paris, 1878, pp. 305-308.

Rambaud, M., *L'Empire Grec au Deuxième Siècle*, Paris, 1870, pp. 220-230.
Robinson, James H., *Medieval and Modern Times*, New York, 1919, Chapters 2 and 3.
Sakuzoff, Yanko, *Bulgarite v Svoyata Istoria* (Bulgaria in Its History), Sofia, 1922, Chapters 1, 2, and 3.
Willis, Mason W., *The Modern World*, New York, 1915, Chapters II and V.
Yearbook of The University of Sofia, Vol. *XLIV*, Book 2, 1948, pp. 1-36.

NOTE

1. M. Paparrhigopoulo, *Histoire de la Civilisation Hellénique*, Paris, 1878, p. 305.

CHAPTER IV

THE ESTABLISHMENT OF THE FIRST BULGARIAN STATE (679-1018): BYZANTIUM RECOGNITION 681

1. SLAVS AND BULGARIANS

The original homeland of the Bulgarians is commonly believed to have been the northern coast of the Caspian Sea, extending as far as India, Persia, and even China. Being one of the numerous Tiranian tribes —Huns, Avars, Turks, Magayars—the Bulgarians had lived a primitive, nomadic life for centuries, that is, until they appeared on the borders of Europe. The various tribes of the Proto-Bulgarians who had settled between the Don and Volga rivers and north of the Caucasus Mountains between the Caspian and Black Seas had formed a tribal league called "Great Bulgaria." This took place about the end of the sixth century (585). The leader of this league was Khan Kubart, educated in Byzantium. After Kubart's death (650), the "Great Bulgaria" began to collapse under the constant pressure of the Avars and Khazars, two powerful tribes. During the second half of the seventh century (670), however, the unification of the seven Slavic tribes took place in Moesia, between the Balkan Mountains and the Danube River. Part of the Proto-Bulgarian tribes, under the leadership of Khan Asparuh, settled in southern Bessarabia, and from here they began their attack against Byzantium; an alliance was formed between the Slavs and the Proto-Bulgarians.

However, the victorious Proto-Bulgarians led by Khan Asparuh had made an agreement with the local Slavic aristocracy, who were at the head of the various tribes. It was at this time that measures were taken for the foundation of a Bulgaro-Slavic state with Pliska as its capital

23

(679). This state was now strong enough to strike not only against Byzantium but also against any other enemy.

Soon after the agreement had been consummated with the Slavic aristocracy, Khan Asparuh renewed the war against Byzantium and advanced south into Byzantine territory or what is now northeastern Bulgaria. The Byzantine emperor Constantine IV (Poganatus) was compelled by the advancing Proto-Bulgarians to sue for peace. A peace treaty was signed in 681 with provisions that Byzantium pay annual indemnity. *And it was by this very act, the new Bulgaro-Slavic state was recognized by Byzantium.*

When the Eastern Goths or Ostrogoths invaded the Danubian province of Byzantium, the Emperor Zino (474-491) for the first time called on the "Bulgarians" for help. This occurred in 480, only several years after the fall of the Empire in the West (476) to the attacks of German tribes under Attila.

Nevertheless, the Byzantine Empire received the most serious blows from the Slavs, and particularly from the Bulgarians. Its history and the geography of the early Middle Ages clearly show this evidence. The ethnographic cast of the Balkan Peninsula is a living witness of these wounds and traces.

As we have noted, some of the invading tribes only passed through the Empire, devastating and plundering its cities and provinces and leaving the country. Such were the Goths, the Huns, the Avars, the Hazars, the Pechenegs, the Koumans, and others. Some of them continued their invasions for centuries, occupied some of its provinces, settled and remained there. Such were the Slavs, who began the influx into the Balkan Peninsula during the fifth and sixth centuries, and later on the Bulgarians during the seventh century. The Slavic tribes seized one by one Moesia, Thrace, Macedonia, Dardania, a large part of Epirus, Thessaly, and the Peloponnesus. The entire region south of the Danube River was referred to as Slavonia. The invading tribes assumed the names of the territory they had occupied, such as Northerners, Branichevs, Kouchevans, Timokchans, Moravians, Bizaks, Strumanians, Somalians, Richins, Sagudats, Dragovitchi, Voinitchi, Vesselichi, Zagorians, Militzi, Ezertsi, and others. The whole of the Peloponnesus was settled by Slavs, mainly by Militzi, Ezertsi, and Dragovitchi. Such settlements were found as far as Laconia, in Sparta, and in Attica—clear to the gates of Athens itself. However, Christianity and the Greek civilization absorbed them. They were assimilated by the more cultured native element; surviving are only the names of their settlements.

In the tenth century, under the jurisdiction of the Larosa episcopacy, there existed the *Ezero* bishopric, which is believed to have derived its name from the Slavs called Ezertsi, or "lake settlers." The Slavs changed the name of the Peloponnesus itself. Since the Middle Ages, its geographical name has generally been Morea. Throughout Morea, the appellations of scores of settlements, mountains, and plains are Slavonic. Such is the case with both Epirus and Thessaly.

Other Slavic tribes settled in Illyria, Bosnia-Herzegovina, Zachloumie, Duclea, Dalmatia, Pannonia, and other places. They were called Serbs, Harvats, Bosnians, Zachloumians, Travonians, Ducleans, Pannonians, Dalmatians and so on. "The Slav Element," writes Rambaud, "changed the language of both geography and history; it compelled the Byzantine authors to speak not only of Moesia, Thrace, Dardania, Epirus, Hellas, and the Peloponnesus but also of Bulgaria, Serbia, Moravia, Slavonia, Zagoria, Morea, and Bersetia. Almost to the walls of Athens, in the sacred Eleusia, is found a Slavic inscription. Lenorman notes down as Slav colonies the villages Vrania, Bastani, Varnaby, Matsi, Tchourka, Brana, lying in the plains and upon the slopes of Marathon and Zouno in the plain of Eleusia.

"On the Peloponnesus we rely upon the accurate evidence collected by Falmerier, who, after scrutinizing the topographical appellations, district by district, and after carefully examining the etymology of each, arrives at the same conclusion as Constantine VII[1] did, viz., that the entire Peninsula had become Slavonian. In the first place, is the very name of Morea, which superseded the old name of the island of Pelops and which in Slavonic means 'maritime country'; the names of mountains, such as Hulm in Achaia, to towns such as Orechovo, Shelmina in Lacomia, of counties such as Slavochorion or Slavonia in Mecenia; Zagora in Arcadia; Veligosta on the ruins of the same Mantinea that had seen the fall of Epaminondas; Goritsa perched upon the site of ancient Tegea; Nicla, which in turn gives over its place to Trigolitza.

"But in citing these results obtained from topographical and etymological investigations made by Falmerier, one should not forget the objections raised against the above assertions. Lick, for example, assures us that in the geography of the Peloponnesus one Slavonic name stands against ten Greek ones.

"The Greek Emperors often waged war against the two Slavonians— against the southern and Macedonian Slavonians."[2]

Referring to this matter, Dr. Constantine Ireček writes: "Not only Epirus and Thessaly, but Hellas itself, the ancient and famous plains of the Peloponnesus, Athens, and Bosnia are covered with Slavonian appellations of localities. Three-fourths of the local names testify of the Slavic settlements now extinct. Helicon is known by the name of Zagory and close to Marathon is found a village called Vranya. Here we discover the mountain Hemos (Hulm) and the well-known villages: Bistritsa, Boucovina, Goritza, Granitza, Kamenitza, Nivitza, Podgora, Tsenitsa, and so on. In a Venetian record of the year A.D. 1293, Tsaconitza is given simply as 'Sclavonia de Morea.' The modern name of the Peloponnesus

Falmerier derives from the Slavic word *more*. Kopitar, however, is opposed to this view, while today Professor Hopf proves that *Morea* is a mere metathesis of *Romea,* la Mourée, l'Amorea."[3]

In his map of the Peloponnesus, Hellas, and Thessaly without the islands, Kiepert,[4] a noted geographer, grades the geographical names in the following proportions: three-fourths Slavic, one-tenth Albanian, one-tenth new Greeks, and only one-tenth ancient.[5]

The Slavic tribes that settled in Moesia, Thrace, Macedonia, and Dardania were more fortunate than their kinsmen in the Peloponnesus, Thessaly, and Epirus. Here they succeeded in preserving their individuality and soon created in the Balkan Peninsula a state of their own, with their own church, literature, and culture.

A Turanian race, akin to the long since vanished Avars and the still surviving Turks, Finns, and Magyars, the Bulgarians crossed the Danube during the sixth and seventh centuries and invaded the various Slavic tribes who had already been settled in what is now Bulgaria, Thrace, and Macedonia. Few in number, the Bulgarians intermarried with the subjugated Slavs and thus they were absorbed into the Slav bloodstream. *Today the name "Bulgar" is the only thing left of the eastern origin of the Bulgarian nation, which by race, language, customs, and local traditions has become entirely Slav.* But the final assimilation of the Bulgarian race was consummated by the adoption of the *Glagolic* alphabet, invented by the two Salonika brothers—Cyril and Methodius—and used in Slavic liturgy and literature.

Referring to the assimilation of the Bulgarians, Professors Kosev, Hristov, and Angelov write: "The conversion of the Slavic-Bulgarian state to Christianity contributed most substantially for the final formation of the Bulgarian nation. Their common religion created conditions in the process of assimilating the Proto-Bulgarian minority within the Slavic mass of people. The Slav language spoken by the vast majority of the population emerged triumphantly, preserved its grammatical structure, its basic speech and vocabulary and continued to develop within its grammatical rules, while that of the Proto-Bulgarian language was constantly losing its quality and gradually disappeared. This disappearance has been so effective that today one can hardly find fifteen Proto-Bulgarian words in the Bulgarian language whose origin is, in part, doubtful."[6]

The Slavs who colonized in the Balkan Peninsula in the fifth and sixth centuries led an isolated tribe life. Some of them established principalities vassal to the Byzantine Empire; others formed loose organizations under the direct control of Constantinople. Under the leadership of Khan Kubrat (584-642) and later of his son, Prince Asparuh (644-701), the Bulgarians appeared in Dobrudja and Moesia, conquered the northern Slavs, and *established the first Bulgarian kingdom in 679, with Pliska as its capital.*

Although it had to face many serious foes, the new kingdom managed to preserve its independence and power. Under Khan Krum (803-814), Bulgaria displayed such energy and dash that it shook the foundations of the Byzantine Empire. The Bulgarians came to the very doors of Constantinople. During Krum's reign, the frontiers of Bulgaria reached beyond the Danube River and as far as the Transylvanian Mountains on the north and almost to the city of Adrianople on the south. Krum also occupied Sofia.

Under Presian (836-852) and Boris I (852-889), Bulgaria extended its limits northwest to Iber River and southwest beyond Ohrid. Almost the whole of Macedonia was included in the Bulgarian state. A century later (892), under Simeon (Symeon, 893-927), who was the first to assume the title of *Tsar*, the Bulgarians founded their first Empire. It extended at first over the whole of Bulgaria, Thrace, Macedonia, and Epirus. But under Tsar Samuel (Samuil, 993-1014), the eastern provinces were lost, leaving only the western part, with its capital of Ohrid, western Macedonia, where it maintained its independence until 1018. The city of Ohrid acquired in the tradition of the Bulgaro-Macedonians a spiritual and sentimental prestige that is still retained.

2. THE EFFORT TO ESTABLISH
THE BULGARIAN CHURCH AND LITERATURE

The Byzantine Emperor Romanus I (920-944) felt the impetuous threat of the Slavs directed by the Bulgarians. Tsar Simeon, too, felt the fascinating power of civilization exerted by Byzantium, which was the work of Romans and Greeks, and which was such a potent instrument for the preservation of the Empire. In the personality of Simeon, Byzantium saw the Slavs no more as "barbarians" armed with weapons only, but as warriors armed also with books and with a culture pushing for more room for its might, energy, and enterprising spirit. Side by side with the Roman and Greek literature, a new one, the Slavic, was making its appearance over the horizon, and Bulgaria, from the time of Tsar Simeon the Great to the fourteenth century, became the center of Slav learning and civilization.

The predominant idea of the Bulgarian Tsars was the consolidation of Slavdom on the Balkan Peninsula and the creation of a Slavic literature and culture able to hold its own against the rival Greek and Latin. The seed of this idea was originally sown by Boris I (852-889), the first Bulgarian Christian Tsar and Slavic saint. In bringing about the conversion to Christianity of the Bulgarian people, Tsar Boris did not make his state spiritually subordinate either to Rome or to Byzantium but founded an independent national church. This was an epochal achievement because at the time of the conversion to Christianity of their respective nations none of the Serbian Jupans (lords), the Russian Grand Dukes, Prince St. Vladimir, or the Hungarian-Wallachian *Voyvoda* (chief) Alexander were able to accomplish this. Although Serbia, Russia, and Romania were politically independent countries, religiously they remained for a long period of time under the jurisdiction of foreign religious authority.

Before going under the spiritual leadership of the Constantinople Greek Patriarchate, that is, after their conversion, the Serbians used the Latin language in their churches. Such was not the case with Tsar Boris. He made the question of conversion a *sine qua non* for a national church. One of the inquiries that he had made through his emissaries to Pope Nicholas I (858-867) was: May Bulgaria have a Patriarch of its own? The same point he raised before the Constantinople Patriarch. By posing this question, however, he had run against the existing church traditions. Neither Rome nor Constantinople recognized an independent church for any particular nation. Because education at that time was connected with the church and represented by it, Tsar Boris was equally apprehensive of both the eastern and western churches. He had other important reasons for assuming this policy. The newly born Slavic literature and education were in need of a special care lest they should be stifled and crushed at their very appearance in the world. Boris's conception of an independent national church was undoubtedly the greatest achievement of the first Bulgarian Christian Tsar.

His son and successor, Simeon (893-927), took up his father's bequest for an independent national church and literature and brought it to its full realization. During his reign, Bulgaria laid the foundation of a state church. He was able to achieve this success through his treaties with the pope, whose benediction sanctioned the new institution. During Simeon's time, Bulgaria, besides a free church, had its own writers and Slavic literature, which quickly spread among the other Slavs, driving out the Greek and Latin.

Under Simeon the Great, the Bulgarian nation experienced its Golden Age of literature and culture. Referring to this period of Bulgarian literature, the great scholar of Slavic linguistics, Vitroslav Iagič (1838-1923), in explaining the character and significance of the Old Bulgarian literature and language, writes: "The ancient Bulgarian literature attained such a phenomenal development in the number of books of a church and religious character able to accumulate that it justly takes its ranks side by side with the richest literature of those days, viz., the Greek and Latin. It certainly surpassed all of other European literature of the same kind. Strictly speaking, during those times, church literature existed in only three languages: Greek, Latin, and Slavic."[7]

Discussing the same subject, two American Slavic scholars, Clarence Manning and Roman Smal-Stoki, write: "Summing up, we may say that this old Bulgarian literature and the period of Bulgarian history in which it was produced are of fundamental importance to the whole Slavdom. Bulgaria succeeded in maintaining and preserving the achievement of the Slavic apostles and educators in Great Moravia; it gave the Slavs a Slavic church language for divine service which soon became the Slavic literary language of the time; it presented to the Slavs a rather impressive literature and thus laid the basis for Slavic education and culture. Bulgaria is the cradle of Slavic civilization. From the earliest times, this Bulgarian-Slavic Christianity was marked by a deep emotional consciousness of race and nationality."[8]

Under Simeon's successor, Peter (927-969), by order of the Byzantine Emperor Romanus I, the Patriarch of Constantinople recognized the autonomy of the Bulgarian church. The integrity of the church continued during the reign of Samuel (993-1014), but, after the fall of the eastern Bulgarian state, he removed the seat of the Bulgarian church to western Bulgaria, first to Sofia (Serdica) and then to Ohrid, western Macedonia. Here it was able to maintain its existence even after the fall of the western Bulgarian kingdom (1018), now under the name of the Ohrid Archbishopric. The Greek Emperor Basilius II, by his three edicts given to the Ochrid Archbishop Joan in 1020, confirmed the religious rights of the Bulgarians and the independence of the Ohrid Archbishopric. In one of these edicts, he defines its dioceses and the number of bishoprics constituting it. The Bulgarian Archbishopric in Ohrid existed until 1767, when the Greek Patriarch of Constantinople prevailed upon the Turkish government to abolish it.

If the conversion of the Bulgarian people was considered an event of great importance during the ninth century, then the conception of a Slavic alphabet was undoubtedly the greatest achievement in the world in general and Slavdom in particular. A challenge to the centuries-old prevailing Greek and Latin alphabet and literature was presented not by Tsar Boris or Simeon the Great but by the Salonika brothers, Cyril and Methodius, who inculcated the same idea into the minds of their numerous Slavic pupils and followers, the majority of whom inhabited Macedonia.

3. STS. CYRIL AND METHODIUS— THE FOUNDERS OF THE SLAVIC ALPHABET— AND THEIR MISSIONARY WORK

The most significant event in the history of the Bulgarian people, occurring in the first half of the ninth century, was the creation of the Slavic alphabet and the subsequent emergence of the first Slavic literature.

The creation of the Slavic alphabet was a historical necessity. In the

Sts. Cyril and Methodious of Salonika

course of three centuries, the Bulgarian state had made considerable social, economic, and political progress; it had become a large and powerful state but it lacked its own national alphabet. To satisfy the cultural and educational needs for its Slavic national element, an alphabet other than that of the Greek was necessary. In Bulgaria, at least, such an alphabet was needed more particularly because of the conversion to Christianity by Tsar Boris in 885.

The creation of the Slavic alphabet was the work of the famous Slavic educators and brothers, Sts. Cyril and Methodius. Both of them were born in Salonika, the capital of Macedonia. St. Methodius was born in 825 and St. Cyril in 827; his secular name was Constantine. Their father, Leon, was a nobleman and a Byzantine magistrate.

Although the two brothers came from a prominent family, they soon renounced secular honors. St. Methodius, after studying law, was appointed governor of the Macedonian province of Strymon, where the Slavic population predominated; but a few years later he abandoned the post and retired to the monastery of St. Basil on Olympus.

St. Cyril studied under the best scholars at the Imperial Court under the reign of Michael III (856-867), specializing in Greek literature, rhetoric, music, and dialectics. Because of his thorough education, he held for a time the office of Secretary to the Patriarchate and Librarian at the Cathedral of St. Sophia in Constantinople.

After a brief retreat to a monastery on the Bosporus, Cyril accepted a professorship at the famous University of Constantinople. It was because of this that Cyril also had the surname "The Philosopher." Soon he entered the priesthood and joined Methodius in the monastery. In their missionary work, Cyril was the philosopher, while Methodius was noted for his administrative ability. Being of Slavic descent, both of them spoke the old Slavic language fluently.

At this time, Cyril had heard that the Slavs could not understand the Divine Service and the Bible. He set himself, therefore, to compose an alphabet to meet all the requirements of the Slavic or "Glagolic" speech, with its many sounds. The two brothers set themselves to inventing the necessary alphabet by taking letters from the Greek, Criptic, and Armenian alphabets. Scholars of the Old Slavic alphabet consider Cyril the author of the more difficult *Glagolitza* script (862), contending that the *Cyrillic* alphabet was invented by his disciple, St. Clement of Ohrid, some decades later. The *Glagolitza* (in the Old Slavic *glagol* means "word," hence a sign that speaks) is still being used in liturgical services in the eastern Slavic countries.

The *Cyrillic* alphabet derives from the Greek uncials (*uncialis*) of the ninth century, to which were added other letters (signs) that express Slavic sounds for which there was no equivalent in Greek. This less complicated alphabet has been and is still used by the Bulgarians,

Russians, Serbs, Ukranians, and others in their liturgical and literary works. Although the Croats, Slovenes, Czechs, Slovaks, and Poles are Slavs, they employ the Latin alphabet in both instances.

Fluent in the then Slavic language, Cyril and Methodius were greatly concerned about the pagan mass of Slavs and how to convert them to Christianity. But their work could not be effective without the translation of the Gospel and liturgical books into the native language. Having composed the alphabet, Cyril in cooperation with his brother, Methodius, began the translation of the Scriptures and the necessary liturgical books. These works were spread not only in Bulgaria but also throughout the Slavic world.

When Photios was elevated to the Patriarchate in 860, both brothers were invited to become active in the life of the church. A people known as Khazars had settled in Crimea and around the Black Sea in southern Russia. In 860, the Khazars petitioned Constantinople to send them Christian missionaries, and the first to be sent there (861) were Cyril and Methodius. With the help of the newly invented alphabet, the *Glagolitza,* they succeeded in Christianizing all of the Khazars. Their Khan (ruling prince) himself was among the converts.

Immediately after the Khazar mission, a delegation arrived (862) in Constantinople from Moravia (now part of Czechoslovakia). Rostislav (846-870), the ruler of Moravia-Bohemia, having established an independent kingdom known as the "Great Moravian Empire," had driven out the German influence and asked for Christian teachers and missionaries who could preach to his people and conduct Divine Service in their Slavonic tongue.

Sts. Cyril and Methodius were again selected for this service. Once in Moravia (863-867), they began translating the Scriptures and liturgical books from the Greek. This activity aroused the German clergy of the neighboring states. They were opposed not so much to the Byzantine rite as to the popular vernacular speech being used as a medium of worship. The German clergy were stressing that only Latin, Hebrew, and Greek could be used in celebrating the Mass, because these languages had been represented in the inscription on Christ's cross. Wearied by continued complaints against the Salonika brothers, the pope (Adrian II) interrupted their three years of missionary work by summoning them to Rome. Convinced by Cyril's arguments that the Slavic language used in the liturgy was the best means of conveying Christianity to the Moravian pagans, the pope sealed his confidence in them by blessing their translations of the Scriptures and by celebrating Mass over them. While in Rome, Cyril and Methodius were both consecrated as bishops. Amid the honors lavished upon them, Cyril fell ill and on February 14, 869, passed away at the age of forty-two. He was buried in the lower Basilica of St. Clement's Church in Rome.

GERMAN EMPIRE

HUNGARY

Danube

Cumans

Dniestr

Pechenegs

Wallachians

Pechenegs

Belgrade

Serbs

CROATIA

Spalato

Ragusa

Antivari

Durazzo

ITALY

Normans

Rome

Bulgarian Preslav

Niš

Sofia

Bulgarians

BYZANTINE EMPIRE

Ochrid

Ioannina

Corfu

Nicopolis

Thessalonica

Larissa

Adrianople

Constantinople

Abydos

Smyrna
Ephesus

Lesbos

Athens

Patras

SICILY
Islam

The Byzantine Empire in the Tenth Century and the Bulgarians

33

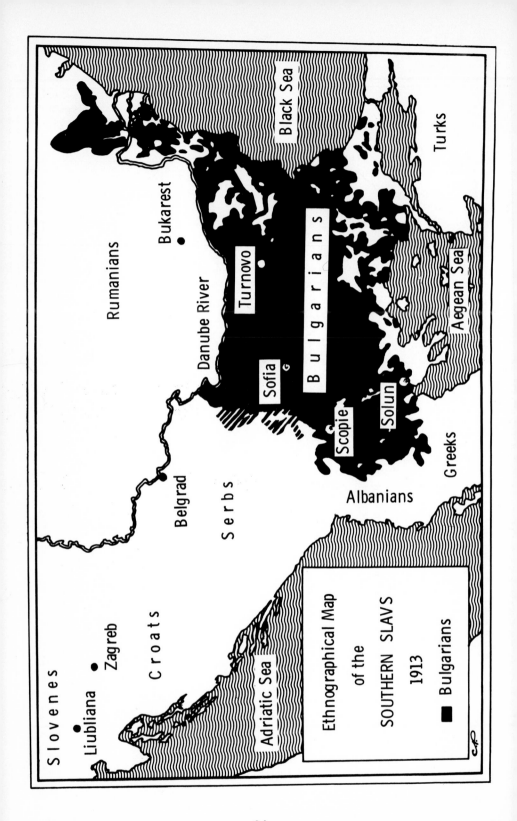

Ethnographical Map
of the
SOUTHERN SLAVS
1913

■ Bulgarians

Black Sea

Turks

Bukarest

Rumanians

Danube River

Turnovo

Bulgarians

Aegean Sea

Sofia

Scopie

Solun

Belgrad

Serbs

Greeks

Albanians

Slovenes

Liubliana

Zagreb

Croats

Adriatic Sea

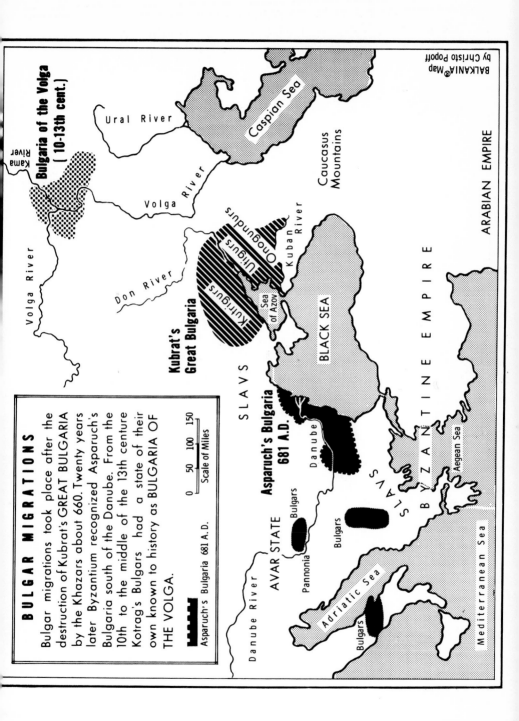

BULGAR MIGRATIONS

Bulgar migrations took place after the destruction of Kubrat's GREAT BULGARIA by the Khazars about 660. Twenty years later Byzantium recognized Asparuch's Bulgaria south of the Danube. From the 10th to the middle of the 13th century Kotrag's Bulgars had a state of their own known to history as BULGARIA OF THE VOLGA.

0   50   100   150
Scale of Miles

Asparuch's Bulgaria 681 A.D.

Bulgaria of the Volga
(10-13th cent.)

Kubrat's
Great Bulgaria

Kutrigurs

Utigurs

Onogundurs

Asparuch's Bulgaria
681 A.D.

AVAR STATE

Pannonia

Bulgars

Bulgars

Bulgars

SLAVS

SLAVS

BYZANTINE EMPIRE

ARABIAN EMPIRE

Caspian Sea

Ural River

Kama River

Volga River

Volga River

Don River

Kuban River

Caucasus Mountains

Sea of Azov

BLACK SEA

Danube

Danube River

Adriatic Sea

Aegean Sea

Mediterranean Sea

BALKANIA® Map
by Christo Popoff

35

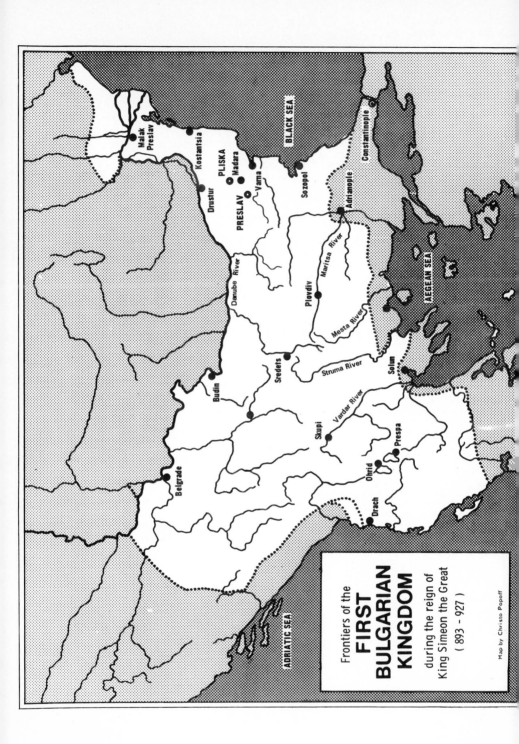

Frontiers of the
FIRST BULGARIAN KINGDOM
during the reign of
King Simeon the Great
(893 - 927)

Map by Christo Popoff

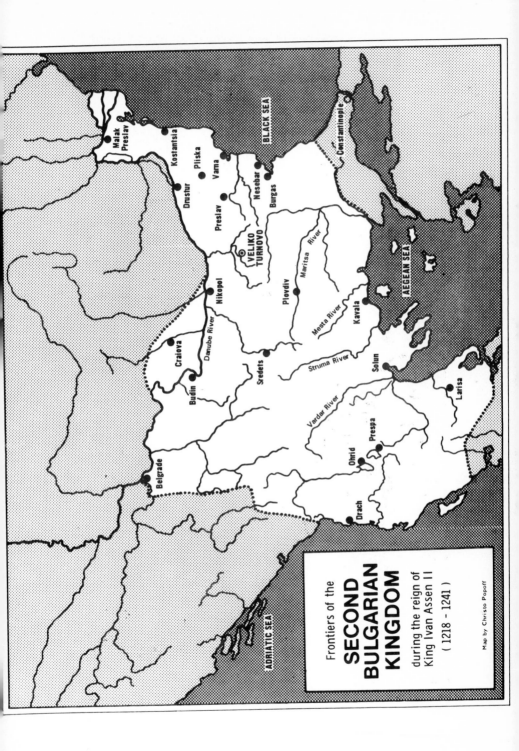

Frontiers of the
SECOND BULGARIAN KINGDOM
during the reign of
King Ivan Assen II
(1218 - 1241)

Map by Christo Popoff

ADRIATIC SEA

BLACK SEA

AEGEAN SEA

Malak Preslav
Kostantsia
Drustur
Pliska
Preslav
Varna
Nesebar
Burgas
Constantinople
VELIKO TURNOVO
Maritsa River
Plovdiv
Mesta River
Kavala
Nikopol
Danube River
Craiova
Sredets
Struma River
Solun
Budin
Vardar River
Larisa
Belgrade
Prespa
Ohrid
Drach

37

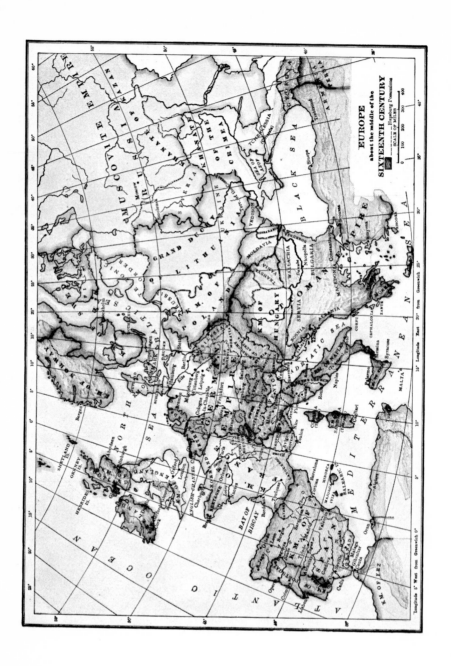

EUROPE
about the middle of the
SIXTEENTH CENTURY

38

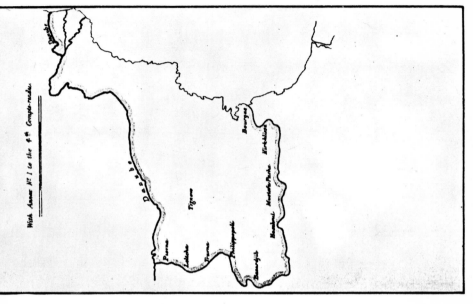

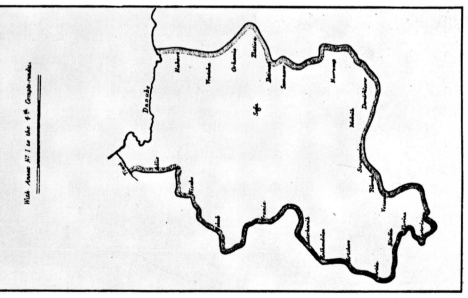

Bulgaria According to the Ambassadorial Conference, Constantinople, 1876

*The Ottoman Empire
in Europe After the
Treaty of Berlin and
the Territorial Reduction
of San Stefano, Bulgaria*

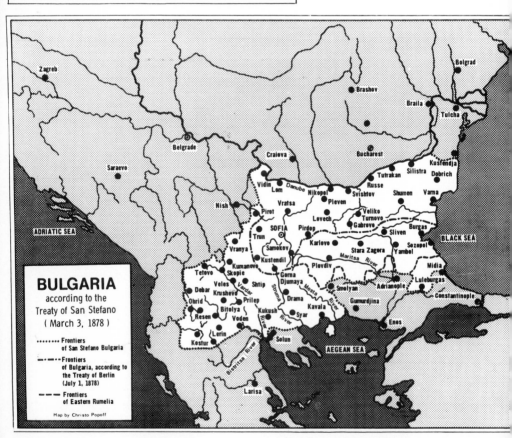

BULGARIA
according to the
Treaty of San Stefano
(March 3, 1878)

········· Frontiers
of San Stefano Bulgaria

-·-·-· Frontiers
of Bulgaria, according to
the Treaty of Berlin
(July 1, 1878)

- - - Frontiers
of Eastern Rumelia

Map by Christo Popoff

After his brother's death, St. Methodius returned to Moravia to continue his missionary work despite the enormous opposition against him. Pope Adrian II (867-872) had created for Methodius the Archbishopric of Sirmium, a site near modern Mitrovica. But Methodius's mission was constantly hampered by the bitter attacks of the German bishops of Salzburg and Passau, who regarded his archbishopric as cutting into their dioceses. Enlisting the help of King Ludwig of Bavaria, the German bishops succeeded in 871 in forcing Methodius to leave his archbishopric. Returning to Constantinople in 882, he undertook to complete the translation of the Bible. Exhausted physically after twenty-two years of missionary work among the Slavs, he died in 885 at the age of sixty.

Because of the continued persecution by the German bishops, the pupils and assistants of Cyril and Methodius in their missionary work in Moravia and Pannonia had been compelled to return to Bulgaria. In need of teachers and preachers in his civilizing mission, Tsar Boris I received them with joy and gratification. They were more than two hundred in number. The most prominent of these pupils and assistants were St. Clement of Ohrid (Macedonia), Naum, Gorasd, Angelarius, and others.

4. ST. CLEMENT OF OHRID

Perhaps the most distinguished pupil and disciple of Sts. Cyril and Methodius was St. Clement of Ohrid (835-916). He and Naum were the first Slavic teachers in Bulgaria. But St. Clement was the first Bulgarian pedagogue. His field of education and evangelical activity was Koutmichevitza in western Macedonia, including Albania, which was then a part of Bulgaria. No less brilliant educational and literary activity was carried on in Macedonia, whose center of culture was the city of Ohrid. In this respect, its guiding spirit was St. Clement, one of the most learned and zealous exponents of Sts. Cyril and Methodius. The educational work of Macedonia was extended by two secondary stations, Glavinitza and Devol in Albania. In this respect, Ohrid vied with Preslav, the capital of Simeon the Great. As in Preslav all literary men received their direction from Tsar Simeon, so in Ohrid all went to St. Clement, who was the central figure; he had for his co-workers his fellow students Naum, a man fond of learning, and Gorasd, a person endowed with strong will and master of the Slav, Latin, and Greek languages.

St. Clement was one of the most active apostles, orators, and teachers and one of the most productive writers during Tsar Simeon's epoch. To him, as we have noted, is attributed the honor of inventing the *Cyrillic* alphabet, while Sts. Cyril and Methodius were the authors of the

Glagolic one. From a social and religious point of view, he played a part second to that of Simeon the Great. St. Clement and Tsar Simeon are two Slavic men of genius in the ninth century. They were the men who have done most for Slavic civilization, while Sts. Cyril and Methodius were the original inspirers.

The foundation for preaching the Gospel was first laid by St. Clement. Seeing that the people were ignorant, that the majority of the priests could only read the Scriptures without understanding them, and that no sermon in the Bulgarian tongue existed, he wrote precepts and sermons for all holy days. Some of the precepts were written in a simple language accessible to the uneducated congregation, while others treated lofty subjects and were expressed in rhetorical style. The first type are Sunday instructions, while the others are praise sermons or panegyrics. St. Clement wrote the biographies of his illustrious teachers—Sts. Cyril and Methodius—and also translated religious books from foreign authors. He was constantly traveling about from place to place in southwestern Macedonia preaching the Gospel. By his activity, St. Clement had the opportunity to teach the reading and writing of the Slavonic language to more than 3,500 students. Many of them became teachers and were assigned among the various districts. Of the above number, he prepared about three hundred as readers, deacons, and priests and sent them out to different parts of Bulgaria. St. Clement was, therefore, the first Slavic pedagogue, the "Pestalozzi" of the ninth century.

The successor to Tsar Boris I, as pointed out above, was his younger son, Simeon. The latter found Bulgaria in most friendly relations with Byzantium. The half a century of peace between these two countries helped Bulgaria to develop not only socially and economically but also culturally. Because of the promotions of cultural and literary works, Slavic scholars consider Simeon's reign as the "Golden Age of Bulgaria." Referring to this period, Dr. Constantine Ireček writes: "The age of Simeon is the Golden epoch of the Bulgarian literature." And Mishev states: "He was, undoubtedly, the best-educated Bulgarian and one of the few great men of learning in Europe during the ninth century." The court of Simeon the Great was the first Bulgarian academy. It was filled with books and was constantly frequented by men of letters. The Tsar himself wrote books and essays.

5. THE BYZANTINE-BULGARIAN WARS —THE END OF THE FIRST BULGARIAN STATE

In the reign of Tsar Peter and Tsar Samuel, the Bulgarian literature continued its course of development but not with such a tempo as it had during the reign of Simeon the Great. The disturbed state of affairs in the country under Tsar Peter was not favorable to literary achievement, and the conditions under Samuel's reign were no more favorable. The entire reign of both Tsars was taken up with wars against the attacks by the rulers of the Byzantine Empire. But the final blow against Tsar Samuel's Bulgaria occurred in October 1014.

Leading a huge army, Vasilius II came from the north and attacked Samuel's troops in the Valley of Kluch, situated between Ograjden and the Belasitsa Mountains. Samuel saved himself only because Gavril Radomir, his son, had somehow helped him to escape. Samuel arrived in Prilep, but fifteen thousand of his troops were made prisoners. The Byzantines put out the eyes of ninety-nine of every hundred of these prisoners, leaving one man in every hundred with *one* eye, to guide the others home. When Samuel saw his blinded troops, he fainted and never again recovered. Neither of his two successors—Gavril Radomir (1014-1015) and Ivan Vladoslav (1015-1018)—was in a position to save the situation, and thereby Samuel's Bulgaria fell under Byzantine rule. Thus the final phase of the First Bulgarian State (679-1018) came to an end.

6. THE BOGOMIL MOVEMENT

Prior to the conversion and even after it, there existed among the Bulgarians not only preachers of Orthodox Christianity but also Christian sects who introduced into Christianity the Iranian (Persian) dualism of deity. The latter were mostly Armenians and Syrians transplanted into Moesia (northern Bulgaria) and Thrace by the Byzantine Emperors. Among these settlers were found Manicheans, Paulicians, and Massilians. Aggressive sectarians, they succeeded in spreading their doctrine among the Slavic people. The reasons for their success were the existence of the following:

1. a pagan Slavic theology;
2. the dogma and rituals of Orthodox Christianity;
3. the alien state and church forms of administration;
4. the sectarian dogmas of the Manicheans, Paulicians, and Massilians;
5. the Roman and Byzantine rivalry to win and spiritually subjugate the Bulgarians, and
6. the failure of the lives and practices of the clerical class to conform with the teachings of Christianity.

The new sectarian doctrine was a protest against the existing religious mode and primarily against the Byzantine church and state organization. This protesting movement, called *Bogomilstvo*, had its start in Bulgaria during the reign of Tsar Peter I, about the end of the tenth century. The movement was named after its founder, Father Bogomil, who was the first Bulgarian Christian reformer. He was, perhaps, the first precursor of

John Wycliff, John Huss, Huldreich Zwingli, Martin Luther, and John Calvin.

The Bogomil doctrine appealed to Christians to free themselves from Rome and Constantinople and seek salvation only in the pure Gospel truths, in the moral and religious perfection of man, and in the liberation of the mind and soul from every authority. As a protest movement against the state and the church, the Bogomil doctrine had two parts: a religious and a political and social one.

The Bogomils' doctrine of belief was dualistic. It recognized two coequal supreme beings: the God of Good and the God of Evil. The first was God the Father; the second Satanael, his son. God the Father was the creator of the invisible world, while Satanael stood at the head of the angels.

The Bogomils rejected the church teaching, the sacraments, hierarchy, rituals, and liturgy. Icon worship was considered idolatry, and they abhorred and turned away from the cross, because it was taken as an instrument of punishment. They did not worship Holy Mary because they did not believe she was the mother of Jesus Christ; they did not consider the relics sacred because they thought that on them stood demons who performed miracles and allured men.

They rejected the Holy Communion because they believed that the water and the bread had been created by Satanael. For the same reason, they rejected baptism with water but accepted the baptism with spirit and fire as it is in the Gospels. They confessed their sins and did penance publicly but without enumerating their sins.

The Bogomils did not believe in the resurrection of the body, which they believed had been created by Satanael, but only in the resurrection of the soul. They built no temples because they believed the demons would live in them, asserting that Satan himself had lived in the temple of Jerusalem and later in the church of St. Sophia (in Constantinople). They prayed four times daily and as often during the night, either outdoors or in their own houses. They read the Lord's Prayer, and whenever they prayed they set the book of the Gospels on a chair covered with a white cover.

The Bogomils rejected the marriage sacraments and were opposed to matrimony. All those who married could annul the marriage whenever one of the parties, especially the husband, wished it.

No holy days were observed by the Bogomils. They even worked on Sunday. They ate no fish, butter, or milk, preferring vegetable food, cabbage, olives, and olive oil. They were in fact vegetarians.

Of the Scriptures they believed only in the Gospel, the Epistles, and the Apocalypse (Revelations).

According to the tenets of the Bogomils, homicide, or the killing of any being whatever, with the exception of snakes, which were considered the work of the devil, constituted the greatest crime. The Bogomil sect was against every form of killing, even in self-defense. They were also against capital punishment and against war. They recognized no spiritual or civil authority. The Bogomils taught disobedience to the authorities, hated the kings, spoke disparagingly of the elders, reproached the *boyars* (lords or privileged class), and instigated the slaves to cease working for their masters.

The Bogomils were divided into *credentes,* or believers, and *perfecti,* or the selected. The believers in their daily life were not distinguished from the other Christians; they were allowed to marry, to serve the state, and to go to war. It was different with the selected. Their life was hard and severe. They were not allowed to be seen at public gatherings, to attend weddings or national festivals, to enter inns, to get angry, to eat meat or drink wine. They observed a most strict fasting and lived only on vegetable food. They shunned society life and devoted themselves to preaching and were always ready to die for the principles they propagated. The *perfecti* or selected were highly respected by the believers for their exalted virtues.

The Bogomils were organized into religious communities, which were strictly democratic. In them, all members enjoyed equal privileges. There was no distinction between believers and the selected, between men and women. Any man or woman having reached majority could become a preacher. The religious communities were represented by three orders: the bishops or father, the apostle or organizer, and the visitor or the man. The religious representatives did not consider themselves invested with any right or authority received at a sacrament; they rather looked upon themselves as authorized members of the communities. The apostles would go from place to place to preach and teach. The Bogomil communities formed parishes at the head of which stood a bishop.

In the reign of Tsar Peter I, the church of Bulgaria was finally reorganized after the fashion of the Byzantine hierarchical government and assumed an important place in the state. The Bulgarian Patriarchy then counted some forty dioceses or bishoprics, as many as were comprised by the Byzantine Patriarchy. Both the Patriarch and the bishops surrounded their seats of authority with a luxury and splendor that vied with the magnificence of their Byzantine rival. The Patriarchal staff in Constantinople included about forty clericals; the same number was adopted for the church officials attached to the court of the Bulgarian Patriarch. Some of the Bulgarian bishops considered it below their dignity to have a staff of less than forty members. In the Byzantine Empire, all civil processes were placed under the jurisdiction of the church. The same thing was introduced in Bulgaria, where the bishops enjoyed still wider privileges. Bulgaria's higher clergy had always acted on the side of the king and his dynasty.

The wealth of the higher clergy and its material opulence developed in it a passion for luxury, which inspired it with a sense of rivalry with the Byzantine church hierarchy. The love for pomposity and a life of dissolution increased its avaricious appetites and its greed for amassing great riches, the realization of which was accompanied with all sorts of abuses. While the clergy rendered partial justce, it, nevertheless, resorted to extortion and wronged the helpless.

The people, naturally, were not and could not be content with the rule of their royal and spiritual leaders. They failed to see in the ranks of the clergy any longer the enthusiastic teachers, diliigieint writers, and preachers of the time of Simeon the Great. Few of the clergy who were able to write were dedicated to teaching and preaching, and fewer still followed the footsteps of St. Clement of Ohrid. The majority of the clericals preferred a prodigal life, pleasures, feasts, and intemperance. The few virtuous members of the clergy, unable to bear the clerical malpractices, withdrew into the mountain monastery fastnesses, where they became hermits. Among these, one should mention Ivan Rilski, the founder of the Monastery, Prochor Pshinski, Gabriel Lesnovski, and Joachim Ossogovski, in whose memory monasteries were built in Macedonia.

The real social and spiritual malefactors at that time were the kings, emperors, popes, patriarchs, feudal landlords, and other oppressors. To fight against them, Father Bogomil appeared on the Balkan scene with Bible in hand. On his evangelical banner were written the words "Slavic democracy, equality, justice, religious, and political freedom."

When the Byzantine general John Zimisces (969-976) entered Preslav, the capital, and occupied Tsar Peter's domains, it was that creed that drew the Bulgarians close to their Tsar Samuel in his struggle against the Greeks, and it was under the inspiration of the same doctrine that a hundred and eighty years later the Bulgarians, led by Assen and Peter, renewed the struggle against the Greeks.

Such then was the Slavic and the human side of the teachings of the Bogomils. Because it was more Slavic than Paulician or Manichean, the Bogomilian belief found acceptance in all Slavic lands—in Bosnia, Dalmatia, Serbia, Bohemia, and other places. Because it was human in its views, it made its way into other countries in western Europe, in Italy, southern France, Germany, and even England. The Bogomilian followers and communities were known under various names. In Bulgaria, they were known as Bogomili, Babuni, Technikeri, and Torbeshi; in Greece, as Bogomili or Tundaiti; in Bosnia and Italy, as Patareni and Cathari; in southern France, as Albigenses or Bulgari, Cathari, and Waldemses; in Germany and England, as Cathares.

In the Slavic lands, the Bogomilian sect was, next to Bulgaria, most widely spread in Bosnia and had least success in Serbia, where it was constantly persecuted by the Serbian kings. In Bosnia, it took deep roots. At the time of Ban (governor) Koulin, the Bogomil doctrine became almost a state religion. Ban Koulin himself and his family were converted to Bogomilianism. However, the phenomenal spread of the Bogomil movement aroused Pope Innocent III (1198-1216), who launched several campaigns against it, not only in southern France but also in Bosnia until the downfall of the country under Turkish rule.

The decline of Bogomilianism in Bulgaria began during the conquest of the country by the Ottoman Turks from 1393 to 1396. Naturally, in Bulgaria a new government was established and a new feudal system introduced by the conqueror. Mohammedanism was established as the dominating religion, along with its own church. The Bulgarian people were thereby subjected to an extremely difficult condition of existence, and were forced to endure and live with it for nearly five hundred years.

7. BOGOMIL LITERATURE

During the Bogomilian epoch, the growth of the romantic or apocryphal literature received a great stimulus. For the most part, literature was made up of translations. In Bulgaria were translated, written, and edited the bulk of the Bogomilian and apocryphal books, which were scattered throughout Slavdom. Bulgaria served for a long period as a literary depot for this kind of literature, as it used to be for liturgical books, rubrics, sermons, biographies, panegyrics, chronicles, and annals. The translations were more from Greek than from Latin, and dealt with Biblical topics. The most important Bogomil book was the apocryphal collection entitled *Sermon on the Holy Cross and on the Enunciation of the Holy Trinity.* It was translated and compiled from the Greek and consists of six books. Its author is believed to be Father Jeromiah, a Bogomil.

The Bogomil literature was more widely disseminated among the people because it answered questions in which the people were interested. The Orthodox Christians read the Bogomil books with no less interest; they exerted such an influence upon them that at times it was impossible to distinguish an Orthodox from a Bogomil. The circulation of Bogomil literature went on more or less unimpeded and side by side with the national literature. It had a free access everywhere, even in foreign countries, such as Serbia, Bosnia, and Russia, where it was translated and read.

SELECT BIBLIOGRAPHY

Benoit, Jean, *Histoire des Albigeois et des Vaudois,* Paris, 1681, pp. 16-25.
Blagoeff, N. P., *Juridicial and Social Views of the Bogomils,* Sofia, 1912, pp. 91-94.
Bury, John B., *History of the Eastern Roman Empire,* London, 1912, pp. 369-371.
Dimitroff, Donko, *Prvo-ouchitelyat, Zhitopis i Obrazi na Constantine Cyril*

Philosopher (The First Educator, Biography, and Images of Constantine Cyril the Philosopher), Sofia, 1969, pp. 52-54.

Drinoff, Marin S., *Works Of*, Sofia, 1881, Vol. I, pp. 349-350; Vol. II, p. 30 and p. 205.

Freedman, E. A., *Historical Geography of Europe* (Edited by J. B. Bury), London, 1903, pp. 373-382.

Guzelev, Vasil, *Knaz Boris the First* (Prince Boris I), Sofia, 1969, pp. 19-530. This is an excellent work covering the second half of the ninth century.

Hosch, Edgard, *The Balkans: A Short History from Greek Times to the Present Day*, New York, 1972, Chapters 2, 3, 4, and 5.

Iagič, V., *History of Serbo-Croatian Literature*, Vienna, 1871, pp. 82-90.

Ireček, Constantine J., *Istoria Bulgar* (History of the Bulgarians), Odessa, 1878, pp. 226-237.

Kosev, D., Hrislov, H., and Angelov, D., *Kratka Istoria na Bulgaria* (A Brief History of Bulgaria), Sofia, 1969, pp. 31-32; 48-49.

Manning, C. A., and Smal-Stoki, R., *The History of Modern Bulgarian Literature*, New York, 1960, pp. 11-29.

Mishew, D., *The Bulgarians in the Past*, Lausanne, 1919, pp. 25-26; 59-60.

Nicoloff, Assen (Monograph), *Samuel's Bulgaria*, Cleveland, Ohio, 1969, pp. 1-32.

Pastoukoff, I., and Stoyanoff, I., *Istoria na Bulgarskia Narod* (History of the Bulgarian People), Plovdiv, 1925, p. 44-50; 67-72.

Philipoff, N., "The Origin of The Bogomils" *Bulgarian Review*, Vol. V, Nos. 5 and 9.

Radeff, Simeon, *Makedonia i Bulgarskoto Vzrajdane v XIX Vek* (Macedonia and the Bulgarian Renaissance in the Nineteenth Century), Sofia, 1927, Part I, pp. 7-48.

Rambaud, M., *L'Empire Grec au Deuxième Siècle*, Paris, 1870, pp. 220-230.

Robinson, James H., *Medieval and Modern Times*, New York, 1919, Chapters 20 and 31.

Sakuzoff, Yanko, *Bulgarite v Svoyafa Istoria* (The Bulgarians in Their History), Sofia, 1922, pp. 58-65; 93-94.

Stanimiroff, Stanomir S., *Istoria na Bulgarskata Tsurkva* (History of the Bulgarian Church), Sofia, 1925, pp. 22-43; 49-57.

Stephanve, Constantine, *The Bulgarians and the Anglo-Saxondom*, Berne, 1919, Chapter I.

Topencharov, Professor Vladimir, *1100 Years Since the Death of Constantine —Cyril the Philosopher*, Sofia, 1970, pp. 1-171.

Zlatarski, V. N., *Bulgarian Revue*, Sofia, Vol. III, No. 2, pp. 32-35; *Revue Macédoniene*, Sofia, 1926, Vol. II, No. 1, pp. 1-32.

NOTES

1. Byzantine Emperor (912-959).
2. M. Rambaud, *L'Empire Grec au Deuxième Siècle*, Paris, 1810, pp. 220-231.
3. Constantine Ireček, *Istoria Bulgar*, Odessa, 1878, pp. 226-227.
4. Heinrick Kiepert (1818-1899).
5. These ratios are in Kiepert's *Inhaltreiche Texte*, p. 29.
6. D. Kosev, H. Hristov, and D. Angelov, *Kratka istoria na Bulgaria*, Sofia, 1969, pp. 28-29.
7. V. Iagič, *History of Serb-Croatian Literature*, Vienna, 1871, p. 82.
8. C. A. Manning and R. Smal-Stoki, *The History of Modern Bulgarian Literature*, New York, 1960, p. 16.

CHAPTER V

BYZANTIUM
AND THE EMERGENCE
OF THE SECOND
BULGARIAN STATE
(1187-1393)

1. *BULGARIA UNDER BYZANTINE RULE*

Bulgaria's incorporation into the Empire proved disastrous to Byzantium. The frequent riots, internal disorders, lack of public control, and loss of authority and prestige in the conquered Bulgarian provinces were sure signs of the decline of the Byzantine Empire.

Following the collapse of the first Bulgarian Empire in 1018, Bulgaria was for more than a century and a half an integral part of Byzantium. The more stringent taxation and other grievances brought about serious revolts. In Bulgaria, the excessive taxation was felt not only as an unbearable burden but also as a terrible curse. The inhabitants were robbed of everything by the greedy tax collectors and other state officials. Their flocks were carried away, their granaries emptied out, and government agents even sold out their lands. This last act touched the Bulgarian population to the quick and forced them to resort to armed resistance and frequent uprisings.

2. *REVOLTS AGAINST BYZANTIUM*

Led by Peter Delyan, a son of Gabriel Radomir, the first revolt occurred in 1040, barely twenty years after Bulgaria's subjugation by Byzantium. Another uprising led by Gheorgi Voitech during 1072 and

1073 never assumed the same proportions and was suppressed without much difficulty. The Bulgarians, however, continued to resist the Byzantine rule at every opportunity.

During the Byzantine period, the country was constantly exposed to marauding raids by the Patzinaks (1048-1054), many of whom settled in northern Bulgaria, and also to the invasion of the Cumans (1064, nomads moving into southern Russia from the east). Defeated by the Emperor Isaac Angelus (1185-1195), the Bulgarians fled to the Cumans and returned with an army of the latter. After raiding into Thrace, they accepted a truce that left them in possession of Bulgaria, north of the Balkan Mountains. But the Bulgarians resumed their raids into Thrace and Macedonia. A Byzantine army led by Emperor Angelus was completely defeated in battle near Berrhoe. Peter Assen succeeded Assen I, who was murdered after the battle by a *boyar* (a noble next in rank below that of the ruling princes) conspirator. Peter, too, fell victim to his *boyar* rivals.

3. THE SECOND BULGARIAN STATE

Assen I was made the first Tsar (King) of the Second Bulgarian State. His chief aim had been to extend the frontiers and consolidate Bulgaria's position in the Balkans. During the reign of his successor, however, Bulgaria once again regained her supremacy on the Balkan Peninsula.

The younger brother of Ivan and Peter, Kaloyan (1197-1207), assumed the leadership. He made peace with the Greeks (1201) and then engaged (1202) in campaigns against the Serbs (taking Nish) and against the Hungarians, whom he drove back over the Danube.

The collapse of the Eastern Empire gave Kaloyan an excellent opportunity to reaffirm his dominion. By recognizing the primacy of the pope, he succeeded in securing the appointment of a primate for Bulgaria and in getting himself crowned king by the papal legate. At the same time, he took over the whole of Macedonia.

Ivan Assen, son of Kaloyan, supported by the Russians, began a revolt in northern Bulgaria in 1217. He besieged and took Turnovo in 1218. With Turnovo as the capital, the reign of Ivan Assen II (1218-1241) marked the highest point of the second Bulgarian Empire. Ivan Assen II was a mild and generous ruler, much beloved even by the Greek population. He succeeded in occupying western Thrace and Macedonia and even northern Albania. Kaloman II, however, was the last of the Assen dynasty.

4. THE DISMEMBERMENT OF THE BULGARIAN STATE

At the end of the thirteenth century there appeared a number of independent regions governed by *boyars* or feudal lords. The most noted of these feudal lords were the four brothers Shishman, Smiletz, Radoslav, and Voysil. Shishman became the master of the northwestern part of the Bulgarian state, while the three other brothers controlled the northern and northeastern part of the country.

As a result of such fragmentation of the country, the authority of the new Bulgarian Tsar, Georghi Terter I (1280-1292), had naturally declined. He found it impossible to govern and was succeeded by Smiletz (1292-1298). But he, too, was soon dethroned and his place taken by Todor Svetoslav (1300-1321). Supported by the feudal lords, Svetoslav succeeded in subduing his opposition and thereby strengthening his authority. Svetoslav's reign was short. He died in 1321 and was succeeded by Georghi Terter II (1321-1323). The country was once again involved in squabbles and administrative rivalries. A number of eastern feudal lords *(boyars)* seceded from the central government and joined Byzantium.

In 1323, Michael Shishman (1323-1330), ruler of the Vidin province, was elected to the throne. Although he succeeded in enlarging his territorial domain, he failed to unify all the Bulgarian lands. His reign was characterized by futile wars that exhausted the vitality of the country.

Soon after northeastern Bulgaria was split into warring feudal domains, the remaining part of the country was divided into two parts: that of Turnovo and that of the Vidin states. This idea of dividing the country was initiated by Ivan Alexander (1331-1371). Both of these states were ruled by Alexander's sons. On the Vidin throne, Ivan Stratsimir was installed, while in the Turnovo state Ivan Shishman was the ruler (1371-1393). This fragmentation of the once powerful Bulgarian state resulted in internecine hostility and made it more vulnerable to external attacks. Thus, the invading Ottoman Turks swept throughout northeastern and western Bulgaria. And with the fall of Veliko Turnovo, the capital, Ivan Shishman's state collapsed in 1393. He was the last Bulgarian Tsar of the Second Bulgarian State.

It is important to state at this point that Patriarch Eftimy Turnovski (1327-1393) was the last Bulgarian Patriarch at the end of the Second Bulgarian State. He was Patriarch from 1375 to 1393 and heroically fought against the invading Turks in the defense of Turnovo. He was one of the casualties in this historic battle.

By the end of the thirteenth century the Serbian state, like others of eastern Europe, had developed a strong secular and clerical aristocracy, which, to a large extent, controlled even the more outstanding rulers. Dynastic conflicts and territorial disruption were very pronounced. Serbia then, as now, was the western neighbor of Bulgaria. In the western Balkans the situation was further complicated by the rivalry of the western and eastern forms of Christianity, to say nothing of the persistence of the Bogomil teaching, especially in Bosnia.

One of the greatest Serbian rulers in the Middle Ages was Stephen Dushan (1331-1355). He began his career by deposing his father. By 1344 he had subjected all of Macedonia, Albania, Thessaly, and Epirus. This territorial expansion was ephemeral. Incessant struggles and rivalry existed within his empire, and Dushan's effort in consolidating the Balkans failed in the face of the growing power of the Ottoman Turks. The latter, at the battle of Kossovo (1389), defeated the Serbs, and thenceforth Serbia was a vassal state of the Turks.

5. MEDIEVAL BULGARIAN CULTURE

The full bloom of Bulgarian culture and art at the time of the First Bulgarian State was followed by over a century and a half of Byzantine rule. During that period, the conquered nation asserted itself by a series of revolts led by Peter Delyan and the two brothers, Peter and Assen, who succeeded in establishing the Second Bulgarian State. Its capital was the city of Veliko Turnovo. After this state was founded in 1187, cultural activities culminated again in a new and varied form. During the Middle Ages many architectural monuments and paintings were created. The new capital of Turnovo became the spiritual and cultural center of Bulgaria.

Following the traditions preserved from the First Bulgarian State, there appeared in the Second Bulgarian State such diversified creative works as the building of fortresses, palaces, monasteries, and churches; the writing of numerous literary works; and the making of artistic miniatures and exquisite wood carvings. Literary schools and schools of fine arts were established and became distinguished for their works of art and other achievements.

Besides the building of fortresses and royal palaces, a considerable number of churches were built in Bulgaria. The most famous city was Turnovo with its numerous churches. It was not only the religious center but also the headquarters of the Bulgarian Patriarchate. One of the churches of the Sts. Forty Martyrs, built in 1230 on the bank of Yantra River by order of Assen II, is still preserved.

Turnovo also became the literary center, where translations were made, and where books were copied and decorated with exquisite miniatures.

Art during the Second Bulgarian State was characterized by the exceptional advance in the applied arts and crafts. Goldsmiths and silversmiths attained a high degree of fine workmanship, producing plate, jewels, ornaments, facing for icons, and other objects.

Bulgaria's artistic traditions reached such heights during the medieval period that they could not be destroyed even by the Turkish domination, and as early as the fifteenth century new monuments of art were created. These traditions are bearers of the continuity of Bulgaria's creative ability from the time of the First Bulgarian State to the present.

The Rila (or Rillo) Monastery was founded in the tenth century and at once became one of the main centers of Bulgarian culture. It followed, naturally, that it was also one of the main centers of icon painting. Unfortunately, owing to Bulgaria's eventful history, full of vicissitudes, not all the treasures of culture collected in it for centuries have come down to us. Nevertheless, a small part of them has been preserved. Among them is a valuable collection of icons in which are some of the oldest and most interesting examples of that art in Bulgaria.

Bulgarian national power reached its zenith under Tsar Simeon the Great (see Chapter IV), a monarch distinguished alike in arts of war and peace. According to Edward Gibbon, "Bulgaria assumed a rank among civilized powers of earth."[1] But after Simeon's death, internecine struggles, the penetration of Byzantine customs, and the preaching of pacifism by the Bogomil sectarians helped to bring about a national demoralization, which eventually culminated in Bulgaria's subjugation by the Byzantine Empire.

The writing of history, like other forms of cultural activity, depended on the intensity and activity of the national life at the time. The principal learned class of the period was of course the clergy. Affected by the course of events, some of them fled to the hills and mountains. Among those who fled to the Rila Mountains was John Rilski (Ivan of Rila), who later became the subject of legends and who was proclaimed "St. John of Rila."

Although medieval art is chiefly impersonal, the outstanding artists and mural painters worked at the St. John of Rila Monastery and its surrounding regions during the fourteenth and fifteenth centuries. Icons of St. John of Rila take a special place in the museum collection.

St. John of Rila has been greatly venerated in Bulgaria and elsewhere in the Balkan Peninsula. Paintings and icons of him are found in many Bulgarian churches, such as the thirteenth-century Boyana Church, the fourteenth-century church of Zemen Monastery, the church of Sts. Peter and Paul in Veliko Turnovo, and the church of the Dragovitsi Monastery near Sofia, dating back to the end of the fourteenth and the early fifteenth centuries. The Boyana Church, near Sofia, with its mural paintings of 1259, is perhaps a forerunner of the Renaissance of western Europe.

To the above-mentioned medieval churches and monasteries, one should also add the Monastery of Batehkovo, the Monastery of Troyan, the Monastery of Preobrozhenski, and the Monastery of Royene. The church "Sveti Spas" (Holy Savior) of Skopie, Macedonia, standing not far from the old Turkish fortress, possesses a valuable treasure—an altar screen of highly artistic wood sculptures, executed by Macedonian artists, as the one preserved on the screen inscription testifies: "The first master Philipoff of Gari, Makaria of Galichnik, Bulgarians from Debra, Mala Peka, 1824."[2] These same sculptor masters have embellished with artistic wood sculptures and carvings other churches in Macedonia.

The Monastery St. Prohor Ptchinski, near Koumanovo, had been a Bulgarian sanctuary since the eleventh century. Moreover, the Cathedral Church St. Clement of Ohrid is a Bulgarian church in which are preserved, among other valuable antiquities, the relics of St. Clement, the disciple of Sts. Cyril and Methodius. As we have seen, he worked in Ohrid at the end of the ninth century as bishop and national educator, for which he is honored and held in esteem by the Bulgarian people. The University of Sofia bears the name of St. Clement. Another landmark of Bulgarianism in Ohrid is St. Naum Monastery, an ancient Bulgarian sanctuary bearing the name of one of the followers of Sts. Cyril and Methodius—St. Naum, a contemporary of St. Clement.[3]

This new form of cultural development consisted of translations and the preparation of texts and historical chronicles of Bulgarian events. However, the most interesting writer in the latter part of the fourteenth century was Patriarch Eftimy, the last Patriarch of the Second Bulgarian State. Most of his work consisted of translations from the Greek. He also wrote letters discussing church matters and reforms in the Slav-language liturgy. These letters, a valuable source of many questions concerning church history, have even been used by Russian chroniclers.

Patriarch Eftimy was at the head of a group that devoted itself to the writing of biographies of Bulgarian saints, such as John Rilsky, Petka, Ilarion, and others. All of these endeavors naturally had some influence in the development of the Bulgarian language. Bulgaria's civilization at this time, if one bases one's judgment on the chronicles of the Crusaders, was on a par with that of the rest of Europe.

6. *BULGARIA UNDER TURKISH RULE (1393-1878)*

In the ninth and tenth centuries, the Turks were converted to Islam and, in the eleventh century, they began to attack the Byzantine Empire. The Seljuks, a branch of the Turks, took Baghdad in 1055 and in the following two centuries built up an imposing empire in Anatolia and the Middle East.

In 1243, the Mongols under the leadership of Genghis Khan defeated the Seljuks at Kosedagh. Anatolia had now become a Mongol suzerainty, and eventually the Seljuk Empire disintegrated. Subsequently, local petty chiefs had appeared along the Aegean coast.

When the tide of Mongol invasion rolled back, Asia Minor was left broken up into a great number of small districts, each ruled by a petty chief. One of these chiefs, named Osman or Othman, was the leader of a small band of Turks that had fled from central Asia. The newcomers, to distinguish themselves from the earlier or Seljukian Turks, took the name of their leader, Othman, and called themselves Ottomans.

Othman (Osman) I (1290-1326) was the traditional founder of the Ottoman dynasty. He gradually extended his territory at the expense of the Byzantine Empire, which was weakened by the transfer of many of its frontier guards to the Balkans. But the Turkish advance in the Balkans and subsequently in southeastern Europe seems to have taken the form of gradual infiltration more than of outright conquest.

The Ottoman Turks first crossed into Europe in 1345, and made their first settlement in Europe on Gallipoli in 1354. Having overrun Thrace in 1361, they took Adrianople four years later and made it their first real capital in Europe. By July 17, 1393, they had occupied Turnovo, the capital of the Second Bulgarian Empire, and in 1396 they reached Vidin, the last Bulgarian stronghold. Thus, the Second Bulgarian Kingdom was conquered by the Turks, who ruled over the Bulgarian lands for nearly five hundred years.

The final Balkan victory of the advancing Turkish forces occurred, as stated above, at the battle of Kossovo in 1389. The Serbians were defeated by the Turkish army under the leadership of Murad I (1359-1389), who was killed by a Serb posing as a deserter. Murad's son Bayazir gained the victory. It was the last resistance against the advancing Turkish army, which by the end of the seventeenth century had reached the vicinity of Vienna.

Seventy-eight years after the establishment of their first capital at Adrianople, the Ottoman Turks laid final siege to Constantinople in 1453. At the end of two months, the city was taken by storm and the last remnants of the Eastern Roman Empire disappeared. The proud city of Constantine and Justinian, which had ruled from the shores of the Bosporus for a thousand years, was pillaged by the occupying Turks.

The capture of Constantinople did not by any means mark the end of the Turkish conquest. During the next two hundred years, their empire continued to expand. In the east, they annexed Syria, Mesopotamia, and Egypt. In Europe, after seizing Bulgaria, Serbia, and Bosnia, they crossed the Danube and conquered the north shores of the Black

Sea, southern Poland, Romania, and most of Hungary. They even advanced into Austria and twice laid siege to Vienna, the second time as late as 1683, under Kara Mustafa during the reign of Mohammed IV (1648-1687). Prior to this, under Suleiman II (1520-1566), they acquired all the territory of Bessarabia, the Crimea, and the Asian and African regions formerly ruled by the Arabs and Byzantium—Armenia, Syria, Arabia, Egypt, Libya, Tunisia, and Algeria. The Black Sea, the eastern Mediterranean, the Adriatic, and the Red Sea were part of the Ottoman Empire. At this time Turkey was at the zenith of its power. Only three centuries after Othman's hordes had appeared at the Byzantine frontiers in Asia Minor, Turkey, at the end of the sixteenth century, had become the West's most powerful empire, threatening all of Europe.

7. THE FEUDAL SOCIAL SYSTEM

In general, a class society had existed for centuries throughout the Dark and Middle Ages. While the disorders of the ninth century were at their worst, any man of courage who could get together an armed force and fortify a dwelling found the neighborhood ready to turn to him as its master. Other, weaker landlords gladly surrendered their lands to him, to receive them later as *fiefs* while they themselves became his *vassals*, acknowledging him as their *lord* and fighting under his banner.

This soldiery afforded protection to other classes. The peasants saw that they were no longer to be slain or made captive by chance encounters with marauders. They ventured to plow and sow. In case of danger they found asylum in the circle of palisades at the foot of the lord's castle. In return they cultivated the lord's crop, acknowledged him as their landlord, and paid him dues for their house and cattle and for each sale or inheritance. The *village* became his village; the inhabitants, his *villeins*.

Besides these resident laborers, who had some claim to consideration, fugitive wretches gathered on the lord's land to receive such measure of mercy as he might choose to grant. These sank into the class of "serfs," of whom already there were many on all large estates.

Both villeins and serfs were largely at the lord's mercy, but one master, however tyrannical, could not be so great an evil as constant anarchy. In return for the protection he gave, the lord assumed many privileges. In later times, these came to be unspeakably obnoxious, but in their origin they were usually connected with some benefit conferred by the lord.

Feudalism seems to us a bad system, but it had a good side. The fief, large or small, became an object of love and devotion to its inhabitants. The lord was admired and almost worshipped by his people, and, in return, however harsh himself, he permitted no one else to injure or insult one of his dependents. An honorable noble, indeed, he lived always under a stern sense of obligation to all the people subject to him. A rough paternalism ruled in society. Perhaps the system was more rough than paternal, but it was better than anarchy and it nourished some virtues peculiar to its own day.

Feudalism came to dominate all the relations of man with man. Other things than land were given and held as hereditary fiefs: the great offices of the kingdom, the right to fish in a stream or to cut wood in a forest. A monastery or a cathedral drew its *revenues* largely from its serfs and villeins and from the church lands cultivated by them, and it provided for its *defense* by giving other lands to nobles on terms of military service. Thus, bishops and abbots became suzerains and they were also vassals for their lands to some other lord.

In the Feudal Age society was divided into three social classes: the "upper classes" composed of clergy and nobles, the "praying class," and the "fighting class." These made up feudal society proper, but they were fed and clothed by an immensely larger number of "ignoble" workers. The workers, whether legally free or servile, did not count in politics and not much in war, and they are hardly referred to in records of the time except as cattle might be mentioned. They had few rights and many duties. Labor was almost wholly agricultural and was performed mainly by serfs and villeins.

This feudal system prevailed in western Europe up to the French Revolution of 1789. With the advent of the Industrial Revolution the class society assumed a different character—that of capitalism.

8. TURKISH FEUDALISM IN THE BULGARIAN LANDS

Along with the conquest of the Second Bulgarian State, the Turkish authorities had abolished its feudal system, which for centuries had been established in Bulgaria. But they did not liberate the subjugated inhabitants from the oppression of the then existing feudalism. They only replaced the Bulgarian feudalism with new forms of feudal exploitation, specific only to Turkey's European possessions. These new forms proved to be far more burdensome than the old. The system, however, contained features of the Turkish feudal system as established in Asia Minor and also of that of Byzantium and Bulgaria.

The means of production for existence was, of course, the land. With the conquest of Bulgaria, the feudal lands became the property of the Turkish state. The land had come under the control of the Sultan, and he alone had the right to dispose of it. It was called *mirie* or *mirieska* land.

Private ownership of land was allowed only around the house—the courtyard and field parcels within a radius of one mile from the village or hamlet. Such land was called *mülk*.

The *mirieska* land was cultivated by the peasantry—both Christian and Mohammedan. A peasant had the right to own land. He had also the right to sell it or give it to his heirs. If in the course of three years he failed to till his part of the land, the latter was taken away from him. To have the mastery of *mirieska* estates, the peasant had to pay feudal annuity.

The *mirieska* lands were partitioned in feudal possessions called *lenove*. These *lenoves* were given out by the Sultan to members of the ruling class in order to receive income or feudal annuity from them. There were two basic groups of *lenove* estates: one given for perpetual ownership and the other for temporary or during one's service to the state. The first could be inherited as a legacy, while the other reverted to the state upon either the dismissal from service or the death of the owner.

Perpetual ownership of *lenoves* was given to the *hasoves* and the *vakufs*. Such lands were also given to members of the Sultan's family and to distinguished military commanders. *Vakufs* were given to Mohammedan religious or charitable institutions, such as Mohammedan churches *(djamy)*, religious schools, and eleemosynary or institutions devoted to charitable purposes. The *vakufs* could not pass to private ownership. Their designated primary purpose was to serve charity.

The *lenoves* estates, given only for temporary exploitation, were divided into three categories, depending on the amount of income received. Such estates were the *timari, ziameti*, and *hasove*. The *timaris* brought an annual income up to 20,000 kurus or piastres (Turkish silver coins), the *ziametis* from 20,000 to 100,000 piastres per year, and the *hasoves* from 100,000 piastres and up.

Timaris, ziametis, and *hasoves* were given by the Sultan only to military, administrative, financial, and judicial functionaries. The holders of such *lenoves* received the annuity from them as long as they served in the army or the various state offices. They were not allowed to pass them on to their heirs, or to exchange, sell, donate them as gifts, or give them to the *vakufs*. They could be acquired only if the heirs were appointed to serve the state in some capacity.

The *lenoves* of all categories consisted of one or a number of villages, depending on the annual income. The holders of the *lenoves* constituted the feudal class. In this class belonged high civil and military officials, high priests, and the *spahees* (a corps of Turkish cavalry). Admission to the feudal class did not necessarily require that one be from an aristocratic family—it all depended on the will of the Sultan.

The feudal class received only a part of the feudal annuity paid by the peasants. Each feudal lord received from the Sultan a *berat* (an Oriental sovereign's patent or instrument granting privileges), specifying what taxes he should collect in his *lenove*. The state allowed only part of the annual income to be retained by any of the feudal lords. No feudal lord ever received the total income from his land or estates.

The Turkish feudal rulers were not given immunity, that is, right of full control over the *len* (lenove). The Sultan's authority was in action throughout the territory of the state. The holders of *lenoves* had the right and obligation only to keep under control the income of the landholding peasantry.

The most numerous and sophisticated Turkish feudal class consisted of the *spahees*. They were obligated to go to war on a call by the Sultan, bringing with them one or more Mohammedan soldiers (depending on the size of their landholding), armed and supported by them. In case of refusal to report for war, the *spahee* was deprived of his landholding.

The peasantry who cultivated the land and paid feudal annuities were called *rayah* (subject or submissive races). The *rayah* were not only the subjugated Christians but also Mohammedans who did not belong to the dominant social class. It was not until the eighteenth century that the term *rayah* was applied only to the Christian population.

The peasant was not allowed to dispose freely of the *mirieska* land that he controlled and cultivated. For any change to be made in his land, such as cultivation of different crops, he had to obtain permission from the feudal owner. Such permission was also necessary if the peasant decided to sell his holding, convert a meadow into a grain field, plant grapevines, cut a tree from the forest, and so on. In any case, the peasant had to pay a fee to the feudal owner.

The peasant had no right to relinquish the part of his land that he controlled and cultivated. Should he do so without the consent or knowledge of the feudal lord, the latter could have it restored, if the ten years of time of limitation had not expired, and he could compel the peasant to pay the unpaid income from that portion of the land. Either way, the peasants were strongly attached to the land.

Feudal Turkey also had slaves. They did not participate in production of any kind, however, and they did not constitute a separate class. They were used exclusively as servants in the Sultan's palaces and in feudal homes, and by the wealthier urban or city inhabitants.

The *rayah* paid a great number of taxes and performed numerous imposed obligations. More than seventy-five basic taxes and services were rendered either to the state or to the feudal lord.

The predominant form of feudal taxation was that on the land. The peasants were obliged to pay one-tenth of their agricultural production income (*yushour*) from grain, fruits, vegetables, hay, honey, and so on. Paid in kind were some of the taxes on stockbreeding.

Other series of taxes were paid by cash. Of these, the most important was the land tax. This tax was paid only by the Christian peasantry. On their part the Mohammedan *rayah* paid only for the maintenance of the holy places—Mecca and Medina.

The Christian *rayah* were obliged to perform a series of duties either to the state or to the feudal lords. By their forced unpaid labor, they constructed roads, military fortifications, municipal buildings, homes, and grain bins for the feudal rulers. For the performance of forced labor, the peasants' draft animals were also required.

Irrespective of the numerous taxes and imposts inflicted, the *rayah* were further burdened with extra payments imposed by the state, especially in case of war—supplying livestock for slaughter, supplying food and clothing materials for the army, and so on.

The city *rayah,* that is, the tradesmen and merchants, also paid feudal taxes, either to the state or to the feudal lords. They were also under obligation to pay extra taxes and perform other duties, such as delivering weapons and accompanying the army to perform craftsmen's tasks.

9. THE ROLE OF THE CONSTANTINOPLE GREEK PATRIARCHATE IN TURKEY

The Turkish invasion of Europe during the fourteenth century brought about great revolts among the Balkan states and eventually changed the map of the Balkan Peninsula. The Turks conquered in succession the Bulgarians, the Serbians, the Greeks, the Romanians, and the Albanians. The states founded by all these peoples vanished, and in their place arose a powerful Ottoman Empire, which was involved in the political affairs in Europe from 1353 until its expulsion from Europe in 1912.

In the beginning, the Turks respected the communal organizations of the Christians. What they cared most about was that the latter should be submissive, pay their taxes, and render all the services that their masters required of them during the almost incessant wars that they waged for the extension of their dominion. These wars naturally kept the Christian people in constant servitude, for they were obliged to supply the Turkish army, without any remuneration, with food, means of transportation, and everything else that they might want. The lawlessness of the troops increased the people's hardships and helped to devastate the regions through which they passed on their expeditions. It was the Sultan's policy, however, to propitiate his Christian subjects as far as he could, because he needed their assistance in his efforts to push his conquest beyond the limits of the Balkan Peninsula.

The sufferings of the Christian subjects of Turkey increased in intensity when the former power of the empire began to wane and internal disintegration, owing to the vices and corruption of the authorities, set in. The *Janissaries*, who were recruited from Christian children and converted to Mohammedanism, were the elite troops by which the Sultans won their splendid victories. The corps, under the loose discipline and bad administration of later weak Sultans, degenerated into a body of legalized plunderers, a terror to the Christians and even a standing menace to the Sultans themselves.

The impossibility of obtaining any outside help for their deliverance from the Turkish yoke or of throwing it off by their own unaided efforts brought about a curious social phenomenon in the life of the Christians, which needs some explanation in order to be understood and appreciated. Its parallel may be found in the story of Robin Hood, so familiar to students of English history. Among civilized people of today brigandage is considered a highly disreputable profession and the brigand a reprobate and an outlaw of society to be despised and hunted down. No further back than the last century, before any of the Balkan states had regained their political independence, the Bulgarian *haidout,* the Serbian *haidook,* and the Greek *klephtis,* all meaning "brigand," were regarded by their fellow countrymen with sympathy and admiration. The people delighted in telling of their deeds, and many a popular ballad, current even today, exalts them as meritorious heroes.

To a foreigner, unacquainted with the social and political conditions under which the Christians had lived for centuries under Turkish rule, this attitude toward brigandage and brigands seems a sign of moral depravity. The Christian brigand, however, was not a sneak thief or a vile cutthroat who took to his profession out of a wanton desire for murder. He was a man who, wronged and outraged in his own person or in that of his family by Turkish misrule and injustice, or unable to bear the sight of Turkish insolence and oppression, preferred to shoulder his gun and lead a life of freedom in the mountains.

These brigands used to go in bands under the leadership of a chief chosen by them, and their main object was to keep the Turkish oppressor in fear and respect and afford protection and defense to the Christians. With the loot that they obtained from the exercise of their profession, they not infrequently, as the popular ballads tell us, helped poor people in distress or made donations to churches and monasteries. Among the leaders of such bands women are also mentioned, and some of them are represented to have been superior to the men in valor and very dextrous in the manipulation of weapons. In the struggle for the independence of Greece, Serbia, and Bulgaria these so-called outlaws took an active part and rendered valuable service as leaders of insurgent bands. With the extinction of Turkish rule, the profession of the brigands fell into disrepute, and if at any time wicked and lawless men, actuated by ferocious instincts, have taken to it they have been quickly and summarily dealt with because their conduct has found no support among the people.

The actual course of events in the Balkans is a very close reproduction of the conditions existing previous to the arrival of the Turks in Europe. Then, and even now, the Christian states were engaged in constant destructive strife for hegemony in the Peninsula. Victory, both in the tenth and again in the thirteenth century, was with the Bulgarian state. Then in the twelfth and fourteenth centuries came the turn of the conquering Serbians.

The collapse of these ephemeral states produced no change in the ethnographic composition of the Peninsula. Political structures fell and rose again without any attempt being made to fuse the populations into any sort of national whole. At that stage, indeed, the national idea was not as closely connected with the state idea as it is now. The Bulgar, the Serb, the Romanian, the Albanian remained Bulgarian, Serbian, Romanian, or Albanian throughout the successive regimes. The ancient ethnographic composition, therefore, remained unaltered until the Turkish conquest came, leveling all the nationalities and preserving them all alike in dormant or inactive condition.

The Turkish regime unconsciously worked for the destruction of the national consciousness of the conquered Balkan peoples in the most effective possible way. The Turks banished or assimilated the ruling class or the warrior class in the conquered countries. In the communities no one remained but the village peasants, whose only ethnic bond was that of religion. Here again, the Turkish regime did much to reduce the ethnic and national significance of the religious element to its lowest terms. The religion of all the conquered nationalities being the same, that is, Eastern Orthodoxy, the Turks ended by recognizing only one clergy as representative of the *rayahs,* or Christian subjects. The one chosen was the prominent Greek clergy in Constantinople. The Phanar (the Greek quarter of Constantinople in which the Greek Patriarchate is situated) finally became the sole Orthodox Church in Turkey. By a special decree of the Greek Patriarchate of Constantinople, the last remains of the autonomous Bulgarian Archbishopric of Ohrid, which was maintained until 1767, and of the Serbian Patriarchate at Ipek which existed until 1766, were abolished. Consequently, a common race name was given to the orthodox population in the official language of the Turkish bureaucracy: they were all *Roum-mileti,* from the name, *Romaios,* of the Greek people, which name the modern Greeks gave themselves down to recent times.

The Turkish establishment upon the Balkans was detrimental to all the Christian inhabitants, but particularly to the Bulgarians. The Greeks, the Serbians, and the Romanians had, indeed, lost their political independence, but they were able to preserve their spiritual integrity, the Greeks for all times, the Serbians and Romanians only for a short period. Of all the Balkan peoples, the Greeks were the people who most easily ingratiated themselves with the Turkish authorities and thus took advantage of the privileged position for the realization of their national ideals. They had lost their political freedom but retained their church and civil rights. The Constantinople Patriarchy remained intact. It not only strengthened its position but also acquired from the Sultans such privileges as it had not enjoyed even under the Byzantine rulers. The Greeks under the name of *Roum-mileti* formed a separate community within the Ottoman Empire endowed with full church and civil autonomy with their Patriarch as its chief.

The abolition of the Bulgarian Archbishopric of Ohrid in 1767 placed the Bulgarians under the direct spiritual jurisdiction of the Greek Patriarch of Constantinople. All the church affairs in the Bulgarian dioceses were administered by Greek bishops, and it was a rare exception that a Bulgarian was appointed a bishop. Because the Patriarch and the bishops acted as the official representatives of the Christians before the central government in Constantinople and the provincial authorities, the Bulgarians and even the Serbians in the Turkish Empire had no representatives of their own race; for all practical purposes, they were represented by Greeks.

The Greek Patriarch, by a special charter granted to him by Sultan Mohammed II, the conqueror of Constantinople (1453), had the rank of the highest Pasha or a Vizier (a minister of state) in the Ottoman Empire; the bishops also had civil ranks corresponding to the administrative hierarchy of the empire.

All authorities on this subject agree in describing as most pitiable the condition of the Greek church under Turkish rule. All offices from the highest to the lowest were sold to the highest bidder, and on account of that the patriarchal throne was sometimes occupied by men who were a disgrace not only to religion itself but also to the principle of morality.

The bishops were as a rule men of low character, greedy and ferocious, and bent upon extorting money from the lower clergy and their Christian flock under various forms and pretexts. In addition, especially since the beginning of the last century, a regular system of Hellenization among the non-Greek populations was begun and zealously pursued. This process of Hellenization was greater in the Bulgarian lands than elsewhere.

In Bulgaria, which was a mere Turkish province without any political and spiritual rights, the jurisdiction of the Greek Patriarch and bishops was intact and absolute. The various excessive tolls levied upon the people by the Greek bishops were the least objectionable part of their rule, but taken in connection with the heavy taxes and extortions of the Turkish government and local officials, they must have weighed very heavily on the people.

Infinitely more obnoxious and menacing was the proscription of the Bulgarian language in the schools and of the Slavic liturgy in the churches. The Bulgarians were called and treated as blockheads, their language was considered barbarous, and everything Bulgarian was despised. In the cities and towns of Bulgaria only Greek schools were tolerated, and every more or less educated Bulgarian, imbued with the spirit of Greek learning, was ashamed to call himself a Bulgarian but prided himself on being a Greek.

As late as the beginning of the last century the Greek Patriarchate of Constantinople had absolute control of the ecclesiastical administration and the schools of the Bulgarian lands. Having a complete mastery of the psychology of the Turks, the Patriarchate was not only the most potent spiritual organization in the Ottoman Empire but was also in a position to play the second political factor in it. In virtue of the tremendous prestige which the Patriarchy enjoyed under the Sultans, it had practically its own way, not only in matters of religion but also in politics.

The Hellenization of all alien races in the empire and more particularly of the compact Bulgarian population adjacent to Constantinople was the greatest aim of the Greek Patriarch of Constantinople. As has already been stated, it had succeeded in 1767 in stamping out the Bulgarian Archbishopric of Ohrid, the heart of Bulgarianism. The Patriarch's influence with the Sultan Mustapha III (1757-1774) was so powerful that the latter was unable to withstand the demand for the abolition of the long-detested Bulgarian Archbishopric of Ohrid.

This event coincides with the epoch of Catherine II (1762-1796) of Russia, the great patron of the Eastern Orthodox Church, and the fiery champion for the restoration of a new Byzantine Empire. Another important event connected with her policy for the restoration of Byzantium was the treaty of alliance concluded between Catherine and the Prussian ruler Frederick the Great (1740-1786), who until then had been an outspoken friend of Turkey. A direct result of the understanding arrived at by Catherine II, Frederick the Great, and the Constantinople Patriarchate was the revolts that subsequently broke out in Morea, Crimea, Montenegro, Serbia, and Bulgaria.

At that period, therefore, the Constantinople Greek Patriarchy was at the zenith of its power and energy. And the suppression of the Bulgarian Archbishopric of Ohrid in 1767 was the greatest triumph achieved over its most hated and dangerous rival, the Bulgarian race. The Bulgarians were thus deprived of their only official spokesman and defender. At that time the Constantinople Patriarchate had succeeded in filling all the Bulgarian sees with Greek or Hellenized prelates. The whole Balkan

Peninsula was now under its full ecclesiastical jurisdiction and dominion. *The Bulgarian church, school, social institutions, liturgy, literature, and even the language were passing through the darkest period in the history of the Bulgarian people. The latter were now not only under the political domination of the Sultan of Turkey but also under the spiritual oppression of the Greek Patriarchate of Constantinople.*

SELECT BIBLIOGRAPHY

Professors Bourmov, A., Kostov, D., and Hristov, H., *Istoria na Bulgaria* (History of Bulgaria), Sofia, 1960, pp. 52-55; 85-89; 90-103.

Floreva, Elena, "Medieval Bulgarian Art," *Slaviany,* Sofia, 1970, Vol. XXIV, No. 7, p. 30.

Gibbon, Edward, *The Decline and Fall of the Roman Empire,* Philadelphia, 1887, Vol. III, pp. 330-334; 602-620.

Hosch, Edgar, *The Balkans,* New York, 1972, pp. 57-68.

Professors Kostov, D., Hristo, H., and Angelov, D., *Katka Istoria na Bulgaria* (A Brief History of Bulgaria), Sofia, 1969, pp. 45-52; 65-70.

McKinley, Albert E., Howland, A. C., Dann, M. L., *World History in the Making,* New York, 1927, pp. 359-374.

Mishew, D., *The Bulgarians in the Past,* Lausanne, 1919, pp. 218-279.

Professor Popoff, Ivan, *Bulgarska Istoria* (Bulgarian History), Sofia, 1920, pp. 120-123.

Radeff, Simeon, *Makedonia i Bulgarskoto Vzrajdane v XIX Vek* (Macedonia and the Bulgarian Renaissance in the Nineteenth Century), Sofia, 1927, Part I, pp. 49-64; 74-85.

Sakuzoff, Yanko, *Bulgarite v Svoyata Istoria* (The Bulgarians in Their History), Sofia, 1922, pp. 90-94; 97-140; 145-155.

Stanimiroff, Stanomir S., *Istoria na Bulgarskata Tsurkva* (History of the Bulgarian Church), Sofia, 1925, pp. 61-63.

Turski Izvori za Bulgarskata Istoria (Turkish Sources for the Bulgarian History), Sofia, 1972, Vol. III, pp. 5-9; 19-523. This documentary work is published by the Bulgarian Academy of Science and shows how the Turkish feudal system operated about the end of the fifteenth and sixteenth centuries. It consists of official Turkish documents.

West, Willis M., *The Modern World,* New York, 1915, pp. 26-29; 98-113.

Wolff, Robert L., *The Balkans in Our Time,* New York, 1967, pp. 50-53.

NOTES

1. Edward Gibbon, *The Decline and Fall of the Roman Empire,* Philadelphia, 1887, Vol. III, p. 333.

2. In 1957, the author had the opportunity to visit Sveti Spas Church in Skopie.

3. In the preface of a recently published (1955) UNESCO Art Series publication, *Yugoslavia—Medieval Frescoes,* Mr. D. Talbot Rice writes: "The plates in this book have been chosen . . . with the object of illustrating the artistic quality of the art of Yugoslavia throughout the centuries . . . (p. 5). The paintings illustrated here came from a number of different

churches, of varying dates and in several styles. The earliest of them, in St. Sofia at Ohrid and at Nerezi, are really Byzantine monuments on Serbian soil" (p. 6). In the introduction to the same publication, Mr. Svetozar Radojcič writes: "The monumental art of the frescoes in St. Sofia at Ohrid has no parallel in the inner districts of Macedonia during the eleventh century. . . . The frescoes at Monastir are now considered the precisely dated Macedonian painting" (p. 16).

In the first place, Ohrid was the capital of the western Bulgarian state under King Šamuel (980-1014) and from 1014 to 1018 of Ivan Vladislav, the last king of the First Bulgarian Kingdom (679-1018). Ohrid was also the center of St. Clement's educational activity, and the seat of the Bulgarian autocephalous church until 1767. The most noted iconographers were those from the mountain village of Galichnik, whose inhabitants were Bulgarians. The "artistic quality of the art of Yugoslavia" is, in fact, a recent fiction. The country as it now stands came into being in 1918, and under the Vidovdan Constitution of 1921 became the Triune Kingdom of "Serbs, Croats, and Slovenes." King Alexander abolished the Triune Kingdom and renamed the country "Yugoslavia" in 1929. Is Mr. Rice trying to impress us with the fact that the medieval art found in the churches of Ohrid was on "Serbian soil" and that the above new name of the country existed "throughout the centuries"? Mr. Radojcič, on the other hand, by the above quotation, is trying to make one believe that there had existed a Macedonian art apart from the Bulgarian. The historical fact is that Macedonia is a part of the Bulgarian lands, as Bavaria or Prussia is a part of Germany. Only in 1944 did the Serbo-Communist movement devise a scheme to create out of the geographic name of the province a "Macedonian nation" with a "Macedonian language" based upon a dialect spoken by some of the Bulgarian Slavs of Macedonia.

CHAPTER VI

PRECURSORS
OF BULGARIAN
SELF-PRESERVATION
AND AWAKENING

The lot of the Bulgarians under the oppressive rule of the Turkish Sultans was, perhaps, the worst of any of the subjugated peoples. The new changes that had taken place in the Balkan Peninsula deprived them of both their political and religious freedom. Soon after the fall of Turnovo in 1393, the Turkish authorities exiled the Turnovo Patriarch Euthymius, a noted writer and scholar. Two years later, by order of the Constantinople Greek Patriarch, the Turnovo patriarchal See was already occupied by a Greek, the Moldavian Metropolitan Jeremiah and, thereby, the Bulgarian Turnovo Patriarchy abolished.

During this period many of the prominent oepple of Turnovo were either put to death or compelled to embrace Mohammedanism. Thousands of Bulgarians saved themselves by escaping abroad. Hundreds of families crossed the frontiers to Romania, Hungary, and Serbia. In Bulgaria itself, the people fled to the mountains, abandoning their demolished cities and devastated plains. As a result, many new towns sprang up in the mountain fastnesses, some of them playing a significant role in the latter part of the nineteenth century. The blow against the Bulgarian people proved to be a deadly one. They fell under two yokes—political and spiritual—and under two masters—Turks and Greeks. The former assumed the right of disposing of their property and life, and the latter of their soul and national self-consciousness.

1. *THE BULGARIAN GUILDS*

How did the Bulgarian people manage to survive the century-old Turkish political and Greek spiritual bondage? As pointed out above, the Bulgarian church ceased to exist and in course of time its literature disappeared; its traditions and memories of the past completely vanished. What then was the prime motive power that helped rejuvenate the spirit of the Bulgarian people?

One would perhaps find the answer to this question in the industry and perseverance of the Bulgarian peasants and of the city craftsmen and their guilds. The latter were associations of merchants or tradesmen formed to protect the interests of their members. In some cases they developed into governing bodies of their respective towns.

The mysterious power that guided the Bulgarian nation and preserved its national character through all of its vicissitudes was, therefore, the spirit of industry. The factors on which the vitality of that power depended were the Bulgarian plowman, the man of the hoe, and the craftsman. Without the plow, the hoe, and the craft, the Bulgarian people would not have been able to survive all of their national disasters; neither would it have been possible to have a subsequent Bulgarian awakening or Bulgarian renaissance, schools, literature, and a restored church and state.

With the plow, the Bulgarian gradually and steadfastly kept on creeping from his mountain stronghold down into the plain until, in course of time, his furrows were touching the very banks of the Danube, the shores of the Black and Aegean Seas. By the skill of his handicraft he finally opened his way to the public market of the Ottoman Empire, where his goods, bearing the mark of his industry and honesty, made his name proverbial. The Bulgarians lived by their plow and skill and with the help of these they gradually imposed themselves upon the Turkish rulers as early as the seventeenth and eighteenth centuries.

Guilds, associations, or trade unions had existed in many cities of the Bulgarian lands, such as Vidin, Nish, Pirot, Vrania, Svishtov, Roustchouk, Turnovo, Samokov, Karlovo, Sliven, Shuman, Plovdiv, Velles (Vélés), Bitolia, Skopie, and nearly all other important Bulgarian towns. The mountain towns of Kalofer, Koprivshtitsa, Sopot, Tchiprovitsi, and other cities were flourishing industrial centers. The Bulgarian guilds became potent industrial and commercial factors. They were firmly organized and their charter was officially recognized by the government. Once their existence was sanctioned by the Porte (Turkish Parliament), the local Turkish authorities were bound to respect them and to recognize their importance. Soon the Ottoman regime began to treat their members as a most useful and honorable group of men. The state considered the guilds synonymous with industry, respectability, and usefulness. The Turkish authorities considered them indispensable and dealt with them constantly. The state workshops in Constantinople were filled with Bulgarian *abadji* (native tailors), who were employed in making uniforms for the Turkish army. Through their artisans, tradesmen, and later on through their contractors and caterers, the Turkish governmental officials had the opportunity of acquainting themselves with the Bulgarians. And though the name *Bulgarian* was eliminated from the official records, the Bulgarian handicrafts and guilds were in due time able to restore its importance and make it respected by the Turkish officialdom. Had it not been for the influence exerted by the guilds, the Bulgarian spirit in the towns would have completely disappeared. In fact, the Bulgarian guilds were in themselves well-organized social groups. They were, therefore, the nucleus of the future Bulgarian local governments and church parishes.

The Bulgarian spirit manifested itself most strongly in the interior districts of Bulgaria, Thrace, and Macedonia, where the Bulgarian character of the people was least affected. As early as 1850, and even earlier, the guilds had created parishes of their own to which they had entrusted the management of all church and school affairs. The guilds not only supplied the local communities and churches with enlightened leaders but were most instrumental in the promotion of the Bulgarian language, books, and education. They were the inspirers of their countrymen to a national awakening and to intellectual, spiritual, and social development.

At the beginning of the eighteenth century, the Bulgarians did not exist as a people. They had no clergy and no public men of their own to lead and represent them. They did not consider themselves in respect to race and language a separate body from the rest of the Orthodox inhabitants. It was just about this period that they began to awaken from their lethargy, in which they had been lost for centuries. The Bulgarian guilds and communities were just commencing their exalted work of economic and intellectual advancement, which was the first step toward national self-assertion.

2. *FATHER PAISSY*

The awakening of the Bulgarians forms a special part of the modern history of the Balkan states; its inception starts with the *Encyclopedists*,[1] who stirred the Western nations during the eighteenth century and whose doctrines were subsequently espoused by the leaders of the French Revolution. The ideas of the Encyclopedists reached Bulgaria many years after they had been embraced by the Greeks, the Serbians, and the Romanians. Thus the period of the Bulgarian national and spiritual renaissance dates roughly from the middle of the eighteenth century until Bulgaria's liberation in 1878.

Bulgarian self-consciousness and thought were mainly evoked by

Father Paissy of Khilandar Monastery. Father Paissy (1722-1798) was by far the greatest awakener of the long-forgotten Bulgarian people. He was born in Bansko, Macedonia, in 1722 and went to the Khilandar Monastery in 1745. Here he entered the Greek Academy of Mount Athos[2] and, in 1762, wrote the famous history book, A History of the Slavic-Bulgarian People, Czars, and Saints, which subsequently set the spark for self-assertion and regeneration of the Bulgarian people. Paissy was a monk of the Khilandar Monastery at the time when Mount Athos was a Greek center of activity and also the birthplace of the famous Greek Academy founded at the Monastery of Vatoped. Here Eugene Bulgaris (a Hellenized Bulgarian), a man of great erudition and liberal ideas, gave his lectures on the philosophy of John Locke, English philosopher (1632-1704), and that of Baron von Leibnitz, German philosopher and mathematician (1646-1716). Father Paissy eagerly absorbed all the knowledge he could obtain at the Greek religious and educational institutions of Mount Athos.

Paissy's History of the Bulgarian People was published in 1762; it is written in a simple but graphic style and was the spark that aroused the dormant patriotism of the Bulgarian people. In reality, it was a panegyric on the history of the Bulgarian nation and a bold protest against the Greek Patriarchate, Bulgaria's religious or spiritual oppressor. Recognizing the significance of a people's consciousness of their nationality and of knowing their history, Paissy warmly exclaimed: "Why are you ashamed to call yourself a Bulgarian? Have not the Bulgarians had a kingdom and dominion of their own? Why should you, oh, impudent man, be ashamed of your race and why should you labor in a foreign tongue? Bulgars! Know your race and your tongue!" Paissy's book was of tremendous influence by reason of its fiery patriotism and its enthusiasm for a great part of the Bulgarian people and a long-neglected language. In Bulgarian history, prose, and poetry, Paissy is acclaimed as the first historian and the resurrector of the long-dormant Bulgarian nation. His book signals the beginning of a literary revival in Bulgaria that culminated a century later in a revolt against the Phanariots' spiritual oppressors and soon afterward in a revolt against the political tyranny of the Turks.

In the days of Father Paissy, there were two kinds of educated Bulgarians; some of them were unconscious of their nationality and their history, while others had never ceased to call themselves Bulgarians. The first called themselves Christian and fused readily with the Greeks, who were the nearest brother Christians. The second felt as Bulgarians and, although they too called themselves Christians, they had managed to keep themselves aloof from the Greeks. A representative of the second type was Father Paissy. He was the first important person who appeared at the threshold of Neo-Bulgarian literature; his ideas and feelings proved much stronger than Eugene's philosophy and the Christian resignation of his Bulgarian followers. Paissy took a determined stand against the Christian resignation to which the Bulgarian people had been led; he appeared on the scene just in time to save his nation from utter annihilation. Through him the ideas of the Encyclopedists reached Bulgaria by way of Mount Athos, where they had been introduced by Eugene Bulgaris. Subsequently Paissy spread them throughout his own country. By means of his history, Paissy not only effected his mission but also was the first to delineate Bulgaria's past.

3. BISHOP SOPHRONY

The most ardent pupil and perpetuator of Paissy's tradition was Bishop Sophrony (Stoyko Vladislavoff, 1735-1815). He was born in Kotel, Bulgaria, and was a pupil and the most noted disciple of Paissy. For more than twenty years, Stoyko was a teacher in his native town, after which he was ordained priest and later became Bishop Sophrony of Vratza. He copied Paissy's history and read it to his pupils and to all who flocked to hear him. In the churches he preached to the people in their vernacular; his sermons, consisting of Sunday discourses and precepts, were printed in 1806 at Rimnik. In 1797, Bishop Sophrony was forced to flee Bulgaria and settled in Bucharest, Romania. He was the first new Bulgarian writer, and his collected sermons were the first Bulgarian book to appear at the beginning of the nineteenth century. The title of his work is *Kyriakodromion* or *Sunday Sermon Book,* but later on it was named in honor of its author, *Sophronie.*

These sermons were didactic in character. For the first time in the lapse of four hundred years the Bulgarians were happy to see in their midst an inspired pastor, to listen to a church sermon spoken in their native tongue, and to read a book printed in Bulgarian. Bishop Sophrony was one of the most noted forerunners of the Bulgarian Renaissance.

About the same time there arose two other prominent monks, Hadji Juakim Kirtchovski of Kitchevo and Cyril Peichenovitch of Teartsi, district of Tetovo, Macedonia. Both of these men wrote and published books in the Slavic-Bulgarian language, by means of which they did a good deal in spreading learning among their own kin—the Bulgarian people.

4. HELLENIZED NOTABLES

The work of Paissy and his disciples and their followers reached only the educated class of the Bulgarian people, particularly the teachers and the clergy who stood faithfully throughout the struggle against the Greek policy of Hellenization. The upper class of the Grecianized Bulgarians turned a deaf ear to the new ideas propounded by Father Paissy and his followers. The Hellenized communities, notables, and merchants looked contemptuously upon the priests and teachers who read and taught in the Slavic-Bulgarian language. They boycotted the schools and churches opened and directed by them and showed disgust with everything that was Bulgarian. They thought of themselves as descendants of Marathonian or Spartan heroes and abhorred any identification with the Bulgarian race, its past and its traditions, and with the history of the Bulgarian people.

The national self-consciousness, weak and glimmering in the monastery cells and isolated Bulgarian settlements, had to be given a push and invigorated. To effect this, it was necessary for it to make its way into the Hellenized Bulgarian communities. It had to de-Hellenize the Bulgarian notables who had been given to the Greek cause. It was, therefore, necessary for the Bulgarian people to have their own representatives in Bulgaria itself and abroad. It was necessary for them to have their own center of culture. To achieve this, another Paissy had to appear on the Bulgarian scene, with better education and greater authority, to awaken political self-consciousness among the Hellenized Bulgarian communities—to regain for Bulgaria its straying sons, to snatch them away from the firm grasp of the Constantinople Greek Patriarchate and bring them back to their own people, whom they had renounced and deserted.

Commenting on this tragic phase of the Bulgarian people, the Russian observer E. Goloubinski writes: "During the first thirty years of the present century, in that part of the Balkan Peninsula inhabited by Bulgarian people whose nationality was questioned, literally speaking, there existed not a single Bulgarian who was conscious of the fact or wished to admit that he was Bulgarian; they passed as Greeks even though praying in their native tongue—the Bulgarian. As is usually the case with all miserable renegades, those self-styled Hellenes showed greater aversion to all Bulgarians and Slavs than the genuine Greeks themselves. . . . Thus the so-called better or higher class of people, which in other countries make up the intellectual and educated portion of the population, here did all it could to disassociate itself from the Bulgarian nationality, which had become a meaningless term, and to ally itself with the Greek which was considered the real one."[3]

5. YURI VENELIN

Every epoch has its great pioneers and creative men. In the early part of the nineteenth century, Bulgaria was fortunate in availing herself of the most valuable services of Yuri Ivanovich Venelin (1802-1839), a Russian historian and Slavist. He had studied the historical past of the Slavs, especially the Bulgarians. A Ukranian Slav, Yuri Venelin is intimately connected with the political revival.

Yuri Venelin (as he is referred to by Bulgarian historiographers) ranks, perhaps next to Father Paissy, as the greatest awakener and historiographer of the Bulgarian people. A native Ukranian, he attended the Kishenev Seminary and became acquainted with Bulgaria through his Bulgarian fellow students enrolled at the Seminary. Later on he went to the Moscow University to study medicine, but here too his interest in the Bulgarians never ceased; he undertook to study the history of the Bulgarian people. One of the results of his historical researches was *The Old and New Bulgaria* (Drevnite i Neneshnie Bulgare), published in 1829. This was the first attempt made by a Russian scholar to study in detail the history of the Bulgarian people. His work was not only well received by the Russian Academy of Science and by Russian scholars but also made tremendous impression on other European and Near Eastern Slavists. Subsequently, the Russian Academy of Science entrusted Venelin with the mission of visiting Bulgaria to familiarize himself with the Bulgarian people on the spot by studying their customs and language. At that time the Russo-Turkish War (1828-1829) was still in progress.[4]

Accompanying the Russian troops, Venelin managed to visit the various parts of Eastern Bulgaria (Dobruja), which was then occupied by the Russians. The result of his sojourn in Bulgaria came out in his work *The Character of the Popular Songs Among the Danubian Slavs and Wallacho-Bulgarian and Daco-Slav Documents*. Yuri Venelin was the first Slav scholar to inform Slavdom of the political and spiritual oppression of the Bulgarian people. Venelin's work exerted significant influence on many Russian and European Balkan scholars. He was the first to speak about the fact that the Bulgarians are also Slavs, and he vehemently defended their national rights. For the first time, European scholars turned their attention to Bulgaria.

6. *VASSIL APRILOFF—BULGARIAN SCHOOL PIONEER*

Venelin's published works also influenced many Bulgarian colonists in Russia and Romania. By means of his writings, and especially through his correspondence with leading Bulgarians abroad, he brought about great changes in the minds of the educated Bulgarians. His published works not only made an impression in Russia itself but also gave a powerful impetus to the awakening of the Bulgarian people. Their regeneration had progressed very slowly during the early part of the nineteenth century.' But Venelin's work *The Old and New Bulgaria,* published in 1829, exerted its influence on all classes of the Bulgarian people; they began to make fast strides toward their national goal. Even the Hellenized Bulgarians availed themselves of Venelin's historical works. The educated and intelligent people, who, at that time, abhorred being called Bulgarians, began to recover from their delusion, returned to their people, and even became outstanding leaders in the Bulgarian national regeneration.

Vassil E. Apriloff (1789-1847), a noted Bulgarian philanthropist, according to his own statement was "born anew" after reading Venelin's works on the history of Bulgaria. Born in the city of Gabrovo, Apriloff came from a craftsman family. As a youth, he went to live in Moscow with his merchant brothers. But he soon enrolled and graduated from the Gymnasium (high eschool) at Brashov (Austria-Hungary). After graduation, he enrolled in the medical school in Vienna. Because of ill health, he dropped out and in 1811 settled in Odessa, where he became a wealthy merchant. Responding to the influence of Hellenism, he helped the Greek liberation movement and educational work.

Then, after reading Yuri Venelin's works on Bulgaria, Apriloff began to feel strongly for his nationality and developed an aversion to his previous Hellenistic tendencies. A similar transformation had occurred in many other Bulgarian merchants and notables residing in Odessa, Bucharest, and other foreign cities. At Odessa, Apriloff took the initiative of organizing a committee for opening a Bulgarian school in Gabrovo, his native city.

Many obstacles had to be surmounted, however, before Vassil Apriloff was able to open a Bulgarian school. Imbued with the spirit of Bulgarian national self-consciousness, his ideas inevitably brought about great apprehension among the Greek bishops occupying Bulgarian dioceses. The Greek Bishop of Turnovo vehemently opposed the establishment of Bulgarian schools. As enemies of the Bulgarian Slavs, and their language and literature, they lost no time in doing all they could to stamp out every sign of the Bulgarian national awakening. Availing themselves of the special position and privilege bestowed on them by the Turkish Sultans, the Greek clergy tried, with the help of the Turkish authorities, to extinguish every effort toward the enlightenment and learning in the vernacular of the Bulgarian people.

Taking advantage of the *Berats* (an investiture) by which the Bulgarians were classified as Greeks or *Roum-mileti,* the Greek bishops utilized all sorts of intrigues to discredit the claims of the Bulgarians before the Turkish government. They accused the apostles of the Bulgarian regeneration of being revolutionists. The Ottoman authorities generally believed these charges, and as a result many Bulgarian pioneers in education and learning were persecuted, imprisoned, interned, or exiled. This explains why the first Bulgarian schools were opened and flourished in those mountain towns and villages where the power of the Greek Constantinople Patriarchy and the Turkish authority was least felt.

Fortunately, the Russo-Turkish War of 1829 brought about some important changes. Turkey was defeated and the Treaty of Adrianople compelled Sultan Mohammed II to introduce reforms for the betterment of his Christian subjects. Availing themselves of this favorable situation, the Odessa Bulgarian community succeeded in obtaining the necessary permit for the establishment of the projected Bulgarian school in Gabrovo. After centuries of Greek spiritual and educational oppression, *the first Bulgarian school was, therefore, opened there in October 2, 1835.* And the first man chosen to teach in this school was Neophite of Rilo (Nikola Poppetroff Benim, 1793-1881). He was a well-known pedagogue and cloister reformer. Before taking up his duties, Neophite was sent to Bucharest (1834), where he spent some time preparing himself for his task ahead. There he studied the Ben-Lanchaster teaching method, wrote a Bulgarian grammar and a book of catechism and developed a sort of rapid calculator. Historically, the Gabrovo school became the hearth of revolutionary teachings. Many of its graduates and teachers participated in the ensuing uprisings of the Bulgarian people. As a result, the school was closed by the Turkish authorities in 1876, only to be reopened after Bulgaria's liberation in 1878. The Gabrovo school was renamed in 1879 as the "Apriloff Gymnasium." Many notable Bulgarians, such as Todor Bourmoff and others, graduated from the Apriloff Gymnasium.

The Gabrovo school was the first Bulgarian institution of learning organized after an European model. Soon the example of the Odessa Bulgarians was followed by other native philanthropists. The number of schools began to multiply and also to widen this scope of work. Only a little over a decade after the opening of the Gabrovo school there came into existence more than eighty other schools throughout Bulgaria, Thrace, and Macedonia. For the most part, they were primary and junior high schools. A business school was soon founded in the city of Vélés, Macedonia.

7. GROWTH OF BULGARIAN SCHOOLS AND EDUCATION

The supremacy of the Greek Patriarchate had been consummated by the suppression of the autocephalous Bulgarian Church of Ohrid in 1767. In the latter half of the eighteenth century, the Greek ascendancy in European Turkey was at its zenith; its decline began soon after the

Greek War of Independence (1821-1829), the establishment of the Greek Kingdom (1830), and the extinction of the Phanariot[5] power in Constantinople. The Greek clergy, however, continued to work with undiminished zeal for the spread of Hellenism among the Slavic population not only in Dobrudja and Moesia but also in Thrace and Macedonia. It was carried on with such zeal "as if to obliterate any possible retention by Bulgarians of national character," writes Professor W. M. Sloane. "Even the literary remains of the onetime powerful Bulgarian Empire, preserved in cloisters or in the patriarchate library of Turnovo, were committed to flame. There survived but a few popular romances and spoken traditions."[6]

Along with the destruction of the Bulgarian literature, the Greek schools in Bulgaria posed one of the greatest dangers of denationalization. To counterbalance the influence of the Greek schools the Bulgarians could rely only on the efforts of a small number of isolated schools scattered throughout Bulgaria, Thrace, and Macedonia. During the period 1750 to 1834 there were about 180 cloisters or private schools, only a few of them in cities. These schools were set up in the medieval monasteries. They taught reading in Slavic, writing, and arithmetic.

The greatest intensity in the growth and development of the Bulgarian education was achieved from 1850 to 1876. This period was unique in the progress of Bulgarian intellectual regeneration. Toward the 1870s there was hardly a village or a town without a school. During 1875 in the Stara-Zagora District (county) there were 129 schools, in the district of Turnovo 129, in the district of Plovdiv 106, and in that of Kustendil 100. And during the school year of 1876, there were in Bulgaria and Thrace, 1,472 male and female primary schools in both towns and villages and 350 similar institutions in Macedonia, or a total of 1,892 schools.[7]

By the end of the eighteenth and the beginning of the nineteenth century, many Bulgarians had obtained their education in Greek schools, which, in fact, had been the only ones available. Some of them had been enrolled either in Athens, on the island of Chios, or in Ionnina, Constantinople, and other cities. It had been a dangerous thing for a young man educated in Greek schools to pose as a Bulgarian. It had been far more risky should one actively identify himself with any occupation that helped to arouse an independent sentiment among the Bulgarian people. Because of such a precarious situation one had to keep secret his ethnic origin and language, at least until he had made his fortune, or had passed as a Greek and thereby had been assimilated for good.

One of the most conspicuous features of the history of the Bulgarian national regeneration during the latter part of the eighteenth and the early part of the nineteenth century was the fact that the first rays of

Bulgarian self-consciousness, as well as the first educational pioneers, came from the Macedonian Bulgarians. Some of the outstanding ones were the previously mentioned Father Paissy, who wrote the first Bulgarian history in 1762. Hadji Iokam Kirkovski of Kichevo and Cyril Peichinovich of Tetovo were the first writers at the beginning of the nineteenth century to publish Bulgarian books based on a Bulgaro-Macedonian dialect. Hadji Theodosi of Doiran founded the first Bulgarian publishing house, in Salonika in 1838. Neophite Rilski from Bansko was the first to take charge of the newly established school of Gabrovo in 1835. He was not only the first to write a Bulgarian grammar, but also the first to translate the Scriptures into the Bulgarian language. Bishop Nathaniel (1820-1906), born in a village near Skopie, was the first in leading a national movement demanding the establishment of an autonomous Bulgarian national church; his literary works and his travels in Russia and other Slavic countries created great sympathy for his fellow countrymen—the Bulgarians. Rayco Zhinziphoff of Vélés was one of the first at the time among the lyrical poets of the new Bulgarian literature. The Miladinoff brothers of Struga, Dimiter (1820-1862) and Constantine (1830-1862), published the first anthology with Bulgarian folklore in 1861. They succeeded in publishing their folklore collections with the aid of Bishop Josef Strossmayer, the great Roman Catholic prelate of Zagreb, who took a lively interest in all Slavic people.

Grigor S. Perlicheff (1830-1893) from Ohrid was educated in Greece. In 1860, he received from Athens University the first prize as the author of a long poem, *Apmatolos*, written in Greek. Subsequently, he wrote another lengthy poem in Greek, titled *Skanderbeg*. This poem was about Georghi Kastrioti (Skanderbeg, 1405-1468), an Albanian national hero who led his people against the Turks. But it was Perlicheff's *Autobiography* that made the greatest impression on the Bulgarian people. It contained some unusual reflections about the life of the Bulgarians under their double oppression—spiritual and political. Perlicheff, like the Miladinoff brothers and many other graduates from Greek educational institutions, taught school in his native city of Ohrid, and in Bitolia, Gabrovo, and Salonika. Highly cultured, he dedicated himself to work against the assimilative policy of the Greek Phanariots.

For all practical purposes, almost every Bulgarian educated in Greek taught school in various parts of the Bulgarian lands. Being able to use the Bulgarian language also, they had excellent opportunities to inculcate Bulgarian national feeling among the people. They even clandestinely taught Bulgarian history and geography, in the spirit of Father Paissy. Because of such activity, many of them suffered the consequences of cruel punishment by the Greek Constantinople Patriarchate.

8. THE STRUGGLE FOR AN
INDEPENDENT NATIONAL CHURCH

In every historical epoch events have occurred that have either hampered or alleviated the spiritual and national destiny of a people. In the case of the Bulgarians in the nineteenth century, history was on their side.

As early as 1833, the inhabitants of the city of Samokov and that of Skopie (Macedonia) demanded from the Patriarchate the appointment of Bulgarian bishops and archbishops in the Bulgarian dioceses, with a definite remuneration fixed for them. The Greek Patriarch not only refused to satisfy their request but intensified the persecution of the Bulgarian leaders. This period marks the beginning of the Bulgaro-Greek controversy over the affairs of the Bulgarian dioceses. *This was the first struggle that the centuries-long oppressed Bulgarian nation entered as a whole and from which experience it was inspired to fight for a higher or political freedom.*

In this national struggle, along with the Bulgarian school pioneers, the Miladinoff brothers, Grigor Perlicheff and scores of others, special reference should be made to two courageous and dedicated clergymen who led the movement for a Bulgarian national church that soon became a reality. These two spiritual leaders were Neophite Bozveli and Ilarion Makariopolski.

Neophite Bozveli (Neophite Khilandarski Bozveli, 1785-1848) was a noted personality during the period of the Bulgarian Revival. Born in the city of Kotel, he had been a student of Sophroni Vratchanski. A disciple of Father Paissy, he became a monk at the Khilandar Monastery. Later on he became a teacher and priest in Svishtov (1814-1836). As such, he launched the movement for an independent Bulgarian national church. Traveling throughout the country, he not only agitated against the Greek spiritual oppression but also demanded the opening of Bulgarian schools and the publication of books and newspapers in the Bulgarian language.

In 1839, he went to Constantinople and organized the local Bulgarian colony, made up mostly of tradesmen, for resistance against the Greek Patriarchate. Here Neophite Bozveli initiated the idea of building a Bulgarian church parish in Constantinople. Because of his overt activity against the Patriarchate, Bozveli was exiled in 1841 to Mount Athos until he managed to escape in 1844. A year later, he, along with Ilarion Makariopolski, returned to Constantinople. At this time, they were given credentials by the Bulgarian settlement to represent them at the Sublime Porte,[8] and also at the Patriarchate. And so they did. Petitions were presented to both the Sublime Porte and the Patriarchate, setting forth the demands of the Bulgarians on the church question.

Neophite Bozveli is the author of *Prosveshteni Evrope* (1802) and *Plachi Mati Bulgari* (1848). Both of these works deal with the political and religious oppression in Bulgaria and urge the people to fight against the Greek spiritual tyranny.

Ilarion Makariopolski (Stoyan Stoyanoff Mihailovski, 1812-1875) was also one of the leading personalities in the struggle for a national Bulgarian church. Born in the city of Elena, he became a monk in 1832. Educated in Greek schools, he taught school at Karaya, the island of Andros, the Greek Gymnasium at Siro, and Athens, and later on in the Greek Institute of higher learning in Constantinople. Here he collaborated with Neophite Hillandarski Bozveli in presenting petitions to the Sublime Potre on the church question. Because of this, he also was exiled to Mount Athos (1845-1850). As a result of Russian intervention, he was released. Upon his return to Constantinople, he was ordained as Bishop of Turnovo but stayed in Constantinople to carry on the fight against the Patriarchate. While celebrating the Divine Easter Liturgy in the Bulgarian church at Constantinople on April 3, 1860, and by the popular demand of the Constantinople Bulgarian church community, Ilarion omitted the name of the Greek Patriarch, thereby rejecting the authority of the Constantinople Patriarchate. He was exiled once again, this time to Asia Minor (1861-1864). After his release, he continued to encourage the Bulgarians to carry on the fight until victory was achieved.

After the establishment of the Bulgarian Exarchate (1870), Ilarion Makariopolski became an *ad hoc* member of the Bulgarian Synod. Ordained a bishop in the Synod in 1872 he was appointed a Metropolitan of Turnovo. His omission of the Patriarch's name in the Divine Easter Liturgy in 1860 was thus the first step toward the attainment of an independent national Bulgarian church only ten years later.

9. THE RESTORATION OF
THE BULGARIAN NATIONAL CHURCH—
THE ESTABLISHMENT OF THE EXARCHATE (1870)

By the Treaty of Paris, which ended the Crimean War (1854-1856), England and France guaranteed the integrity of the Ottoman state (Article 7). In return, the Sultan Abdul Medjid I (1839-1861), promised them that he would introduce certain reforms (foreseen by Article 9) in favor of his Christian subjects. Indeed, on January 18, 1856, the Sultan issued a *Hatti-Humayun* (proclamation), whereby he announced equality among Moslems and Christians.

Encouraged by this proclamation, the Bulgarians renewed their struggle with much greater enthusiasm against the Greek Patriarch. This was manifested in various parts of Bulgaria. The citizens of Turnovo, Plovdiv, and Vidin rose against their Greek bishops. Simultaneously, the Bulgarian people sent their representatives to Constantinople. This step was significant because it was the first representation of the Bulgarian people in the capital of the Sultan since the downfall of the Second Bulgarian Kingdom in 1393. Petitions were presented to the Sublime Porte asking for a separate Bulgarian church. Even more significantly, in April 1860 the Bulgarians unanimously resolved not to recognize the Greek bishops as heads of the Bulgarian dioceses.

Prior to this event and because of the continued resistance of the Greek Patriarchate to the demands of the Bulgarians, in 1859 the citizens of Kukush, Macedonia, petitioned Pope Pius IX to take them under his protection, on condition that the pope appoint Bulgarian priests in their church parishes. This movement began to spread in other towns in Macedonia, and many of their citizens were converted to Catholicism; they were allowed to practice the Eastern rite in their churches. Even to the present, many Macedonian Bulgarians have remained Catholics. They are referred to as Uniates. Apprehensive of the Uniate movement, the Greek Patriarch was compelled to appoint Partheny Zographski as Bulgarian bishop of the Kukush diocese. This was the first Bulgarian victory over the Constantinople Phanariots. Indeed, the Uniate movement posed a threat to Eastern Orthodoxy.

Russia now began to show an interest in the Bulgarian cause. Her representative in Constantinople, Graf Nikolay Pavlovich Ignatieff (1832-1908), energetically assisted the Bulgarian demands. He was Russian ambassador to Turkey from 1864 to 1877. The Bulgarian movement began to grow stronger as numerous armed bands appeared in the Balkans. The Sublime Porte, seeing that the movement had assumed a political character, finally decided to settle the Bulgarian church question. Thus, on March 11, 1870, Ali Pasha, the great *Vizar* (equivalent to a Secretary of State) issued a *Firman* (a Royal Decree), whereby the "Exarchate of all Bulgarians" was established. Thus, the church controversy between the Bulgarians and the Greek Patriarchate was terminated.

It is interesting to point out that even after the political liberation of Bulgaria in 1878, the Bulgarian Exarchs resided neither in Turnovo, the seat of the medieval patriarchs, nor in Sofia, Bulgaria's capital, but at Constantinople, thus accentuating their claim to ecclesiastical jurisdiction over the unredeemed Bulgarians of European Turkey.

The *Firman*, however, sanctioned the spiritual affairs of the Bulgarian people to be under the control of Bulgarian ecclesiastics. To this extent, the Bulgarians of what is now Bulgaria proper, Thrace, and most of

Macedonia were united—spiritually at least. The *Firman* also provided that for those districts in Macedonia that were left outside the jurisdiction of the Exarchate (Article X of the *Firman*),[9] Bulgarian bishops might be appointed should two-thirds of the inhabitants so desire.

It was not until 1891 that the districts of southwestern Macedonia *were provided with Bulgarian prelates.* The Sublime Porte, at the insistance of Stephan N. Stamboloff (1854-1895) the then Bulgarian prime minister, whose demands were supported by the Triple Alliance and Great Britain, issued a *berat* for Bulgarian bishops at Ohrid and Uskub (Skopie). The dioceses of Vélés and Nevrokop received Bulgarian prelates in 1894 and those of Bitolia, Strumitsa, in 1898. Thus, the districts that had been left outside the jurisdiction of the Exarchate by the *Firman* of 1870 were now placed under the supervision of the Exarchy at Constantinople. The Bulgarian leaders, animated by the spirit of learning, believed that the safest and quickest way to political freedom was through the restoration of a Bulgarian national church.

But Ohrid, Uskub, and the other dioceses mentioned above are in Macedonia. *The question of Macedonia had thus definitely arisen for the first time in Balkan history.* The Greeks, however, would not admit their defeat. The Patriarch refused to accept the *Firman.* The Bulgarians, supported by the Turks, retorted by electing their first Exarch, Antim I, and thereby making a formal proclamation (May 11, 1872) of the independence of their church. Four months later, the Greek Patriarch in Constantinople excommunicated the new church and declared it schismatic. In fact, before 1872, the Greeks had already contended in Macedonia with the Slavs. But it had not occurred to the Serbians and Bulgarians to dispute about it themselves. The young radicals in Serbia and Bulgaria who, between 1860 and 1870, disseminated the idea of a Southern Slav Federation accepted the proposition that the populations of Thrace and Macedonia were as Bulgarian as those of Bulgaria, as a settled fact, traditionally established.

The Bulgarian publicist Luben Karaveloff wrote the following in 1869-1870: "The Greeks show no interest in knowing what kind of people live in such a country as Macedonia. It is true that they say that the country formerly belonged to the Greeks and therefore ought to belong to them again. . . . But we are in the nineteenth century and historical and canonical rights have lost all significance. Every people, like every individual, ought to be free and every nation has the right to live for itself. Thrace and Macedonia ought then to be Bulgarian since the people who live there are Bulgarians."

His Serbian friend Vladimir Yoranovich agreed and regarded Bosnia-Herzegovina as the only Serbian lands in Turkey, that is Old Serbia in the most limited sense of the term, which shows that he accepted the view of Macedonia as Bulgarian.

10. LITERATURE PRIOR TO
BULGARIA'S LIBERATION

Parallel with the growth and development of schools and education, Bulgarian literature began to make strides. At the beginning of the nineteenth century, the first printed books were of a religious character. Bishop Sophrony's *Kyriakodromion,* published in 1806 and later named *Sophronie,* was followed by a number of books either prepared or translated by Hadji Joakim Kirtchovski and Cyril Peichenovitch. These works also had religious contents. The authors and translators of these books used them in the cloister or in the private schools in which they themselves were engaged as teachers.

The first Bulgarian author and highly educated pedagogue was Dr. Peter Beron (Peter Hadjievich Beron, 1800-1871), a native of Kotel. He brought about radical changes in the educational system that was in vogue in the so-called cloister or monastery schools. Dr. Beron taught school in Bucharest and Brashov and later graduated from the medical school in Munich. He practiced medicine in Bucharest and Kraiova, lived for some time in Paris, and traveled in England, Germany, and Austria-Hungary. For all practical purposes, however, he dedicated himself to education and writing. During 1824, while he was in Brashov, Dr. Beron prepared and published a Bulgarian reader for the Bulgarian schools under the title: *Boukvar c Razlichny Pouchenia* (A Reader with Various Precepts). The *Reader* was subsequently called *Riben Boukvar* (Fish Primer), simply because on its cover page there was a picture of a fish. This publication was a great contribution to early Bulgarian school literature. By eliminating the medieval system of instruction, Dr. Beron came to be considered the first Bulgarian pedagogue and educational reformer.

After 1840 a series of textbooks on philosophy, Bulgarian history, geography, natural science, mathematics, and other subjects were published. Along with Neophite of Rilo's grammar, a number of other works were published prior to 1870. Christani Pavlovich (1804-1848) was the author of an arithmetic textbook (1833) and of a *Slavo-Bulgarian Grammar* (1836). The most important grammar textbooks were written by Ivan N. Momtchiloff (1819-1869) and Ioakim P. Grueff (1828-1912). Momtchiloff is the author of the *Grammar of the Old Bulgarian Language* (1865) and *Grammar of the New Bulgarian Language* (1868). While Grueff is the author of the *Basis of the Bulgarian Grammar* (1858), he was also one of the first translators from foreign languages.

Other Bulgarian scholars began working on philological problems to establish a uniform spelling. The most active in this field were Gavril

Baeff Krustevitch (1820-1898), Naiden Gheroff (1823-1900), Nikola Purvanoff (1845-1872), and Marin Stoyan Drinoff (1838-1906), a Bulgarian historian and professor in Russia. Dr. Marin Drinoff is the man whom Bulgarian scholars consider the most authoritative historian. In 1889, he published two remarkable works: *A Historical Review of the Growth of the Bulgarian Church* and *Origin of the Bulgarian People and Early Period of Bulgarian History* (1869). In 1873 and 1876, Drinoff published in Russian two more research works: *The Settlement of the Slavs in the Balkans* and *The Southern Slavs and Byzantium in the Tenth Century*. The last two works constituted his dissertation for his Ph.D. in history. By his works, Dr. Drinoff established his reputation not only in Europe but also as a distinguished Slavist.

Prior to the publication of Dr. Drinoff's works, Gavril Krustevitch, in addition to his work on philology, published the first volume of his *Bulgarian History*. Dr. Peter Beron, in addition to his famous *Riben Primer*, published works on physics, mathematics, and Slavic philosophy. Most of his scientific works were published in French, German, and even in Greek. Following are some of his works in French: *The Deluge and the Life of Plants* (1858), *Meteorological Atlas* (1860), *Celestial Physics* (3 Vols., 1864), *Physical Chemistry* (1870), and *Slavic Philosophy* (in German).

In 1852 the philologist Naiden Gheroff published his work *A Few Thoughts About the Bulgarian Language* and also compiled the first *Dictionary of the Bulgarian Language* (1895-1904). Nikola Purvanoff (1845-1872), active in the promotion of the "Reading Rooms," wrote *The Inference of the Bulgarian Grammar* (1870). Dragan K. Tsankoff (1828-1911) was editor and publisher of the newspaper *Bulgaria* (1859-1863) and an ardent supporter of the Uniate movement in Bulgaria.

One should emphasize the fact, however, that all the Bulgarian intellectuals prior to and during the period of the Renaissance had attained their higher education in Greek, Russian, French, and German universities. Practically all of them taught in Greek schools and under the Exarchate or abroad, in Romania, Russia, and even Germany.

By virtue of their bilingualism, many translations have been made from the works of such noted Russian writers as Pushkin and Gogol or from German dramatists such as Schiller and others. Translations also were made from Voltaire, Victor Hugo, and others.

In addition to their participation in the struggle for national regeneration, the subject matter of the writers in the early part of the nineteenth century had been concerned either with church affairs or connected with Bulgaria's national goal.

The works that represent pure literature are those of Petko R. Slavaikoff (1827-1895), Dobry Chintouloff (1822-1886), Rayco Zhinziphoff (1839-1877), Luben S. Karaveloff (1834-1879), Dobry P. Voynikoff

(1833-1878), Vasil Drumeff, (1838-1901) and Christo Boteff (1848-1876).

Slavaikoff was the foremost Bulgarian poet in the middle of the nineteenth century and an outstanding writer and publicist. In 1850, he published in Bucharest three volumes of poems and in 1852 translated Aesop's *Fables* and published another volume of songs and short stories. In 1872, he published in the periodical *Tchitalishte* the most beautiful poems and stories. Dobry Chintouloff, after graduating from Greek school, studied in Odessa and there he began to write verse. His songs, full of revolutionary sentiment, spread widely among the youths of the Bulgarian schools.

Rayco Zhinziphoff wrote poetry and short stories about the life of the Macedonian Bulgarians. Luben S. Karaveloff was mostly noted for his short stories and novels. Dobry P. Voynikoff wrote dramas and comedies. Vasil Drumoff, later ordained as Bishop Clement (1838), studied in Russia and wrote several novels and dramas.

Christo Boteff was the most dominant figure in Bulgarian life and thought during the years immediately preceding the liberation of Bulgaria. He was the first Bulgarian poet of undisputed literary talent, and his twenty-two poems are almost all among the classics of Bulgarian literature. Boteff's poems might be classified in three groups: (1) that of the *Haidouts*, (2) revolutionary, and (3) social.

In addition to the participation in the struggle for an independent Bulgarian national church, which became a reality in 1870, many of the above-mentioned creative writers lived long enough to see the political liberation of the Bulgarian people.

11. THE OPENING OF READING ROOMS AND SUNDAY SCHOOLS

To hasten the development of education among the Bulgarian people, it was found necessary to establish special schools not only for children but also for illiterate adults. These institutions were the Tchitalishta (reading rooms) and the Sunday schools. The heart of Bulgarian education and culture at the time was in these institutions.

In addition to the already established schools, the first reading room came into being after the Crimean War. In 1856, reading rooms were established in Shoumen, Lom, Svishtov, and later in many other cities. After the liberation of Bulgaria (1878), there were more than 130 national reading rooms. For the administration of the reading rooms, there ensued a sharp struggle between the "old ones" and the "young ones." More often, the latter were victorious. In many places the reading rooms were centers of revolutionary propaganda. Outside Bulgaria the most famous reading rooms were "Bratska Lubov" (Brotherly Love) in Bucharest and the one in Constantinople where the *Tchitalishte* magazine had been published.

In addition to the reading rooms, Sunday schools were established. These schools came into being toward the middle of the nineteenth century. Their primary purpose was to render instruction to young boys and girls and also to illiterate adults who had no opportunity to attend the regular schools. The greatest number of Bulgarian Sunday or holiday schools were established during the period 1869 to 1874. Evening schools were also opened. The most popular Sunday schools were established in the cities of Turnovo, Stara Zagora, Sliven, Kotel, Vidin, Svishtov, Constantinople, and other places. The instruction in these schools was free.

The Bulgarian Sunday schools appeared as a reaction against the Greek spiritual influence. The instruction in these schools was in the Bulgarian language. In most of the Sunday schools, the subject matter taught was reading, writing, and arithmetic, while in some of them brief courses were offered in Bulgarian history, Bulgarian grammar, geography, physics, mathematics, agriculture, home economics, business education, and other subjects.

Although these educational institutions appeared under very difficult conditions of Ottoman rule and lasted for a short period of time, the Sunday schools and the reading rooms during Bulgaria's Renaissance made their contribution to the educational and cultural uplifting of the Bulgarian people; they inculcated in them the spirit to participate in the struggle of national liberation. Because the instructors were conscious of their Bulgarianism, the Greek language was completely dropped from the course of study.

12. THE DECLINE OF TURKEY IN EUROPE

The Ottoman Turkish Balkan ascendancy was largely due to its military might. The breaking up of the Seljuk and Byzantine rulers in Asia Minor, and the pulling apart of the Byzantine and Slavic Balkan states, created the most favorable situation for the Turkish military success. The organization of her military forces was patterned on the then existing state of conditions. Her military might was felt even in the Western world. Turkey's advance reached Vienna, where the Turks met a formidable resistance by better organized Western states. After the termination of the religious wars in Europe (1618-1629) and the consolidation of the absolute monarchies in the West, Turkey began to lose territory at the end of each war in which she was engaged with Western European states. This was largely due to the breaking up and weakness of her internal administration. The Turkish military strength was no longer able to cope with the new conditions. Internally chaotic, Turkey failed to make any significant social and economic progress, and politically she continued to deteriorate; a strong central governmental organization was lacking.

The military organization upon which Turkey had relied for centuries eventually turned against the Sultan's government. The Janizary (or Janissary) Corps, a body of infantry that existed from the fourteenth to the nineteenth centuries, were the conscripts and the sons of subject Christians seized in their childhood as tribute. They had been deeply indoctrinated in Mohammedanism and were peculiarly privileged; they formed the main fighting force of the Turks. The Janizaries finally became so unruly that, in a revolt by them in 1826, many thousands were killed, and the rest dispersed; eventually the organization disbanded.

Resisting any kind of reform that might alter the oriental feudal way of life, the large landowners, the civil servants, and military governors who had no loyalty to the central government were concerned only with their own enrichment at the expense of the Christian subject races. Because of their very low remuneration, the Janizaries too indulged in bribery and corruption. Turkey was indeed in dire need, not only of the reorganization of her army but also of her civil administration. It had come to a point that neither the armament nor the tactics of the feudal Ottoman army were strong enough to resist any attack by a Western power.

Sultan Abdul Hamid I (1774-1789) was the last ruler of medieval Turkey. His successor, Sultan Selim III (1789-1807), was the first one to introduce reforms that created a regular army patterned after the armies of Western Europe. Because of this, he was killed in a revolt by the Janizaries. Under the reign of Mohammed II (1808-1839), the old conditions were restored. After the successful Serbian and Greek uprisings and the attainment of their independence, however, Turkey was compelled to abolish the Janizary Corps and thereby introduce the Western European military system. And from the time of Mohammed II on many pressing painful internal reforms were introduced as a result of the awakening of the Christian nationalities in Turkey. These agonizing reforms were forced upon Turkey by the Great Powers throughout the reign of Sultans Abdul Medjid (1839-1861), Abdul Aziz (1861-1876), and Abdul Hamid II (1876-1908). With the constant intervention in the internal affairs of Turkey, the latter ceased to exist as a great power. Alexander I of Russia (1801-1825) was the first to refer to Turkey as the "sick man of Europe."

SELECT BIBLIOGRAPHY

Arnaoudoff, Michael, *Grigor Purlicheff*, Sofia, 1969, pp. 11-238.
Belejity Bulgari, 1396-1878 (Notable Bulgarians, 1396-1878), Sofia, 1969, Vol. III, pp. 11-31; 409-422.
Elibe, Halide, *Turkey Faces West*, Yale University Press, 1930, pp. 18-25.
Goloubinski, E., *A Short Description of the History of the Orthodox Bulgarian, Serbian, and Romanian Churches*, Moscow, 1881, pp. 176-178.
Les Macédoniens dans la vie Culturo-Politique de la Bulgarie (Enquête du Comité Executif Macédonien), Sofia, 1919, pp. 3-21.
Mach, Von R., *The Bulgarian Exarchate: Its History and Extent of Its Authority in Turkey*, London, 1907, pp. 10-105.
Manning, A., and Smal-Stocki, R., *Modern Bulgarian Literature*, New York, 1960, pp. 45-51.
Miller, William, *The Ottoman Empire, 1801-1913*, Cambridge, 1913, pp. 292-299 and p. 345.
Mishew, D., *The Bulgarians in the Past*, Lausanne, 1919, pp. 218-280; 314-318; 397-464.
Monroe, Willis S., *Bulgaria and Her People*, Boston, 1914, pp. 27-28.
Pastoukoff, I., and Stoyanoff, I., *Istoria na Bulgarskia Narod* (History of the Bulgarian People), Plovdiv, 1925, pp. 140-150; 199-202.
Popoff, Ivan, *Bulgarska Istoria* (Bulgarian History), Sofia, 1920, pp. 116-129; 130-141.
Radeff, Simeon, *Makedonia i Bulgarskoto Vzrajdane v XIX Vek* (Macedonia and the Bulgarian Renaissance in the Nineteenth Century), Sofia, 1927, Part I, pp. 86-103, Part II, pp. 177-308.
Sakuzoff, Yanko, *Bulgaria v Svoyata Istoria* (The Bulgarians in Their History), Sofia, 1922, pp. 165-169; 179-187.
Slavonic Encyclopaedia, New York, 1949; p. 121; pp. 914-915.
Sloane, W. M., *The Balkans: A Laboratory of History*, New York, 1914, pp. 2-3 and p. 102.
Stanimiroff, Stanimir S., *Istoria na Bulgarskata Tsurkva* (History of the Bulgarian Church), Sofia, 1925, pp. 122-135; 160-163.

NOTES

1. The Encyclopedists were radical French thinkers, such as Rousseau (1712-1778), Voltaire (1694-1778), and Montesquieu (1689-1755), who attacked religious intolerance, the slave trade, and especially the practices of the Old Regime in France. Next to Great Britain, France contained the most numerous, prosperous, and influential middle class. Members of this class furnished the Revolution with its principal leaders, such as Marat, Danton, and Robespierre. Even the nobility and clergy included many men, notably the Marquis de Lafayette, who condemned the abuses of the Old Regime.

2. Mount Athos (Holy Mountain) is a mountainous tip of the Chalcidice Peninsula jutting into the Aegean Sea. It was the center of Orthodox monasticism and Orthodox learning at that time.

3. E. Goloubinski, *A Short Description of the History of the Orthodox Bulgarian, Serbian, and Romanian Churches*, Moscow, 1881, p. 176.

4. The war against Turkey started as a result of the Greek Revolution of 1821-1828. With regard to Greece, by the Treaty of Adrianople, 1829, Turkey agreed to accept the London Conference (November 30, 1829), which decided to give Greece complete independence.

5. As noted, the term *Phanar* (Phanariots) is applied to that quarter of Constantinople in which the Greek Patriarch resides. It was the center of a Greek aristocracy, half hierarchical and half commercial, which lent its services to the Turks.

6. W. M. Sloane, *The Balkans: A Laboratory of History*, New York, 1914, p. 102.

7. D. Mishew, *The Bulgarian in the Past*, Lausanne, 1919, p. 316.

8. The government of the Turkish Empire.

9. Article X of the *Firman* of March 11, 1870, states, among other things: "If the whole Orthodox population or at least two-thirds thereof desire to establish an Exarchy for the control of their spiritual affairs in localities other than those indicated above and this desire be clearly established, they may be permitted to do as they wish. Such permissions, however, may be accorded only with the consent or upon the request of the whole population or at least two-thirds thereof."

CHAPTER VII

THE HAIDUTI-MOUNTAINEER
NATIONAL DEFENDERS

The situation of the Christian subject races of European Turkey, particularly in the last two centuries of Turkish rule, was the darkest of their history. Their destiny was wholly determined by the will of the individual Turkish local governors—*Beys* or *Pashas*. The tyranny of the Turkish civil and military officials was unrestrained. Moreover, the Turkish landlords forced the Christian subjects to work on their lands without remuneration even on Sunday or other Christian holy days. This Turkish imposition of forced labor or *angary* (unpaid labor) was practiced until Turkey was driven out of Europe. This practice was taken advantage of not only by the wealthy landlords but also by the poorer Turkish element. The latter also forced and exacted free labor from the helpless Christian villagers. Thus a great many of the peasantry were reduced to mere slavery.

More unbearable still was the practice that allowed a Turk, when he cast his eyes on the young wife of a peasant or his daughter or sister or mother, to offend her, rape her, or carry her away. The husband, father, or brother, fearing terrible vengeance and possessing no weapons, had to submit.

Bulgarian historians point out that Turks came into Bulgarian villages and were quartered there for a number of days, eating three times a day without paying. On their way out, with pistols in their hands, each demanded from his host eight to ten *piastres* for their teeth "because they were wearing out while eating Bulgarian chickens."[1] Such conditions existed throughout Bulgaria and Macedonia under Turkish ascendancy. The Bulgarians and more particularly the Macedonian Bulgars were the last to experience the severity of the Ottoman rule

1. CAUSES FOR THE HAIDUTI MOVEMENT

Even in the darkest days of their subjugation, the Bulgarians had not been without protection. This was rendered by the *Haiduti* "outlaw"

bands. Like Robin Hood in the English ballads, they were represented
as the protectors of the poor and the weak, the friends of the Christians,
and the ruthless scourge of the Turkish oppressors. The latter had been
inflicting barbaric practices and unbearable offenses upon the Christian
subject races. Because of this difficult and cruel situation the *Haiduti*
movment evolved. In the beginning it had no political purpose; it was
not a movement with an idea of working for the liberation of their
subjugated and maltreated fellow countrymen. Their chief object was
retaliation—to avenge themselves on the rapacious and unrestrained
Turks.

It would be interesting to point out a number of the incidents that
forced some of the Bulgarians to join the *Haiduti* bands. The causes
were the following:

1. one's parents slain by a Turkish civil or military officials;
2. the burning of one's house and pillage of property;
3. the ruin of one's business;
4. an attack upon the honor of a family;
5. an offense upon a wife;
6. the rape of a daughter or a sister;
7. abduction.

Such horrible conditions were common in European Turkey. When they
reached such a state that no one could bear such disgraceful inflictions,
many vigilant and fearless Bulgarians left their plows and businesses,
left their wives and children and took to the mountain ranges.

The *Haiduti* movement became a form of resistance against the
Turkish oppressors of the Bulgarian people. The *Haidutis* operated not
only in Bulgaria and Macedonia but also among the other Balkan
Christian people. These popular Balkan heroes appeared in Serbia under
the name *Haiduk*, in Bulgaria and Macedonia as *Haiduti*, and in Greece
under the name of *Kleftis*. The latter were active in the southern part of
Macedonia long after the liberation of Greece. They were in fact thieves.
The word *Kleftis* means "thieves." They were true brigands and worked
for their own personal gains. They did not carry out their work with the
same romantic idealism as the Bulgarian *Haiduti* or the Serbian *Haiduks*.

The earliest accounts about the *Haiduti* in Bulgaria relate to the
exploits of the *Voyvoda* (Chief) Radich in 1454. His band roamed
around the mountainous area of Sofia. Other noted chiefs of *Haiduti*
bands during the seventeenth and eighteenth centuries in Bulgaria were
Khoseluo Velko and Brzak *Voyvoda*, while those in Macedonia were
Babou and Balcho *Voyvoda*. There were also women *Haiduti Voyvodas*,
such as Rada, Boyanka, Bourgana, Todorka, and others. During the
intermittent squabbles of the Ottoman feudal rulers in the eighteenth
and nineteenth centuries, the most noted *Haiduti Voyvodas* were Indje,

Chavdar, Lalush, Manush, Strahil, Velko, Alten Stoyan, Detelin *Voyvoda Haiduti* Velko, Philip Totyo, and scores of others. Their exploits are praised by Bulgarian poets and prose writers—sung in lyrics and poems. In time, the *Haiduti* turned into a movement of resistance against Turkish rule. The movement continued until the liberation of Bulgaria in 1878.

2. THE ORGANIZATION OF THE HAIDUTI BANDS

In order to carry on their work more successfully, *Haiduti* formed companies of fifteen, thirty, fifty, and at times up to two hundred. The most experienced and fearless man of the band was elected *Voyvoda* or chief. He in turn appointed one of his men as standard-bearer. Strict discipline was maintained. The *Haiduti* took an oath of loyalty and mutual help. They usually gathered in previously designated places referred to as "*Haiduti* rallying points." They took off to the forests, hills, and mountains about the middle of April and roamed in their districts until September, after which they returned to their villages and towns, staying in hiding.

During the period of their activity, the *Haiduti* managed to procure their food either as helpers to the village peasants in their fieldwork or by getting their supplies through the mountain shepherds. In this respect, the Bulgarian peasants cheerfully supported them.

The *Haiduti* further swore that no member should commit a crime of stealing or an offense to a woman or attack a Christian. Those who were suspected of violating their oath were immediately expelled from the company or severely punished. Thousands of legends and songs are connected with the exploits of the *Haiduti;* their ranks were recruited from all those who had insults to avenge or nothing but their lives to lose. If a Bulgarian once joined them, his only chance of safety was to be loyal to his fellows, for he had put himself beyond the pale. The hand of every Turk was against him and his hand was against every voracious Turk. The villagers, "groaning beneath the exactions of their lords, welcomed the *Haiduti* as deliverers. Women were sacred in the eyes of these chivalrous cutthroats, for they firmly believed that whoever touches a helpless damsel would die in a Turkish gaol."[2]

In the official Turkish documents the *Haiduti* were referred to as "bandits," and they were relentlessly pursued by the Turkish army. Should a member of a *Haiduti* be apprehended, his head was cruelly severed from his body, nailed on a pole, and carried through villages, towns, and cities in order to frighten the rebellious Christian subjects. This type of cruelty was carried on until the expulsion of Turkey from Europe in 1912.[3]

3. APOSTOL PETKOFF—
MACEDONIA'S LEGENDARY HAIDUT

One of the most popular and legendary *Haiduti* in Macedonia in the latter part of the nineteenth century was Apostol Petkoff. He began as a *Haidut* and his sphere of activity was the Enidje-Vardar district in the southeastern part of Macedonia. Apostol's band of *Haiduti* was active long before the launching of the Internal Macedonian Revolutionary Organization.⁴ When the latter was organized in 1893, Apostol Petkoff gave up his independent activity and joined the newly formed organization. After that, Apostol's career, as Enidje-Vardar *Voyvoda* (chief of band), was a series of sensational affairs. He operated in the southernmost part of Macedonia to the river Bistritsa. He was known by Turks and European diplomatic agents in Turkey because of his complete command of the well-known Enidje-Vardar marsh. Many times the Turkish forces surrounded the marsh to seize him and exterminate his band, but they always failed. Apostol distinguished himself in numerous skirmishes with the Turkish army. He was the most hated "rebellious *giaour*" (infidel) subject to Abdul Hamid II. His popularity, as a result of his daring clashes with the Turks, impelled foreign *gendarmerie* officers and consular officials to open secret negotiations with him in order to get his views on the various questions of reform.

Being totally ignorant of the nature and development of the underground Macedonian movement, these foreigners saw in Apostol Petkoff the representative of Macedonia's peasantry and regarded him as the soul and body of the rebellious element. Even the Sultan Abdul Hamid considered Apostol as such. The Sultan on several occasions invited Apostol to talk terms for the pacification of the clamorous Macedonian Bulgarians. During the reform period after the 1903 insurrection in southwestern Macedonia,⁵ the Sultan sent one of his relatives to offer Apostol his own terms to withdraw from the revolutionary movement. But Apostol refused to accept the handsome offer of Sultan Abdul Hamid II.

When Apostol showed willingness to meet the Sultan's envoy, chiefly for sheer curiosity, he received the following letter from the envoy: "To the Voyvoda Apostol, Chief of *Chetas*,⁶ greetings from Sheik Achmed Kemal Bey. I shall arrive at the appointed place tomorrow to enjoy the supreme pleasure of an evening conversation with you and your associates."⁷ The mission of Kemal Bey was to ask Apostol to come to Constantinople to be the guest of the Sultan for one month. He obviously recognized in Apostol a man of military and administrative ability and also a leader of the people. Abdul Hamid wanted to learn in detail the desires of his subjects directly from their leader. During the visit, moreover, all troops were to be withdrawn from Apostol's *rayon* (district of operation) and he might communicate with his subordinates daily by his own special couriers. Apostol was to be received and entertained with royal honors. Apostol, however, unconditionally declined the Sultan's proposal.

The Sultan, as well as some of the foreign consular agents in Turkey, were not able to see where the true leadership of the revolutionary movement in Macedonia lay. To them, Apostol Petkoff was simply one of the many Macedonian Bulgar chiefs of bands who were following orders from a higher revolutionary body. Nevertheless, Apostol was one of Macedonia's Robin Hoods. For more than twenty years he followed the war trails. At first, roaming the mountains and hiding in the swamps, he was one of those picturesque *Haiduti* who later cheerfully joined the Internal Macedonian Revolutionary Organization and followed the orders of the Central Revolutionary Committee. He was no longer a *Haidut* but a *comitaji*.[8]

Apostol and his band had many armed encounters. Trapped with thirty-eight men, comrades-in-arms, in a village situated on the Vardar River, Apostol engaged a whole division in a twelve-hour fight. The Turks were compelled to reinforce their troops by bringing artillery and cavalry from Salonika. The uneven struggle was sharp. The band was finally destroyed, only two being able to escape by plunging into the river after dark. Apostol was one of them. "Three hundred *asker* (infantry troops) had fallen," writes Albert Sonnichsen, an American journalist who had joined the Macedonian revolutionary bands and knew Apostol personally, "but the government did not mind that, for they believed Apostol was finally killed. A week later, Vali Pasha[9] received a letter bearing Apostol's seal, announcing his recovery from a slight flesh wound. But this unwelcome intelligence was not published. Instead, an emissary was sent to Apostol's wife in his native village offering him a fat pension abroad if he would stay dead. Even then, when I met him in the swamp, it was not generally known in Bulgaria that he was alive, and Turkish officers were walking about the streets in Salonika wearing medals awarded them for participating in Apostol's killing."[10] Finally, Apostol was betrayed and met a tragic death on August 15, 1911. Such was the end of this romantic person, the precursor of the later systematic organization for the liberation of Macedonia.

The *Haiduti* (called outlaws by the Turks) were the precursors of the true movement that preceded the liberation of Bulgaria in 1878. Shortly before the liberation of Bulgaria, the *Haiduti* movement ceased and in its place the Revolutionary Committee was organized by Rakovsky, Karaveloff, Levsky, Boteff, and others; its activities precipitated the Russo-Turkish War of 1877. With the advent of these men at the head of the Revolutionary Committee the movement took on a national political character.

The case with Macedonia was similar. It was not until the intellectuals, such as Grueff, Delcheff, Tosheft, Matoff and others, took hold of the situation after the result of the Congress of Berlin (1878) that the Macedonian liberation movement was organized and assumed a national political character. It was essentially the work of the Macedonian liberation movement that brought about the Balkan War of 1912 and the expulsion of the Turks from Europe.

4. EMERGING NATIONALITIES IN THE BALKANS

By the provision of the Karlowitz Peace Treaty of 1699, Turkey yielded all of Hungary except Temesvar. And by the peace of Küchük Kainarja of 1774, which ended the Russo-Turkish war, Turkey renounced suzerainty over the Crimea and elsewhere in the Black Sea region and gave Russia the indefinite *right to protect* the Orthodox churches in the Turkish Empire. It was not destined for the Sultans of Turkey to remain long in peace. Although external attacks had ceased, internal troubles were constantly arising. By the end of the eighteenth century four subject races were beginning to agitate for freedom. In 1799, the Sultan was forced to recognize the independence of the tiny mountain state of Montenegro on the Adriatic. In 1805 the Serbians, under the leadership of Kara George, rose against the Sultan. Although their first attempt failed, it was not without results. In 1821 the Greeks also rose against the Turks. In 1827 the Treaty of London, signed by Great Britain, Russia, and France, demanded that Turkey make Greece an autonomous state. Turkey refused and the naval battle of Navarino took place. Later, Russia and France sent armies and Turkey was defeated.

At about the same time, the Romanians too were agitating for independence. In connection with the final settlement by the Treaty of Adrianople in 1829, Turkey recognized the independence of Greece and granted to the Romanian provinces of Moldavia and Wallachia and Serbia a large measure of self-government with their own rulers, tributary, however, to the Turkish Empire. This arrangement remained until the Congress of Berlin in 1878. The independence of Greece and that of Serbia and Romania were not without a direct effect upon the Bulgarian subjects in the remainder of European Turkey. And from this period on began the so-called *Near Eastern question* in diplomacy. *It was in fact the question of the Bulgarian people.* It became a problem of what the interested European powers should do with the "sick man's" European lands.

5. BULGARIAN POLITICAL DEMANDS

We have noted the dissatisfaction, indignation, and continuous protests of the Bulgarians during the first half of the nineteenth century. Ironically, the social class that was closely connected with the Turkish government and the Greek church hierarchy was the Bulgarian *chorbadji*. The latter, in the Bulgarian lands, were the rich money changers, rich merchants and money lenders, big landowners and suppliers of the Turkish army. The source of their income was the merciless exploitation not only of the Turks but also of their own people. Their economic interests were closely related to those of the Turkish feudal despotism, and they played the role of the most reactionary element during the Bulgarian national liberation movement.

The Bulgarian *chorbadjis* were not interested in any national cause. They were content with the existing social order and cared nothing for any movement of national liberation. They even became the main obstacles in preventing the struggling Bulgarians from meeting with either the Turkish ruling authorities or the Greek ecclesiastical hierarchy. Many of them were Grecianized plutocrats. In his *Mati Bulgaria* (Mother Bulgaria) Neophit Bozveli called upon the Bulgarians to set themselves against these Grecianized *chorbadjis*. The Bulgarian small merchants, craftsmen associations, and young intellectuals directed their struggle first and foremost against the *chorbadjis*.

The church and school struggle that the Bulgarians undertook in the second half of the nineteenth century was entirely without political undertone. Their demands were the first step in the fight for national independence and thus they assumed the character of political demands.

The legal rights of the Christian population were guaranteed to a certain degree by the issuance of the *Gulhane' Hati-i-Sherif* and the *Hati-i-Sherif* of 1839. The Bulgarian merchants and craftsmen associations anxiously waited to see what the Sultan's regime would grant to the Christian subjects. In the *Memoir* of Alexander Exarch (1810-1891) to the European powers in 1843 and also in the Petition of Neophit Bozveli and Ilarion Makariopolski delivered to the Turkish government in the name of the Constantinople Bulgarian community in 1845, along with the question of the independent church, there was also a demand for political representation.

One of the demands in this Petition was for an intermediary between the Sublime Porte and the Bulgarian people in regard to the national creed. It asked for four lay representatives—a demand that Ilarion, in his meeting with the Grand Vizar, closely connected with the internal peace of the country. Meanwhile, in the periodical *Mirozrenieto* (World's

View) published by Ivan Dobrovsky (1812-1896) there appeared in 1851 a demand that Bulgaria should be governed by a prince who would have two of his own representatives in Constantinople.

But the most sharply expressed political demand was contained in the Petition presented to the Turkish government in 1856 by the Bulgarian community of Constantinople. It begged the Sultan to allow the Bulgarian people to elect, without the intervention of the Greeks, a clergyman and a layman as leaders; the first would be an Archbishop and the other the political leader of the Bulgarians. The Bulgarians also asked for their own courts of law in civil matters, with judges to be elected by the people and confirmed by the two above-mentioned leaders. In the districts where the population was predominantly Bulgarian or mixed, under the Turkish governor there should be a Bulgarian assistant or lieutenant governor. The Bulgarians should be allowed to serve in the army, but their companies should be separate from those of the Turks. Bulgarian youths should be allowed to enroll in the school for officers.

These were the strongest political demands ever presented by the Bulgarian craftsmen associations and businessmen until that time. Outside these groups and even among them, however, there had appeared and developed rebellious movements that were more and more arousing the national consciousness of the awakening Bulgarian citizenry.

6. LEADERS OF THE BULGARIAN REVOLUTIONARY MOVEMENT

Scores of revolutionary leaders throughout the country were agitating and preparing the Bulgarian people for revolt against the five-centuries-old Turkish regime. Each contributed to Bulgaria's cause.

The foremost and most daring intellectual leaders of the revolutionary movement for Bulgaria's liberation were Georgi S. Rakovsky (1821-1867), Luben Karaveloff (1834-1879), Christo Boteff (1848-1876), Vasil Ivanoff Levsky (1837-1873), and Georgi Benkovsky (1841-1876).

Georgi S. Rakovsky was educated in Athens and later studied in Paris. As a successful lawyer and merchant in Constantinople, he was also an employee of the Turkish state. He soon gave up all of that and devoted his life to obtaining the freedom of his people—the Bulgarians. He was a poet-journalist, and his first book of poems was published in 1857 under the title *Gorskia Putnik* (The Forest Traveler). In his poems, Rakovsky describes the suffering of the Bulgarians and glorifies the heroism of the Bulgarian *Haiduti*. His activities were carried on in Paris, Belgrade, and Bucharest. In Bucharest, where there was a large settlement of Bulgarian refugees, Rakovsky began to publish the newspaper *Dunavsky Lebed* (The Danube Swan), and later the *Budeshtnost* (Futurity). While in

Bucharest, he began to organize, equip, and dispatch a number of freedom-fighting groups into Bulgaria. Through his work the latter half of the nineteenth century became the most tumultuous period in the struggle for Bulgarian freedom, and Rakovsky is considered "the Patriarch of the Bulgarian revolution."

Luben Karaveloff was a poet, a journalist, and a noted publicist. He was the intellectual leader of the Bulgarians abroad in the struggle for freedom. Karaveloff traveled in Russia, Serbia, and Romania. While in the latter country, he collaborated closely with Vasil Levsky and Christo Boteff. He succeeded Rakovsky, upon the latter's death, as the head of the Secret Central Revolutionary Committee organized in 1866. In Bucharest he soon began to publish the newspaper *Svoboda* (Liberty). Karaveloff was the only one of this group who survived to see Bulgaria liberated.

Christo Boteff was an outstanding and daring leader of the revolt against Turkey in 1876. Boteff is the foremost figure in the history of Bulgarian literature. At the age of fifteen he began to write poetry. His poetical works are by far the best in Bulgarian literature. Prior to the Bulgarian revolt of 1876, Boteff was in Bucharest editing the newspaper *Zname* (Flag). When the revolt broke out, he put himself at the head of two hundred men, left Romania, captured the Austrian riverboat *Radelski*, and forced the captain of the boat to land his band somewhere on Bulgarian soil. While on his way to Vratsa, where an uprising was taking place, his band was met by a large Turkish army and in the ensuing battle Boteff was mortally wounded on May 20, 1876.

Vasil Ivanoff Levsky was the most legendary apostle of the Bulgarian revolt against Turkish rule. He left Bucharest and entered Bulgaria in order to carry on his legendary apostolic work. Levsky was the first freedom fighter to cross Bulgaria from the Danube River to the Rhodope Mountains and from the Black Sea to the Serbian border. He succeeded in organizing more than two hundred local revolutionary committees. His name became the most popular among the subjugated Bulgarians but his whereabouts was undetectable by the Turkish police. Finally betrayed and captured by the Turks in 1872, Levsky was executed in Sofia on February 6, 1873. Levsky was referred to as the "Apostle of Freedom."

Georgi Benkovsky was at first engaged in his family's wholesale business. Traveling in different parts of the Ottoman Empire—Asia Minor, Egypt, and elsewhere—he soon began to think about the freedom of his people. While on a trip to Bucharest, he came in contact with members of the Revolutionary Committee, such as Levsky and Boteff. He soon embraced the revolutionary movement. In connection with the preparation of the Starazagora uprising in 1875, Benkovsky, with others, was assigned by the Revolutionary Committee to set Constantinople afire. But his mission failed. Returning to Romania, he was ordered back to

Bulgaria to agitate and organize the people in the Plovdiv district for the projected April 1876 revolt. Here he succeeded in organizing a series of local revolutionary committees, encouraged the people to buy arms, and trained them in military tactics. Benkovsky led the uprising in Panagurishte and later organized the *Hvrchovata Cheta* (riding or cavalry group), thereby visiting many rebellious points. He was engaged in many skirmishes with Turkish troops, but after the suppression of the general uprising he withdrew with a small group into the Balkan Mountains. Betrayed, he was besieged and mortally wounded near the village of Ribiritsa in 1876.

7. THE BULGARIAN INSURRECTION OF 1876

The Turkish rapine and oppression of the inhabitants of Bulgaria and the other Turkish possessions such as Bosnia and Herzegovina resulted in a bloody outbreak against Ottoman rule. During 1874, 1875, and 1876, the economic conditions of the Christian subject races—the *rayahs*—of European Turkey were becoming unbearable. The failure of the crop at this time was of the greatest consequence. The peasants of Bosnia and Herzegovina, as well as those of Bulgaria, were undergoing a severe economic hardship. In spite of these conditions, the Turks continued to raise taxes and collect them with unnecessary brutality. Never before in the history of the *rayahs* had Turkish oppression and rapine reached such a degree as at this period.

The first conflagration of a widespread revolt against Turkish rule manifested itself in the small province of Herzegovina. Bosnia and Herzegovina were the outermost provinces in the possessions of European Turkey in the latter part of the nineteenth century. It was the Slav inhabitants of the village of Nevesinje in Herzegovina, who, in the summer of 1875, gave the signal for the outbreak of an insurrection that quickly involved the whole of the Slavic subjects in Turkey and that, before it was suppressed, led to another war between Russia and Turkey. The primary causes of the original rising in Herzegovina were not so much political as social and economic. In July 1875, the peasants of Herzegovina refused to pay their taxes or to perform their accustomed labor services *(angari)*. When confronted with the Turkish forces their defeat was inevitable. Sympathizers from Serbia and Montenegro flocked to their assistance. Things began to look dark when the Great Powers intervened with an attempt to mediate between the Turkish government and its discontented subjects.

While this development was taking place, the Bulgarian leaders became convinced that no better opportunity to strike for freedom would ever arise and they vigorously began preparations for a general insurrection in Bulgaria. On April 19, 1876, the citizens of the town of Koprivshtitsa declared a state of insurrection. The population of the mountain towns and villages, such as Panagurishte, Klisoura, and Batack, well known for their alertness and love of freedom, hastened to the mountains, where they were barely able to hold their own against the Turkish forces.

8. THE BULGARIAN HORRORS OF 1876

The Turkish authorities in the revolutionary districts were so alarmed that they demanded military aid from Constantinople. Meanwhile, the Mohammedan inhabitants quickly armed themselves, forming irregular hordes—*bashi bazuks*—and hastened to the areas of the uprisings. The fury of the Turks knew no bounds; they resolved wholly to exterminate the disloyal *giaours*. The vengeance of the Turks was carried to such atrocious proportions that there is hardly a parallel in all the history of European peoples. Villages and towns were burned mercilessly; the tops of the Rodope and Sredua Gora mountains were illuminated by the burning towns of the surrounding districts; on the northern slope of the Rhodope, as the result of the atrocities inflicted by the regular Turkish army and the accompanying *bashi bazuks*, occurred one of those terrible incidents in which no less than forty thousand men, women, and children lost their lives. The seven thousand inhabitants of the town of Batak suffered to the extent that only a few hundred persons escaped the fury, as if by a miracle.

All of these horrors took place shortly after the Bulgarian insurrection. The European powers were not aware of these horrible incidents. The Turks exercised a complete freedom of action. There was no reason why they should not. Was not Sultan Abdul Aziz I aware of the fact that the European powers, because of their mutual jealousy, would not interfere in the internal affairs of Turkey? He knew well of the aspirations of Russia, but he also knew that he had the Turkophile Benjamin Disraeli of England on his side, which alone was enough to guarantee his method of suppressing the Bulgarian insurrection.

The outside world knew nothing of the Turkish ferocity in suppressing the Bulgarian insurrection. However, some intelligence began to arrive in Constantinople, either with the Bulgarian Exarch or with Dr. George Washburn and Dr. Albert L. Long, president and vice president, respectively, of Robert College.[11] The priest Taleff of Tatar-Pazardjik informed them of the happenings in the area of revolt by letters sent by special courier. Dr. Washburn and Dr. Long translated these letters into English and made them known to Edwin Pears, foreign correspondent of the *London Daily News*, and also to A. Gallanga, correspondent for the *London Times*. Fortunately, the foreigners in Constantinople were able to transmit the news of the atrocities to their native lands. Edwin Pears was really the first foreigner in Constantinople to write to the *Daily News* on the "Moslem Atrocities in Bulgaria." This account appeared in the *Daily News* on June 23, 1876. Pears gave an account of the atrocities as gathered from the facts related to him by Dr. Washburn and Dr. Long. Pears's report in the *Daily News*, in the words of William Ewart Gladstone, "first sounded the alarm in Europe."

The correspondent of the *London Times*, A. Gallanga, quoted only one letter, which appeared in the *Times* on July 8, 1876. Its brief content showed the character of Turkish action. It states:

The Government here has probably not ordered any general massacre of unarmed villagers but it is directly responsible for these outrages, because it has known of them and made no effort to stop them, because it has ordered the disarming of the whole Bulgarian population and then armed the Circassians and Bashi-Bazouks and turned them loose upon the helpless towns.

What has been done by these savages?

1. More than 100 Bulgarian towns have been utterly destroyed, although no pretext of revolutionary movements existed in regard to more than five or six of these. A Province formerly bringing in a revenue of a million of pounds to the Government has been devastated. The names of these towns and all the particulars can be furnished to anyone who wishes to see them.

2. At least 25,000 unarmed and inoffensive people have been massacred in cold blood. According to the Turkish papers of Constantinople, at least 40,000.

3. More than 1,000 Bulgarian children have been taken and sold as slaves. They have been sold publicly in the streets of Adrianople and Philippopolis (now Plovdiv).

4. Horrible tortures of every description have been inflicted on thousands of those not murdered.

5. The outrages upon women have been more general and more brutal than in any case I have ever read of. These outrages are more terrible because Bulgarian women have higher ideas of virtue and chastity than those of any other nationality in the East. If the women of England could know the facts, such a cry of indignation would go up as would rouse all Europe to action.

6. At least 10,000 Bulgarians are now in prison and are undergoing tortures, many of them, such as have not been known in Europe since the Middle Ages and which were formerly declared to be abolished in Turkey by the Sultan Abdul Medjid.

7. Many thousand refugees are crowded in the large towns where they suffer all kinds of abuse from the Turkish population, and are starving to death because the Bulgarians are not allowed to help them.

The subject of the Bulgarian atrocities was brought up in the House of Commons by W. E. Forster and in the House of Lords by the Duke of Argyle. Benjamin Disraeli, the Prime Minister, doubted whether such atrocities had really occurred and even resorted to forged telegrams from the British Ambassador in Constantinople, Sir Henry G. Elliot, to show that the stories published in the *Daily News* and *Times* were "gross exaggerations." English public opinion carried on a heated discussion over the news reports and the skeptical attitude held by Disraeli. At the same time, Gladstone, the opposition leader in the House of Commons, took up the issue of the Bulgarian atrocities. In speeches and debates he accused Disraeli's government of inaction. And on September 6, 1876, Gladstone published the famous sixty-four-page pamphlet *Bulgarian Horrors and the Question of the East.* As a result, public indignation spread not only in England but throughout the civilized world. Compassionate in spirit, Gladstone called for the total expulsion of Turkey from Europe, "bag and baggage." He closed with the following words, which became the most famous in the public debates at the time:

An old servant of the Crown and the State, I entreat my countrymen, upon whom far more than perhaps any other people of Europe it depends, to require and to insist that our Government, which has been working in one direction, shall work in the other and shall apply all its vigour to concur with the other States of Europe in obtaining the extinction of the Turkish executive power in Bulgaria. Let the Turks now carry away their abuses in the only possible manner, namely by carrying off themselves. Their Zaptehs and their Mudirs, their Bimbashis and their Yuzbachis, their Kaimakams and their Pashas, one and all, bag and baggage, shall, I hope, clear out from the provinces they have desolated and profaned. This thorough riddance, this most blessed deliverance, is the only reparation we can make to the memory of those heaps on heaps of dead; to the violated purity alike of matrons, of maiden and of child; to the civilization which has been affronted and shamed; to the laws of God or, if you like, of Allah; to the moral sense of mankind at large. There is not a criminal in an European goal, there is not a cannibal in the South Sea Islands, whose indignation would not rise and overboil at the recital of that which has been done, which has too late been examined, but which remains unavenged; which has left behind all the foul and all the fierce passions that produced it, and which may again spring up in another murderous harvest from the soil soaked and reeking with blood, and in the air tainted with every imaginable deed of crime and shame. . . . We may ransack the annals of the world, but I know not what research can furnish us with so portentous an example of the fiendish misuse of the powers established by God "for the punishment of evildoers, and for the encouragement of them that do well." No Government ever has so sinned; none has so proved itself incorrigible in sin or which is the same so impotent for reformation. If it be allowed that the Executive power of Turkey should renew at this great crisis, by permission or authority of Europe, the charter of its existence in Bulgaria, then there is not on record, since the beginning of political society, a protest that man has lodged against intolerable misgovernment or a stroke he has dealt at loathsome tyranny that ought not henceforward to be branded as a crime.

The situation had developed to such an extent that even Disraeli (now Lord Beaconsfield) served notice to the Sublime Porte of the possible consequences of its acts. He ordered the British Ambassador in Constantinople, Sir Henry G. Elliot, to undertake an investigation on the very spot.

9. AMERICANS IN BULGARIA'S HISTORY

Had it not been for the Americans at Robert College, especially Dr. Washburn, Dr. Long, and others, who had urged the American Minister in Constantinople, Horace Maynard, to send a special officer to the suffering areas affected by the Turkish atrocities and thereby ascertain whether or not the published newspaper stories were correct, the world would have soon forgotten about the cruel suppression of the Bulgarian April insurrection. It would have merely been considered another Balkan event. Credit is really due, however, to two courageous Americans who had arrived at the devastated spot to observe and graphically describe the actual occurrences. These two men were the diplomat Eugene Schuyler and the Irish-American journalist Januarious A. MacGahn.

In 1867, Eugene Schuyler was appointed American consul-general in Moscow and, in 1869, Secretary of the American Legation in Petrograd (now Leningrad). In the summer of 1876, Schuyler had been transferred to the American Legation in Constantinople. At that time, the April insurrection had already been suppressed. But when Schuyler took his post as consul-general, the topic of conversation in the diplomatic offices and the press was the "Eastern Question"—a synonym for the Bulgarian question. At the same time, however, Dr. Washburn and Dr. Long had urged the American Minister in Constantinople, Horace Maynard, to send a special officer to the suffering areas affected by the Turkish atrocities and thereby confirm whether or not the published stories were correct. Maynard had decided to send the newly arrived Eugene Schuyler. The latter was ordered to go to Adrianople and from there to Philippopolis (Plovdiv) and the Tatar-Pazardjik regions.

Meanwhile, the *London Daily News* sent a special correspondent to investigate the reported massacres on the spot. This man was the very eminent journalist J. A. MacGahn, who, as military correspondent for the *New York World,* had covered the Franco-Prussian War of 1871. Eugene Schuyler, accompanied by Peter Dimitroff, a graduate from Robert College, as an interpreter, along with MacGahn, who acted as Schuyler's secretary, arrived at the designated regions in Bulgaria. They set out from Constantinople on July 23, 1876. Letters and telegrams had been sent to the *Daily News* confirming the stories about the atrocities. Visiting the town of Batak, MacGahn and Schuyler were shocked at the sight of the devastated town.

On August 7, the *Daily News* published a telegram describing what they saw. On approaching Batak, said the telegram, they "found on the spot a number of skulls scattered about and one ghastly heap of skeletons with clothing. I counted them from the saddle a hundred skulls, picked and licked clean; all of women and children. We entered the town. On every side were skulls and skeletons charred among the ruins or lying entire where they fell in their clothing. There were skeletons of girls and women with long brown hair hanging to the skulls. We approached the church. There these remains were more frequent, until the ground was literally covered with skeletons, skulls and putrefying bodies in clothing. Between the church and the school there were heaps. The stench was fearful. We entered the churchyard. The sight was more dreadful. The whole churchyard for three feet deep was festering with dead bodies partly covered—hands, legs, arms and heads projected in ghastly confusion. I saw many little hands, heads and feet of children of three years of age and girls with heads covered with beautiful hair. The church was still worse. The floor was covered with rotting bodies quite uncovered. I never imagined anything so fearful. There were 3,000 bodies in the churchyard and church. . . . In the school, a fine building, 200 women and children had been burnt alive. All over the town there were the same scenes. . . . The man who did all this, Achmed Aga, had been promoted and is still Governor of the district. The newspaper accounts were not exaggerated. They could not be. No crime invented by Turkish ferocity was left uncommitted."

But MacGahn's letter of August 2, 1876, sent from Tatar-Pazardjik and published in the *Daily News,* provoked the inevitable Russo-Turkish War. The letter not only reflected the shock of what MacGahn saw but also expressed sympathy for the people who struggled to realize the same ideals for which the American people had fought only a century before. MacGahn never saw the creation of a free Bulgarian state, for which he shook the conscience of Europe. On June 9, 1878, on the eve of the International Congress of Berlin, he was stricken with a malignant fever, died in Constantinople, and was buried in Pera, with the distinguished Russian General Mihail D. Skoboleff (1843-1882) attending his funeral.

The American people paid tribute to the memory of this freedom-loving man in an unusual way. In 1884, his remains were disinterred at Constantinople and brought to America on the U.S. steamer *Powhatan.* In New York and in Columbus, Ohio, where his remains lay in state for a day, as well as at the funeral in New Lexington, Ohio, thousands of Americans paid tribute to the memory of MacGahn. Seventeen years later, on the Fourth of July—American Independence Day—the monument of Januarious Aloysius MacGahn was unveiled, with the epitaph "MacGahn, Liberator of Bulgaria."

SELECT BIBLIOGRAPHY

Anastasoff, Christ, *The Tragic Peninsula*, St. Louis, Mo., 1938, pp. 1-21; 343-345.

Blagoeff, Dimiter, "Vasil Levsky i negovata revolutsiona deinost" (Vasil Levski and His Revolutionary Activity), *Novo Vreme*, Sofia, 1898, pp. 211-214.

Belezhiti Bulgary (Noted Bulgarians), Sofia, 1968, Vol. II, pp. 11-21; 25-51; 197-202; 241-267; 311-325; 339-355; 367-389; 451-483; 501-516.

Gladstone, W. E., *Bulgarian Horrors and Question of the East*, London, 1876, pp. 1-64.

Haitov, Nikolay, *Haiduti*, Sofia, 1968, pp. 15-303. This very interesting work of 303 pages deals with a number of distinguished Bulgarian *Haiduti* and their exploits against Turkish rule prior to the liberation of Bulgaria.

Harris, David, *Britain and the Bulgarian Horrors of 1876*, Chicago, 1939, pp. 160-162; 201-218; 231-236. This work of 437 pages deals only with the event that the title indicates. It is one of the most comprehensive works published in English.

MacDermott, Marcia, *The Apostle of Freedom*, London, 1967, pp. 19-393.

Miller, William, *The Balkans: Romania, Bulgaria, Serbia and Montenegro*, New York, 1909, pp. 190-210.

Mishev, D., *The Bulgarians in the Past*, Lausanne, 1919, pp. 333-396.

Pastouhoff and Stoyanoff, *Istoria na Bulgarskia narod* (History of the Bulgarian People), Plovdiv, 1925, pp. 192-196.

Sakuzoff, Yanko, *Bulgarite v svoyata istoria* (The Bulgarians in Their History), Sofia, 1922, pp. 153-156; 190-214.

Sonnichsen, Albert, *Confession of a Macedonian Bandit*, New York, 1909, pp. 170-178.

NOTES

1. Pastouhoff and Stoyanoff, *Istoria na Bulgarskia Narod*, Plovdiv, 1925, p. 193.
2. William Miller, *The Balkans: Romania, Bulgaria, Servia and Montenegro*, New York, 1907, p. 200.
3. C. Anastasoff, *The Tragic Peninsula*, St. Louis, Mo., 1938, pp. 343-345.
4. See Chapter IX below.
5. See Chapter X below.
6. Armed groups of freedom fighters.
7. A. Sonnichsen, *Confession of a Macedonian Bandit*, New York, 1909, pp. 170-178.
8. The Turks called the Bulgarian insurgents *comitaji* because they were members of a revolutionary committee.
9. The Governor of the *Vilayet* (province) of Salonika.
10. A. Sonnichsen, *supra*, n. 7, p. 36.
11. This American educational institution was established in 1863 by a New York businessman and philanthropist, Christopher Robert. A number of Bulgarians graduated from this college and became noted statesmen after the liberation of Bulgaria.

CHAPTER VIII

THE ESTABLISHMENT OF THE THIRD BULGARIAN STATE (MARCH 3, 1878)

1. THE CONSTANTINOPLE AMBASSADORIAL CONFERENCE (1876)

In the general desire of the European powers to maintain peace, it was definitely recognized that this was impossible unless Turkey adopted a program of reforms embracing the volatile region of Bulgaria and Bosnia-Herzegovina. In a supreme effort to prevent further developments, the Great Powers—England, Russia, Germany, France, Austria-Hungary, and Italy—along with Turkey called for an International Ambassadorial Conference to be held in Constantinople in order to consider the problem of the Bulgarian April insurrection and thereby resolve the Bulgarian question.

The European Conference of Ambassadors convened in Constantinople at the invitation of Lord Derby, then the British Foreign Secretary. The distinguished diplomats who attended the Conference were the Marquis of Salisbury, the Special British Delegate; Sir Henry Elliott, the British Ambassador; Baron Werther, the German Ambassador; Count Zichy, the Delegate of Austria-Hungary; Count Bourgogné, the French Ambassador; Count Chaudordy, the Special French Delegate; Graf Ignatieff, the Russian Ambassador; Count Cori, the Italian Ambassador; and others.

After the first prolonged session of the Constantinople Conference in December 1877, attended by the above representatives, and after the opening speech of the President, Savfet Pasha, the Turkish minister of Foreign Affairs, and after the speeches of Salisbury, Ignatieff, Zichy, and Chaudordy, they presented to the foreign representatives six projects, the third of which was the project for the Organic Statute of Bulgaria, having the following form:

Bulgaria—Project for an Organic Statute

1. Out of the territories designated below there will be formed, conformably with the annexed map, two Vilayets (Provinces) which will be administered in the forms set forth in detail below.

The *Eastern Vilayet,* which will have Turnovo for its capital, will be composed of the sandjaks of Roustchouk, Turnovo, Tultcha, Varna, Sliven, Philippopolis (except Sultan Yeri and Achir-Tchelebi) and the Kazas of *Kirk-Kilisseh,* Mustapha Pasha, and Kazil-Aatch.

The *Western Vilayet,* with Sofia for the capital, will be composed of the Sanjak of Sofia, Viddin, *Nish, Uskub, Bitolia (except two Kazas of the south), a part of the Sanjak of Seres (three Kazas of the north), and the Kazas of Strumitza, Tikvesh, Veles, and Castoria (Kostour).*[1]

The ethnic boundaries for Bulgaria drawn up by the Constantinople Ambassadors Conference were based upon the work of such Balkan scholars as Louis Leger, Dr. G. B. Washburn, Professor P. N. Milyukoff, Sir Arthur Evans, and others. They were based upon historical, ethnographical, philological, and geographical data, and on the actual state of things. It is noteworthy fact Otto Von Bismarck, who was one of the principal members of the Congress of Berlin, which, for political reasons, diminished the frontiers of Bulgaria to a minimum, possessed a very definite knowledge of the ethnic area occupied by the Bulgarian people. It may be judged by the following statement elicited from him in the German Reichstag itself through an interpellation as regards the condition of things in the Balkans made by Benningsen, leader of the National Liberals.

"The ethnographical situation of Bulgaria," said Bismarck, "as I know it from authentic sources and as it appears in the best map I know—that of Kiepert—is this: *The boundaries of the Bulgarian nationality descend on the west, almost without any mixture, even beyond Salonica and reach in the east with a very small admixture of Turkish elements as far as the Black Sea.* The Constantinople Conference, however, as may be seen from its decisions, has stopped in East Bulgaria a little to the north of the Bulgarian nationality and, in exchange, it may be, it has in the west added to Bulgaria more territory inhabited exclusively by Bulgarian population."

The French diplomat Adolph Avril has made Bismarck's words ring with greater resonance and authenticity by commenting upon them in the following manner:

We have hitherto known the Chancellor in many forms but Bismarck as ethnographer has a great interest of its own. In the first place, it is well to show his green competitors and his ripe rivals that the Chancellor of the Empire has felt bound to know and, therefore, to investigate the Bulgarian question. And so, he is well acquainted with his Kiepert.

Secondly, *an ethnographic declaration from Bismarck is more than an opinion, it is an event.* This declaration has a special weight independently of its inherent value. Let us observe, in passing, that the Chancellor of the German Empire admits, speaking ethnographically, the great Bulgaria of the Constantinople Conference and of the San Stefano Treaty.

However, tacitly supported by the British, the Turkish government rejected the plan proposed by the Powers. At the same time it served notice to the assembled diplomats that the Sublime Porte had granted a Constitution guaranteeing the rights and freedom of the nationalities in European Turkey. Doubtless, this scheme was devised to allow Turkey to gain time. But since the above proposal was rejected, Lord Salisbury declared the Conference to be at an end.[2]

2. RUSSO-TURKISH WAR OF LIBERATION

An armed conflict was now inevitable, for Russia was at the end of her patience. Of all European states, Russia alone was the first to claim the right to protect the Christians living within the Ottoman Empire (as per Karlowitz Treaty of 1699). On April 24, 1877, Russia declared war on Turkey and by June 27 a Russian army crossed the Danube River and moved to the Balkans. In the early part of 1878, the Turkish army was devastatingly defeated. The road to Constantinople was clear. The victorious Russian army, assisted by thousands of Bulgarian volunteers, advanced almost within sight of the minarets of Constantinople.

Meanwhile, the British government was taking momentous action. The British ambassador in Constantinople was transferred to Vienna, and Layard, who had been minister to Madrid, was sent to Constantinople. Layard was known as a Turkophile and in some respects "more Turkish than the Turks themselves." The Ottoman government took this as a proof on the part of the British government that it would stand on the Turkish side against Russian advances toward the Straits and Constantinople. Notwithstanding the war fever in London, the Turks broke down and were compelled to sign an armistice at Adrianople, as well as an agreement whose basis was peace. Russia now entered into a treaty with Turkey—the famous Treaty of San Stefano, which assured the population of the Christian provinces almost complete independence.

3. THE SAN STEFANO TREATY

Turkey was now defeated. The Russians occupied the little town of San Stefano, which was about ten miles west from the capital of Turkey

—Constantinople. England had formally served notice that Russian troops should not, even temporarily, occupy Constantinople. To support its policy, the British government sent a part of its Mediterranean fleet to the Sea of Marmara. England prepared for war. Austria-Hungary lent her support to England. The Russian government, aware of the fact that it could not involve itself in war with such a European coalition, accepted the Turkish proposal for peace. *A peace treaty was, therefore, signed in the town of San Stefano on March 3, 1878*—hence the name San Stefano Treaty.

According to the above treaty, an autonomous Bulgarian state was created, including northern and southern Bulgaria, Thrace, and almost the whole of Macedonia. A Russian army was allowed to remain there for two years until the organization of the new Bulgarian state was completed. The San Stefano Treaty granted complete independence to the principalities of Serbia, Montenegro, and Romania.

The main provisions of this treaty were, of course, the rehabilitation of the old Bulgarian kingdom, by creating a new Great Bulgarian state. The latter extended from the Danube River on the north to Thessaly on the south, and from the Black Sea on the east to Albania on the west, thus including the whole of the present state of Bulgaria, most of Thrace, the whole of Macedonia, and the western districts of Nish, Pirot, Zaichar, and Vrania. The Great State of Bulgaria thus created was based essentially on historical and ethnic considerations; the preponderant character of the population was Bulgarian.[3]

In considering the San Stefano Treaty, Professor Oscar Browning, in his work *A History of the Modern World*, London, 1912, pages 294-297, writes: "The Treaty of San Stefano was the wisest measure ever proposed for the pacification of the Balkan Peninsula. It was by no means favorable to Russian ambition and, indeed, suggested the suspicion that it was drawn up by Ignatiev with exaggerated moderation, because he knew that as soon as it was concluded it would be torn to pieces by Great Britain. It created a large Bulgaria, founded on knowledge of history of that country and her claim, through her energy and steadfastness, to be the dominant power in the Peninsula. It recognized that Turnovo and Ohrida are the two foci of the Bulgarian nation, just as Moscow and Kiev are of Russia, one the civil and the other the religious capital. The new Bulgaria received Kavala on the Aegean as a port for the exportation of her produce. She was recognized as a free Christian province of the Turkish Empire, with an elective prince. Thus constituted, she could not have been a satellite of Russia but was far more likely to become ungrateful to the power which had created her and thus be an effective barrier to the advance of Russia towards Constantinople. In their ignorance, the bulk of British statesmen knew nothing of this; they had no knowledge of Bulgarian history and an incorrect map was issued to members of Parliament which entirely distorted the true state of affairs—as we have said, the map of the Balkan Peninsula distributed to members of Parliament was of mendacious character. Reference to authoritative sources, such as Petermann's *Mitteilungen*, would have shown that the Bulgarians were the predominant power in the Peninsula and that the Greeks had no claim to consideration. Salisbury knew little or nothing about Bulgarian history or the conditions on which alone a stable government could be erected. . . . Salisbury admitted afterwards that he was wrong; but it was poor reparation for a disastrous error to say some years afterwards that you 'put your money on a wrong horse.' "

4. THE CONGRESS OF BERLIN AND ITS OBJECTIVE

For selfish reasons, the British government flatly refused to recognize the Treaty of San Stefano. Obviously, England feared that by creating a great Bulgarian state on the Balkan Peninsula, Russia would be in a position to strengthen her sphere of influence there. England also feared that Bulgaria thus created might become a powerful ally of Russia. And in order to impress on the latter England's dislike of the San Stefano Treaty, the Tories voted money for armaments, sent a fleet to the Aegean Sea, ordered troops from India, and then informed Russia that the Treaty of San Stefano must be torn up and that the whole matter must be submitted to a Congress of Berlin.

In order to avoid a possible confrontation among the Great Powers, Bismarck, the German Chancellor, offered himself to act as peace mediator. He issued invitations for a Congress to be held in Berlin to discuss the contents of the Treaty of San Stefano. Russia, after some delay and discussion, gave in to the British and Austro-Hungarian pressure and agreed to accept the invitation, in spite of the fact that she had fought the war for the liberation of the Bulgarians without the aid of any of the powers and that it had cost her hundreds of millions of dollars and the lives of many thousands of soldiers. It was finally agreed that a Congress should assemble in Berlin on June 1, 1878. England was represented by Lord Beaconsfield (Disraeli) and Lord Salisbury. Lord Beaconsfield's policy in this Congress, in the words of Professor J. A. R. Mariott, "actually obstructed the development of the Balkan nationalities."

As stated above, the San Stefano Treaty with one stroke had solved the Bulgarian question most satisfactorily. The Bulgarian people considered themselves not only liberated but also politically united. But soon their momentary unity ended in deep affliction. For the Congress of Berlin destroyed the united Bulgarian nation, and the chief engineer planning its destruction was Disraeli. One month later, the Treaty of Berlin was signed, on July 1, 1878, and the partition of united Bulgaria accomplished. The country was now divided into five parts. Out of the northern part of the country, including the province of Sofia, a Bulgarian principality was created under the suzerainty of the Sultan;[4] from southern Bulgaria was created an autonomous province under the name of Eastern Rumelia, which was to remain under the political and military authority of the Sultan of Turkey; for its internal affairs it was to have a sort of "administrative authority" with a Christian as its governor; the districts (counties) of Nish, Pirot, Zaikar, and Vrania, in the western part of Bulgaria, were given to Serbia; Macedonia and Thrace, along with the Sandjak of Novi-Bazar, were given back to the Sultan; while Bosnia-Herzegovina was handed to Austria-Hungary for the purpose of "administration."[5]

What the concerted European powers failed to do in 1876, Russia tried to effect alone in the following year. In his manifest to the Russian people, Tsar Alexander II stated that the chief motive for declaring war on Turkey was her failure to execute the decisions of the Ambassadorial Conference, providing for the final liberation of the Bulgarian people.

As pointed out above, Turkey had been crushed and compelled to sign the San Stefano Treaty. The latter was another and more solemn recognition of the legitimate Bulgarian claim to national reunion.

England, Germany, and Austria-Hungary, however, jealous of Russia's political preponderance in the Near East and fearing that the creation of a strong Bulgarian state in the Balkans would prove a mere Russian vanguard toward the Dardanelles, intervened in behalf of Turkey, and caused the convocation of the Berlin Congress for the revision of the San Stefano Treaty.

At Berlin, Europe went back on its word and rescinded its decisions taken by its representatives of the Constantinople Conference. Thus, the good work of the latter was undone because of the rival designs cherished by the various European powers.

In this manner Bulgaria was sacrificed on the altar of the selfish interests of a suspicious Europe. Considering this matter, the great authority Dr. G. B. Washburn writes: "The Treaty of San Stefano had created a Bulgaria essentially on the lines agreed to by the Powers at the Conference of Constantinople. The Treaty of Berlin divided Bulgaria into five sections, giving one part (Nish, Pirot, etc.) to Serbia, one (Dobrudja) to Romania, one to an autonomous province called East Roumelia, one (Macedonia) to Turkey and one to constitute the principality of Bulgaria under the suzerainty of the Sultan; and it was

England especially that insisted upon this and also upon the right of Turkey to occupy and fortify the range of the Balkans all with the object of making it impossible for the Bulgarians to form a viable state which might be friendly to Russia. The Englishmen who knew Bulgaria, all our friends, understood the folly and wickedness of this at the time. All England has learned it since. Thus far, the results have been the revolution of 1885 which resulted in the union of Bulgaria and Eastern Rumelia, the war with Serbia, the insurrection in Macedonia and the Province of Adrianople and all the massacres and unspeakable horrors of the last thirty-nine years in Macedonia, to say nothing of what Bulgaria has suffered from the intrigues of foreign powers ever since the Treaty of Berlin. The awful massacres and persecutions from which the Armenians have suffered since 1886 have been equally the result of this treaty."[6]

Because the Macedonian question was a direct outcome of the work of the Congress of Berlin, the story of Macedonia and the subsequent tragic Balkan situation will be considered below.

Although the Bulgarian people were first spiritually united by the *Firman* of February 1870, which created the national Bulgarian church, and seven years later by the San Stefano Treaty, unfortunately the Congress of Berlin performed the first political division, while the Treaty of Bucharest (1913)[7] effected the second political division of the Bulgarian nation. Because of such unjust and shameful distribution of the Bulgarian people from one sovereignty to another, as a result of European rivalry, bloodshed has occurred on the Balkan Peninsula for the past eight decades, and it may erupt again.

5. FRIENDLY ROMANIAN-BULGARIAN
RELATIONS IMPAIRED

Until the Congress of Berlin, Romania and Bulgaria were living as good neighbors and friends. Throughout the revolutionary period, preparatory to the great struggle of 1876, the Bulgarian patriots found in Romania a most hearty welcome and encouragement. Braila, Bucharest, Galatz, and Jassi had become great centers for Bulgarian intellectual and insurrectionary activities. Turkish persecution had driven thousands of Bulgarians to Romania. Hundreds of Bulgarian students flocked across the Danube. In Braila was founded the Bulgarian Literary Society, which after the liberation of Bulgaria was moved to Sofia and was developed into the Bulgarian Academy of Sciences. In 1867, a secret agreement was concluded between the Romanian government and the Bulgarian Revolutionary Organization for joint action against Turkey.

In 1877, by capturing the Grivitza Redoubt, the Romanians, as allies of Russia, had won a great military victory and the eternal gratitude of the Bulgarian people. For ages past the Danube had been a most convenient natural boundary that separated the two neighbors. Their relations were so friendly that when, in 1878, toward the close of the Russo-Turkish peace negotiations, Prince Charles I of Romania (1866-1881) was notified by the Russian government of its intention to retain Bessarabia, in exchange for which Romania was to receive Dobrudja, he wrote Tsar Alexander II a touching letter of protest, ending with the words, "The friendship of a nation is more precious than a piece of territory."

Once Romania acquired Dobrudja, on the other side of the Danube, an end was put to the good relations between the two countries. From then on, Romania became apprehensive about the unlawful acquisition and felt insecure because of the discontent created in the hearts of the Bulgarians. One of the first anxieties of every Romanian government was how best to protect Dobrudja from a future attack on the part of the Bulgarians. The Romanians were not too happy with the Congress of Berlin decision, nor with the provision of the Treaty of Berlin. This may be surmised from the fact that at its session of June 28, 1878, the Romanian National Assembly passed a resolution that ended with the following: "*An annexation to Romania of a territory found on the other side of the Danube is not in the interest of Romania, which does not wish to become the cause for future disturbances and, therefore, she under no circumstances would agree to the annexation of Dobrudja.*"

But what could a small country like Romania do against the declared will of an imperialistic Europe? Thus the Berlin decisions destroyed the traditional friendship of the two countries, which nature had provided with a frontier at once defensible and natural. Thereafter the relations between Romania and Bulgaria, for one reason or another, remained strained. Romania, conceiving the idea that, in order to ensure the safety of her trans-Danubian possessions, she needed a greater hinterland to the south, developed an ambition to acquire the Danube-Tourtoukai-Balchik "triangle." That dream led to the unprovoked aggression and invasion of 1913. By the Treaty of Bucharest (August 10, 1913), Romania wrested another slice of territory from Bulgaria. The Romanian-Bulgarian conflict of 1916 was another disastrous sequel to the policy inculcated in Romania by the powers signatory to the Treaty of Berlin.

Such has been the sad history of the Romanian-Bulgarian relations ever since 1878, when an evil fate decreed that Dobrudja—the cradle of the Bulgarian race, the land of Asparuh, Krum, and Simeon, known for more than seven centuries as Black Bulgaria, Maritime Bulgaria, Danubian Bulgaria—should be handled in such a way as to break up the firm friendship of two young states merely for a "piece of territory." All of this was a direct result of the Berlin Treaty.

Had it not been for the evil designs of the Great Powers in 1878, Romania and Bulgaria would have to this day remained the best of friends and a model of neighbors, and the Balkans and Europe would have been spared so much unnecessary turmoil, conflict, and bloodshed.

6. STRAINED SERBO-BULGARIAN RELATIONS

The decisions taken at the Berlin Congress proved equally disastrous to the fraternal relationship between the Serbian and the Bulgarian people. Until then, Serbs and Bulgars had taken part side by side in all the struggles directed against Turkey. It is sufficient to point out that in the various Russo-Turkish wars of 1806, 1811, 1829, 1854, and 1877 Serbians and Bulgarians had taken a most active part. Bulgarian and Macedonian contingents always responded to the revolutionary movements of Serbia, Greece, and Romania. In 1862, a Bulgarian legion led by Georgi Rakovsky and consisting of veteran fighters from Bulgaria and Macedonia rendered great help to the Serbian troops that attacked the Turkish garrison stationed in Belgrade.

The purely Bulgarian uprisings of Pomoravia, 1806-1809, of Pirot in 1830, of Nish in 1841, of Vidin in 1851, were always treated as such by the entire Serbian press, government, and public opinion, and when in 1867 there was concluded the secret agreement between the Serbian government and the Bulgarian Revolutionary Committee abroad, the territories of Bulgaria proper, Bulgarian Morava, and Macedonia were never considered other than Bulgarian lands.

Until the Berlin Treaty, Pomoravia was recognized by all as part of Bulgaria *irredenta*. The religious and political struggles of the inhabitants of this territory were always in harmony with the general efforts of the Bulgarians at large for their regeneration and liberation.

The Congress of Berlin, however, which had turned over Dobrudja as a "compensation" to Romania, in 1878 gave in the same way to Serbia the districts of Nish, Pirot, Zaichar, and Vrania, disregarding the repeated protests of the patriotic Bulgarian population. From this date on began the fratricidal friction, conflicts, and wars between the two Balkan Slavic peoples who are so closely related in many respects. And from July 1, 1878, the eyes of the Serbian state were fixed toward the south. The Serbs, too, were induced to look for more secure boundary lines in order to assure the retention of the newly acquired territories, which they knew were alien to them in spirit and traditions.

What instigated Serbia's policy in a southerly direction when her legitimate national interests were found to the northwest, in the Serbo-Croatian lands then under the Dual Monarchy rule, was the fact that, according to a secret treaty, Russia, in 1878, to gain the goodwill of Austria-Hungary in her own acquisition of Bessarabia and other territory wrested from Turkey, had sanctioned Austria-Hungary's occupation of Bosnia-Herzegovina. That was, indeed, a deadly blow to the national aspiration of the Serbians. The latter would have preferred those kindred provinces to have remained under the domination of Turkey rather than to have been transferred to another, though more refined rule. The anguish was, indeed, felt by the Serbians. And yet the Serbians themselves, by virtue of certain stipulations of the Berlin Treaty, had become the masters of a number of districts inhabited by Bulgarians, whose bitter protests were heeded neither by them nor by selfish Europe and not even by Russia, their liberator from the Ottoman despotism.

In fact, the Bosnians and Herzegovinians had little to complain of against an Austrian regime under which they were allowed to have their own churches and schools, to use their own language, and to enjoy a communal autonomy.

How different was the lot of the unfortunate Bulgarian lands that were forcibly incorporated into the Principality of Serbia! Ever conscious of its own weakness and of the strong Bulgarian spirit of the Pomoravians, the Serbian government employed all possible means and methods for smothering the last vestige of Bulgarianism among them. A revolt of these people was quenched in cold blood by the Serbian regime. Hundreds of the leading citizens were imprisoned, others were forced to flee to Bulgaria or were shot as "rebels."

These events, obviously enough, were of a nature to foster unfriendly feelings between the two Slav and neighboring states. The Bulgarian Principality, reduced in area to a minimum, was too young and too weak to come to the rescue of its oppressed kindred, not only in Serbia but also in Romania and Macedonia, whose lot was now getting to be more cruel and unbearable than ever. Patiently and silently the Bulgarian people endured provocation after provocation heaped upon them from all sides by their covetous and envious neighbors. The Serbians thenceforth could not be looked upon by the Bulgarians in any other light than as oppressors and enemies of the Bulgarian people.

The overt manifestation of chauvinistic Serbian propaganda about Macedonia found its support by intellectuals connected with the University of Belgrade. It began in 1873, three years after the establishment of the Bulgarian Exarchate and five years before the political liberation of Bulgaria, when Milosh S. Milojevič read a paper at the Serbian Royal Academy in Belgrade. The contents of this paper bewildered the audience at the Academy. "Its theme was," writes Professor Wilkinson, "that the Serb language and culture extend much farther south than hitherto generally has been believed. Milojević argued in fact that Macedonia was Serb and not Bulgarian territory and he produced a map to support his contention. It was a Serbian, Stoyan Novaković, a distinguished member of the Academy, who exposed the shallowness of his argument. In fact, a great deal of the evidence submitted was proven to be forged. Milojević emerged as a cheap, mischievous chauvinist, ignominiously condemned by his fellow countrymen for having committed an unfriendly act against a good neighbor. . . . However, a clash between the Serbians and the Bulgarians in Macedonia was not to develop until Serbian expansionists, diverted by the march of events, turned their face from the Adriatic towards the Aegean."[8]

Doubtless, Milojević's arguments found support in some political circles in Belgrade. But almost all independent Serbian newspapers condemned him for sowing discord between the Bulgarian and the Serbian peoples, breeding not brotherhood and friendship but enemies and adversaries. The Serbian newspaper *Javnost* (Herald), wrote at the time the following:

> We would like to assure our brothers, the Bulgarians, that the Serbian public opinion fully opposes the foolish and quixotic ideas of Milosh Milojević and his group. We cannot even say how stupid we consider this behavior. For a long time now Mr. M. Milojević has been looked upon as a charlatan in our literary circles or as a man much closer to the "blind man Jeremiah" and to his kin than to people who go in for scholarly truth. Our conclusion is supported by Mr. Novaković and (Milan) Kojundič, of his recent effort, submitted to the Serb Society of Science. We have known for a long time that Mr. Milojević has been waging a war against the Bulgarian nationality in Macedonia but we never thought that any Serbian government could participate in such things.[9]

To help carry out the expansionist policy, the Serbian government relied on the advice of two prominent professors of Belgrade University —Jovan Cvijič and Stoyan Novaković, who was also a politician.

Jovan Cvijič (1865-1927), as professor of the University of Belgrade (since 1897) and president of the Serbian Academy of Science (since 1921), had acquired a reputation among European scholars as a geologist, physical geographer, and cartographer. As head of the Department of Geography, he was in a position to carry out intensive research in the Balkans. Almost inevitably his work was affected by his country's political aspirations. "To conform with the expansionistic policy of Belgrade," writes Professor Wilkinson, "Cvijič began to modify his ethnographic map of Macedonia. Conceiving the idea of 'Macedo-Slavs,' he modified his ethnographic maps of 1906, 1907 and 1910, so as to incorporate practically all of Macedonia as part of South or Old Serbia. If, declared Cvijič, the Macedonian Slavs were to be incorporated into the Serbian state, they would very soon become Serbian in nationality—a prophecy which was never fulfilled."[10]

As for Stoyan Novakovič (1842-1915), an eminent Serbian scholar who was following scientific principles and who ridiculed the chauvinistic pretensions of Milosh Milojevič, he, also as a politician, soon turned about and became an exponent of the idea of "Macedonianism."

In his report to the Ministry of Education in Belgrade, Novakovič expounds his idea about the new stage in the activities of the Serbian propaganda in its struggle against the Bulgarian Exarchate, as well as his plan for a transitional period in Serbianizing the Macedonian Bulgarians. Wrote Novakovič in 1887:

> Since the Bulgarian idea, as it is well known, is deeply rooted in Macedonia, I think it is almost impossible to be shaken completely by opposing to it only a purely Serbian idea. This idea, we are afraid, merely as bare opposition, will not suppress the Bulgarian idea. That is why the Serbian idea will need an ally that could stand in direct opposition to Bulgarism and could possess in itself the elements which would attract the people and their feelings and thus sever them from it. I see this ally in Macedonianism.[11]

It was, therefore, such "scientific" manipulations that brought about animosity and conflicts between the two Balkan Slavic states Serbia and Bulgaria. Because of the intentional confusion created by the Belgrade exponents of expansionism, some Slavic scholars often refer to the Macedonian Bulgarian language as a "Slav dialect akin to both Serbian and Bulgarian" or to the "Macedonian Slavs" as distinct from the Bulgarians.

7. THE ELECTION OF PRINCE ALEXANDER
OF BATTENBERG

Article VII of the Berlin Treaty provided that, after its ratification by the signatory powers, the Russian army of occupation would not remain in Bulgaria more than nine months. After a meeting of Bulgarian notables to be held in Turnovo (Article IV) to draft an Organic Statute for the administration of the country, the next step was to proceed with the election of a prince, after which Bulgaria would assume its autonomous status.

Prior to the election of a prince, the administrative head in Bulgaria was General Alexander Dondoukoff-Korsakoff (1820-1893). He was a distinguished Russian officer who had participated in the Crimean War of 1854 and also in the Russo-Turkish War of 1877 to 1878 as supreme commander of the Eighth Corps of the eastern detachment. He was appointed chief imperial commissar in Bulgaria on May 20, 1878, and charged with the task of organizing the government of the newly created Bulgarian Principality. Evidence shows that Dondoukoff-Korsakoff had entertained the idea that he might eventually be elected head of the Bulgarian state. Because of a possible negative attitude on the part of the Western powers, however, it was agreed upon that no Russian citizen should be elected head of the Bulgarian state. The reasons were quite obvious. A Russian at the head of the Bulgarian government would have been considered by the interested powers, particularly England and Austria-Hungary, as leading to the creation of another Russian *goubernia* (province).

In the period of nine months specified by the Treaty, Dondoukoff-Korsakoff had prepared the Organic Statute, which created the central and local administrative units and laid the foundation of the Bulgarian army. On February 10, 1879, a Constituent Assembly was held in Turnovo, the old Bulgarian capital, to approve the draft Constitution of Bulgaria. And on April 7, 1879, the Grand National Assembly was convened in Turnovo to elect the ruling head of the Principality. Antim I (Atanas M. Chalkoff, 1816-1880), the first Bulgarian Exarch, presided over both the Constituent and the Grand National Assembly. The latter proceeded, with the election of Alexander of Battenberg (1857-1893), a German, as Prince Alexander I of Bulgaria (1879-1886). He was elected because of the wish and recommendation of his uncle, Tsar Alexander II of Russia. Only a few years later, on April 27, 1881, Prince Battenberg caused some changes to be made in the Turnovo Constitution; it appeared too liberal to him. This aroused dissatisfaction among the masses of the people and he was compelled, on September 7, 1883, to restore the altered provisions of the original Constitution.

After the assassination of Tsar Alexander II in 1881, Prince Alexander I of Bulgaria began to pursue a pro-Western policy. He now began to look toward Austria-Hungary and England rather than Russia. The relation between Battenberg's policy and that of Tsar Alexander III of Russia became strained. The political parties in Bulgaria were then divided as either Russophiles or Russophobes. The former succeeded in dethroning Prince Alexander I of Bulgaria, who abdicated on August 29, 1886. Before his abdication, and in accord with the provisions of the Turnovo Constitution, Prince Alexander I appointed a Council of Regents (1886-1887) made up of Stephan N. Stamboloff (1854-1895), Petko S. Karaveloff (1845-1903), and Lieutenant Colonel Sava A. Moutkouroff (1852-1891). Because of disagreement of the Russophobes, Karaveloff resigned, and Georgi A. Zhivkoff (1844-1899) was elected in his place. The Regency thus constituted followed a pro-British and pro-Austria-Hungary policy.

Naturally, the political crisis of the country was sharpened. The urgency for electing a head of state was paramount. The third Grand National Assembly was held on October 19, 1886, and the first point on its agenda was the election of a prince. A deputation led by Stamboloff had visited several European palaces looking for a candidate. On June 25, 1887, the deputation approached Ferdinand of Austria and, on June 27, he announced that he would accept the Bulgarian throne. Thus, the third Grand National Assembly elected Prince Ferdinand I of Saxe-Coburg-Gotha (1861-1929), and thereby the Regency terminated.

8. UNIFICATION OF EASTERN RUMELIA WITH THE PRINCIPALITY OF BULGARIA

Article 13 of the Berlin Treaty stated that south of the Balkans there was to be a province under the name of "Eastern Rumelia," which was to remain under the direct political and military control of the Sultan. This province was to have an "autonomous government" with a Christian governor-general appointed by the Sublime Porte and with the approval by the European Powers (Article 17); after the ratification of the Treaty there was to be created a European commission to work out, with the concurrence of the Porte, a plan for the organization of Eastern Rumelia (Article 18). But after the announcement of the Berlin Treaty, the general indignation and widespread of revolts in Eastern Rumelia prevented the International Commission from carrying on its designated work. The Commission, however, which was constituted of foreign and Turkish representatives, remained in Constantinople.

The first general-governor of the province was Prince Alexander Bogorodi (Aleko Pasha, 1823-1910), whose term of office expired in 1884. He was succeeded by Gavril B. Krstevitch (1820-1898), who had studied law in Paris. Because of his legal profession, he had been appointed to important positions in Turkey's judicial hierarchy. He had participated in and was, indeed, of great help in struggle for the Bulgarian Church and in the national movement during the period 1860 to 1870. After the liberation of Bulgaria from the five-centuries-old Turkish yoke, Krstevitch was appointed by the Sublime Porte as secretary-general and minister of internal affairs of Eastern Rumelia. Meanwhile, he was closely connected with the movement for the unification of Eastern Rumelia with the Principality of Bulgaria.

Because the vast majority of the population of Eastern Rumelia was Bulgarian, the movement for unity with Bulgaria found strength not only among the masses of the people but also among persons connected with the militia of the province. Of the many prominent leaders of the movement, one should at least point out those who actually led the revolt and succeeded in accomplishing its objective. The most prominent member of the underground movement was Zahari D. Stoyanoff (1850-1889). He was a noted writer, publicist, Bulgaria's representative of memoirs and biographical literature, and also a devout revolutionary. He participated in the April uprising in 1876. In Plovdiv, the capital of East Rumelia, he published the newspaper *Borba* (Struggle), which advocated unity with Bulgaria. He was a member of the Bulgarian Secret Central Revolutionary Committee, which led the fight for the unification. Zahari Stoyanoff and his followers helped the cause of the liberation of Macedonia. This help was given to the Macedonian revolutionary committees that were being organized in Bulgaria.

The two military officers who had plotted the revolt in 1885 were Major Raycho Nikoloff (1840-1885), commandant of the gendarmerie (cavalrymen), and Major Danail T. Nikolaeff (1852-1942), commandant of the second battalion in Plovdiv. It was secretly agreed that the revolt should take place in the early part of September in Plovdiv. About this time military maneuvers were taking place not only in Eastern Rumelia but also by the Bulgarian army. The latter's maneuvers took place in the Shumen area, a northern Bulgarian district near the Turkish border in Rumelia. Under the leadership of Major Nikoloff, the revolutionists took every possible measure to make the coup a success. Before the government of Eastern Rumelia had a chance to avert the conspiracy, Zahari Stoyanoff, Major Nikolaeff, and Major Nikoloff entered Plovdiv, surrounded the residence of the governor-general, Krstevitch, and forced him to surrender. On September 6, 1885, they proclaimed the unification of Eastern Rumelia with the Principality of Bulgaria.

Neither Turkey nor the signatory powers of the Berlin Treaty showed any threat for this action on the part of the Eastern Rumelian Bulgarians.

But the achieved unification of Eastern Rumelia with Bulgaria was not in accord with the wishes of Tsar Alexander III of Russia. It was said that he had even urged the Sultan to invade Eastern Rumelia, and, to punish the disobedient Principality of Bulgaria, he recalled all Russian officers from the country, thus severely handicapping the military resistance of the young Principality. Fortunately, the English Ambassador in Turkey at that time was the distinguished diplomat Sir William White, a great friend of Dr. G. B. Washburn, president of Robert College. Ambassador White alone, for nearly all of his colleagues in Constantinople were on the side of Russia, warned Turkey that any rash act on her part might cost her her very existence. The Sultan was awed and dared not to move, and thus the day was won for Bulgaria and her reunion realized. The *coup d'etat* of 1885 was successful only because of the support of the British government effectively manifested through Sir William White.

If the convocation of the Berlin Congress at which Bulgaria, Rumelia, Macedonia, Pomoravia, Thrace, and Dobrudja were cut off from their bigger sister, Bulgaria, was the work of a mistaken British diplomacy, the union of Rumelia and Bulgaria in 1885 was also effected by British statesmen, who were now anxious to repair the political conscience of Great Britain, which had been largely responsible for the partition of San Stefano Bulgaria.

9. THE SERBO-BULGARIAN WAR OF 1885

Without any provocation on the part of the seven-year-old Principality of Bulgaria, King Milan of Serbia (1882-1889), under the pretext of maintaining the balance of power, rushed in with a regular and veteran army toward Sofia, expecting to reap a rich territorial crop at the expense of a small and inexperienced state, as Bulgaria was then.

Russia, which, in the short period of seven years had found out that Bulgaria, contrary to Russia's expectations, would never act as a Tsarist vanguard in the Balkans, ordered her military instructors and officers to abandon the Principality to its fate; she firmly believed that a Turkish reoccupation of Bulgaria would present her another opportunity for a rescue expedition in the Near East. Fortunately for Bulgaria, her lieutenants and subalterns—there were only a few native officers holding the rank of major and captain—were able in a short period of time to drive back the invader. Only the threat of Austria-Hungary prevented the victorious Bulgarian army and militia from entering Belgrade.

Serbian military provocations were occurring all along the western frontier of Bulgaria. After the unification of Eastern Rumelia and the Principality of Bulgaria on September 6, 1885, Serbia declared war on Bulgaria on November 14 of the same year. King Milan made this known to the Serbian people in the following manifesto:

To the Serbian people,

True to the traditional policy of the Obrenoviches for the defense of the highest interests of the fatherland, I, with the help of the loyal representatives of my beloved people, undertook all possible measures, against the provocation on the part of the Bulgarian Principality by its brutal violation of the Berlin Treaty and to make it clear and voiceful that Serbia cannot be unconcerned toward the change of balance of power among the people of the Balkan Peninsula, especially when this is exclusively in favor of a state, which at every moment since its liberation is being used to prove to Serbia, that she is a bad neighbor and that she does not wish to respect her rights and even her territory. . . .

By announcing this to my beloved people, I, in this serious moment rely upon its love toward the fatherland and on its dedication toward the Serbian act.

Milan[12]

After this manifesto, Serbia soon felt the effects of the humiliating defeat by the inexperienced Bulgarian army and militia, led by young officers, mainly captains. Brilliant victories were achieved at the battles at Slivnitsa, Tsrev, Tri-Ushi, Dragoman, Gourgulyat, Tsaribroad, Pirot, and Vidin. For decades during the national struggle, the young generations of Bulgarians were educated to love their fatherland and follow in the steps of their fathers and forefathers. Their enthusiasm and dedication to fight for the defense of their seven-year-old free country transcended the Prussian military tactical training of the Serbian army. And had it not been for the Austro-Hungarian warning to the Principality of Bulgaria, the latter's young army would have even occupied Belgrade.

It was not difficult to guess that the real instigator for the fratricidal war between Serbia and Bulgaria was none other than Austria-Hungary, whose aim was to distract the attention of the Serbians, with their vision of territorial acquisition everywhere except northwest. How skillfully the Dual Monarchy managed its *protégé* may be gathered from the fact that already on June 28, 1881, Austria-Hungary had, on the strength of the secret treaty concluded between her and Serbia, succeeded in inducing the latter to renounce her claim to Bosnia-Herzegovina, in return for which Austria-Hungary pledged herself to support a Serbian policy in Macedonia.[13] Thus, under the patronage of the Hapsburgs, there was laid the foundation of a strong Serbian propaganda in that ill-fated land, which ever since the conclusion of the Berlin Treaty had been an arena where the hostile interests of Greeks and Serbians clashed with the aspirations of the preponderant and compact Bulgarian population, who were trying to unite with their brethren of free Bulgaria, as the Eastern Rumelians had in 1885.

The Turkish government found it advantageous to encourage, now one, now the other faction, believing the principle of *divide et impera* to be the only expedient for maintaining its existence in Europe—an existence that was artificially prolonged at the Berlin Congress by means of Disraeli's political chicanery. The historical enmities between Greeks and Bulgarians, now augmented by a determined Serbian campaign, alternately manipulated by Turkey, Austria-Hungary, and Russia, converted Macedonia into a veritable hell. The Bulgarian population, being the most formidable element in the province, became the target for attack on the part of all other nationalities, inspired and instigated from Belgrade, Athens, and Constantinople, which in turn were receiving their directions either from Vienna or from Petrograd.

As has already been pointed out, Austria-Hungary's policy was an important factor in bringing about the war of 1885. She was against the unity of Eastern Rumelia with Bulgaria. Austria-Hungary, however, would have recognized the unification, provided that "Serbia was given territorial compensation" at the expense of Bulgaria. The joke of the matter was Bismarck's indirect manipulation. Although he rejected the Austrian thesis of the "change of equilibrium on the Balkan Peninsula" and the idea of "territorial compensation" to Serbia, Bismarck was cunningly trying to involve Russia in the Balkan conflict, which would inevitably bring about the straining of relations between Russia and England. His scheme, however, did not materialize. The unification of Eastern Rumelia with the Principality of Bulgaria became a *fait accompli*. Serbia tried her luck but lost. The Bulgarian captains defeated the Serbian generals, and the war of 1885 was over.

10. THE CULTURAL DEVELOPMENT OF BULGARIA AFTER ITS LIBERATION

The liberation of Bulgaria from Turkish domination gave a stimulus for its cultural development. The efforts of the people were now directed not only to building up the new state but also toward its cultural and spiritual development.

After the liberation of the country, the cultural development was built upon that of the period of Bulgaria's renaissance. The ideas of that renaissance during the eighteenth and nineteenth centuries continued to agitate the minds of the masses of the people even after the liberation.

Several decades after the liberation of Bulgaria came the introduction of various kinds of philosophical ideologies, natural science, and sociological teachings, which found wide acceptance by the intelligentsia. The new concepts came either from Russia or from the Western European countries. Prior to the liberation, many Bulgarian intellectuals had attained their higher education abroad. This in itself was of great help for the educational and cultural development of the new country.

The main factor in Bulgaria's educational and cultural growth after the liberation was the opening of a school of higher learning, with departments of history, philosophy, physics, mathematics, and law; this school later became the Sofia State University. A school of fine arts was opened in Sofia in 1895. Many noted Bulgarian artists graduated from this school. The opening of Sofia University created opportunities for scien-

tific research in the various academic disciplines. Much research was
done in the natural and social sciences. The most distinguished figures
in this area were the biologist Porphiny I. Bahmatieff (1860-1913), the
chemist P. N. Raynoff, the geologist Georgi N. Zlatarski (1854-1909), the
historian Vasil N. Zlatarski (1866-1935), the archeologist Gavriel Ilieff
Katsaroff (1874-1958), and the linguist Alexander Theodorov-Balan
(1859-1959). After the liberation of Bulgaria a number of scientists and
specialists from other Slavic and European countries arrived to assist in
the development of Bulgarian science and culture. In the newly created
Bulgarian Principality the prominent Czech historian Constantine J.
Jireček, author of valuable researches on the history and geographical
extent of the Bulgarian lands, served for a time as chief secretary and
minister of national education.

Significant progress was also made in the national educational system
when Professor Marin Drinoff became director in charge of national
education, during the latter period of the temporary Russian administration of Bulgaria. In organizing the educational system, Drinoff had observed the traditions created during the epoch of Bulgaria's renaissance.
From 1879 to 1910, the number of schools tripled and the number of
students increased fivefold. In 1910, the literacy of the urban population
reached sixty-three percent, and that of the villages thirty-five percent.[14]
Until the wars of 1912 to 1918, national education in Bulgaria increased
rapidly. Numerous reading rooms and libraries were opened for the
masses of the people. In Sofia in 1879, the foundation was laid for the
National Library, Kiril and Methodi, which became the greatest national literary center.

Soon after the liberation, a series of newspapers and periodicals
began to appear. The early journals were *Maritsa, Tirnovska Consti-
tutsia, Bulgarian Glas, Nezavisimost,* and others. Periodicals dealing with
sociopolitical, economic, and literary questions were also published.
After the unification of Eastern Rumelia and Bulgaria and at the beginning of the twentieth century, the publication of daily newspapers increased. Some of the noted journalists were Stoyan Chilingaroff, editor
of the independent daily *Dnevnik* and *Outro,* whose director and owner
was Atanas Damianoff; Ivan Zlateff, editor of *Narodni Prava;* Vladimir
Boboshevsky, editor of the independent daily *Balkanska Tribuna;* Luben
Harizanoff, editor of *Mir;* Peter G. Bakaloff, who reported the debates
during the constitutional changes made by the Fifth Grand National
Assembly and who was publisher of the *Almanac of the Bulgarian Constitution* (1911); Vasil Paskoff, editor of the newspaper *Preporets;*
Krusto Stancheff, editor and owner of the daily *Kambana;* Todor Vlaikoff,
editor of the newspaper *Radical;* Todor Astarzhieff, editor of *Rech;* and
others.

About this time, socialist ideas were introduced in Bulgaria, mainly by Dimiter Blagoeff (1855-1924), a noted Marxist theoretician. Socialist newspapers and periodicals, such as *Rabotnik* and *Rabotnicheski Vestnik* and the periodical *Novo Vreme,* were published.

During the early years after the liberation, much progress was made in the development of Bulgarian literature. The writers and poets at this time were under the influence of the events connected with the heroic struggle of the Bulgarian people for national freedom. The Russo-Turkish war of liberation had also exerted considerable influence on them. Their works were mainly based upon these tumultuous events. It was to these events that the greatest Bulgarian national poet and writer, Ivan M. Vazoff (1850-1921), dedicated his talent. During this period of storm and stress and gradual stabilization of the Bulgarian political, economic, and cultural life Vazoff did his work. The period called for literature of a type very different from that of the insurrectionary days before the liberation; the country faced problems of a different character, and it was Vazoff who gave the predominant tone to literature for the next decades.

Ivan Vazoff's most important works are: *Pod Igoto* (Under the Yoke), a novel about the life of the Bulgarian people on the eve of the liberation (1876); the narrative *Nemili ne Dragi* (Outcasts); and the poetical collections *Pryaporetz i Gousla* (Banner and Ribec) and *Tugite na Bulgaria* (The Afflictions of Bulgaria). Of the other voluminous works of prose and poetry, Vazoff's *Epopea na Zabravenite* (Epic of the Forgotten) is the most outstanding. In this epic, he glorifies the exploits and patriotism of the most prominent national revolutionists and freedom fighters.

Soon after the liberation, writing on the same theme were Zahari Stoyanoff and Constantine Velichkoff. Stoyanoff was the author of several memoirs and biographical publications, of which the most important are his *Zapiski po Bulgarskite Vostania* (Notes About the Bulgarian Insurrections) and the biographies of Vasil Levsky and Hristo Boteff. Constantine Velichkoff wrote his memoirs, *V Tumnitsata* (In the Dungeon).

After the unification of Eastern Rumelia with northern Bulgaria, there appeared a new nationalistic literary current. Its typical representatives were Todor Vlaykoff, Hristo Maksimoff, Anton Strashimiroff, Mihail Georgieff, Elin Pelin, and the poets Tsanko Tserkovsky and Peyo Yavoroff (1878-1914). Yavoroff was by far the most prominent poet of this period. For a time, he was editor of *Delo* (The Cause) and later of the newspaper *Makedonia* (Macedonia). In 1908, he became associated with the Bulgarian National Theater in Sofia, for which he wrote the two plays, *In the Foothills of Vitosha* and *When the Thunder Strikes.* In 1907, he published his collections *Insomnia* and *Visions.* And in 1911 appeared his last collection, *The Breath of the Shadows on the Clouds.*

An important contribution to Bulgarian literature after the liberation was the works of Aleko Constantinoff (1863-1897), *Bai Ganuo* (Old Man Ganuo) and *To Chicago and Back* (1893). In the first work, Constantinoff tells incredible stories about a contemporary Bulgarian—his covetousness, unscrupulousness, lack of culture, self-seeking, and so on. Critical satire is also found in the works of Stoyan Mihailovsky.

At the beginning of the twentieth century there appeared in Bulgaria an idealistic-symbolic current, whose most typical representatives were Pencho Slaveykoff (1866-1912), Theodor Traykoff, Nikolay Lileff, and others. The ideological leader and defender of this current was the literary critic and editor of the periodical *Misel* (Thought, 1892-1907), Dr. Krustu Krusteff (1866-1919).

Along with the development of literature, significant strides were made in the theater, music, the fine arts, and architecture. Plays were performed in Bulgaria even before the liberation, and at this time the first Bulgarian dramas were written. After the liberation, the first theatrical companies were organized in Plovdiv and Sofia. The first professional theatrical troupe was formed in Sofia after the Serbo-Bulgarian War of 1885. There, too, a special theater was built. In 1892, the Sofia actors founded the troupe "Slzi i Smyah" (Tears and Laugh), which later became the Bulgarian National Theater, supported by the state. The outstanding actors were Krustu P. Saraphoff (1876-1952), Adriana Budevska, Stoyan Bchvaroff, Vasil Kirkoff, Hristo Gancheff, and others. The plays written by Bulgarians were *Ivanko* by V. Droumeff, *Heshove* (Bravados) by Ivan Vazoff, and others. Later on, the performers of opera came into being. The first opera presentation was given by Dragomir Kazakoff and Ivan Vouleff. Soon the first Bulgarian composers appeared. The outstanding composer was Emanuel Manoloff. Together with Dobry Hristoff, he composed a series of group songs that are still used by vocal societies in Bulgaria.

The first Bulgarian operas were based on the ordinary life of the people and on the national liberation struggles. Such were *Kamen and Tsena* by Ivan Vazoff and V. Kautsky, *Tahir Begovitsa* by Dimiter Hadjigeorgieff, and *Gergana* by Georghi Atanasoff.

Other works of art also made significant progress. After the liberation, the noted historical painter was Nikolai Pavlovich. A number of other realistic works of art appeared; they were based on the national way of life of the people. The most prominent artists of this type were Ivan Mrkvichka and Yaroslav Veshin. Of particular artistic value are the paintings *Horo* (Dance) and *Rchenitsa* by Ivan Mrkovichka, and *Haiduti* by Y. Veshin, who also emerged as the best artist, as shown by his paintings *Na Nozh* and the *Otstplenieto na Tourtsite Pri Lule-Burgas* (The Retreat of the Turks at Lule-Burgas). Other contemporary artists were Anton Mitoff, painter of *Pazar v Sofia* (Market Place in Sofia), and

Ivan Angeloff, *Bog dal Bog Vsel* (God Giveth and God Taketh), and others. And the most prominent sculptors were Zheko II. Spiridonoff (1867-1945) and Boris Shtits.

Bulgarian architecture began to develop after the liberation. Prior to this, most of the architects had been foreigners. Gradually, Bulgarian architects, who had obtained their education abroad, began working along with them. In commemoration of the national liberation struggles and also of the help rendered by Russia, many monuments were built by Bulgarian architects. The most impressive of these monuments are the Alexander Nevsky Memorial Church and the Statue of Alexander II, both of which are in the center of Sofia.

SELECT BIBLIOGRAPHY

Almanac of The Bulgarian Constitution (on the occasion of the establishment of the third Bulgarian kingdom), Plovdiv, 1911. The Constitution of the Bulgarian Principality (in Bulgarian), pp. 327-353; the full text of the San Stefano Treaty (in Bulgarian), pp. 45-67; the full text of the Berlin Treaty (in Bulgarian), pp. 71-104.

Bourmov, A., Kosev, D., and Hristov, Hr., *Istoria na Bulgaria* (History of Bulgaria), Sofia, 1960, pp. 139-156; 237-241.

Hristov, Hristo, *Osvobozhdenieto na Bulgaria i Politikata na Zapaonte Drzhavi —1876-1879* (The Liberation of Bulgaria and the Western European States—1876-1879), Sofia, 1968, pp. 49-95; 96-122; 132-158.

Istoria na Srubsko-Bulgarskata Voyna 1885 (History of the Serbo-Bulgarian War of 1885), Sofia, 1971, pp. 10-443. This work is published by the Ministry of National Defense of the Historical Section.

Kiril, Patriarch of Bulgaria (1953-1971), *Bulgarskata Exarchia v Odrinsko i Makedonia Sled Osvoboditelnata Voyna 1877-1878* (The Bulgarian Exarchate in the Province of Adrianople and in Macedonia After the Russo-Turkish War of 1877-1878), Sofia, 1969, Vol., pp. 11-89.

Kosev, D., Hristov, Hr., Angelov, D., *Kratka Istoria na Bulgaria* (A Brief History of Bulgaria), Sofia, 1962, pp. 148-166; 174-178.

Panaretoff, Stephen, *Near Eastern Affairs and Conditions*, New York, 1922, pp. 156-183.

Pantev, Andrey, *Anglia Streshtou Roussia na Balkanite—1879-1894* (England Versus Russia in the Balkans, 1879-1894), Sofia, 1972, pp. 29-282. *Note:* This scholarly research work is based on documents issued at the time in England, Russia, France, Germany, Italy, and other interested countries.

Radeff, Simeon, *Stroytelite na Svremena Bulgaria* (The Builders of Contemporary Bulgaria), Sofia, 1911, Vol. I, pp. 3-49; 107-159; 485-559; 629-688.

Sakuzoff, Yanko, *Bulgarite v Svoyata Istoria* (The Bulgarians in Their History), Sofia, 1922, pp. 195-212; 215-227.

Stephanove, Constantine, *The Bulgarians and Anglo-Saxondom*, Berne, 1919, pp. 18-53; 70-78; 185-212.

Stoyanoff, Zahary, *Zapiski po Bulgarskite Vostania* (Notes About the Bulgarian Insurrections), Sofia, 1962, Vol. I, pp. 95-118; 201-317, Vol. II, pp. 323-481.

NOTES

1. The British *Blue Book*, Turkey, No. 2, p. 153.
2. For an abstract of the proceedings of this Conference, see Edward Hertslet, *The Map of Europe by Treaty*, IV, pp. 2526-2530 and 2541.
3. See Article VI of the San Stefano Treaty.
4. See Articles I and II of the Treaty of Berlin.
5. *Ibid.*, Articles XXV.
6. Dr. G. B. Washburn, *Fifty Years in Constantinople*, Boston, 1909, pp. 183-184.
7. See Chapter XI below.
8. Professor H. R. Wilkinson, *Maps and Politics—A Review of the Ethnographic Cartography of Macedonia*, Liverpool University Press, Liverpool, 1951, p. 93.
9. *Documents and Materials on the History of the Bulgarian People*, published by the Bulgarian Academy of Sciences, Sofia, 1969, p. 190.
10. Wilkinson, *supra*, Chapter VIII, n. 8, p. 149.
11. *Documents and Materials*, *supra*, Chapter VIII, n. 9, p. 245. See Cl. Djambazovski, "Stoyan Novaković and Macedonianism." *Historical Magazine*, Vol. XIV, Skopie, 1964, p. 141.
12. *Istoria na Surbsko-Bulgarskata Voyna of 1885*, Sofia, 1971, pp. 168-169. *Note:* This book of 490 pages is published by the Bulgarian Ministry of National Defense.
13. See the Treaty of Alliance between Austria-Hungary and Serbia, Belgrade, June 16-28, 1881, and the "Personal Declaration of Prince Milan that he would carry out the Treaty without restriction" in A. F. Pribram, *The Secret Treaties of Austria-Hungary, 1879-1914*, I, pp. 50-56.
14. A. Bourmov, D. Kosev, and Hr. Hristov, *Istoria na Bulgaria*, Sofia, 1960, p. 239.

CHAPTER IX

THE MACEDONIAN QUESTION: AN APPLE OF DISCORD

1. THE ORIGIN OF THE MACEDONIAN QUESTION

In modern history the Macedonian question is rather new. It first appeared on the Balkan scene in connection with the struggles for an independent Bulgarian national church. The triumph of these struggles culminated with the issuance of the *Firman* of March 11, 1870. The latter outlined the territorial extent of the Bulgarian lands in European Turkey. Macedonia was thereby included in the spiritual unity of the Bulgarian people. As we have seen, under the San Stefano Treaty of March 3, 1878, the whole of Macedonia, except Salonika and the Chalcidice Peninsula, was included in the projected state of Bulgaria. Macedonia was even considered as part of the Bulgarian lands by the Constantinople Ambassadorial Conference in 1876. Only five months later, however, the provisions of the San Stefano Treaty were completely reversed by the Congress of Berlin. By the subsequent Treaty of Berlin of July 13, 1878, Macedonia was left under continued Turkish rule. Thus *the Macedonian question appeared for the second time on the political Balkan scene in 1878, and thereby came the rivalry of the Balkan states for her disposition.* The "sick man" of Europe was soon expected to vanish, and Macedonia became an arena of Serbian and Greek propaganda, encouraged covertly by interested European powers.

2. THE GEOGRAPHIC EXTENT AND THE POPULATION OF MACEDONIA

Macedonia, of course, constituted by far the largest province of European Turkey. Because of its geographic location in the heart of the western half of the Balkan Peninsula, Macedonia occupied a valuable strategic position, both for commerce and for military strategy. The country is traversed by the only natural and shortest roads from north to south; these connect middle Europe with the Aegean Sea and thereby the Near East. In order to understand the political meaning of the Macedonian question, it would be of interest to give a brief sketch of the country.

In general, the topographic features of Macedonia are quite irregular and rather mountainous; the geographic boundaries of the country are for the most part natural. On the east, Macedonia is bound by the Mesta River and the Rhodope Mountains. On the north, she is bound by a range of mountains starting with Shar Planina (Shar Mountain), Cherna Gora (Black Forest), and the Osogov Planina. These mountains extend from west to east, with some irregularities, which assume a northeastern (Cherna Gora) and southern direction (Osogov Planina). The western boundary of Macedonia is a line along the eastern part of the Albanian border, running in a rather southerly direction, passing west of Lake Ohrid. The southern border of Macedonia is the Bistritsa River, which originates in the southern Albanian mountains and runs west and south of the Kostour (Kastoria) district to the Gulf of Salonika (see map).

As indicated by her geographic boundaries, Macedonia is surrounded almost entirely by high mountains, except for her outlet to the Aegean Sea. Thus, she assumes an inclined plane that slopes southward. There are three rivers—the Vardar, the Struma, and the Mesta—which run through from north to south and empty into the Aegean Sea. The most important valley, however, is that of the Vardar. First, because the Vardar River is the largest and therefore the most useful for commercial purposes and, second, because the Vardar Valley is connected through the low mountain passes near Vrania with the Valley of Morava, which leads to the Danube and thus opens the way toward Middle Europe. Thus Macedonia occupies a central position in the southwestern part of the Balkan Peninsula, with Thrace and Bulgaria on the east, Albania on the west, the Aegean Sea and Greece on the south, and Shar Mountain and Serbia on the north.

Within these boundaries, Macedonia covers nearly 26,000 square miles, just about the size of South Carolina or the combined areas of Connecticut, Delaware, Maryland, and Massachusetts. Although the country shows a mountainous character, it, nevertheless, contains numerous fertile plains. The climatic conditions are quite favorable for residence, agriculture, and livestock husbandry, which is, of course, the main industry.

The total population of Macedonia, as estimated in 1912, before Turkey was driven out of the country by the Balkan War of 1912, was 2,260,000, of which 55 percent were Bulgarians, 20 percent Turkish, 10 percent Greek, 5 percent Albanian, 5 percent Jews and Arumanians (Vlacks), and 5 percent Gypsies and others. From this statistical data, one would note the heterogeneous character of the inhabitants; nevertheless, the predominating group, the one that had played the major role in the affairs of Macedonia, was the Bulgaro-Macedonians.

The *Report* of the International Commission to Inquire into the Causes and Conduct of the Balkan Wars gives the following information:

Official Turkish statistics admitted only one principle of discrimination between the ethnic groups dwelling in Macedonia, namely, religion. Thus, all the Mohammedans formed a single group, although there might be among them Turks, Albanians, Bulgarians, "pomaks," and so on; all the patriarchists in the same way were grouped together as "Greeks," although there might be among them Serbians, Wallachians, Bulgarians, and so on. Only in the "exarchist" group did religion coincide more or less with Bulgarian nationality. The Turkish official registers include men only; women were not mentioned because the registers served only for the purpose of military service and taxation. Often, nothing was set down but the number of "households." This explains the lack of anything approaching exact statistics of the Macedonian population. Owing to the different principles and methods of calculation employed, national propagandists arrived at wholly discrepant results, generally exaggerated in the interest of their own nationality. The table subjoined shows how great is this divergence in estimate and calculation:

Bulgarian Statistics (Mr. Kantchev, 1900)

Turks	499,204
Bulgarians	1,181,336
Greeks	228,702
Albanians	128,711
Wallachians	80,767
Jews	67,840
Gypsies	54,557
Serbians	700
Miscellaneous	16,407
TOTAL	2,258,224

Serbian Statistics (Mr. Gopcevic, 1889)*

Turks	231,400
Bulgarians	57,600
Greeks	210,140
Albanians	165,620
Wallachians	69,665
Jews	64,645
Gypsies	28,730
Serbians	2,048,320
Miscellaneous	3,500
TOTAL	2,879,620

*Recent Serbian authorities avoid giving general figures, or else, like Mr. Guersine, suggest a total for the Macedonian Slav population that approximates more closely to Mr. Kantchev's figures.

Greek Statistics (Mr. Delyani, 1904)
(Kosovo Vilayet omitted)

Turks	634,017
Bulgarians	332,162
Greeks	652,795
Albanians	—
Wallachians	25,101
Jews	53,147
Gypsies	8,911
Serbians	—
Miscellaneous	18,685
TOTAL	1,724,818*

The Bulgarian statistics alone take into account the national conscious-ness of the people themselves. The Serbian calculations are generally based on the results of the study of dialect and on the identity to cus-toms: they are, therefore, largely theoretical and abstract in character. The Greek calculations are even more artificial because their ethnic standard is the influence exercised by Greek civilization on the urban population and even the recollections and traces of classical antiquity.

The same difficulties meet us when we leave population statistics and turn to geographical distribution. From an ethnographical point of view, the population of Macedonia is extremely mixed. The old maps of Ami Bóe (1847) and thereafter follow tradition regarding the Slav popula-tion of Macedonia as Bulgarian. Later, local charts make the whole country either Serbian or Greek. Any attempt at more exact deliniation, based on topical study, is of recent date. There are, for example, Mr. Kantchev's maps, representing Bulgarian opinion, and the better known one of Mr. Tsviyits (J. Cvijič), representing the Serbian. But Mr. Tsviyits's ethnographic ideas vary also with the development of Serbia's political pretensions. In 1909, he gave "Old Serbia" a different outline from that he gave it in 1911 (see his map published in the "Petermann" series), and in the hour of Serbian victory on the eve of the second Balkan war, another professor at Belgrade University, Mr. Belits (Belič), published his map, based on a study of dialects, a map that satisfies the most recent immoderate pretensions. The Serbo-Bulgarian frontier rec-ognized by the treaty of March 1913 is plainly inspired by the ideas of Mr. Tsviyits, while the line drawn by Belits reveals and explains the causes of the breaking of treaty and the war between the allies.[1]

As has already been pointed out, after the Congress of Berlin, Austria-Hungary entered into closer relations with King Milan of Serbia. In the

---

*See also *infra*, Appendix VIII.

secret treaties signed in 1881 and renewed in 1889, Austria promised in clear, even terms "to aid the extension of Serbia in the direction of the Vardar Valley." Thus, at the very moment when the Dual Monarchy was depriving Serbia of any possibility of westward extension by joining the section of the Serbian population inhabiting Bosnia-Herzegovina to herself, Austrian diplomacy was holding out, by way of compensation, the hope of an extension toward the south, in those territories whose population, up to the period 1860 to 1870, had been universally recognized as Bulgarian even by the Serbians.

"From this point on," states the *Report* of the Carnegie International Commission of 1914, "nationalism distinctly gained ground in Serbia. The whole of Macedonia was identified with 'Old Serbia' and 'Young Serbia' in its map, claiming the entire territory occupied under the rule of Stephen Doushan, in the fourteenth century. At this period, the network of Serbian schools spread especially fast, thanks to the aid of the Turks, who here as elsewhere followed their habitual policy of playing off the Serbian and Greek minorities against the stronger and more dangerous minority of the Bulgarian exarchists. In 1899, the Serbian school manuals were for the first time published at Constantinople with ministerial sanction, and the Serbian school soon ceased to be secret and persecuted. In 1895-1896, according to official Serbian statistics, there were 157 schools with 6,831 scholars and 238 male and female teachers. It is, however, noteworthy that 80 of these schools, comprising 3,958 scholars and 120 male and female teachers, were situated in Old Serbia properly so-called, that is to say, that more than half of them belonged to counties that were undoubtedly Serbian.

"Here are the statistics for the Bulgarian exarchist schools for the same period: there were in Macedonia, 1896-1897, 843 such schools (against 77 Serbian schools); 1,306 teachers (Serbian, 118); 31,719 scholars (Serbian, 2,873); children in the kindergarten, 14,713.

"These figures show that, at the close of the nineteenth century, the overwhelming majority of the Slav population of Macedonia was sending its children to the exarchist Bulgarian school. The school became, henceforth, an auxiliary of the national movement and independent of the church. The movement changed both its character and its object. Side by side with the ecclesiastical movement led by priests and assisted by the religious council of the community, there arose in about 1895 a revolutionary movement directed against the Turkish regime whose object was political autonomy and whose leaders were recruited from the schoolteachers. On the other hand, the resistance of the minorities, supported by the Turks, grew more pronounced. 'Patriarchism' and 'exarchism' became the rallying cries of the two conflicting nations. From this time on the ethnographic composition of Macedonia was to be elucidated only by an enumeration of 'exarchist' and 'patriarchist' households—a most uncertain and fluctuating method since the strife grew more complicated, so that one and the same family would sometimes be divided into 'Bulgarians,' 'Greeks,' 'Wallachians,' and 'Serbians,' according to the church attended by this or that member."[2]

Referring to Vassil Kantchev's *Makedonia—Ethnographia i Statistika,* Colonel L. Lamouche, in his book *Quinze Ans D'Histoire Balkanique* (1904-1918), states that Dr. Gustav Weigand's statistics[3] and those of the Czech scholar Vladimir Sis approach those of Kantchev's. Writes Colonel Lamouche:

Je ne puis garantir absolument la précision des chiffres de détail, mais ce que est certain, c'est que, comme j'ai pu m'en rendre compte sur place, les nationalites indiquées pour les différents villages sont exactes, ainsi que la proportion des éléments dans les localites mixtés. On pent donc en conclure que les proportions, sur l'ensemble de la population, se rapprochent beaucoup de la vérité.

M. G. Weigand, professeur a l'Université de Leipzig, savant ethnographie et linguiste, qui à, a plusieurs reprises, parcouru la Macédoine dont il connâit parfaitement les langues et les dialectes, attribue aussi une serieuse valeur á l'ouvrage de V. Kantchev, dont il a pu contrôler les donées.

D'après V. Kantchev, la population de la Macédoine dan les limites indiquées, aurait été, dan la période de 1895 à 1900, de 2,252,000 âmes se décomposant comme suit, entre les nationalités et les cultes.

	Chrétiens	Israélites	Musulmans	Total
Bulgares	1,032,000		147,000	1,179,000
Turcs			498,000	498,000
Grecs	211,000		14,000	225,000
Macédo-Roumains	78,000			78,000
Albanais	8,500		116,500	125,000
Tsiganes	10,000		45,000	55,000
Israelites		70,000		70,000
Divers	22,000			22,000
TOTAL	1,361,500	70,000	820,500	2,252,000

M. Vladimir Sis, de nationalté tchèque, dan une étude publiée en 1918,[4] donne des chiffres se rapprochant beaucoup de ceux de Kantchev.[5]

3. THE LAUNCHING OF A LIBERATION MOVEMENT BY THE MACEDONIAN BULGARIANS

The revolt against the Berlin settlement first manifested itself in Macedonia. In 1878 and 1880, a series of uprisings occurred in Ohrid, Prilep, Demir-Hissar, Krushevo, Resen, Debra, and other Macedonian districts. Article XXIII of the Berlin Treaty was supposed to ameliorate the conditions of Turkey's Christian subjects. It states:

> The Sublime Porte undertakes scrupulously to apply in the Island of Crete the Organic Law of 1868 with such modifications as may be considered equitable.

> Similar laws adapted to local requirements, excepting as regards the exemption from taxation to Crete, shall also be introduced into the other parts of Turkey in Europe for which no special organization has been provided by the present treaty.

> The Sublime Porte shall depute special commissions, in which the native element shall be largely represented, to settle the details of the new laws of each province.

> The schemes of organization resulting from these labors shall be submitted for examination to the Sublime Porte, which, before promulgating the Acts, shall consult the European Commission for Eastern Rumelia.

Ever since the settlement of the Congress of Berlin, the Macedonian Bulgarians had hoped for their deliverance from Russia; but the union of Eastern Rumelia with the Principality of Bulgaria in 1885 swept aside this hope, because Russia's attitude toward Bulgaria became antagonistic. The Macedonians now looked toward Bulgaria itself for their deliverance. Macedonia, moreover, was considered *Bulgaria irredenta* or "Unredeemed Bulgaria." The desire to round out the Bulgarian kingdom by adding to it *Bulgaria irredenta* was one of the reasons that led Bulgaria to take the side of the Triple Alliance in World War I.

But the political situation in the Balkans toward the end of the nineteenth century was such that it was impossible for Bulgaria to render any help to the cause of Macedonia. Russia now definitely opposed any move on the part of Bulgaria and, in fact, took the side of the Turks. England, who had been responsible for the destruction of the united Bulgarian state of San Stefano, became a much better friend of Bulgaria than was Russia. The European rivalry over the Balkan situation certainly diminished the expectation that the Macedonians would be delivered by the Great Powers. It was because of this unfortunate situation that the Macedonian leaders began to rely upon their own efforts for freedom. They soon realized that Article XXIII of the Berlin Treaty had become a dead letter. Seeing that they could obtain no redress for their sufferings either from the Ottoman government or from the European powers, the Bulgarian population of Macedonia, along with that of Thrace, set themselves to organize a revolutionary movement of their own under the order of a Revolutionary Central Committee.

Although the first Bulgarian insurgents had called themselves *Haiduti*, later on the Turks began referring to them as *comitajis* (armed bands of freedom fighters) because they were now under the command of a revolutionary committee. The Bulgarians in Macedonia took up arms almost immediately after the restoration of Macedonia to the Turks in 1878. However, their earlier protests and revolts were of sporadic nature and there was no unanimity of action—no solidarity. Their action became more systematic and organized only in 1893, when the Internal Macedono-Odrin (Adrianople) Revolutionary Organization (IMORO) came into being (henceforth to be referred to only as IMRO). Its avowed purpose was the autonomy of Macedonia and Thrace. But a certain number of its leaders were for attaching these provinces to Bulgaria in accordance with the San Stefano Treaty.

The pro-Bulgarian tendency naturally found encouragement in the palace of Sofia, while the autonomists were to lay the basis for eventual self-government in Macedonia and Thrace.

At the head of the movement aiming to restore the San Stefano Bulgaria were Macedonians, officers in the Bulgarian army such as General T. Tsoncheff, Colonel Iankoff, and others.

Late in the autumn of 1902, General Tsoncheff proclaimed a general uprising to be led by men from Bulgaria. He crossed the frontier in November with about four hundred men and, in the districts of Djoumaya and Razlog near the Bulgarian frontier, he carried on a guerrilla campaign for more than three weeks. But the IMRO opposed his enterprise and there was no general uprising, even in the very limited area he had invaded. By December, all fighting was at an end. Tsoncheff and his band returned to Bulgaria, and the peasants of the invaded districts were left to bear the brunt of Turkish vengeance. Although the IMRO had no share in these events and even tried to frustrate General Tsoncheff's wild enterprise, the Turks made no discrimination, and all over Macedonia the burden of the Turkish yoke grew heavier. As a result of Tsoncheff's revolt in the Djoumaya and Razlog districts there were:

45 Bulgarians killed
67 houses burned
807 houses pillaged
438 men and women tortured
111 women outraged
3,000 found refuge in Bulgaria.[6]

4. FRENCH DIPLOMATIC AGENTS' REPORTS ABOUT THE UPRISING IN MACEDONIA

The stronger the revolutionary movement became, the more clearly the Turkish authorities and the European consuls saw that an uprising was being prepared. Many diplomatic documents confirm this. The following are taken from the *French Yellow Book of 1902*. M. Choublier, the French consul of Monastir (Bitolia), in report to his superior of March 4, 1902, writes:

> Everywhere they are talking about an uprising which is to come this spring. It is impossible to say what part of Macedonia is most threatened by a Bulgarian movement; however, the revolutionary bands have concentrated their efforts along a line running across Macedonia through the mountainous and forest districts of Shtip, Velles, Prilep, Kroushevo, Monastir, and Kastoria (Kostour).
>
> The bands have been weakened in their activity by the war which the leaders of the Greeks and their proselytes, supported by the Turkish authorities, have carried on against them. The Bulgarians, who joined the Greek elements, have been especially harmful, for they keep revealing the plans of the Bulgarians. The Greek church authorities in Monastir take the side of the Turks against the Christian population, which they expect to be joined to Greece some day. . . . The Greeks clamor for severe measures against the Bulgarians.
>
> The Serbian propaganda on the other hand is not hostile to the Bulgarian movement. The Serbian consul advises all who come to him for advice not to join the Bulgarian bands under any circumstances but to preserve a favorable neutrality and even to help the revolutionists to escape when they are being pursued by the Turks. The Serbian propaganda is very weak in these localities and so poorly organized that it would only be taking useless risks if it followed the example of the Bulgarians. On the other hand, if the Serbians opposed the revolutionary movement they would lose the sympathy of the inhabitants, who are not so very patriotic but who want to be freed from their present intolerable situation and would accept any liberator with joy wherever he might come from.

M. Choublier, however, did not properly gauge the national consciousness of the struggling Macedonian Bulgarians.

On March 6, 1902, the French ambassador in Constantinople, M. Constans, wrote to M. Delcassé, the minister of foreign affairs, as follows:

> From the conversations which I have recently had with my colleagues and among others with the Russian ambassador, it appears that they also have received unusually disturbing reports concerning the activities of the Bulgarian and Macedonian bands, which are making serious preparation for an uprising in the spring. It is true that such reports are circulated every year about this time but, according to my opinion, we must give more credence to these rumors now than during past years. The preparations for the revolutionary movement have assumed such proportions that it will be harder now than ever before to keep it from breaking out.

On July 29, 1902, M. Bapst, the French chargé d'affaires at Constantinople, wrote to M. Delcassé the following:

According to the reports which I receive, the most unsettled part of Macedonia at the present time is the Monastir district, where the bands are most numerous and where they have succeeded not only in arming themselves but also in arming the civilian population with "Gra" guns brought in across the Greek border. It is plain that nothing but a strict administrative, financial, and judicial control will be able to bring even a degree of moral tranquility and material welfare to these people who have suffered so much, but it is doubtful even now whether the reforms so much desired and so long expected will take form at the deliberations of the Commission, which at present is sitting at the Grand Vizeriat.

In Bulgaria, there were scores of thousands of Macedonian refugees. There existed a legal Macedonian organization, the aim of which was to further in a moral and material way the efforts of the people in enslaved Macedonia, who were fighting for their liberation. The Tsoncheff-Mihailovski Committee, which was at the head of this organization in 1902, violated its rules and regulations by sending bands into the districts of Gorna Djoumaya, Razlog, and Petritch to start an uprising. This action was strongly opposed by the leadership of Internal Macedonian Revolutionary Organization.

On December 3, 1902, M. Steeg, the French consul-general in Salonika, in his report to M. Delcassé, wrote the following about the revolutionary movement:

It is well established now that the last attempt at an insurrection was the work of the Sofia committee of which General Tsoncheff is the president, and that the purpose of the uprising was to precipitate events and thus get control of the Macedonian national movement. As far as the purely Macedonian committees are concerned, the Internal Organization, which is surrounded by more mystery than ever before and the ideal of which— an autonomous Macedonia—is in conflict with the annexationist aspirations of Tsoncheff's committee, they have not been content merely to refrain from taking part in the recent movement but have vigorously opposed it as a premature venture condemned to certain failure.

Furthermore, as far as I have been able to learn, the adherents of the Macedonian Revolutionary Organization are more numerous and better organized than those of the Sofia committee and it is this organization to which should be ascribed the summary executions and the acts of terror which so often occur in this country. Furthermore, we have a right to believe that when this organization decides that the day has come for an action to the one undertaken by the Tsoncheff committee, the insurrectionary movement, without having any better chances of success, perhaps, will assume much larger proportions. There are indications which seem to show that the organization has made serious preparations for an insurrection next spring.[7]

Even before writing this report, M. Steeg had already sent to the French government (October 28, 1902) a scheme for reforms in Macedonia.[8]

5. LEADERS OF MACEDONIA'S
REVOLUTIONARY MOVEMENT

At the head of the autonomist movement were men who actually took part in the organization of the IMRO and whose names are venerated by the Macedonian Bulgarians. These men were Damian Iv. Grueff (1871-1906), Gotse N. Delcheff (1872-1903), Hristo A. Matoff (1872-1922), Pere N. Tosheff (1866-1912), Dr. Hristo N. Tatarcheff (1869-1952), Boris P. Sarafoff (1872-1907), and others. Under the leadership of this group of men, the IMRO had its way during the next several decades; it became the most powerful underground movement, with a well-organized secret administration. It was the work of these men—Grueff, Delcheff, Tosheff, Matoff, Sarafoff, and others—that shattered Sultan Abdul Hamid's possessions in Europe. The lives of these men were, in fact, the history of the whole Macedonian liberation movement. Their idealism and devotion to the cause of freedom and human rights deserve one's admiration. They were true apostles and martyrs for the cause of freedom and self-determination of Macedonia.

Damian (Dame) Iv. Grueff was born in 1871 in the village of Smilevo, district of Bitolia, southwestern Macedonia. After receiving an elementary education in his native village, he later studied in Ressen, Bitolia, Salonik, and at the University of Sofia. While still a student at the Bulgarian Gymnasium in Salonika, Grueff felt the unbearable Turkish oppression and maltreatment of his fellow countrymen. Soon after he graduated from the Gymnasium he went to Bulgaria and there, in 1889-1890, enrolled at the University of Sofia to specialize in history. There Grueff found an opportunity to study the history of the Bulgarians but more particularly the methods and tactics of the Bulgarian revolutionists—Rakovsky, Karaveloff, Boteff, Levsky, and others—who had been greatly responsible for the freedom of Bulgaria. Following the method used by the Bulgarian revolutionists prior to the liberation of Bulgaria, Grueff thought about the formation of a similar organization in Macedonia for the deliverance of the Bulgarians still held in bondage by the Sultan of Turkey.

He left the University of Sofia and returned to Macedonia for the sole purpose of organizing the Macedonian people. To avert any suspicion by the Turkish authorities, Grueff decided to become a schoolteacher. For two years he taught school, first in his native village and then in the city of Shtip. These two years of teaching served him as orientation for the work of the great conspiracy against the corrupt and rapacious regime of Sultan Abdul Hamid.

Later on he settled in Salonika and there, with the cooperation of

Dr. Hristo N. Tatarcheff, Peter Pop Arsoff, and others, formulated in the summer of 1894 the constitution and bylaws of the IMRO, under the chairmanship of Dr. Tatarcheff. It was to be a secret organization under the directives of the Revolutionary Central Committee, at the head of which were Dr. Tatarcheff, Pere N. Tosheff, and Hristo A. Matoff.[9]

From 1894 to 1900, Grueff was an untiring apostle—a new Levsky—preaching and recruiting adherents to the revolutionary movement. In the summer of 1894, he organized the first local revolutionary group in the town of Negotin, and soon after, along with Pere Tosheff, he organized the first district committee in the city of Shtip. Thereafter, Grueff also visited the cities of Ressen, Ohrid, and Struga and found wide acceptance of his revolutionary ideas. In the city of Shtip, however, the conditions for organizational work were even more favorable and here he remained as a teacher during the academic year of 1894-1895. In the fall of the same year, Gotse Delcheff, who had independently conceived the same idea as Grueff—that of organizing a secret revolutionary organization—arrived in Shtip to work for that purpose. Here Grueff and Delcheff met for the first time. Soon after their acquaintance they found the similarity of their common mission. Delcheff accepted the scheme of work that had already been outlined by the Salonika Central Committee. After this, both Grueff and Delcheff worked together in Shtip and its surounding settlements.[10]

In the years 1895 to 1897, Grueff settled in Salonika in the capacity of an Exarchist school inspector.[11] Grueff now became the body and soul of the Revolutionary Central Committee. Under the direction of the former they began to issue secret underground revolutionary newspapers, introduced ciphers or messages in code, used pseudonyms, and established channels for secret communication among the various local committees and also with its representatives abroad. One of its trusted men were sent to Sofia for the purpose of purchasing arms and ammunition and other supplies for the IMRO.

Grueff's roaming from village to village and from one city to another resulted into a systematic revolutionary organization throughout the province of Macedonia and the Vilayet of Adrianople.[12] For purely political reasons and to safeguard itself from any complication, the Exarchy decided to dismiss Grueff in 1898.[13] Soon after his dismissal, Grueff moved to Bitolia and there, with the cooperation of Slaveico Arsoff and others, he began to issue another undergorund newspaper. Sunday schools were opened, money was collected through a special "revolutionary tax," and a quantity of war materials was purchased. Once again Grueff was appointed to the teaching staff of the Bulgarian Gymnasium (high school) in Bitolia, and in this capacity he actively assumed the management of the revolutionary movement in Bitolia Vilayet.[14]

The effects of Grueff's activities in the Bitolia district were felt by the Turkish authorities. The numerous revolutionary *chetas* (armed bands or freedom fighters) that infested the mountains began to terrorize the tyrannical Turkish oppressors. Grueff, however, was suspected of revolutionary activity and was arrested on August 6, 1900, and held in the Bitolia prison until May 1902. In the latter part of May of 1902, he was sentenced and sent into exile in Podroum-Kale prison in Asia Minor, where he also found his exiled co-workers, Hristo Matoff and Dr. Hristo Tatarcheff. On the occasion of a general amnesty on Easter of 1903, they were released from prison.

The chief engineer of the Macedonian liberation movement was Gotse (Georghi) N. Delcheff. Born in 1872 in the city of Koukoush, northeastern Macedonia, he received his elementary education in the local Bulgarian school and later enrolled in Gymnasia in Salonika. There he became one of the most popular students, not only because of his scholarship but also as a youthful agitator and advocate of Macedonia's freedom and independence. While in Salonika, Delcheff familiarized himself with various European socialistic movements. Notwithstanding his social philosophic concepts, he enrolled in the Military School in Sofia in 1891. There he found himself in an entirely different environment. As a cadet confined to the barracks, he found that his life had become too monotonous. He was not in a position to indulge in the discussion of or to participate in any movement concerning Macedonia. In spite of the strict discipline, Delcheff managed secretly to procure and read socialist literature. Suspected of being a "socialist," he was expelled from the Military School in 1903.

While Grueff, Tosheff, Matoff, Dr. Tatarcheff, and others were organizing secret revolutionary groups in Salonika, Serres, Shtip, and other places, Delcheff was doing the same thing independently among the Macedonian immigrants in Bulgaria. When he heard about the formation of a Central Revolutionary Committee in Salonika, he immediately returned to Macedonia. Upon his arrival in Shtip, Delcheff met Grueff for the first time; the latter had already founded a local revolutionary committee. The two became intimate friends and co-workers. Delcheff and Grueff undertook the whole work of the conspiracy. To make the work more effective and less suspicious, they both decided to teach in Macedonia. Through request and pressure on the Exarchy, they were appointed to teach, Grueff in the city of Shtip, and Delcheff in the nearby village of Novo-Selo. These two apostles now became the supreme masters of the conspiracy of the IMRO.

Delcheff, either as teacher or a disguised peddler, as a merchant or an unsuspected villager, was spreading the gospel of freedom. "I conceive the world," said Delcheff, "only as a place for cultural rivalry of the nations."[15] With the cooperation of others, he undertook to organize the peasants and city dwellers in the districts of Shtip, Serres, Salonika, Bitolia, Ohrid, Lerin, Kostour, and other places. There was not a corner in the eastern, northeastern, southern, or southwestern part of Macedonia that he failed to visit. He thereby became a true apostle of freedom for Macedonia. He preached the principle of the autonomy of Macedonia, based upon Gladstone's pronouncement: *"Macedonia for the Macedonians."*

Unfortunately, Delcheff's death was a tragic one—quite usual in the annals of Macedonia's martyrology. While roaming through the southern part of Macedonia in preparation for the anticipated general insurrection, which was to take place on August 2, 1903, he arrived in the village of Banitza, district of Serres. Simultaneously, two other *chetas* (armed freedom fighters) arrived, one under the leadership of the *voyvoda* (chief) Georghi Brodiliata, and the other under the *voyvoda* Dimiter Goushanoff. Altogether there were twenty men. They settled for the evening in two houses. The next day, before daybreak, the village was surrounded by an army of more than a thousand Turkish soldiers. While searching for arms, the Turks approached the two houses where Delcheff and his comrades lodged. Escape was impossible—the battle was on! The ferocious struggle went on while the village blazed. Delcheff and his men burst out of the house in the evening, hoping by means of volleys and bayonets to break the Turkish line. They were outnumbered fifty to one! Not one of the besieged *comitajis* was captured alive. They kept up the fight to the last man! More than one hundred soldiers were slain. So were Delcheff and his comrades-in-arms—to the last man! This tragic episode occurred on April 21, 1903, a little over three months before the general insurrection was officially declared. Such was the end of Delcheff's romantic career; he was the most venerated Macedonian freedom fighter.

The third outstanding and intimate associate of Dame Grueff and Gotse Delcheff was Peter (Pere) Tosheff, an unpretentious schoolteacher. He was one of the most popular of the Triumvirate of the IMRO. The names of these three men are outstanding in the annals of Macedonia's revolutionary movement.

Born in the city of Shtip, western Macedonia, in 1867, Pere Tosheff received his education in the local Bulgarian school and later studied in Sofia and Plovdiv. When the unification of Eastern Rumelia with the Principality of Bulgaria took place in 1885, Tosheff was still in Plovdiv. The declaration of war by Serbia against Bulgaria because of the above event caused many Macedonian Bulgarians who were then in Bulgaria to hasten to the aid of the young Bulgarian state. Tosheff therefore enlisted in the Macedonian Volunteer Corps to fight against the unprovoked Serbian attack. Distinguishing himself for bravery in this war, he was awarded a cross for heroism. At the conclusion of the Serbo-Bulgarian

War of 1885, Tosheff returned to his native country and thereafter dedicated his life to the cause of the Macedonian people. In order to carry on his revolutionary gospel, and to avoid any suspicion on the part of the Turkish authorities, he chose, as Grueff and Delcheff had, to become a schoolteacher. As such, and later appointed as Exarchist school inspector, Tosheff was able to visit the various local revolutionary committees. After 1894 he was a regular member of IMRO's Central Revolutionary Committee.

In the spring of 1901, an explosion occurred in the Salonika Ottoman Bank; it was attributed to an act of the IMRO. Pere Tosheff was arrested, tried, and sentenced to exile in Podroum-Kale, Asia Minor. At the instance of an amnesty in 1902, he was released. He returned to Salonika and soon went to Bitolia. When the general insurrection was proclaimed in August 1903, Tosheff put himself at the head of a *cheta*. During the period of the insurrection, he was engaged in numerous skirmishes with the Turkish troops. He survived, however, and witnessed later developments in Macedonia, such as the so-called "Young Turks Revolution" and other political changes. Nevertheless, Tosheff remained a marked man by the Young Turks. For the latter, he was too dangerous a *giaour*,[16] because he was one of the three most beloved revolutionists still alive. Upon his return from a visit to Sofia in the spring of 1912, and while on his way to Prilep, his home town, Tosheff was ambushed and assassinated. Thus the last of the trio—Grueff, Delcheff, and Tosheff, leaders of the famous IMRO—was killed by agents of the Young Turks.[17]

While Grueff, Delcheff, and Tosheff were organizing the Macedonian peasants and spreading the gospel of freedom, Hristo Matoff, through his literary works, was shaping the form, method, and tactics of the IMRO. There was hardly another man in the Vilayet of Skopie (Uskub) more hated, despised, and imprisoned for every little suspicion by the Turkish authorities than Hristo Matoff. From 1895 until his death in 1922, he was the intellectual exponent of the IMRO.

Born in March 1872, in the city of Struga, western Macedonia, Matoff received his education in the Bulgarian schools in Macedonia. He chose the teaching profession as his life career. In 1895, while in Salonika, Matoff was initiated into the IMRO by Dame Grueff. His education, however, qualified him to be appointed the director of the Bulgarian pedagogical school in Skopie. As head of this important school he attained an unusual influence in the entire Vilayet of Skopie. With the cooperation of Peter Matsanoff, Stefan Petroff, and Vladimir Boyadjieff, he organized a local revolutionary committee in Skopie.[18] Matoff's influence and activity in the Skopie Vilayet were of great consequence for the growth of the IMRO. As head of the Bulgarian pedagogical school in Skopie, he succeeded in less than one year in organizing, with the cooperation of other men, a revolutionary committee in each and every town and village of the Skopie Vilayet. In 1898, he was elected a member of the Central Revolutionary Committee in Salonik. As such, he was first to suggest the formation of armed revolutionary bands *(chetas)* for each district in Macedonia. His idea was readily accepted by the other members of the Central Committee, and its result was astounding. With the organization of the armed revolutionary *chetas* in the various districts throughout Macedonia, the IMRO became not only a fighting but also a retaliative force. Matoff was also credited with the formation of the village *chetas* or militia. The latter became, as we shall see below, an indispensable force, and, together with IMRO's active *chetas*, they carried out many daring actions against the Turks.

When the Salonik outrage occurred in 1901, Matoff was imprisoned in Edy-Koule, the famous fortress-prison of Salonik, the Bastille of Macedonia.[19] Later, he was exiled to Podroum-Kale in Asia Minor. There he found both Grueff and Toseff also in exile. Because of the general amnesty in 1902, he was released and later went to Sofia as IMRO's Central Committee representative abroad.

Matoff was the acknowledged constitutionalist of the Macedonian liberation movement. All of his literary works are concerned with Macedonia's struggle for freedom and independence. He wrote several books and a number of pamphlets, including (1) *Za Dustroystvoto na Vtreshnata Organizatsia*, (2) *Vostanichesky Deystvia*, (3) *Za Oupravlenieto na Vtreshnata Revolutsiona Organzatsia*, (4) *Osnovi na Vtreshnata Revlutsiona Organizatsia*, (5) *Shto Behme-Shto Sme*, and (6) *Repressaly Protiv Grtskata Vo-oroujena Propaganda*. While in prison, he wrote a number of poems: *Vinishkata Pessen*, which became the marching song of the freedom fighters (IMRO's *chetas*), *Zatochnick* (The Exile), and *Mayka i Sin* (Mother and Son). Because of the political situation under the Young Turks regime in Macedonia, Matoff was compelled to emigrate to Bulgaria, where he died in Sofia on February 10, 1922. He was the last of the original leaders that brought about the organization of the Internal Macedonian Revolutionary Organization (IMRO).

6. AN ATTEMPT FOR FREEDOM— THE ILINDEN INSURRECTION OF 1903

In determining the nature of their activity, the founders of the Internal Macedonian Revolutionary Organization named it "Internal" to distinguish it from the external organization of Macedonian emigrants abroad. They kept in mind the decisions of the Congress of Berlin, the schemes of the Balkan states to increase their territories by dividing Macedonia, and the heterogeneous population of Macedonia. They had to devise a method of action that would not violate international treaties, that would attract the nationalities in Macedonia, and that would keep the country from becoming a victim of the struggle that the Balkan states were carrying on for hegemony.

In Article I of IMRO's constitution, one reads:

"The purpose of the Macedonian Revolutionary Committee is to gain complete political autonomy for Macedonia."

Article XXIII of the Treaty of Berlin provided that the European possessions of Turkey should be under the control of an organization similar to the one worked out for the island of Crete in 1868, but this article was never put into force. It served as the basis on which the Macedonian revolutionists made their demands, and it was well chosen because it had already received international recognition. The methods that the Central Revolutionary Committee and all the subordinate revolutionary committees in the districts, subdistricts, towns, and villages employed in order to attain the end for which the organization was created, namely, *an autonomous Macedonia,* were to arouse in the people an attitude of self-defense, to disseminate revolutionary ideas among them by means of the written and spoken word, and after suitable preparation to start a revolution simultaneously in all parts of Macedonia.

The first article of the "Rules and Regulations of the Internal Macedono-Adrianople Revolutionary Organization" reads as follows:

"Every one who lives in European Turkey, regardless of sex, nationality, religion, or personal beliefs, may become a member of the Internal Macedono-Adrianople Revolutionary Organization."

The idea of an armed uprising was well received, and in a short time the revolutionary net enveloped the whole country. The IMRO had its own system of administration, its own police force, courts, post offices, and soldiers—the revolutionary armed bands. It became a state within a state.

It was not until the middle of November 1897 that the Turks discovered the secret of the whole conspiracy. This incident has been known in the revolutionary annals of the IMRO as the "Vinishkata Affera," the affair of Vinitza. Chance opened the eyes of the Turks, unmasked the whole conspiracy, and forced it into the open. The period of secret preparation was brought to an abrupt close and a period of action was inaugurated. *This was the first hint to Europe that a Macedonian question existed.*

In its strenuous work of preparedness, a group of revolutionists invaded the village of Vinitza in the Vilayet of Skopie. It captured a local Turkish Bey (land proprietor), exacted £T800 from him, and, fearing that he might avenge himself on the helpless villagers, murdered him.

This was one method by which the revolutionists were raising money for arms and ammunition. The search instituted by the authorities in the neighboring villages was carried out with the usual brutality; wholesale arrests were made; torture was applied to extract confessions; and rape and robbery were committed by the soldiery. During the tortures and inquisitions that followed, the Turkish troops came suddenly upon a hidden store of dynamite and rifles. Further inquiry revealed the work that for four years the Revolutionary Committee had been carrying on under the eyes of the indolent authorities. For two months, a veritable reign of terror oppressed the whole Vilayet of Skopie. Referring to this affair, Dr. N. H. Brailsford writes:

> The search for hidden arms was conducted in every Bulgarian village and the Turks, seized with a madness which sprang partly from panic and partly from anger, indulged in more than cruelty. Torture and violence were freely used and it was the intellectual leader of the people—the priest and still more the schoolmaster—who suffered most severely. Over five hundred partisans of the committee in the Uskub Vilayet were flung into prison and about three hundred fled to Bulgaria.[20]

This incident had far-reaching consequences. On one hand, it revealed to the Turks the existence of a widespread conspiracy and consequently exposed the Bulgarian element to every sort of persecution. On the other hand, it led to a complete change of tactics by the IMRO. The latter now employed measures of action and was transformed into a retaliatory organization, whose decisions were executed by the *chetas*. Every year that followed witnessed fresh excesses on the part of the Turks and fresh reprisals on the part of the Revolutionary Committee. Assassination was the only weapon the latter possessed and they did not hesitate to have recourse to it, "more especially against Greeks who acted as the secret police of the Turks and thus . . . committed murder by proxy."[21]

There was no peace for the Christians in general, but particularly none for the Bulgarians, unless they obeyed the fatal proverb that experience had taught them: "The sword does not strike when the head is bowed." If they did not cringe, they had to fight. The Macedonians were driven to servility or bloodshed. The Bulgarians of Macedonia felt that industry was useless and that life itself was precarious. They were constantly seeing their chastity outraged and their religious faith insulted. Such being the general situation, the precipitation of a general insurrection became not only inevitable but even imperative.

The moment for which the Bulgarians of Macedonia had been preparing for ten years arrived on the evening of Sunday, August 2, 1903. It was the festival day of the Prophet St. Ilia, hence the name of the rising—*Ilindenskoto Vostanie* (The Ilinden Insurrection). In the territory of the IMRO, there were the following nationalities: Bulgarians, Turks, Greeks, Grecomans (renegade Bulgarians), Serbomans (also renegade Bulgarians), Romanians (Vlachs), Albanians, Jews, Gypsies, and others. The Ilinden Insurrection, however, was not the work of the combined efforts of these nationalities; it was an attempt by only one of them—the Bulgarians. The other Christian subject races either assisted, tolerated, or actually opposed the insurrection.

A revolutionary congress was convened in Smilevo—Grueff's native village—to decide on the actual date for the proclamation of the insurrection. All revolutionary districts were represented. After deciding on the date for the revolt, the Revolutionary Congress proceeded to elect a General Revolutionary Staff of three to command the activity of the insurrection. The General Staff consisted of Grueff, Boris Sarafoff, and Lozancheff. A Circular Letter announcing the time of the insurrection was issued by the Staff on July 28, 1903, only five days before the actual revolt began.

The period of preparation, which consisted of agitation, the procuring of arms, and the training of the inhabitants in the use of them, lasted ten years, from 1893 to 1903.

The first hostility began on August 2, 1903, in the village of Smilevo, near the city of Bitolia. One hundred and fifty insurgents battled for nineteen hours against an army of 2,300 Turks. An immediate response followed from all sides. In the remaining revolutionary districts of Skopie, Salonik, Pirin (the area of Serres and Drama), the uprising took the form of guerilla warfare carried on by reinforced revolutionary bands. In the Bitolia Vilayet, where the insurrection actually took place, the insurgents captured three cities, Kroushevo, Klissoura, and Neveska, and for a time were masters of the villages. The people, however, made costly sacrifices in their struggle for liberation and self-government, both during the period of preparation and during the insurrection itself.

Thus, according to the data recorded at the time, the revolutionists, who were often betrayed to the authorities or discovered by them, suffered the following losses during the period of preparation:

Arrested	3,764
Tortured	2,503
Died from torture	22
Beaten	90
Killed (unarmed people)	354
Wounded (unarmed people)	95
Sentenced to die	28
Sentenced to life	49
Sentenced from 3 to 15 years	454
Exiled	103
Burned houses	385

Burned alive	7
Pillaged houses	825
Outraged women and girls	146[22]

The official report of the IMRO—*Le Memoire de l'Organisation intérieure (1893-1903)*—records that as many as 132 skirmishes took place in the period from 1898 to the middle of 1903, that is, prior to the insurrection. The total casualties were 512 insurgents and 4,373 Turkish soldiers killed. The following table shows the number of engagements in the different Vilayets, the ratio between the combatants, and the number killed on each side:

The Vilayet of Salonik—(1893-1903)

Number of skirmishes		46
Combatants	Insurgents	1,846
	Troops	37,269
Killed	Insurgents	164
	Troops	1,582

The Vilayet of Monastir (Bitolia) (1901-1903)

Number of skirmishes		55
Combatants	Insurgents	1,154
	Troops	15,358
Killed	Insurgents	145
	Troops	1,088

The Vilayet of Uskub (Skopie) (1902-1903)

Number of skirmishes		21
Combatants	Insurgents	1,080
	Troops	19,015
Killed	Insurgents	185
	Troops	1,501

The Vilayet of Adrianople—(1901-1903)

Number of skirmishes		10
Combatants	Insurgents	182
	Troops	2,593
Killed	Insurgents	19
	Troops	202

Adding all these figures:

Skirmishes	132
Insurgents (engaged)	4,262
Troops (engaged)	74,235
Killed (Insurgents)	513
Killed (Troops)	4,373[23]

Such was the balance sheet *before* the tragic end of the Ilinden Insurrection of August 2, 1903.

Of the 239 skirmishes that occurred during the actual period of the uprising, that is, from August 2 to about the middle of September 1903, more than 150 took place in the revolutionary Vilayet of Bitolia—the actual territory of the insurrection. And throughout the period of the revolt, the struggle was not equal. The average proportion between the insurgents and the Turkish troops was one insurgent to fifteen soldiers, or taken by districts the ratio was as follows:

In the district of Kitchevo	1:25
In the district of Ohrid	1:22
In the district of Bitolia	1:15.6
In the district of Florina	1:13.8
In the district of Kostour	1:7.3[24]

As has been pointed out, the epic Ilinden struggle was credited with a number of ephemeral victories. The Turks and even the European representatives in Macedonia were taken by surprise. No one believed that the Macedonian peasants, crushed and brutalized, were really capable of a serious military demonstration on a scale that would entitle it to be referred to as a "Great Insurrection."

In the early part of the uprising the Turkish forces were under the command of Omar Ruchdi Pasha. About August 25, he was replaced by the more resolute and merciless Nazir Pasha. The latter took command and began to apply a systematic campaign by burning villages of rebelling Bulgarians so that he might drive the insurgents into a corner. He had assembled enough men to enable him to carry out his campaign. The rebellious district in which he had to operate was not very extensive, though difficult to traverse. From August 25 onward, the revolutionists were acting purely on the defensive. They maintained their ground fairly well until the middle of September, usually evading the Turks with success, but were occasionally forced into a general engagement. After September, the fighting was very desultory, and on November 2 the insurrection was officially declared at an end.

From the time of the uprising on August 2 until its fall, November 2, there were 239 skirmishes, and 994 insurgents and 5,328 Turkish soldiers killed. The total number of insurgents was about 27,000, against a Turkish army of 351,000.[25] During the suppression of the insurrection 200 Bulgarian villages were ruined by Turkish vengeance; 12,000 houses burned; 5,000 women outraged; 4,700 inhabitants slain; and 71,000 made homeless.[26] Such was indeed the heroic but tragic end of IMRO's Great Insurrection of 1903.

Dame Grueff put himself to work touring the various rebellious districts, disarming the insurgents, and storing the war materials for future use. The years 1903 to 1904 were the most disastrous for the Macedonian people. But Grueff and his fellow workers kept up the spirit of the peasants and continued the work of organization in preparation for another opportune time to strike once more. "For great affairs," said Grueff, "are necessary great forces. Liberty is a great thing; it requires great sacrifices." Grueff was an untiring worker. He rebuilt the temporarily wrecked organization, made it more systematic and more powerful. Unfortunately, on his way through the village of Rousinovo, Malishenko district, Grueff and his *cheta* were betrayed to the Turks. In a violent and heroic struggle with numerous Turkish troops, he was slain on December 23, 1906.

When the Turkish authorities heard that Grueff was among those killed they immediately telegraphed the local Turkish governor to uncover the buried bodies and take a photograph of Grueff. The autocratic bureaucracy of Constantinople wanted to convince themselves of the fact that the great *giauor*, Grueff—the disturber of the Empire—was really dead. Thus ended the epic life of Macedonia's apostle of freedom, Dame Grueff.

Referring to this incident, the American journalist A. D. H. Smith, who had for two years been a member of a Bulgarian revolutionary band in Macedonia, writes:

> Damian Grueff, the great chief of the Bulgars, was treacherously slain. Grueff's name will live in song and story long after the Turk has been cast from Europe. Of course, one is not expected to believe all the stories told about a popular hero but if one tithe of these narrated by his old comrades-in-arms is true he was an adventurer fit to stand with William Wallace and Robin Hood. He was a bayard in gallantry—of that there can be no dispute.

> His little escort of eight men was lying for the night in the hut of a Greek shepherd somewhere in the mountains of Serres. It was bitter cold or they would have slept out of doors as is the custom of the insurgents. They trusted the Greek because he had received kindness from them in the past and had always pleaded friendship, unlike most of his countrymen who hate the Bulgars worse than they do the Turks.

> The Greek gave the *chetniks* goats milk and *sireeny*, the white cheese of the country, and when they were settled down to sleep he slipped out to watch his flock, he said. But he travelled as rapidly as he could through

the snow to the nearest Turkish outpost and at dawn the *asker* (Turkish regular troops) broke from the forest edge upon the hut in which lay Grueff and his men. The fight was short and sharp.

Outnumbered as they were, the *chetniks* smashed a hole in the Turkish ranks with a well aimed volley from their Manlichers. Then they closed in and fought bitterly with bayonets and revolvers. Two *chetniks* went down but the rest broke through and the running fight was kept up for hours along the narrow trails. At last, when only four were left, a bullet struck Grueff in the thigh. The wound bled freely but he could walk and his comrades begged to be permitted to stay with him.

He refused. He knew that the *asker* would have no trouble following the trails left by his bloody bandages and he gave his men strict orders to leave him and make their way to the place where the Congress was to meet. "Ask their blessing for me," he said. "Leave me as many cartridges as you can spare and go." They went—weeping. This is a fact—not fiction, be it remembered.[27]

SELECT BIBLIOGRAPHY

Anastasoff, Christ, *The Tragic Peninsula,* St. Louis, Missouri, 1938, pp. 22-55; 69-96.
Bajdaroff, G., *Douhat na Makedonia* (The Spirit of Macedonia), Sofia, 1923, pp. 5-190. *Note:* This book contains thirty-seven biographical sketches of the most distinguished leaders of the IMRO in the struggle for a free and independent Macedonia.
Bajdaroff, G., *The Macedonian Question: Yesterday and Today,* Sofia, 1926, pp. 3-17.
Brailsford, H. N., *Macedonia: Its Races and Their Future,* pp. 134-173.
Krainikowsky, Dr. A. I., *La Question de Macédoine et la Diplomatie Européenne,* pp. 33-109.
Lamouche, Colonel L., *Quinze Ans D'Histoire Balkanique (1904-1918),* Paris, 1928, pp. 7-31. *Note:* Colonel Lamouche was a former member of the French section of the International Mission for the Re-Organization of the Ottoman Gendarmerie. During his fourteen years of residence in the Balkans, he had an excellent opportunity to study the Macedonian problem and the people of the country itself.
Long, George (Editor), *An Atlas of Classical Geography,* New York, 1856. For the ancient boundaries of Macedonia see pages 21 and 57 and the map on Plate 14. The latter shows also the extent of Lower and Upper Moesia and Thrace. The editor was formerly professor of Ancient Languages at the University of Virginia.
Rappoport, Alfred, *Au Pays des Martyrs—Notes et souvenirs d'un Ancient Consul Général D'Autriche—Hongrie En Macédoine (1904-1909),* Paris, 1927, pp. 122-134.
Report of the International Commission to Inquire into the Causes and Conduct of the Balkan Wars, Washington, D.C., 1914, pp. 21-38.
Sylianoff, Hristo, *Osvoboditelnite Borbi na Makedonia* (The Liberation Struggles of Macedonia) Vol. I, pp. 197-444.
Tosheff, Svetozar Dr., *Po Kervav Put* (By the Bloody Road), Plovdiv, 1969, pp. 13-222.

Wilkinson, H. R., *Maps and Politics—A Review of the Ethnographic Cartography of Macedonia*, Liverpool, 1951, pp. 1-7; 27-57; 92-111; 318-325.
Yavoroff, P. K., *Biographia na Gotse Delcheff* (The Biography of Gotse Delcheff), Sofia, 1904, pp. 18-34.

NOTES

1. *Report of The International Commission to Inquire into the Causes and Conduct of the Balkan Wars*, Washington, D.C., 1914, pp. 43-44 (henceforth referred to as the Carnegie International Commission). See also Professor Wilkinson, *supra*, Chapter VIII, n. 8, pp. 146-150.
2. *Ibid.*, pp. 26-27. The members of the Carnegie International Commission of Inquiry who prepared the *Report* of 417 pages were: Austria—Dr. Joseph Redlich, professor of Public Law at the University of Vienna; France—Baron d'Estourneelle de Constant, senator and president of the commission; Germany—Dr. Walter Schucking, professor of Law at the University of Marberg; Great Britain—Francis W. Hirst, Esq., editor of *The Economist*, and Dr. H. N. Brailsford, journalist; Russia—Professor Paul Milyukoff, member of the Duma; United States—Dr. Samuel T. Dutton, professor in Teachers College, Columbia University.
3. Professor Dr. Gustav Weigand, *Ethnographie von Makedonien*, Leipzig, 1924, p. 81.
4. Vladimir Sis, *Mazedonien*, Zurich, 1918.
5. Colonel Lamouche, *Quinze Ans D'Histoire Balkanique (1904-1918)*, Paris, 1918, pp. 12-13.
6. C. Anastasoff, *supra*, Chapter VII, n. 3, p. 77.
7. G. Bazhdaroff, *The Macedonian Question: Yesterday and Today*, Sofia, 1926, pp. 16-17.
8. C. Anastasoff, *supra*, Chapter VII, n. 3, p. 320.
9. Grueff's *Spomeny* (Memoirs), p. 21. *Note:* Grueff's *Memoirs* were published in Sofia, 1927, by Professor Luben Miletich.
10. *Ibid.*, p. 121.
11. Although the Bulgarian Exarch in Constantinople was reluctant to cooperate with the IMRO, yet the latter's pressure upon the Exarch was so great that he was compelled to appoint leading men of the IMRO to important teaching positions in Macedonia. All Bulgarian schools in European Turkey, that is, Thrace and Macedonia, were under the jurisdiction of the Exarchate in Constantinople, and, therefore, the Exarch had the authority to appoint teachers, principals, and school inspectors. The object of such a policy on the part of the IMRO was to facilitate and make more effective its conspiratorial work.
12. For administrative purposes, European Turkey was divided into five *Vilayets* (provinces): (1) Adrianople, (2) Salonika, (3) Uskub (Skopie), (4) Monastir (Bitolia), and (5) Korcha (Korcë).
13. Grueff, *supra*, n. 9, p. 9.
14. Of course, this was not a part of his teaching at the Gymnasium. This part of his work was strictly secret—not even known to the Exarchy itself.
15. G. Bazhdaroff, *Douhat na Makedonia* (The Spirit of Macedonia), Sofia, 1925, p. 22.
16. A contemptuous Turkish word for an infidel, especially Christian.

17. See K. Perlicheff's "Essay on Peter Tosheff" in *Makedonia*, I, Book 3, March 1922. G. Bazhdaroff, *supra*, n. 7, pp. 35-41.

18. Matoff's Pamphlet, *Za Svoyata Revolutsiona Deynost* (About My Revolutionary Activity), 1928, p. 7

19. As a result of this incident, Matoff is pictured as the hero in Pierre d'Espagnt's romance (published in 1902) *Avant le Massacre*. The author of this interesting romance happened to be in Salonika during the explosion of the Ottoman Bank and subsequent imprisonment of the leading men of the IMRO. See *La Memoire de L'Organisation Intérieure (1893-1903)*, pp. 47-49.

20. N. H. Brailsford, *Macedonia: Its Races and Their Future*, London, 1906, p. 127.

21. See Section 45 of the Annual Report for Bulgaria for the year 1906, *British Foreign Office*, 371-202. See also Gooch and Temperly, *British Documents on the Origin of the War 1898-1914*, V, p. 101.

22. G. Bazhdaroff, *supra*, n. 7, pp. 22-23.

23. *Le Memoire de l'Organisation*, *supra*, n. 19, p. 76; Colonel Lamouche, *supra*, n. 5, p. 28; C. Anastasòff, *supra*, Chapter VII, n. 3, pp. 78-80.

24. C. Anastasoff, *ibid*, pp. 69-96; *Le Memoire de l'Organisation*, *supra*, n. 19, p. 182. *Report of the Carnegie International Commission, supra*, n. 1, p. 34.

25. *Ibid.* (Carnegie Report).

26. *Ibid.*

27. A. D. H. Smith, *Fighting the Turks in the Balkans*, New York, 1906, pp. 33-34.

CHAPTER X

THE GREAT POWERS AND THE MACEDONIAN QUESTION

1. THE AUSTRO-RUSSIAN AGREEMENT OF 1897

When, in 1878, Macedonia was handed back to Turkey, the latter solemnly promised to give equal rights to her Christian subjects. The powers signatory to the Berlin Treaty assumed at the same time the obligation to see that Turkey kept her promises and, if necessary, to compel her to introduce the promised reforms. As has already been pointed out above, Article XXIII of the treaty provided for the introduction of reforms analogous to those of the Cretan Organic Statute of 1868. Unfortunately, neither the contracting parties of the Berlin Treaty nor Turkey kept their promise. The tragedy of European diplomacy was manifested by a sudden change of policy toward Turkey and the Balkans. Russia, the "liberator of Bulgaria," met with defeat at the Congress of Berlin. But the defeat of Russia was, indeed, a great victory of Austria-Hungary, the latter being supported in her effort by the dictates of Bismarck's Germany. Nevertheless, Austria-Hungary and Russia soon became the decisive factors in shaping the fate of the Balkans.

These two self-appointed powers were endeavoring to settle the estate in the event of a sudden death of Sultan Abdul Hamid II, the "sick man of Europe." Accordingly, in 1897, Emperor Francis Joseph of Austria-Hungary visited the Tsar of Russia, and an agreement was contracted between Russia and Austria.[1] The substance of the 1897 agreement was, first, that the *status quo* in the Balkans would be maintained, and, second, that the powers, by excluding the other signatories of the Treaty of Berlin, would undertake for themselves the settlement of the Macedonian Question. This agreement was one of the most mischievous ever accomplished by the two "interested powers." It is worth noting, however, that Russia, being at this time unable to hold under her influence the newly created Principality of Bulgaria, had assumed an anti-Bulgarian policy. It did not matter to her that the Macedonian Bulgarians were the prime victims of the above agreement. The Sultan of Turkey was thereby assured that he would remain absolute master of Macedonia, over which two ambitious powers kept watching each other.

Although Turkish cruelty, massacres, arrests, burning of villages, plundering, and police crimes had reached unspeakable proportions, successive British and French cabinets "washed their hands" of any responsibility toward the Christians in European Turkey. The reason for such an attitude on their part, of course, was obvious: Pan-Islamism was their fear. They could not afford to arouse Mohammedan sentiment against them in their then extensive colonial possessions in Asia and Africa.

While England and France declined for one reason or another to insist upon the fulfillment of the Sultan's promises with regard to the reforms in Macedonia, Germany on the other hand declined to hold Abdul Hamid II to his promises. Germany was, in fact, at that time, the only friend Turkey had in Europe. When Kaiser Wilhelm II went to Constantinople to visit his friend Abdul Hamid in 1898, the German emperor also made a pilgrimage to Jerusalem. In Damascus on November 8, 1898, he made a most sensational speech, aiming to seal his friendship with the Mohammedan world. Said the Kaiser: "The two hundred million Mohammedans who, dwelling dispersed throughout the East, reverence in H. M. the Sultan Abdul Hamid their Khalif, may rest assured that at all times the German emperor will be their friend."[2] By such a speech, the Kaiser hoped to promote Germany's expansionist policy of *Drang nach Osten*. Berlin and Constantinople concurred in combating all efforts directed toward the Straits and the Dardanelles on the part of Russia. Should the latter succeed in penetrating the Balkans or even seize Constantinople, that would in itself put an end to Germany's plan to build a railroad from Berlin to Baghdad and the Persian Gulf and thereby control a vast trade with the Orient. Germany had already arranged or rather obtained a concession from Turkey for the construction of this road, and it was well under way when World War I broke out.

In 1888, certain concessions for railway construction in Asia Minor were granted by the Porte to German interests. In 1889, under the auspices of certain banking interests of Berlin and Stuttgart, the Ottoman Company of Anatolian Railways was promoted. In 1902, the convention for the construction of a railway from Constantinople to Baghdad was finally concluded. This was only one of the lines stretching from Hamburg, Vienna, Budapest, Belgrade, and Nish to Constantinople, with an extension from Baghdad to Bersa. Thus, Berlin was to be connected by railways with the Persian Gulf.[3]

Because of her *Drang nach Sudosten* aspiration, Germany pursued a special policy toward the Balkans. This German policy, however, was directed more or less through her then subservient ally—Austria-Hungary. Because Serbia lay stretched across the path of Berlin-Baghdad, it is not difficult to explain why Austria-Hungary was allowed to occupy the provinces of Bosnia-Herzegovina and later to annex them contrary to the treaty stipulations of 1878. Thus the only territorial connection friendly to Germany as well as to Austria that would permit an easy and uninterrupted connection between Berlin and the Near East was the Turkish possession of the Sandjak of Novi-Bazar. Was it strange, therefore, that Austria was insisting on building a railway through the Sandjak of Novi-Bazar to the main line in Macedonia? Although this was not the shortest and most natural way from Berlin to Turkey in Asia, it would have avoided unnecessary friction, which was otherwise unavoidable. It was because of this aspiration of Germany that the latter was causing dissensions among the Balkan nationalities. Otto von Bismarck was being quoted as saying: "In Serbia, we are Austrians; in Bulgaria, we are Russians." Such being Gemany's Balkan policy, one would readily see the reasons for all the misfortunes in the Balkans, and particularly in Macedonia. With Russia an accommodating friend of Austria-Hungary and the latter a willing servant of Germany, the two worked hand in hand to create the unfortunate political situation for the Macedonian Bulgarians—all for the sole benefit of German imperialism.

2. DIPLOMATIC CONCERN OVER THE MACEDONIAN QUESTION

In the early part of 1902, the Archduke Ferdinand of Austria visited St. Petersburg (Petrograd) in order to confirm the Austro-Russian agreement of 1897. On February 28, 1902, M. de Montebello, the French Ambassador in St. Petersburg, described the revolutionary agitation in Macedonia to M. Delcassé, the French Foreign Minister: "It might have been hoped that the visit to St. Petersburg of the Archduke Ferdinand of Austria would have produced a salutary impression and arrested, for some time at least, the intrigues of the agitators in Macedonia. It must have been known, in fact, that the voyage of the Archduke had confirmed the agreement established between Russia and Austria at the time of the visit of the Emperor Francis Joseph in 1897. The present agitation is therefore of a character all the more serious in that it shows itself more active than ever, in spite of the political events which should have checked it."[4]

Although Austria and Russia showed great displeasure over the disturbance in Macedonia caused by the IMRO, the latter's revolutionary manifestations reached even higher points. The diplomatic agents of the European powers began to issue a series of reports to their respective governments on the critical political situation in Macedonia. In a previous chapter we have seen the revolutionary development in the year 1902, that is, prior to the Great Ilinden Insurrection of 1903. On October 20, 1902, M. J. de la Boulinière, Minister of France at Sofia, wrote: "If the Powers wish to exercise a moderating influence on coming events, they must take the initiative in a plan of reforms to be imposed on Turkey. Only the winter separates us, perhaps, from occurrences which, if they are not averted, may be all the more serious in that not only Bulgarian but Slav sympathies are leading up to them and will increase their importance."[5] A week later, on October 28, 1902, M. Steeg, the French consul-general at Salonik, sketched more or less a program of more practical reforms. M. Steeg wrote:

The critical situation of the Bulgarian villager of Macedonia is well known. On the one hand, he is without defense against all the violence of the revolutionary bands and on the other, he is exposed to all the exactions of the Turkish gendarmerie, who are recruited from a bad class, irregularly paid, and obliged to "live off the inhabitants."

The organization of a sufficiently numerous gendarmerie, well paid, well selected, and commanded by first-class officers would suffice, it seems, to make more and more difficult the movement of the revolutionary bands and to reassure the peasants, who, from the moment they ceased to fear reprisal, would probably support the authorities. Such a reform would certainly cost less than the mobilization of *redifs* and the dispatch of troops, to which the Ottoman Government is more and more frequently forced to have recourse.

It is well known, on the other hand, how many abuses arise from the system of farming the tithes, which are almost always awarded to influential beys, who use their authority from the state as a pretext to make all sorts of exactions. If proof was wanting of the gravity of this question, it could be found in the fact that the two last insurrectionary movements began by the massacre of civil agents charged with collecting the tithes.

Now it happens that in the greater part of Macedonia, the tithes being appropriated to the securities of the railway (Salonika-Monastir and Salonika Dedeagatch), the produce of the adjudications is paid into the Public Debt. A rule obliging that the administration collect these revenues by its officials would doubtless suffice to put an end to abuses which are often intolerable.

It seems that if, by the reform of the gendarmerie and of the system of collecting the tithes, a minimum of security were assured to the Macedonian populations, they could not but be sensible of having made a step forward. Other important points, such as the freer admission of the Christian element into the magistracy and the administration, could be discussed afterwards more at leisure, and even the ringleaders would find themselves obliged to subordinate the realization of their political aspirations to consideration of the moment.[6]

This was the first plan ever suggested for immediate reforms in Macedonia. And according to M. Steeg the reformation of the gendarmerie and of the system of collecting the tithes was sufficient to calm the discontented peasants of Macedonia. Nevertheless, French diplomacy began an earnest effort to induce the other powers to compel the Sultan to grant the minimum reforms which he had promised. M. Delcassé, the French Foreign Minister at the time, as a result of the suggestions made by his diplomatic agents in the Balkans, negotiated with the various foreign governments with respect to the reforms for Macedonia. M. Bapst, the French charge d'affaires at Constantinople, wrote the following on December 1, 1902:

In view of the attitude taken by the principal Powers, the Sultan has just instituted two commissions: One to proceed to study on the spot the "ameliorations" to be applied to the situation in Macedonia, the other at the Porte to examine the proposals of the first. It seems as if these decisions have been taken in order to elude the demands of the Russian ambassador, who has been charged by the emperor to demand efficacious reforms, and who in his last audience brought strong pressure to bear upon the Sultan. But Mr. Zinovieff has just told me that he would not be put off with palliatives and that he had received formal orders from the emperor to insist on reforms.

Harassed during these last days by the remonstrances of the ambassadors, the Porte wishes to have taken into consideration all that has been said to it and to consent to some reforms in Macedonia; but it requires no very close examination of the version given to the press to see that the government has no serious intentions in mind.

The inspector who has been appointed is to "superintend and carry out the measures recently decreed for the Vilayets of European Turkey and approved by imperial *irade*." Now, except the sending of troops to Macedonia, no measures were decreed by the sovereign; it is then with repression by the strong arm that Hussein Hilmi Pasha is expected to "superintend and carry out."

Why, also, should Macedonia—that is to say, the redeemed part of the Greater Bulgaria of the Treaty of San Stefano—be classed together under the name of the "Vilayets of European Turkey," with Albania, Epirus, and the Greek or Turkish districts of the Vilayets of Adrianople or Salonika? Reforms appropriate to one of these regions would not be suitable to others; this incompatibility affords a prextext for making no change.[7]

It appeared that French diplomacy was trying to show a possible solution to the difficult situation in Macedonia. Had the other powers cooperated in alleviating the existing state of conditions, the resulting events of 1903 would have been averted, with thousands of lives saved and less destruction in Macedonia.

3. EUROPEAN INTERVENTION FOR
REFORMS IN MACEDONIA

A. The Austro-Russian or "Vienna Plan"

The year 1902 was characterized by a number of disorders and insurrectionary eruptions. To prevent future uprisings, the Sultan, on December 1, 1902, issued a sort of "Instructions concerning the Vilayets of European Turkey," and thereby appointed two commissions: one to proceed to study on the spot the "ameliorations" to be applied to the situation in Macedonia, the other at the Sublime Porte to examine the proposals of the first. Hussein Hilmi Pasha was appointed to the one commission as an "inspector of reforms." Soon after this farcical gesture of the Sultan, the Tsar of Russia sent his emissary to Bulgaria to caution her to remain quiet. To make the tragicomedy more realistic, Count Lamsdorff, the Russian minister of foreign affairs, was soon to visit Vienna so that he might convey the impression to the world that the two "concerned" powers were taking active measures in common.

Meanwhile, what was the result of the Sultan's own scheme of reforms? How far did Hilmi Pasha carry out the Sultan's scheme? Ironically, Hilmi Pasha, the "inspector general" of Macedonia, not only failed to carry out the meager plan of the Sultan, but his "real occupation during the seven months of his tenure of office was not reform but repression. The insurrection of August was the fruit of his activity."[8] This Turkish farce was well known to the Western powers and, having no confidence in the Sultan's scheme of reforms, they began to introduce, through their ambassadors, new and more practical measures of reforms. Thus, M. Delcassé, the French minister of foreign affairs, applied pressure in Petrograd by informing the Russian government that the British ambassador at Constantinople, Sir N. O'Connor, was presenting a scheme for a new organization of the administration in Macedonia.[9] As a consequence, in the latter part of December 1902, Count Lamsdorff arrived in Vienna, conferred with the Austrian chancellor, Count Goluchowski, and later with the emperor. Their discussion was centered about the following vital considerations:

a. What was necessary to alleviate the lot of the Christians in Macedonia?

b. What was the best way to bring about the desired result, without altering the status quo and without curtailing the sovereignty of the Sultan in Macedonia?

The discussion was, of course, within the spirit of the Austro-Russian agreement of 1897. But the contents of the "Vienna Plan" of February

25, 1903, with which they claimed the Sultan was in accord, are shown in the following document presented to the Sublime Porte:

1. In order to assure the success of the mission by virtue of the Sultan's *irade*, the appointed inspector general will be maintained at his post for a period of seven years and he will not be recalled before the expiration of his term, unless the powers have been previously consulted on the subject. He will be empowered to make use of the Ottoman troops, if necessary, for the maintenance of public order, without having to apply each time to the central government.

2. The Valis will be required to give implicit obedience to his orders.

3. In the reorganization of the police and gendarmerie, the Ottoman Government will call in the assistance of foreign specialists. The gendarmerie will be composed of Christians and of Mussulmans in a proportion analogous to that of the populations of the localities in question.

4. The rural policemen shall be Christian where the majority of the population is Christian.

5. In view of the molestation and excesses from which the Christian population has so often suffered at the hands of certain *arnaut* malefactors and in view of the fact that the crimes and misdemeanors of the latter for the most part escape punishment, the Ottoman Government will consider without delay measures to put an end to this state of things.

6. The numerous arrests made on the occasion of the last disorders in the three Vilayets having caused much excitement there, the Ottoman Government, in order to hasten a return of normal feeling, will grant an amnesty to all accused of, or condemned for political offences, as well as to those who have emigrated.

7. In order to assure the regular working of the local institutions, a budget of the revenues and expenses will be made out in each Vilayet, and the provincial collections, controlled by the Ottoman Imperial Bank, will be applied in the first place, to the needs of the local administration, payment of the civil and military services being included therein. The manner of collecting the tithes will be modified, and the system of farming the tithes wholesale will be abolished.

8. At the same time there will be instituted in certain localities of the three Vilayets, under the direction of the ambassadors at Constantinople, active consular supervision of the application of the reforms agreed upon.[10]

In the above "Vienna Plan" of reforms there are features previously proposed by the Sultan himself. But the only provision of the Vienna Plan put in operation was the creation of rural guards of village communities—the *beckchi*. The application of this "reform" resulted in what the inhabitants of Macedonia referred to in jest as "the reformation of the village watchmen." Although the plan provided a series of other reforms to be instituted in the three Vilayets in Macedonia, it, in fact, remained an empty promise. One thing, however, was significant: it recognized the right of Austria and Russia, as the two "interested" powers, to devise a scheme of reforms and to supervise its application. Their consular staff acquired a privileged position, which ensured them precedence over the other four powers—England, France, Italy, and Germany—also signatories of the Berlin Treaty. The scheme itself, however, was feeble and halfhearted. It remained a dead letter.

B. The British Plan of Reforms

The Austro-Russian intervention in the affairs of Macedonia in the course of 1903 became an apparent failure. The Western powers could no longer put reliance on the schemes of control by the "two concerned" powers. England was the first Western power to formulate a new plan of reforms. Thus, on September 29, 1903, Lord Lansdowne, the British foreign minister, made a number of more practical suggestions for arranging the affairs in Macedonia. Lord Lansdowne, being informed of the arrival in Vienna of Count Lamsdorff and having in view the approaching meeting between the Tsar of Russia and Francis Joseph of Austria, determined to confront the two powers responsible for the fate of Macedonia with a number of practical reforms compatible with Western European tendencies. Consequently, he instructed his ambassador in Vienna to present the following five points to the Russian and Austrian ministers for their consideration:

1. According to our opinion, no scheme will give satisfactory results, if its application is placed in the hands of a Mohammedan governor responsible to the Turkish government only and independent of foreign control. We shall point out two alternatives:

   a) The appointment of a Christian governor in no way connected with the Balkan Peninsula nor with the Powers which signed the Treaty of Berlin or

   b) The continuance of a Mohammedan governor with the assistance of European counselors. We shall be agreed to have these last appointed by the two powers concerned.

2. The appointment of enough European officers and under-officers to reorganize the gendarmerie.

3. All undisciplined soldiers to be removed from Macedonia and regular troops only to be kept there.

4. Each of the two powers to delegate six officers to accompany the Turkish troops in order to restrain them and to secure reliable information.

5. Provision of facilities for the distribution of aid to the thousands of people who have been driven from their homes and scattered throughout the country in utter destitution.[11]

It was, therefore, the result of the Macedonian insurrection and the resulting repressions, persecution, and tortures that followed that reminded Europe of the promise made by the Treaty of Berlin. The Great Powers, though reluctant, were compelled to intervene. England took the initiative by proposing the above scheme of reforms.

C. The Second Austro-Russian Plan—The Murzsteg Program

With the intervention of Great Britain, Vienna and Petrograd grew uneasy. The monopoly of the two powers was seriously menaced. Would Vienna and St. Petersburg (Petrograd) capitulate and let the other powers intervene in the internal affairs of Turkey? It was apparent to Austria-Hungary and Russia that their exclusive right to superintend the affairs of European Turkey was challenged by Lord Lansdowne's plan of reforms. As a result, Emperor Francis Joseph and the Tsar of Russia, Nicholas II, felt the necessity to strike public imagination by a solemn act. On September 30, 1903, they held a meeting at Murzsteg, near Vienna, and as a consequence of their deliberations a second Austro-Russian plan of reforms was promulgated, usually referred to as the "Murzsteg Program." In order that this plan might be approved by all the Great Powers, the Austro-Russian diplomats devised a scheme of control by dividing Macedonia into five sectors, each to be controlled by one of the powers.[12] The following nine points constituted the Murzsteg scheme of reforms:

1. In order to establish a control over the activity of the local Ottoman authorities concerned in the application of the reforms, the Inspector General Hilmi Pasha should be accompanied everywhere by special civil agents of Austria-Hungary and Russia, whose duty it would be to call the attention to the needs of the Christian population, to point out the abuses of the local authorities, to convey the necessary recommendations to their respective ambassadors at Constantinople, and to inform their respective governments of all which occurs in the country. As their assistants the agents might appoint secretaries and dragomen charged with the execution of their orders and authorized to tour the districts in order to question the inhabitants of the Christian villages, to superintend the local authorities, etc.

   The task of the civil agents being to supervise the introduction of the reforms and to calm the population, their tenure of office shall terminate within two years after their appointment.

   The Sublime Porte shall direct the local authorities to render to these agents all necessary facilities in order to enable them to fulfill their mission.

2. Since the reorganization of the Turkish police and gendarmerie constitutes one of the most essential measures for the pacification of the country, the introduction of this reform should be urgently required from the Porte.

Considering the fact that the officers employed at present are ignorant of the language and local conditions, and have not been able to render themselves useful, it would be desirable to introduce the following modifications and additions to the original project:

a) The task of reorganizing the gendarmerie in the three Vilayets shall be confined to a general of foreign nationality, in the service of the Ottoman Imperial Government, who might be assisted by military men from the Great Powers, who shall divide among themselves the districts in which they shall act as commanders, instructors, and organizers. In this way they would be in a position to watch the behavior of the troops toward the population.

b) These officers may ask, if they think it necessary, for the addition of a number of officers and subalterns of foreign nationality.

3. As soon as the pacification of the country is effected, the modification of the boundaries of the administrative units should be demanded from the Ottoman Government, with a view to the more regular grouping of the nationalities.

4. The administrative and judicial institutions should be reorganized, and Christians be admitted to the public service, thus to encourage the development of local autonomy.

5. There should immediately be established, in the principal centers of the Vilayets, mixed commissions made up of an equal number of Christians and Mohammedans in order to inquire into and investigate the political crimes, and other offenses, committed during the recent troubles. In these commissions should participate the consular representatives of Austria-Hungary and Russia.

6. Turkey should pay for the reparations of Christian refugees and the rebuilding of houses, churches, and schools destroyed by the Turks. The money should be distributed by committees on which Christian notables would sit, while Austrian and Russian consuls should supervise.

7. A year's taxes should be remitted to the Christian inhabitants of the burned villages.

8. The Ottoman Government should undertake to introduce the reforms mentioned in the project of last February, without delay.

9. Since the greater part of the excesses and cruelties have been committed by the *ilaves* (*redifs* of the second class) and *bashi-bazouks*, the Porte must cease to employ these two categories and replace them with regular troops.[13]

The Murzsteg Program differed from the proposal of Lord Lansdowne in that it modified his conditions and thus made them more acceptable to the Sublime Porte. For instance, instead of a Christian governor-general, it was agreed that the chief inspector, Hilmi Pasha, was to be assisted by two civilian agents, one Austrian and the other Russian, to act as a controlling body of two members. The reformation of the gendarmerie was to be entrusted to officers delegated by the

Great Powers and distributed throughout the Macedonian districts. The other points of the Murzsteg Program were about the same as those proposed by Lord Lansdowne. Although these reforms were drawn up on October 2, 1903, it was not until April of 1904 that they were put into operation in Macedonia.

4. THE APPLICATION OF THE REFORMS
—ITS FIASCO

In order to see that the reforms called for in the Murzsteg Program were carried out by the Turkish authorities, the Great Powers had divided Macedonia into five administrative sectors, each assigned to a power to oversee the application of the reforms. Thus, Russia obtained the city of Salonika and the western part of the Vilayet;[14] Austria-Hungary settled in Skopie (Uskub); to Italy was given the city of Monastir and the surrounding districts; France obtained the city and Sandjak of Serres, a very populous district near the Bulgarian frontier; while England received the district of Drama. Such was the method used in overseeing the application of the reforms in Macedonia. However, the administrative schemes of the powers in the above districts accomplished nothing. The whole affair, as a result of the allotment of the above areas, presented a thorny diplomatic problem. "The Powers debated the question as if they were delimiting spheres of influence or partitioning Macedonian territory, instead of merely assigning districts to be reformed."[15]

The Murzsteg Program of reforms failed to achieve its purpose. It ended with a double *fiasco;* first, because the Austro-Russian intervention in the internal affairs of the then European Turkey caused Macedonia to become more disturbed, more anarchical, thus making chaos worse than ever, and, second, because the scheme failed to prevent the intervention of other powers, and particularly of England.

5. GREEK AND SERBIAN BANDS AID
THE TURKS AGAINST THE BULGARIANS

The insurrection of August 1903 had left Europe with the impression that the Bulgarians were the dominant element, because they alone, aided by some Romanians, had rebelled against the centuries-old Turkish rule. The Murzsteg scheme of reforms did not achieve anything of consequence to alleviate the political and economic conditions in Macedonia. The IMRO had not disarmed. It was futile to talk of suppressing it. The Turks were incapable of such a task, for the IMRO had behind it an obstinate and virile race, a race that was ready to make sacrifices to win its freedom. In fact, its ranks were augmented, and soon disorders again prevailed in Macedonia.

In June of 1904 several explosions had occurred on the trains going from Skopie to Salonika, and from the latter to Dedeagach. In July, a skirmish took place at Geumendje between a Bulgarian *cheta* of freedom fighters and a detachment of Turkish soldiers. Such incidents began to occur more frequently. During the fall, the consuls began to report the activities of Greek and Serbian bands. Indeed, the Turkish authorities welcomed them as allies against the powerful Bulgarian liberation movement. On November 2, 1904, M. Bapst, the French chargé d'affaires at Constantinople, wrote the following:

> This summer passed off without any violent uprising in Macedonia in comparison to what occurred last summer. There was no open insurrection nor was there much devastation. But the evil is greater than before, perhaps, for an insurrection can always be put down by force of arms but this movement which breaks out simultaneously in different places in the form of isolated crimes and brigandage eludes the actions of the troops and cannot be effectively opposed except by the police and the gendarmerie. Furthermore, the movement has manifested itself in great violence during the last few weeks, the conflicts between the races are becoming ever more furious, murders increase, and the terrorized inhabitants hope for a change of regime.

After the Ilinden insurrection, just as after the Russo-Turkish War of 1877, the Greek archbishops and consuls tried to take advantage of the hostility felt by the Turkish authorities toward the Bulgarians in Macedonia, who were fighting for the freedom of all nationalities and who had invited all Macedonians, regardless of nationality or religion, to take their stand under the flag of liberty. Bands, armed in Greece, invaded Macedonia for the purpose of forcing Bulgarians and Romanians to place themselves under the jurisdiction of the Greek Patriarchate in Constantinople. A French authority on the Balkans, M. Victor Bérard writes:

> Hellenized Macedonia furnished very few combatants; but the Greek propaganda has recruited bands in Crete, the islands, Morea, and Epirus, which are supported from Athens and commanded by Greek officers. These foreigners treat their "sectors" as vanquished territory, and the fury of their patriotism is directed against the Wallachians, whom the Romanian propaganda is pushing toward a schism.

> During the fall of 1904, anarchy reigned in Monastir. Greek officers, sent from Athens, terrorized the Wallachian villages; letters found upon them made it more than certain that they were aided by the Greek consuls and the clergy of the Patriarchate.[16]

To show the terror and anarchy that had prevailed, we shall refer to several incidents that had occurred while Macedonia was under European control. Thus, on January 17, 1905, a band of thirty-two armed men, of whom twenty were Turks and twelve Greeks, invaded the Bulgarian village of Marvinitzi, county of Doyran, where they arrested twenty-six notables of the village and looted several houses. The chief of the band violated a young bride called Velika Christova.

Leaving Marvinitzi, the band carried off the twenty-six notables, and at a quarter of an hour's walk from the village fired several volleys at them, leaving on the ground ten killed and five severely wounded, of whom three died the same day. The other eleven villagers managed to escape.

An hour after the departure of the band, which had taken the road for the Turkish village of Kazandali, thirty soldiers arrived at Marvinitzi, but, instead of pursuing the band, they only verified the fact of the outrage and departed.

The next day, the *caimacam* (prefect) of Doyran, accompanied by a lieutenant and a detachment of soldiers, went to Marvinitzi. A great number of men and women wished to go to Salonika to tell the authorities of the affair; the lieutenant prevented them from going.

The inhabitants of Marvinitzi recognized in the band Mile Chana of Bogdantzi and Anton Dimtcheff of Gartchista, two adherents of the Greeks, who belonged to the Greek band of seven men that had operated two months before at Bogdantzi; these two men, had been arrested then, but had been released by the authorities of Ghevgheli.

On April 6, 1905, at nightfall, a Greek band of two hundred and three men surrounded the Bulgarian village of Zagoritchani. Having heard the sounds of a trumpet, the inhabitants of the village believed it was Ottoman troops arriving. The next day was the feast of the Annunciation. Early in the morning, at the moment when the people were going to the church, they were surprised by shots fired from all sides. All persons in the streets and about the church were massacred, after which the band attacked the remainder of the inhabitants in their houses, of which they burned several and destroyed others with dynamite bombs. Sixty people were killed, among them women and children, and seven were wounded. Fifteen houses and twenty-eight huts and granaries were burned or destroyed.

For two terrible hours this band did its monstrous work, putting the village to fire and sword and retiring only at the news of the approach of a detachment of Ottoman soldiers commanded by Sub-Lieutenant Nazir Bey. It was positively asserted that the band was headed by three officers and fifteen soldiers of the Greek army.

The consuls of Austria-Hungary and of Russia, as well as the officers of the Italian section, went to Zagoritchani and verified the account of horrors committed by the band. In the streets around the church many corpses had been mutilated; skulls smashed, eyes torn out, hands and limbs cut off. Women had their hands cut off; children of five years were disemboweled. One of the priests of the village, an old man of seventy, had been murdered; his body was covered with wounds. An entire family had been killed by bombs thrown into the house; the father and mother and their children had been horribly mutilated by the splinters of the bombs. One of their little girls, who had tried to escape by the door, had been ripped up by bayonets.

Appalled by the horrible fate of their coreligionists of Zagoritchani, the inhabitants of the neighboring villages abandoned their homes and took refuge in the fields and woods. Thus, when the consuls went to Zagoritchani they did not find a living soul in the village of Bobishta.

That the Greek band which attacked Zagoritchani could not have committed the outrage without the complicity of the Ottoman authorities is proven by the following circumstances:

1. It is inconceivable that a band of more than two hundred men could have organized itself and gone to Zagoritchani without being noticed by the agents of the authorities, when numerous detachments of gendarmes and troops continually patrolled the roads and villages and knew how to discover the hiding place of the smallest Bulgarian bands reported to be in this or that locality.

2. Some days before the outrage, a detachment of troops had arrived in Zagoritchani to make house-to-house searches; the chief on entering the village commanded the trumpets to sound. At this sound the panic-stricken inhabitants began to flee. The Ottoman officer having stopped them and asking why they were running away, they replied that they feared that the sound of the trumpet meant the arrival of a Greek band. The officer quieted them by saying that only the *asker* (troops) could use the trumpet. Nevertheless, some days after, the Greek band that surrounded the village also used a trumpet, and the inhabitants did not disturb themselves, believing it was more troops arriving! Coincidence or not, this fact deserves to be noted.

3. On the fourteenth of March, some peasants of Zelenitche had transmitted a request to one of the Italian officers, asking him for protection against the Greek party of Belkaman and Eleovo, county of Kastoria (Kostour), who, at the instigation of their spiritual chiefs, were projecting an attack on their village. The Italian officer called the attention of the *caimacam* (prefect) twice to the projects of the Greeks and the doings of a Greek engineer in the service of the state at Florina, who was thought to be a chief of Greek bands. In spite of this warning, the caimacam took no measures of protection nor

even of precaution; he did not have the movements of the Greek bands watched and they, instead of Zelenitche, attacked Zagoritchani.

The facts just set forth are significant enough, and the inescapable conclusion is that the local authorities and, in particular, the prefects of Florina and Kastoria, as well as the Greek bishops of those two towns,[17] were personally responsible for what happened at Zagoritchani.[18]

On November 11, 1905, about nine o'clock in the evening, a Greek band of about eighty to a hundred men, armed with Mauser and Gra rifles, entered the village of Nevoliani, county of Florina. They surrounded the house of Georghi Yaneff, where a party of fifty relatives and friends was assembled for a marriage. The Greeks began to fire shots through the doors and windows. Then, seeing that the wedding party did not come out, the bandits set fire to the house. A certain number of guests and the newly married couple managed to escape by a little door of the inner court, and they took refuge in the neighboring house. There were thirteen killed and eight wounded, some of them young boys and girls.[19]

On September 6, 1906, a detachment of eighty men belonging to the Thirty-sixth Infantry Regiment under the command of Lieutenant Ixan, entered the village of Gorno-Rodevo, near the city of Voden (Edhessa). The mayor, two notables, and two peasants were killed, as well as an old man of seventy, a child of ten, and another of four. Two women and a child of four were wounded. The detachment afterward plundered the village and beat the inhabitants. The following day, the Russian officer Bairaktaroff, who resided at Voden, arrived at the scene to make an inquiry and ascertain the facts of the horror.[20]

Hundreds of similar cases show the Turkish brutality during the period in which Macedonia was under the supervision of the powers and when the various schemes of reforms were "introduced." Although the chief aim of the Murzsteg Program was to bring some measure of appeasement, to restore order, to reestablish confidence, to repair devastation, and to remove the motives for rebellion, it failed and its failure actually aggravated the abnormal state of conditions in Macedonia.

During the first eleven months of 1905, under the reforms, there had occurred 1,010 murders of peaceful Bulgarians. These murders were committed by the following malefactors:

330 were due to Albanian bands or individuals.
195, to the regular troops.
451, to Greek bands or agents.
34, to Serbian bands or agents.

As regards 1906, Sir Edward Grey, the British minister of foreign affairs, declared in the House of Commons that, according to infor-

mation supplied by the consuls, there had been from the first of January
to September 30:

> 577 Christians killed in the Vilayet of Salonik.
> 431 Christians, in the Vilayet of Monastir.
> 183 Christians, in the Vilayet of Uskub.

Therefore, in the first nine months of 1906, there were 1,191 political
murders, and from January 1, 1905, to September 30, 1906, the total
number of murders was 2,201. These grim figures give a better and
clearer idea of the inefficiency of the reforms.[21]

The failure of the Murzsteg scheme of reforms was assured because
the Powers attempted to "reform" Macedonia without reckoning with
the Macedonians.

6. ANGLO-RUSSIAN INTERVENTION
FOR REFORMS IN MACEDONIA

While the Great Powers were maneuvering with the various schemes
of reforms and arguing over the methods of applying them, the revolutionary movement in Macedonia developed to a point where another
blow was to be struck against the Turkish regime. Notwithstanding the
fact that the IMRO now had to battle against the Greek and Serbian
bands, its strength and aggressiveness surpassed that of the insurrectionary period of 1903. Reprisals against Turkish brutality and skirmishes
with the regular troops became more and more frequent; the prospects
for another blow against the existing regime were apparent. Meanwhile,
the Turks undertook a more systematic method of repression and persecution. Their brutality reached such a degree of intensity that public
opinion once more began to be agitated. The voices of the horror-stricken
Christian races in Macedonia were once more heard by the European
statesmen and diplomats. For, if nothing practical was accomplished
by the various attempts for reforms, there was, however, this: that the
Great Powers advertised the Macedonian question and the world conceived it as a vital, living one.

The year 1907 was characterized particularly by the number of
meetings held by the monarchs of the various powers. There were three
outstanding problems before the different cabinets at that time; namely,
the Moroccan question, the question concerning Asia, and the Macedonian question. These were of greatest concern to European diplomacy.
Thus, from the third to the seventh of August 1907, there was a meeting
between Kaiser Wilhelm II and Tsar Nicholas II; on August 14, between
the Kaiser and King Edward VII; on August 15, between Edward and

Emperor Francis Joseph of Austria-Hungary;[22] on August 21, between Edward and Premier Georges Clemenceau of France; on August 24, between the Austrian and Italian ministers of foreign affairs, Achrenthal and Tittoni; on the same date, between Jules Cambon, the French ambassador at Berlin, and Count Bulou, the German chancellor. At these meetings, among other things, the question of Macedonia occupied a large part on the agenda.[23]

The mandate of the Murzsteg scheme of reforms in Macedonia was due to expire in 1907, and the Turkish government expressed willingness to prolong it for seven years more; that is, until 1914. But Sir Edward Grey, the British foreign secretary, made a proposal to the various European cabinets that, after the expiration of the mandates of the officers in charge of the reforms, a governor-general approved by the powers be appointed for Macedonia.

Meanwhile, an unexpected development took place in Constantinople that caused a stir in England and Russia. The success of Germany in acquiring in Constantinople certain guarantees for the projected Berlin-to-Baghdad railroad greatly reflected on the Anglo-Russian policy toward the Near East. Neither of these powers desired to see German hegemony in Asia. It was mainly due to mutual fear of the German peaceful penetration in Asia that the Anglo-Russian agreement of 1907 was brought about.

As a consequence, however, on June 9, 1908, a meeting was held in Raval by King Edward VII, Tsar Nicholas II, the Russian minister of foreign affairs, Izvolsky, and the British ambassador at St. Petersburg, Sir Hardwig. As a result of this meeting, an agreement concerning an Anglo-Russian scheme of reforms was formulated. The following was the British proposal:

English Scheme of Reforms for Macedonia
of March 3, 1908[24]

Foreign Office, March 3, 1908.

Your Excellency is aware that on the 18th December last His Majesty's Government made certain proposals to the Great Powers with a view to the restoration of order in the Macedonian vilayets.

These proposals were to the effect that General Degiorgis and the foreign staff officers should be intrusted with a full measure of executive control, and that the force under their command should be properly qualified for effective action by a substantial increase in numbers and an adequate equipment. It was further recommended that the Powers should represent to the Sublime-Porte that the chargers on the Macedonian Budget in respect of the maintenance of the Turkish troops were out of all proportion to the services which, as shown by experience, they could render in the maintenance of public security, and that the funds requisite for the increased gendarmerie should be provided by a corresponding reduction of the existing garrison.

Replies have now been received from all the Governments concerned, intimating their inability to support the recommendations of His Majesty's Government, and the Austro-Hungarian and Russian Governments have expressed their views on the situation in some detail in an identic Memorandum dated the 28th January, of which a copy is inclosed for your Excellency's information.

His Majesty's Government have received these communications with great regret. They fully recognize the difficulty of devising practical measures to put an end to the deplorable state of affairs in Macedonia which the continued activity of the bands has brought about, and with which the Turkish authorities have totally failed to deal effectively. It was therefore only after careful consideration, and with a full sense, of the moral responsibility which rests upon them, in common with the other Great Powers, to make an endeavour to alleviate the sufferings of the population and to avert the dangers to the European peace which may result from the present situation, that His Majesty's Government made suggestions which, in their view, were calculated to bring about the restoration of order and the security of life and property.

They cannot fail, therefore, to experience a feeling of disappointment that, while their proposals have met with an unfavourable reception, no alternative scheme is yet forthcoming to deal with a situation which imperatively requires immediate and energetic treatment.

With regard to the first objection raised by the Austro-Hungarian and Russian Governments in their Memorandum, His Majesty's Government would point out that the question of employing the gendarmerie for the repression of the bands was discussed at the recent Conference of the "Adjoints" of the Great Powers at Salonica at their meetings on the 15th, 16th, and 17th October last. The results of these discussions were communicated to the Ambassadors of the Great Powers at Constantinople in a Memorandum signed by those present, including the "Adjoints" of Austria-Hungary and Russia. Paragraph II of this Memorandum deals with a proposal presented by the "Adjoint" of Austria-Hungary, proposing that the pursuit of the bands should be intrusted to the gendarmerie, whose numbers should be considerably increased. Two alternative suggestions for carrying out this scheme were put forward by the Austro-Hungarian and Russian "Adjoints" respectively, and both were approved by the Conference. In view of this unanimous expression of opinion by the military experts on the spot, His Majesty's Government cannot admit that the principle of employing an increased and mobile gendarmerie in place of the Turkish troops for the repression of the bands is either impractical or impossible, and they regret to find that the Austro-Hungarian and Russian Governments have found themselves unable to support the proposals put forward or supported by their own "Adjoints."

The financial difficulties which the Austro-Hungarian and Russian Governments apprehend do not appear to His Majesty's Government to be insuperable. If the Turkish troops are relieved of the task of suppressing the bands, it is obvious that a considerable reduction in their numbers would become possible. The number of extra European officers suggested by the Austro-Hungarian "Adjoint" at the Salonica Conference would not exceed twenty, and the expense thus involved, as well as that of the extra men to be added to the force, could be provided for out of the saving effected on the reduction of the Turkish regular troops.

The Austro-Hungarian and Russian Governments further apprehend that the arrangement would never receive the consent of the Sublime-Porte.

His Majesty's Government are not aware that the attitude of the Turkish authorities towards the measures proposed is one of uncompromising hostility. His Majesty's Ambassador at Constantinople has already on more than one occasion, in conversation with the Sultan, suggested the employment of the gendarmerie in place of Turkish troops for the repression of the bands, and his suggestions were received by His Majesty in a friendly spirit. His Majesty's Government feel convinced that if a strong and unanimous representation to the Turkish Government were made by the Great Powers it could not fail to be effective.

The Austro-Hungarian and Russian Governments are further of opinion that the present moment is inopportune for making fresh proposals. With regard to this point, His Majesty's Government can only observe that the present condition of the three vilayets is so serious as to call for immediate and effective action. To await a moment which might be considered specially opportune for taking such action would involve an indefinite continuance of the state of anarchy which at present prevails, and lay the Powers open to the grave charge of indifference to the sufferings of the population.

His Majesty's Government recognize that the question of the position of the foreign officers may possibly give rise to difficulties. His Majesty's Government have no reason to believe that the difficulties are insuperable. They are not, at any rate, of so formidable a nature as to justify the abandonment of the scheme. With the exercise of tact and discretion on the part of the officers it should be quite possible to avoid friction and insure harmonious wording.

Finally, the Austro-Hungarian and Russian Governments remark that the immediate responsibility for the suppression of the bands rests with the Turkish Government. This is no doubt the case. But as the Turkish Government have signally failed to carry out the duties which naturally devolve upon them, a grave moral responsibility will rest upon the Great Powers signatory of the Treaty of Berlin if the present deplorable situation is permitted to continue.

His Majesty's Government recognize the difficulty of carrying out any proposal for reforms in Macedonia unless it has not only the consent, but the willing and wholehearted cooperation, of the other Great Powers.

They are deeply impressed by the danger of taking separate action which would break up the European concert. Underneath the Macedonian question lies the Turkish question. An attempt to settle the question of Macedonia that caused a division amongst the Powers might raise the Turkish question without settling that of Macedonia. If this were to happen, reforms in Macedonia would be lost to sight, while the Turkish question, if once the concert of the Powers was broken, might prove, as it has done more than once before, a danger to the peace of Europe. On the other hand it is certain that serious consequences may ensue from a continuance of the present state of disorder and violence in the vilayets, especially if it is believed that the European concert is unable or unwilling to find a remedy.

In reviewing the course of events in Macedonia during the last few years, it appears to His Majesty's Government that the special evils which induced first Austria and Russia, and then the other Powers, to take up the question of Macedonian reforms have been ameliorated. Outrages by

Turkish troops and officials have been greatly diminished by the presence of European officers and the creation of the gendarmerie. The collection and management of the finances has been improved by the Financial Commission. But, while from this point of view the situation has improved, other evils have arisen which have counteracted, or even more than counteracted, the good effect of the whole of the improvement.

The strife between the different nationalities and the outrages committed by armed bands have made life and property in Macedonia more insecure than ever, and have been accompanied by revolting crimes, such as that at Dragosh recently, where five men, ten women, and eleven children were deliberately burned alive in their houses.

The enormous number of the Turkish troops kept in Macedonia and charged upon the Budget of the three vilayets remains an intolerable financial burden upon it.

The renewal of the mandates of the Civil Agents and of the Financial Commissioners, together with the proposed judicial reforms, if carried out, would no doubt continue the amelioration of Turkish administration which has been referred to above.

But they would not pacify the country, and they would not lessen, or touch appreciably, the worst evils from which the country is now suffering, nor could they arrest the campaign of murder and violence. On the other hand, it has to be borne in mind that if the note on judicial reforms is not presented, and if it is understood that the Powers have dropped this project without putting forward any other proposal of reform, the effect will be most deplorable, and the situation in Macedonia, which is already bad, will become desperate.

The renewal of the mandates of the Civil Agents and of the Financial Commissioners cannot be regarded as a step forward; it is at best a mere continuance of the present state of things, which was contemplated as a logical consequence and condition of the increase of the customs duties, without which the revenue thus allocated to the Macedonian vilayets could not be satisfactorily employed.

His Majesty's Government are greatly impressed by the seriousness of this situation, and by apprehension of the consequences to which it may lead if it continues to get worse—consequences which would be especially serious and embarrassing for those Governments who by their geographical position have more direct and political interest in the Balkans than His Majesty's Government.

In dealing with this question of Macedonia, His Majesty's Government have been influenced by no political motives, but solely by a desire to discharge the responsibility, which they have felt rests upon them in common with the other Powers who signed the Treaty of Berlin and more especially the obligations incurred under Article XXIII of that Treaty, to do what is possible to promote reforms. They have felt that the continuance of these evils in the Turkish Empire must in the end be a source of weakness and danger to the Turkish Government, and a danger to peace. They have desired, in the interests of humanity and political quiet, to do all in their power to mitigate these evils. They feel, now, that the situation has reached a critical stage, at which it would be well for the Powers to deal with it as a whole, and thoroughly.

The situation is not beyond remedy, but it cannot be remedied by half-measures.

Were a Governor of Macedonia to be appointed who would be given a free hand and be irremovable for a term of years except with the consent of the Powers, and were an adequate force of gendarmerie and European officers placed at his disposal. His Majesty's Government are convinced that the country might be cleared of bands and be pacified in a short time. Violence and outrage, such as have existed for so long, would disappear, and civil and financial reforms would progress rapidly on the foundations which have already been laid. The Governor would be a Turkish subject, and the question of whether he should be a Christian or a Mussulman would be of comparatively slight importance, if other conditions as to his personal character, his powers, and position were satisfactory.

His Majesty's Government desire to emphasize the fact that religious difference is not in any way involved in this question. It is not now a case of strife between Christian and Moslem; it is simply a question of putting an end to anarchy and violence, and of establishing a state of tranquility and of security for life and property by which all the inhabitants, Christian and Moslem, would benefit alike.

In order to render the Governor independent of the control of the Palace, his pension should be guaranteed by the Powers and provision made for it in the Macedonian Budget. In these circumstances His Majesty's Government would have no objection to the favourable consideration of the proposal that the Civil Agents, the Financial Commissioners, and the "Adjoints" should be in the service of the Sultan.

To finance this Administration, it would be necessary that the Turkish troops at present kept by the Macedonian Budget should be largely reduced in number, and His Majesty's Government recognize that, if this were done, the Powers who were parties to the arrangement should guarantee the integrity and external security of this part of the Sultan's dominions as long as the arrangement continued, and proved effective in securing reform and satisfactory to the Powers.

At the same time pressure should continually be exerted at Athens, Sophia, and Belgrade with a view to arresting the passage of bands across the frontier and restraining their activity in the Macedonian vilayets.

Believing that it is urgently necessary that the actual situation should be firmly grasped, in order to avoid evils even worse than those which already exist, and that such reforms as they have indicated would be a complete remedy, both prompt and effective, His Majesty's Government earnestly recommend them to the favourable consideration of the Powers.

If other proposals are put forward by other Powers, His Majesty's Government are ready to consider them, and whether it be the reforms suggested in this despatch or some others deemed preferable by the Powers and as likely to be effective which are adopted, His Majesty's Government will be ready to cooperate with the rest of the Powers in taking whatever measures are necessary to secure them, or to agree to such measures being taken by any Powers who are prepared to act on behalf of the concert.

His Majesty's Government cannot regard the fact that objections will be raised by the Turkish Government as a reason for not putting forward proposals at Constantinople. All proposals, whether large or small, have hitherto met with objections at Constantinople, and if it is admitted that this fact is an obstacle which cannot be overcome, it is fatal to any further proposal at all. His Majesty's Government believe that if all the Powers make it known that they are equally in earnest and resolved, they can secure the acceptance of any proposal which does not involve a disintegration of Ottoman territory. If, on the other hand, the Powers are not prepared to assume this attitude, they will, in effect, declare that they are powerless to secure anything, and that the Concert, as an instrument for securing reforms, has ceased to exist a conclusion which His Majesty's Government most earnestly deprecate and desire to avoid.

I request that your Excellency will read this despatch to the Minister for Foreign Affairs, and leave a copy with his Excellency should he desire it.[25]

7. THE "YOUNG TURKS" REVOLT OF 1908

The first attempt by a group of Turkish refugees and exiles to conspire against Abdul Hamid's regime took place in Geneva in 1891. Here they formed an association that later developed into a secret society known as the "Committee of Liberty." But shortly after its organization, it transferred its operation to Paris, where it amalgamated with the "Ottoman Committee of Union and Progress." Paris became the working center of this organization and from there secret propaganda was formulated for distribution in Turkey. About the year 1901, the Ottoman Committee of Union and Progress (henceforth to be referred to as OCUP) established its secret headquarters in Salonika. Ahmed Riza, an exile and leader of the Paris branch of the OCUP, remained there in order to further the cause of the Young Turks movement.

The impetus given to the movement at this time was not so much because of the tyranny of the home administration as it was of the aggressive policies of the Great Powers in relation to Turkey. The naval demonstration initiated by Lord Lansdowne at the end of 1906 had just taken place. The constant talk among the Balkan states for the partition of Macedonia and the withdrawal of England from the Concert of Europe, followed by her alliance with Russia to act in the internal affairs of Turkey, created an alarming situation in Turkey, which consequently stimulated the Young Turks movement. For if things were to continue as they actually were, the province of Macedonia would be lost to the Empire. It was therefore high time for the Young Turks to make definite preparations and to initiate a definite policy toward their national evils. They wished also to have their state administrative machinery taken out of the grip of the corrupt element and the influence of the Palace so that they might be able to establish a modern democratic state.

The greatest success of the OCUP was in the army. The leading and most energetic men at the head of the movement in Macedonia were army officers. It was necessary and imperative to win the army to their side. Considering the strength of the Third Army Corps in Macedonia whose headquarters were in Salonika, it would have been useless without its aid for the Young Turks to make any attempt at revolt. Their main reliance, therefore, was on the army. Thus by winning the army in Macedonia to their side, the Young Turks were able to spread their influence beyond the confines of European Turkey. They also succeeded in winning to their cause a considerable number of the officers of the Second Army Corps stationed in Asia Minor with headquarters in Smyrna. Disguised as a preacher among the regiments stationed there, Niazi Bey, one of the leading men of the Young Turks revolt, had been working in Asia Minor for eighteen months before the revolt took place.

The seriousness of the situation became so alarming to the Sultan's Palace and the corruptive element around it that the Sultan began to use a peculiar form of diplomacy, that of fostering schemes of promotions for the leading officers of the OCUP movement. The Sultan invited Enver Bey, the most popular man of the Young Turks movement, to come to the capital, promising him promotion in rank. Enver Bey had been educated in Germany. He was greatly responsible for winning the Third Army Corps at Salonika to the Young Turks' cause. Although he was well known to the Palace for his activity in the OCUP movement against the Sultan, he was not threatened with punishment but with a promise of promotion. But Enver Bey knew better. He knew perfectly well what the invitation was worth and that the only promotion he was likely to get, in the words of Buxton, "was the promotion to the bottom of Bosphorus." Although it had been calculated by the leaders of the movement that the time would not be ripe for their projected revolt until the autumn of 1909, the apparent foreign intervention in Macedonia and the institution of an active campaign against the OCUP, which the Palace was intending to inaugurate in the early part of 1908, precipitated the revolt.

The first overt act took place in the mountainous town of Ressen in the Vilayet of Monastir (Bitolia) on July 5, 1908. Here Niazi Bey, the renowned persecutor of the Bulgarian revolutionists of the IMRO, first raised the standard of revolt. He was a major in the regular army at this period and had gained a reputation for his ferocious operations against the rebels of the subject races. His military duties had brought him into contact with the Bulgarian *comitajis* of the IMRO. During the great insurrection of 1903, Niazi Bey took an energetic part in an attempt to exterminate the "rebellious *giauors.*" Even to the peaceful *rayahs* of the Vilayet of Monastir he became a terror. His activity against the IMRO's freedom fighters was governed by a somewhat hostile policy. Nevertheless, after the year 1905 he had assumed a certain degree of sympathy toward the IMRO. Although he was compelled, as a matter of military duty, to persecute the Bulgarian revolutionists, he often expressed his sympathy with their cause.[26]

Niazi Bey was convinced that the idealism of the IMRO was far more beneficial to the destiny of Macedonia than the despotism of the Sultan and his corrupt bureaucracy in Constantinople. When he proclaimed his revolt against the old Turkish regime, Niazi Bey calmed the terrified population in Macedonia by issuing the following proclamation:

> We have come out to fight despotism, if necessary. But our objects are pacific and liberal. We call upon all Ottoman subjects to inaugurate a new era of equality. To you Christians we say, the Great Powers and the Balkan states have done nothing for you. They have only sowed discord between you while playing for their own hand. Our government is also to blame. Let us work together for our country. I promise freedom to every race and creed on condition that they renounce all ideas of annexation to other countries. So long as a Turk remains alive, the country will belong to the Ottomans. I appeal to all bands to report themselves to me and arrange a common program.[27]

Abdul Hamid began to seek assistance from his hirelings, the Greeks. All other races in Macedonia accepted the call of the Young Turks for a common action. The Greek element remained indifferent but generally antagonistic to the Young Turks' action. Writes Mr. Knight:

> The one doubtful element of the population was the Greek. It appears that the Palace had not only sent Munir Pasha to Athens to seek the assistance of those intriguing subjects of King George who used to equip the brigand bands that had been the curse of Macedonia; but it also issued instructions to General Osman Pasha in Monastir to persuade the Greek bands within his district by means of what bribes or promises I cannot say, to hunt down and capture Niazi and the other leaders of the insurrection. It is undoubtedly the fact that the Greek bands, assisted by hired Mussulman desperados, were displaying great activity at this period, and that the Greek clergy were directing a vigorous persecution of the Bulgarian exarchists.[28] The Committee of Union and Progress dealt firmly with this one disturbing element in an otherwise peaceful and united country.[29]

From July 5, the date of Niazi Bey's revolt at Ressen, to July 22, the state of affairs was such that the government still nominally ruled and administered the three Vilayets of Macedonia—those of Monastir, Salonika, and Skopie—but its authority had been reduced to impotence. Nevertheless, on July 23, 1908, a definite ultimatum was presented to the Sultan from the OCUP at Salonika. The ultimatum stated that unless the Constitution of 1876 was granted within twenty-four hours, the troops of the Second and Third Army Corps would march on the capital.

The Council of Ministers was called together to deliberate on the OCUP's ultimatum. Although it met with some opposition, the opinions of Kiamil Pasha and Said Pasha, both leading statesmen and somewhat liberal-minded, were strongly in favor of giving in. Before the twenty-four hours of the ultimatum had elapsed, in the early morning of July 24, the Sultan's acceptance was telegraphed to Salonika. Thus, while Niazi Bey revolted in Ressen, and Enver Bey proclaimed the Constitution at Salonika, Abdul Hamid acknowledged its validity. Subsequently, the *Huriet* (liberty) was proclaimed, and political equality, thenceforth, was to be enjoyed by all the subject races in the Empire. The principle of liberty, equality, and fraternity, phrases borrowed from the French Revolution, was to be the foundation of the new *Huriet* in Turkey—in European Turkey at any rate. And as a result of the Young Turks' *coup d'etat* a sudden change toward the Ottoman Empire took place in European diplomacy. The Great Powers recalled the reformers during the month of September 1908 and left the situation of Macedonia in the hands of the new regime—that of the Ottoman Committee of Union and Progress.

8. THE IMRO DISBANDS— THE FORMATION OF "CONSTITUTIONAL CLUBS" ONLY TO BE OUTLAWED

The chief exponents of the OCUP declared that an era of freedom, equality, and brotherhood was dawning in the Ottoman Empire. Delegates were sent to the leaders of the IMRO to assure them that the rights they were fighting for existed already and that the cooperation of all nationalities was sought in this attempt at reforming the state. The Bulgarians and the Vlachs (Romanians) of Macedonia accepted the promises without misgivings. Thousands of revolutionists of the regular *chetas* (bands) of the IMRO lay down their arms and journeyed to the big towns. Thus, the armed members of the IMRO came into the open, descended from their hiding places in the mountains, and came into the cities. The wish of the Bulgarians in Macedonia was that the Ottoman Empire might become a federal state and that Macedonia and Thrace might be separate states in the federation. Because of such a desire and hopeful expectation, the Bulgarians gave hearty cooperation to the Young Turks. The Greeks, on the other hand, who perfidiously used the weakness of the old regime to further their own propaganda, accepted the *coup d'etat* coolly. The Albanian Mohammedans were not pleased with the change, for they had enjoyed certain privileges under the old regime and their national awakening had just begun.

By proclaiming the Constitution of Midhat Pasha, the new regime created a certain amount of freedom and made an attempt to guarantee some political rights to the various races and creeds in the Empire. Although the stipulated rights were not explicit, it was possible to carry on the struggle for more and better reforms in a legal manner on the basis of constitutionality. The Bulgarians in Macedonia, therefore, suspended their revolutionary activity, disbanded the powerful IMRO, and formed constitutional clubs with the following program:

1. The granting of local self-government to new administrative units to be made up of the various nationalities in the Turkish Empire, organized, as far as possible, into homogeneous groups.
2. The granting of equal suffrage to all male Ottoman subjects of thirty years or over; voting to be direct and secret. The protection of the rights of the minorities to be guaranteed.
3. Complete freedom of speech, press, conscience, meetings, organizations, and the individual.
4. The introduction of self-government in all the municipalities, which are to be the first administrative units.
5. A new system of administrative organization, based upon homogeneous ethnical groups with elective councils and permanent committees.
6. The language of the schools to be the mother tongue of each race.
7. The Bulgarians in Turkey to retain all the rights providing for free religious and political development, secured on the strength of the various state documents issued by the supreme executive authority.
8. The subjects of the various races to use their tongue in the official institutions.[30]

Meanwhile, the Greeks in Macedonia gathered about their bishops in the so-called "syllogues."

To the vast majority of the Turkish population, constitutional government however, was a meaningless term. No one knew anything definite about it. Even the ruling caste—the bureaucracy—had no conception of parliamentary government. The unique position of the average Turk in the community rendered the election system useless as far as the Musulmans were concerned. How could a ruling caste, corrupt to the core, adapt itself to such a radical change as a government by the consent of the governed? The age-long traditions of the Turks with regard to ruling, oppression, rapine, and massacre were not to be magically altered overnight. The average Turk felt in his heart the impracticability of the visionary Young Turks. Constitution, liberty, elections, parliamentary government were so much devilish imposition by the *giaours* upon the reckless and visionary members of the OCUP!

The Young Turks, however, who were pronounced nationalists, soon began to oppose the nationalistic aspirations of the other peoples and in 1909 the National Assembly passed a law against the national organizations of non-Turkish groups. The Bulgarian constitutional clubs were forcibly broken up. Arbitrary rules were made to govern the elections; for example, while one delegate fell to every 250 Mohammedans, only one fell to every 750 Christians, and besides that the national representatives were not chosen directly by the electors but by their delegates.[31]

The OCUP endeavored to put all their strength into an attempt at assimilation and Ottomanization of the other subject races. Their first act toward this objective was to destroy the privileges of the Bulgarian and Greek Orthodox Church.[32] The Turks believed that these privileges constituted a strong barrier to the assimilation of the races in the Empire. Consequently, the OCUP set out to Ottomanize the various nationalities and subsequently began to restrict the rights of the religious communities of the Greek Patriarchate as well as those of the Bulgarian Exarchists. The Bulgarian constitutional clubs, which had been organized immediately after the disbandment of the *IMRO* as a result of the *Huriet* of 1908 were ordered to be closed; legislative acts were passed and laws enacted prohibiting the rights of assembly and public and cultural meetings. Because of these unconstitutional acts of the so-called "constitutional" regime of Turkey, the Bulgarians and Greeks in Macedonia united in 1911 for the first time in their history for a common action in order to maintain their school and church privileges.

The world was now convinced that the bloodless "revolution" of the Young Turks, performed under the banner of the Ottoman Committee of Union and Progress, was a mere gesture—a sham performance. How could a conservative and backward nation such as Turkey was at that time ever change from a government of absolute despotism to a constitutional form of government, and that overnight? It was an Englishman who once said that the Turks never change. Social and political evolution is a gradual development. Thanks to the Young Turks' fanaticism and reactionary policy, they brought about the complete destruction of the once powerful Ottoman Empire in Europe.

SELECT BIBLIOGRAPHY

Anastasoff, C., *The Tragic Peninsula*, St. Louis, Mo., 1938, pp. 97-154.
Bazhdaroff, G., *The Macedonian Question—Yesterday and Today*, Sofia, 1926, pp. 3-34.
Brailsford, H. N., *Macedonia: Its Races and Their Future*, London, 1906, pp. 290-322.
Draganof, M., *Macedonia and The Reforms*, London, 1908, pp. 107-290. *Note:* This work contains documentary evidence on the massacres, burning, plundering, police crimes, arrests, and, in general, the bloody repression of the Bulgarians in Macedonia.
Documents Diplomatique—Affaires étrangères, Paris, Vol. XXXIV—*Affaires de Macédoine*, 1902.

Krainkowsky, Dr. A. Iv., *La Question de Macédoine et la Diplomatiè Euro-péene*, Part II, pp. 109-225.
Lamouche, Colonel L., *Quinze Ans D'Histoire Balkanique (1904-1918)*, Paris, 1928, pp. 48-114.
Marriott, J. A. R., *The Eastern Question: A Historical Study of European Di-plomacy*, Oxford, 1917, pp. 341-380.
Panaretff, Stephen, *Near East Affairs and Conditions*, New York, 1922, pp. 126-155.
Rappoport, Alfred, *Au Pays des Martyrs en Macédoine (1904-1909)*, pp. 24-59.
Usher, Dr. Roland D., *Pan-Germanism*, New York, 1913, pp. 203-229.

NOTES

1. See the official documents between Russia and Austria with regard to this agreement in Alfred F. Pribram, *supra*, Chapter VIII, n. 13, I, pp. 184-190.
2. J. A. R. Marriott, *The Eastern Question: A Historical Study of European Diplomacy*, Oxford, 1917, p. 341.
3. *Ibid.*, p. 359. For the diplomatic phase of the Berlin-to-Baghdad project, see Gooch and Temperley (Editors), *British Documents on the Origins of the War (1898-1914)*, VI, Chapter LIV, also Appendix VII and VIII. Note also the map on page 796 showing railways and railway projects in Asian Turkey, 1907.
4. M. Draganof, *Macedonia and the Reforms*, London, 1908, p. 3.
5. *Ibid.*, p. 54.
6. *Ibid.*, pp. 54-55.
7. *Ibid.*, p. 56. All diplomatic documents quoted may also be found in the *French Yellow Book of 1902* and the *English Blue Book of 1902-1904*.
8. N. H. Brailsford, *supra*, Chapter IX, n. 20, p. 300.
9. G. P. Gooch and H. Temperley (Editors), *British Documents on the Origin of the War, 1898-1914*, London, 1928, V, pp. 50-53; 59-68.
10. C. Anastasoff, *supra*, Chapter VII, n. 3, pp. 109-110.
11. C. Anastasoff, *supra*, Chapter VII, n. 3, pp. 116-117; M. Draganof, *supra*, n. 4, p. 60.
12. Germany flatly refused to take any part in the internal affairs of Turkey.
13. C. Anastasoff, *supra*, Chapter VII, n. 3, pp. 118-120.
14. The term *Vilayet* may be translated "province." There were six vilayets then in the possession of European Turkey. Two were to the west, in Albania, Jannina, and Scutari. Three in the center were Macedonian— Salonika, Monastir (Bitolia), and Skopie (Uskub). To the east lay Adrianople. The governor of a vilayet was called Vali and had the rank of a Pasha (equal to a military general). A large Vilayet was subdivided into two or three Sandjaks, the governor of which was called a Mutessarif, who also had the rank of a Pasha. Next came the Caza (department or county), governed by a Caimakam (prefect), who had the rank of a Bey, and was equal to a military colonel. The smallest division was the Nahié (district), governed by a Mudir (subprefect).
15. N. H. Brailsford, *supra*, Chapter IX, n. 20, p. 307.
16. V. Bérard, *La Revolution Turque*, Paris, 1909, p. 203.
17. See also *infra*, Appendix VI.
18. M. Draganof, *supra*, n. 4, pp. 219-221.

19. Nevoliani consisted of about three hundred houses. The inhabitants of the village were half Bulgarian and half Turkish. Nevoliani is only fifteen minutes' walking distance east of Florina, where a Turkish garrison of two thousand troops was stationed. Neither the armed Turkish inhabitants of the village nor the troops in Florina made any effort to pursue the Greek band.

20. The names and ages of the victims as ascertained by Bairaktaroff are found in M. Draganof, *supra*, n. 4, p. 108.

21. C. Anastasoff, *supra*, Chapter VII, n. 3, p. 130.

22. Gooch and Temperley, *supra*, n. 9, Chapter VI, Part II; Chapter XLII and V; Chapter XXXVI, pp. 208-211; also Sir Sidney Lee, *King Edward VII* (1927), II, pp. 549-550.

23. *Ibid.*, pp. 258-259; 264-266; 592-593; 624-625.

24. For the Russian Scheme of Reforms in Macedonia of March 26, 1908, see Appendix I. The text is in French.

25. Turkey n. 1 (1908): *Further correspondence respecting proposals by His Majesty's Government for reforms in Macedonia*, London, 1908, docum. N6. Had the Anglo-Russian scheme of reforms been applied, it would certainly have resulted in the autonomy of Macedonia.

26. See also *infra*, Appendix II.

27. C. R. Buxton, *Turkey in Revolution*, London, 1909, p. 58.

28. See also *infra*, Appendix III.

29. E. F. Knight, *The Awakening of Turkey*, London, 1909, p. 199.

30. G. Bazhdaroff, *supra*, Chapter IX, n. 7, p. 47; C. Anastasoff, *supra*, Chapter VII, n. 3, p. 145.

31. G. Bazhdaroff, *supra*, Chapter IX, n. 7, p. 27.

32. Writing about the later tendencies of the Young Turks' "revolution," the Carnegie International Commission makes the following statement: "Far from satisfying the tendencies of re-awakening nationalism, it sets itself a task to which the absolutism of the Sultan had never ventured; to reconstruct the Turkey of the Caliphate and transform it into a modern state, beginning by the complete abolition of the rights and privileges of the different ethnic groups. These rights and privileges, confirmed by *firmans* and guaranteed by European diplomacy, were the sole means by which the Christian nationalities could safeguard their language, their beliefs and their ancient civilizations. These barriers once down, they felt themselves threatened by Ottoman assimilation in a way that had never been threatened before in the course of the ages since the capture of Constantinople by Mohammed II. This assimilation, this 'Ottomanization,' was the avowed aim of the victor, the committee of 'Union and Progress.'" *Report of the Carnegie International Commission*, p. 35.

CHAPTER XI

BULGARIA'S WARS FOR THE LIBERATION OF THE BULGARIANS IN MACEDONIA AND THRACE (THE BALKAN WARS OF 1912-1913)

1. THE YOUNG TURKS' DOMESTIC POLICY

In Macedonia, as elsewhere in the Turkish Empire, the lot of the Christian populations became steadily worse. The avowed object of the OCUP's policy was unrelenting Ottomanization of the various ethnic groups. The Young Turks launched a policy to make Turkey a nation of Turks. They considered themselves a strong, virile race into which the other races were to be fused. Turkey was weak, they declared, because "the ancient regime was to blame for the powerlessness it had shown in Macedonia. They, on the other hand, would have made an end of it in a few months or at least a few years."[1] Such a policy, therefore, the Turkification and extermination of the Christian races, was the result of a deliberate plan on the part of the Young Turks. To solve the Macedonian and Thracian problems, it was necessary to clear those two provinces of their Bulgarian and Christian inhabitants.

The assimilation of heterogeneous population could only be effected slowly, regardless of how severe might be the measures threatening the future existence of the various nationalities. The leaders of the OCUP wished to destroy their enemies—the Christian subject races—while they were still in power. Because national rivalries in Macedonia offered an ever-ready pretext for the intervention of the powers, the Young Turks decided to put an end to the question with all possible celerity.

182

The process of assimilation or Turkification was to be forced by every form of outrage and persecution. "In Macedonia and Thrace, in the Aegean Islands and along the coast of Asia Minor," writes Dr. Gibbons, "the bishops and clergy suffered untold persecution. Some were even assassinated. I shall never forget a memorable interview I had with Jachim III. . . . 'They treat us like dogs,' he cried. 'Never under Abdul Hamid or any Sultan have my people suffered as they are suffering now. But we are too strong for them. We refuse to be exterminated. I see all Europe stained with blood because of this.' "[2] "But the power of the Young Turks," writes Dr. Marriott, "was unequal to their ambition; their deeds, though brutal wherever they were strong, were less potent than their words. The denunciation of tyranny was all sound and fury; in effect signified nothing."[3]

To augment the chaos of the country, the Young Turks began to use other brutal methods. Local secret Turkish bands fostered by the government began to kill the Bulgarian Macedonian freedom fighters from ambush. The leaders of the Bulgarian revolutionary bands of the IMRO, who had loyally and earnestly assisted the Young Turks in their effort to overthrow Abdul Hamid, were now subjected to extermination. A considerable number of the outstanding IMRO leaders were assassinated. The situation was further aggravated by the *mohadjirs*—Moslem colonists —who were brought from Bosnia and Herzegovina by the Turkish government to force the Bulgarian peasants from the lands which their fathers, grandfathers, and great-grandfathers had cultivated for them. Such conditions favored the reappearance of the former inclination on the part of the people to resort to an armed struggle. As a consequence, the IMRO once more began its conspiratory work. Thousands of Bulgarian Macedonians, members of the IMRO, took to the mountains. Their work now consisted mainly of placing bombs along the railway lines and in government institutions. Thus, from 1910 to 1912, that is, prior to the Balkan War of 1912 against Turkey, the following outrages occurred in Macedonia:

1. The stations of Adjalar (district of Koumanovo), Koumanovo, Boyanovo, and Mirovtsi (near Preshovo) were seriously damaged.
2. The seat of government in the village of Konore (near Skopie) was destroyed.
3. Bombs were exploded at the stations of Zelenich (near Skopie) and Kilinder, in the vicinity of Koukoush, as well as at the gendarmerie post of Vélés.
4. Near Doiran, a dynamite attack was made on a train on the railroad line Salonika-Constantinople.
5. The freight depot at the Vélés station was destroyed.
6. Bombs were exploded at Radovitch, Monastir (Bitolia), Ohrid,

Kavadartsi, Prilep, Kroushevo, and Kitchevo, as well as at the Austrian postoffice[4] and the streetcar station in Salonika.
7. Bomb outrages occurred also at Doiran, Shtip, and Kotchani, after which the Turkish civilian population massacred the Bulgarian inhabitants.[5]

In spite of such a melancholic and desperate attitude on the part of the Bulgarians of Macedonia, the Bulgarian government was still hopeful for an understanding with Turkey. Such a policy was motivated and often fostered by previous Bulgarian cabinets because they were aware of the fact that if Bulgaria had to resort to a rapprochement with any of the other Balkan states it would be possible only at the expense of the Bulgarian nation; that is, the Bulgarians of Macedonia. It was their conflicting interests in Macedonia that was the great barrier to *entente* among the Balkan states. Bulgaria, for example, insistently favored a policy of autonomy for Macedonia. Serbia and Greece on the other hand "advocated not autonomy but partition."[6] Public opinion in Bulgaria would invariably be against such a transaction. "Rather Macedonia autonomous as a whole under Turkish suzerainty than independent on condition of partition. Such has always been the Bulgarian point of view."[7]

Ivan E. Gueshoff (1867-1938), the prime minister of Bulgaria (1911-1913), used all his efforts in the early part of 1911 to induce an understanding between Bulgaria and Turkey. "All through the summer of 1911," writes he, "I continued my talks with the Turkish minister in Sofia on the subject of a possible understanding between Turkey and Bulgaria. Assim Bey pretended to agree with me, blaming the policy of the Turkish government, and meditated upon a round of visits to Monastir, Salonika, and Adrianople, in order to impress the local Turkish authorities with the need of a change in their attitude towards the Bulgarians. He was, however, recalled to Constantinople before carrying out his intention and became the minister of foreign affairs. In the meantime, Italy declared war on Turkey, who now had every reason to be on friendly terms with Bulgaria. Unfortunately . . . the minister did nothing to inaugurate a new policy towards Bulgaria."[8]

Although Bulgaria made every possible effort to arrive at an understanding with the Young Turks regime, the latter not only intensified the persecution of the Bulgarians in Macedonia, but also created a number of provocations against the kingdom of Bulgaria. Discredited before the Mohammedan world because of the failure of their internal policy and above all the loss of Tripoli (Libya) to Italy, the Young Turks felt an urge to divert public opinion from their internal political failures by provoking war against Bulgaria. To accelerate their provocative work, the Young Turks regime encouraged massacres in Shtip and Kotchani in 1912, murders of Bulgarian notables, torture and persecutions of the Macedonian peasantry, and a systematic ill-treatment of the Macedonian Bulgarians serving in the Turkish army.

The outrages against the Bulgarians were not confined to the provinces of Macedonia and Thrace. Frontier incidents that exasperated public opinion in Bulgaria became more frequent. The Turks committed acts that directly concerned the kingdom of Bulgaria; for example, the killing of Captain Nikola Georgieff in May 1911 while he was on his tour of inspection of the border outposts; the killing of two corporals, Ignatieff and Golvesky, of the border outpost at Kara-Tepe (Chepinsko), and similar incidents at Seretash, Veselinova Mahala, Saujak, Deve-bair, Ouzem, Goulesh, Karamanitsa, and Tash-Tepe. Such incidents were of the greatest consequence in the Bulgaro-Turkish relationship. Notwithstanding the reign of chaos in Macedonia and the above border incidents, the Turkish government massed troops on the Bulgarian frontiers, which clearly demonstrated Turkey's intention to make war on Bulgaria. James David Bourchier (1850-1921), the Balkan correspondent of the London *Times* (1888-1921), in an article of May 1, 1912, concerning the political situation in the Balkans, made the following observation: "The conditions in the Near East were never so dark and restless. . . . The declaration of war between Italy and Turkey, engendered a common danger for a cataclysm in the Balkans. . . . But the real danger will never come from the neighbors of Turkey but from the internal disorders of Turkey itself."

Although Bulgaria remonstrated against the Turkish excesses, the Sublime Porte remained unresponsive. Worse still, to encourage a warlike attitude and hatred against the Bulgarians, the Turkish officials, military officers, the *hodjas* (Mohammedan priests), and more particularly the newspapers were constantly uttering threats against Bulgaria. The spokesman of the new Turkish regime at that time was Kiazim Bey, the Vali (governor) of Salonika. In an article published in September 1912, in the newspaper *Tanin*, he wrote: "In order to save the Turkish domination and Ottomanization of Macedonia, I find no other means except the crushing of that Balkan state (Bulgaria), which is the chief cause for the disorders and annoyance of our country. . . . Only by means of a war would we be able to save the Turkish authority in Macedonia. It is necessary, therefore, to create an opportunity so that we may destroy the roots of the widely entertained idea about the decay of Turkey. . . . This is an unalterable urge."[9]

Such being the state of mind of the high priest, the exponent of the new Turkish regime, one cannot fail to understand the general course of Turkey's attitude toward her despised neighbor, Bulgaria. War against the latter was, therefore, a *sine qua non* for the perpetuation of "Turkish authority in Macedonia." Hence the numerous provocations not only against the Bulgarians in Macedonia but also against Bulgaria itself, so as to "create" a favorable "opportunity" for war upon Bulgaria.

2. THE BALKAN ALLIANCE

In view of what was taking place in Turkey, Bulgarian public opinion began to be greatly alarmed. The Bulgarian government at the same time took momentous action. "No Bulgarian statesman, responsible for the future of the Bulgarian nation," writes Mr. Gueshoff, "could remain indifferent to such a condition of things, or ignore the open threats of the Turks to aggravate the measures aiming at the annihilation of the Bulgarians in Macedonia. . . . Among the various methods that suggested themselves, the most important consisted in an understanding not with Turkey, who had rejected our advance, but with our neighbors. Such a policy was greatly facilitated by the unanimity with which public opinion in Bulgaria had recently greeted the meetings of the Serbian and Bulgarian economists and the visit of the Bulgarian students to Athens in April 1911. Matters were further simplified by the fact that in 1904 a secret agreement had been signed with Serbia and that the latter country since made repeated efforts . . . to conclude an offensive and defensive alliance with Bulgaria."[10]

By 1904, however, the diplomats of Belgrade and Sofia were discussing schemes for an offensive and defensive alliance as a means of securing the autonomy of Old Serbia and of Macedonia. This was to be accomplished as far as possible by peaceful means but, in case of difficulty, by force of arms. Difficulties arose as soon as the frontiers began to be spoken of. The diplomats soon proposed a geographical interpretation of the term "Old Serbia." According to the Serbians, Old Serbia was to extend so as to cover the whole of the Sandjak of Novi-Bazar and a considerable part of the Vilayet of Skopie (Uskub). The Bulgarians considered the Serbian claims exorbitant, and finally the idea of an offensive alliance was given up.

On April 25, 1904, however, Balkan diplomats knew well enough that the "sick man of Europe" was incurable. They were anxious to be ready to act when the hour of Turkey's dissolution arrived. To this end, M. Milanovitch, the prime minister of Serbia, vainly proposed in 1904 to extend Serbia's claim over Skopie and Koumanovo. What is more interesting is that by this time Russian diplomacy was quite interested in the formation of a Balkan alliance to include even Turkey. Russia was now well on her way to fostering under her tutelage a Balkan alliance to extend from east to west—from the Black Sea to the Adriatic—for the purpose of checking the north-to-south tendencies of Austria-Hungary and Germany. In 1910, conferences were held in St. Petersburg by Milanovitch and Alexander P. Malinoff (1867-1938), the Bulgarian prime minister (1908-1911). The result of these conferences was fruitless because the same old difficulties about partition arose. "Bulgaria," states the *Report* of the Carnegie International Commission, "was by no means disposed to sanction the Serbian tendencies favored by Russian diplomacy, even in the highly general form of a possible extension of Old Serbia, proper so-called, towards the south."[11]

The principles that were to establish the Bulgaro-Serbian understanding were written in a memorandum. The points embodied in the memorandum as indispensable conditions for a treaty of alliance were the following:

1. The renewal of the Treaty of 1904, *mutatis mutandis:*
   Instead of reforms for Macedonia, they were to ask for autonomy; if that should prove impossible, Macedonia was to be divided.
2. In case of partition, Bulgaria was to receive:
   a. the river Pchina to the west of Vardar, all the way to its source;
   b. the boundaries of the Sandjak of Prizrend and Uskub, to the west of the Vardar.
3. Determination of *casus foederis:*
   a. attack on Serbia and Bulgaria, from whichever quarter it may come;
   b. attack by Turkey on any one of the Balkan states;
   c. an offensive alliance against Turkey with the object of
   (1) liberating Macedonia and Old Serbia, in circumstances deemed favorable to both countries, and
   (2) putting an end to the anarchy or massacres in the Turkish provinces where the vital interests of either country are at stake.[12]

Among the other things in the report to the king and the Ministerial Council about his interview with Milovanovitch, Gueshoff makes the following remark:

When I remarked to Mr. Milovanovitch that if our attempts at liberating Macedonia and Old Serbia take a character of annexation, our task will be greatly complicated, owing to the touchiness of our neighbors, he agreed that it would be better to ask for autonomy, although that solution did not particularly appeal to him. He kept insisting on a partition of the territories liberated and said for some of them there could be no discussion between us. Adrianople must revert to Bulgaria, in the same way as Old Serbia, to the north of Shar Mountain, must belong to Serbia. As regards

Macedonia, the greater part of the province will fall to the Bulgarians. But a section of northern Macedonia must be given to Serbia and the best way would be to reserve the partition for the arbitration of the Russian Emperor. Let us draw no dividing line at the present.[13]

The principle of Milovanovitch, however, was accepted by the Ministerial Council of Bulgaria, and the latter authorized Gueshoff to institute negotiations for an alliance with Serbia. This move was further hastened because of the fact that Turkey had already called up her reserves and had begun to mass troops in Thrace. Serbia accepted, more or less, the Bulgarian formula on the subject of Macedonian autonomy and agreed that the two zones—the uncontested Serbian zone and the contested one—were to constitute a "contested zone," which included the entire Vilayet of Uskub and as far south as the Lake of Ohrid (see map). The instrumentality of Russia was quite a factor in eliminating the apparent difficulties that had arisen between the negotiating parties, for the Gueshoff-Daneff[14] coalition was really the first Bulgarian Russophile cabinet since the union of Eastern Rumelia with the Principality of Bulgaria in 1885. Nekludoff, the Russian minister in Sofia, and Colonel Romanovsky, the Russian military attaché there, were greaty responsible for the harmony reached by the representatives of Serbia and Bulgaria. *But, after all, it was the first time that a Bulgarian government recognized the necessity and possibility for territorial concession in Macedonia by ceding the Vilayet of Uskub to the claim of Serbia.* After determining the frontiers of the "contested zone," a protocol to that effect was signed on March 7, 1912, and six days later, March 13, 1912, a definite treaty of alliance and friendship was concluded between Bulgaria and Serbia. To this treaty was also attached a secret annex— an agreement providing for the disposal of the territorial acquisitions in case of a successful war on the part of the allies against Turkey.

Article two of the secret annex to the treaty states:

> All territorial gains which might eventually be realized through a common action, in confirmation of the first two clauses of the treaty and the first clause of this secret supplement, are to become common possessions—*condominium*—of the allied states. Their final disposition, which will take place within a period of three months, at the most, after the restoration of peace will be made on the following basis:
>
> Serbia recognized the right of Bulgaria to all territories east of the Rhodope Mountains and the River Struma; Bulgaria recognized the right of Serbia to all those which are situated north and west of the Shar Mountains.
>
> As for the territories lying between the Rhodope and Shar Mountains, the Aegean Sea and Lake Ochrida, if both parties become convinced that these cannot be organized into a separate, autonomous province then in view of the common interests of the Bulgarian and Serbian nationalities and because of other considerations of an internal and external character they will be disposed of in the manner indicated below:

Serbia promises not to make any claim on the territories situated beyond the line indicated on the inclosed map, which begins at the peak Golem (north of Krivorechna Polanka) and follows a general southwestern course of the Lake of Ochrida. [There follows a list of the places through which the line passes. See map.]

Bulgaria promises to accept this boundary in case His Majesty, the Russian Emperor, who will be considered the supreme arbiter in the matter, pronounces himself in favor of it. It is understood that the two contracting parties promise to accept as final the boundary which His Majesty, the Russian Emperor, within the above-mentioned limits, shall find as best answering to the rights and interests of the two parties.[15]

As will be seen from the provisions of the above clauses of the treaty and the secret annex to this treaty, the two contracting parties, after deciding on eventual partition, reverted to the idea of autonomy. Partition was to take place only in case the organization of the conquered countries "into a separate, autonomous province" should be found impossible in the conviction of both parties. Before partition was to take place the occupied territories were to be regarded as "common possessions of the allied states." The treaty was to remain defensive purely while the two parties came to an agreement for a "common military action." This "action" was to be obligatory. Turkey, of course, had been expressly designated as the objective of action, but it also included any of the Great Powers that should attempt to annex any portion whatsoever of the territories of the Balkan Peninsula.

While the Bulgaro-Serbian negotiations progressed, Eleftherios Venizelos, the prime minister of Greece (1910-1915), became quite anxious to conclude a Greco-Bulgarian agreement. Venizelos made a proposal to Gueshoff in March 1911 not merely for an agreement to defend the privileges of the Christians in Turkey but also for a defensive alliance in case of an attack by Turkey on one of the contracting parties. No reply was made to this proposition by the Bulgarian government, but thanks to the Balkan correspondent of the London *Times*, J. D. Bourchier, the Greco-Bulgarian rapprochement was made possible. Bourchier acted as the intermediary between Athens and Sofia. It is interesting to note the occasion that made possible the Greco-Bulgarian agreement. It was during the Easter holidays of 1911 when Venizelos undertook an excursion to Pillion. Here Bourchier paid him a visit and they discussed at length the question of a possible Balkan federation. At that very moment, Venizelos charged Bourchier to bear the following message to the Bulgarian government upon his return to Sofia:

Important as the differences are which separate Greece and Bulgaria, they ought not to be considered insurmountable. Their congeners in Macedonia are in danger of being exterminated by the Young Turks. As a consequence, common interest behooves that the two states should get to understand each other as quickly as possible.[16]

On May 11, Bourchier raised the question for a Bulgaro-Greek understanding. The atmosphere was quite favorable at this time. The visit of the Bulgarian students to Athens in the spring of 1911, and the friendly reception that had been accorded to them in Greece, had created a situation highly propitious to an exchange of ideas, paving the path for an understanding between the two countries. "Mr. Bourchier was given to understand," writes Gueshoff, "that the Bulgarian government was in no way opposed to such an exchange of views. Matters, however, remained at a standstill until the Turko-Italian War and the conduct of the Young Turks towards us, especially their unprovoked mobilization against the Bulgarians at the beginning of October 1911, forced us to commence negotiations with Greece."[17] Soon after the Bulgaro-Serbian treaty of alliance and friendship was signed, Mr. Panas, then the Greek minister in Sofia, presented a note to Gueshoff, enclosing a draft for a defensive alliance between the two countries. But in this project not only was nothing said about autonomy for Macedonia and Thrace but even those privileges that had been granted to the Christian population of European Turkey by various international acts, particularly Article XXIII of the Treaty of Berlin,[18] were passed over in silence. Such an attitude on the part of Greece was contrary to the traditional policy of the Bulgarian government. "We could not accept their project," writes Mr. Gueshoff, "as long as Greece did not declare explicitly that she would raise no objection to autonomy."[19] With this objection in view, Gueshoff submitted to Panas the following working formula:

"Greece undertakes not to offer any opposition to an eventual demand by Bulgaria of administrative autonomy for Macedonia and the Vilayet of Adrianople, guaranteeing equal rights to the nationalities there."[20]

The Greek government objected to Gueshoff's formula, but because Bulgaria refused to sign any treaty that did not embody the principle of autonomy for Macedonia, Greece was compelled to alter her objections. Consequently, on May 23, 1912, Panas informed Gueshoff that the Greek government had agreed to his formula concerning the privileges and rights secured by international treaties. Thus clearing the way from the barrier of misunderstanding, a treaty of defensive alliance between Bulgaria and Greece was concluded in Sofia on May 29, 1912. This treaty contained no such detailed provisions for the distribution of eventual territorial gains in case of war with Turkey. The treaty merely provided that the two parties would render mutual aid and would support every action before the Turkish government and the Great Powers of which the purpose was to procure and secure the rights once granted to the Bulgarian and Greek nationality and to gain "inviolable constitutional privileges."[21]

There was no written agreement with Montenegro. The Bulgarian government authorized Kolousheff, the Bulgarian minister at Setinje, to negotiate an understanding with that country. The Bulgaro-Montenegrin understanding was, therefore, an oral agreement that provided for mutual action.

3. THE FIRST BALKAN WAR
(OCTOBER 18, 1912)

With the Bulgaro-Serbian and the Greco-Bulgarian treaties and the military conventions concluded between the Serbian and Bulgarian and the Greek and Bulgarian general staffs, the greatest miracle in the story of European diplomacy took place—the Balkan states were brought together into a formidable alliance. Simultaneously with the forming of the Balkan Alliance, numerous developments of a political character took place. Public opinion in Bulgaria was now unanimous for a decisive action against Turkey. Thus, for example, on August 14, 1912, a great popular demonstration with representatives of all parts of Bulgaria was organized in Sofia to protest the massacres of the Bulgarian inhabitants of Kotchani and Shtip, provoked by the *mohadjirs* and Albanian desperados, and to demand autonomy for Macedonia and Thrace or, in default, that immediate war be declared against Turkey. Ten days later a congress representing the various brotherhoods of Macedonian and Thracian Bulgarian refugees in Bulgaria opened its session in Sofia. The resolutions of the congress were identical with those of the popular demonstration.

In the midst of the excitement aroused by these meetings there arrived from Cetinje a proposal for immediate action, because in April an arrangement had been arrived at between Montenegro and Bulgaria. On August 26, the die was cast and Bulgaria agreed that in October war should be declared. On September 29, on the pretext of carrying out maneuvers in the districts of Adrianople, Turkey mobilized her army. On the first of October, the Balkan states ordered a mobilization of their military forces.[22]

A week later, October 8, 1912, the Russian and Austrian governments informed the Balkan states that they were decidedly against every disturbance of the peace and promised to take into their hands the carrying out of the reforms provided for in Article XXIII of the Treaty of Berlin and added that if war broke out they would permit no change in the territorial *status quo* in European Turkey.[23] Simultaneously, the ambassadors of the Great Powers (Italy was still at war with Turkey) handed a note to the Sublime Porte in which they declared that they wanted to discuss immediately with Turkey the reforms provided for in Article XXIII of the Treaty of Berlin and the law of 1880, which con-

formed to the publicly expressed intention of Turkey to introduce such
reforms.[24] As was to be expected, the government of the Young Turks
declared in answer that it was opposed to foreign intervention in the
internal affairs of the Empire and stated that it would present to
parliament the law of 1880 regarding the Macedonian Vilayets.

On October 12, Bulgaria in the name of the three allies (Montenegro
had already begun military operations on October 8) sent a note to the
Great Powers and to Turkey with an explanatory supplement that contained the following demands:

1. The confirmation of all the ethnic autonomy of the nationalities in
   the Empire, with all that it involves.
2. Proportional representation of every nationality in the Ottoman
   Parliament.
3. The appointment of Christians to all public offices in the districts
   inhabited by Christians.
4. That all grades and varieties of Christian schools be recognized as
   equal to the Ottoman schools of the same kind and rank.
5. That the Sublime Porte be required to desist from its attempt to
   change the racial character of certain provinces in the Empire by
   establishing Mohammedan settlers in them.
6. Regional enlistment for military service and the placing of Christians
   in Christian companies. Enlistment to cease until such companies
   are formed.
7. The reorganization of the gendarmerie in the provinces of European
   Turkey under the efficient control of Swiss and Belgian organizers.
8. That in the districts inhabited by Christians there shall be Swiss
   and Belgian governors approved by the powers and aided by counselors chosen by the district electors.
9. That in connection with the Grand Vizarat a supreme council shall
   be instituted, consisting of an equal number of Christians and
   Mohammedans, whose duty it shall be to see that the reforms are
   applied. The ambassadors of the Great Powers, in conjunction with
   the ministers of the four Balkan states, shall supervise the work of
   this council.[25]

The government of the Young Turks sent no answer to this note.
On October 14, the three allies presented their ultimatum. On October
18 (the same day that the Turko-Italian peace treaty at Lausanne was
signed), Turkey declared war on Bulgaria and Serbia, and on the same
day Greece declared war on Turkey.

The people of the Balkan states received the declaration of war with
great enthusiasm. The decisions of their governments were welcomed,
because this was to be a war of liberation—the Cross against the

Crescent. With specific manifestos the governments of Sofia, Belgrade, and Athens informed their fellow countrymen that they were to fight for a common cause in the name of liberty and against Turkish tyranny. It was believed, too, that the Christians in the Balkans would have on their side the sympathies of all other countries that valued the rights of men, liberty, and human dignity. There was a general rejoicing and outbursts of popular gratitude toward the liberators. The Macedonian revolutionaries (IMRO) had foreseen and encouraged this feeling. The Macedonian brotherhoods in Bulgaria on October 18 issued the following proclamation:

> Brothers!—Your sufferings and your pains have touched the heart of your kindred. Moved by the sacred duty of fraternal compassion, they came to your aid to free you from the Turkish yoke. In return for their sacrifices they desire nothing but to reestablish peace and order in the land of our birth. Come to meet these brave knights of freedom therefore with triumphal crowns. Cover the way before their feet with flowers and glory. And be magnanimous to those who yesterday were your masters. As true Christians, give them not evil for evil. Long live liberty! Long live the brave army of liberation.[26]

Such was the general enthusiasm and conviction after the centuries-old political and economic oppression of the Christian inhabitants in Macedonia and Thrace. The hope and expected outcome of the war was a free and self-governing Macedonia.

Hostility began on all frontiers of European Turkey. Military operations in Thrace, the principal theater of war, developed very rapidly. The Bulgarian army advanced quickly; it invaded the Turkish territory all along the Thracian front on the first day of hostilities. After the first big battle between the Bulgarian and Turkish armies at Selioglu, on October 23, Kirklisse fell. On October 29, Adrianople was besieged. On November 3, the principal Turkish forces were beaten at Loule-Bourgas. On November 15, the Bulgarian army reached Tchataldja, Constantinople's last defense.

The Serbian armies that operated in Macedonia against numerically inferior Turkish forces beat them twice; once at Koumanovo on October 24 and a second time at Monastir (Bitolia) on November 17. However, a division of the Bulgarian army (the Seventh Rilo Division) contributed to the victory of Koumanovo by beating the Turkish army at Kotchani and on November 6 reached the outskirts of Salonika.

The task of the Greek army was the lightest of all, for it was opposed by insignificant Turkish forces. Only at Enidje-Vardar on the first and second of November did the Turkish army show them any resistance worth mentioning. Although the Greek army was farther from Salonika than the Bulgarian Rilo division, the Turks surrendered Salonika to them.

Nevertheless, the general belief among some of the European powers, particularly the central ones, was that the Balkan Alliance would be defeated. They would not have been sorry to see the allies given a drubbing by the Turkish forces, whom everybody in Europe regarded as infinitely their superiors. But to their surprise within one brief period of a few months the Balkan Alliance struck a devastating blow at the Ottoman Empire. Four small states with a total population of less than 10,000,000 people defeating a power whose inhabitants numbered over 25,000,000 was a great victory.

On December 3, the belligerents accepted an armistice proposed to them by the Great Powers. From this armistice, however, the Greeks were, at the instance of the allies, expressly excluded. The Balkan allies could not afford to permit the activity of the Greek fleet in the Aegean to be even temporarily interrupted, for fear that the Turks might transport troops from Asia. The military situation of Turkey was so desperate that when the armistice was concluded the Turks remained in possession only of Constantinople, Adrianople, Janina, and Scutari in Albania. Outside the walls of those four cities they no longer held a square mile of ground in Europe. Ten days after the conclusion of the armistice, representatives from the belligerent states met in London. Side by side with the conference of delegates sat a second conference composed of the ambassadors accredited to the Court of St. James's by the five Great Powers.[27] The latter sat continuously under the presidency of Sir Edward Grey, the British minister of foreign affairs, from December 1912 through August 1913.

By January 22, 1913, all difficulties had been more or less overcome and Turkey had agreed to accept, as a boundary between herself and Bulgaria, a line drawn from Midia on the Black Sea to Enos on the Aegean Sea (see map), thus surrendering Adrianople. But the London conference of the ambassadors, as well as that of the belligerents, reckoned without the general consent of the Young Turks' leaders in Constantinople. On January 23, Enver Bey, at the head of a military deputation, burst into the chamber where the Council was sitting in Constantinople, denounced the proposal to surrender Adrianople, insisted on the resignation of the Grand Vizier, Kiamil Pasha, and shot Nazim Pasha, the Turkish commander in chief.

The coup d'etat of Enver Pasha brought the London negotiations to an abrupt conclusion, and on February 1 the conference broke up. Mahmud Shevket Pasha replaced Kiamil Pasha as Grand Vizier and the Turks renewed military operations. The allies denounced the armistice on January 29 and, on February 4, resumed the attack on Adrianople. On February 8, a big battle occurred at Boulager, where the Turkish army suffered another defeat. On Mach 26, the famous fortress of

Adrianople was taken by storm by the Bulgarians. On April 12, Janina surrendered to the Greeks and, on April 23, the Montenegrins entered Scutari. A few days before the fall of Scutari, a second armistice was concluded between Turkey and the Balkan Alliance. The latter agreed to accept unconditionally the mediation of the powers but reserved the right to discuss with the powers the question of the frontiers of Thrace and Albania and the future of the Aegean islands. Negotiations were accordingly reopened in London on May 20, and ten days later the Treaty of London was signed. Everything beyond the Enos-Midia line and the island of Crete was ceded by the Porte to the Balkan allies, while the question of Albania and of the Aegean islands was left in the hands of the powers.[28]

4. THE SERBO-GREEK SECRET AGREEMENT AGAINST BULGARIA

At the cost of immense sacrifices and through matchless heroism, the allied armies were able to crush Turkish despotism, the centuries-old enemy of the Balkan nationalities. The Balkan allied states waged a war against the Turkish regime in order to free their fellow nationals, who were still held under the scepter of the Sultan. At least, such were the provisions of the various treaties of the alliance. The war against Turkey appeared to be a war in defense of the weak and for the cause of liberty and independence; it was a protest against the violence on the weak by the strong. Because of the acclaimed purpose and nature of the war on Turkey, it was glorious and popular throughout the freedom-loving world.

Unfortunately, dissensions and a struggle for hegemony quickly developed among the victorious allies. Serbia demanded the revision of her treaty of alliance and friendship with Bulgaria. Serbia now demanded the extension of her territorial claims far beyond the line agreed upon in the Bulgaro-Serbian Treaty of March 13, 1912. Serbia in fact began to claim all the territory occupied by her army. "After the overthrow of the Turks during the first month of the war," writes Gueshoff, "we obtained documents and received information in Sofia which disclosed on the part of our allies sentiments and purposes entirely at variance with the object which we had set before ourselves and with the letter and spirit of our treaties of alliance. Pashich,[29] the Serbian prime minister, began to insist upon the revision of the treaty of alliance so as to extend Serbian claims over such cities as Prilep, Kitchevo, Vélés, Ohrid, etc., together with their surroundings. This, however, was a deliberate violation of the treaty of alliance between the kingdoms of Serbia and Bulgaria. To assure the retention of the lands which she had occupied, Serbia resorted to secret negotiations with Greece for the purpose of arranging an alliance against Bulgaria. . . . At the same time, reports began to reach us from various sources, confirming a dispatch from M. Hadji-Misheff, our minister in Athens, that efforts were being made to conclude, if not a regular alliance within the existing one, at least an understanding against Bulgaria. We also learned how badly the Greeks and the Serbians were treating the Bulgarian patriots in Macedonia."[30]

Serbia as well as Greece, not being sure of their confrontations with Bulgaria, began to negotiate with Romania and even with Turkey—their enemy of yesterday—for a common action against Bulgaria. Thus, on April 19, 1913, Rustich, the Serbian minister in Bucharest, asked T. Maiosesco, the Romanian minister of foreign affairs, whether his government would be disposed to conclude a defensive alliance with Serbia against Bulgaria. A series of diplomatic communications was being exchanged by representatives at Petrograd, Belgrade, Sofia, Bucharest, and Athens. These conspiratorial negotiations were taking place while the Bulgarian armies were still battling the Turks at Tchataldja, the last defense of Constantinople.

As a result of the above diplomatic negotiations, the Greco-Serbian secret treaty of June 1, 1913, was concluded. It was supposed to be kept "most secret" (Article 11) and its contents not divulged to any other power, either as a whole or in part. Article IV outlined the Serbo-Bulgarian and Greco-Bulgarian frontiers upon the principle of their actual territorial occupation in Macedonia, and Article V states: "In case there arises disagreement with Bulgaria in regard to the above outlined frontiers and in case a more desirable agreement becomes impossible, the two contracting countries reserve the right to propose to Bulgaria, by common agreement, that the dispute to be submitted for mediation or arbitration to the sovereign Great Powers of the Triple Entente or the chiefs of other states. In case Bulgaria should refuse to accept this method of peaceful solution of the dispute and should she undertake a hostile position against either one of the two kingdoms or should she attempt to impose her pretentions by force, the two high contracting countries are obliged to render mutual help with all their armed forces and not to subsequently conclude peace, except by mutual consent."[31]

The secret Greco-Serbian alliance was concluded in principle during the month of January 1913, at the same time that the Bulgarian armies were still engaged in fighting the Turks. The diplomatic controversy that ensued among the allies was obviously so intense that it presented itself in the form of a break. Now it was high time for Venizelos and Pashich to ask Romania and Turkey to join in a coalition against Bulgaria.

5. THE SECOND BALKAN WAR
(JUNE 29, 1913)

Bound by secret agreements, Serbia, Greece, Romania, and Turkey were now looking for an incident to attack Bulgaria. The development of events took place rapidly. On April 7, Bulgaria and Greece appointed a joint committee to delimit their frontier in Macedonia, but on May 9 it broke up without reaching an agreement. Romania, too, was tugging at Bulgaria with regard to a rectification of the frontiers in Dobrudja. On May 7, 1913, an agreement was signed by which Bulgaria assented to the cession of Silistra and its fortifications, including a strip of territory from Bulgarian Dobrudja. Notwithstanding this agreement, a military convention was concluded among Serbia, Greece, and Romania, and, on May 28, Serbia demanded that the treaty concluded between herself and Bulgaria on March 13, 1912, should undergo a thorough revision so as to compensate her with more territory in Macedonia because of the formation of an autonomous Albania. Meanwhile, as stated above, Greece and Serbia concluded an offensive and defensive alliance against Bulgaria.

The efforts of Bulgaria to effect an understanding failed to materialize. While Dr. Stoyan P. Daneff (1858-1948), the new Bulgarian prime minister (June 1 to July 4, 1913), was preparing to start for Petrograd and a Russian gunboat was waiting at Varna to convey him to Odessa, war had broken out on the frontier. This war had not been sanctioned by the Bulgarian government. The then Bulgarian chief of staff, General Savoff, without waiting for the result of the supreme effort of the Bulgarian government to reach a solution to the difficult situation, yielded to public excitement and on his own responsibility ordered, on June 29, a general attack on the Serbian and Greek fronts in Macedonia.[32] As soon as the Bulgarian government learned about this fatal step, it discharged General Savoff at once, and the order was given for an immediate cessation of operations. But the battle had begun and the Serbians and the Greeks rejected the offer of Bulgaria for the cessation of hostilities. There is no doubt that the Serbian government was greatly influenced by the Russian minister in Belgrade, Hartwig, who constantly advised the Serbians not to take the first step but, rather, holding Macedonia, to wait until Bulgaria lost her patience and started action, so that she would be blamed for the first attack on her allies. Unfortunately, Hartwig's supposition came true. This Russian diplomat was, therefore, greatly responsible for the destruction of the Balkan Alliance. The action that resulted from the reckless order of General Savoff placed Bulgaria before world public opinion in a position to be blamed for a war that her allies had actually provoked and made inevitable because of their vicious intent.[33]

The fatal incident of June 29, however, culminated in an interallied war. This was the beginning of the so-called Second Balkan War. Bulgaria was now to combat not only her former allies—Serbia, Greece, and Montenegro—but also her new and old adversaries, Romania and Turkey, respectively. Two days before the outbreak of hostilities, Romania, encouraged by Russia, declared to Bulgaria that she reserved for herself entire liberty of action in the event of war. Turkey, meanwhile, assumed a more and more aggressive and intransigent attitude. "A veritable avalanche of misfortune, indeed," in the words of Carnegie International Commission, "descended upon Bulgaria." The latter alone had to combat five states, Slavic and non-Slavic, Greek Orthodox and Mohammedan. The rage of battle began on all sides of besieged Bulgaria; she was completely isolated from the rest of the world. The Bulgarian army was completely exhausted from the campaign against the Turks; the Serbian and Greek armies, on the other hand, were rested and well entrenched; they were resting and preparing against Bulgaria, while the latter was using every available soldier against the Turks. Bulgaria was at a disadvantage in every respect; all the odds were against her.

Fighting desperately for what was right, the Bulgarian armies began to show signs of defeat. They were not able to hold the positions behind the River Zletovska, Bregalnitsa, Kriva Lakavitsa; they were stopped and driven back after several days' assault. On July 7 and 8, the Serbian army took the offensive. On July 8, the Serbians took Radovitch; the Greeks, Strumitsa. On July 11, the Romanian army completed its mobilization and crossed the Bulgarian frontiers without encountering any opposition. On July 12, the Turkish army of Tchataldja began reconquering Thrace. On July 21, it was at Lule Bourgas and Kirk Klisse; the following day it recaptured Adrianople, which had been hastily evacuated by the Bulgarians. On July 14, the Serbians took Kriva Palanka. On July 23, Bulgaria made its first appeal to the Tsar of Russia to mediate, and without waiting for the results of this last proposal Dr. Daneff resigned in despair.[34]

During the first week of the crisis, the enemies' armies continued their march, and the Romanians advanced to Sofia. A telegram from Ferdinand to Francis Joseph of Austria demanded mediation for Romania: on his advice Ferdinand sent a telegram directly to King Carol of Romania. The latter demanded the cession of the triangle Danube-Tourtoukai-Balchik as the condition of peace. His demand was accepted on July 21, but the Bulgarians still had to fight the Greeks, who had reached the frontiers of Bulgaria at Djoumaya while the Serbians were besieging Vidin. Negotiations were at last opened at

Bucharest on July 31. On August 4, they were extended for four days. The peace of Bucharest was signed on August 10, and peace with Turkey was concluded on September 29, 1913.

Bulgaria was unable to overcome her adversaries; she was compelled to capitulate and go to Bucharest to submit herself to the peace dictated by the victors. Alone, left to her own forces on the battlefield against overwhelming enemies, she found herself also isolated in the conference of Bucharest. No one asked the victors for leniency in the settlement with Bulgaria. Russia, the then champion of Pan-Slavism, was no longer interested in the affairs of the existing critical situation of Bulgaria. The diplomatic agents of Russia were now directed to the building of a more powerful Serbian state, because Serbia had proved a willing servant for Russia's Balkan interests. The Treaty of Bucharest, which concluded the Second Balkan War, divided Macedonia between Serbia and Greece, and an insignificant part only was left to Bulgaria. Not only did Bulgaria lose in Macedonia but also in her own territory by surrendering to Romania a considerable part of Bulgarian Dobrudja.[35]

Thus, the once San Stefano Bulgaria was divided for the second time in thirty-five years; first, in 1878 in Berlin and, secondly, in 1913 in Bucharest. Although by the Treaty of Bucharest the second division of the Bulgarian nation was performed, it was the first time that Macedonia had been partitioned—whence, the subsequent perplexity in the Balkan dilemma.

6. THE FATE OF THE BULGARIANS IN DIVIDED MACEDONIA

By the Treaty of Bucharest, Macedonia was divided mainly between Serbia and Greece, with an unimportant district given to Bulgaria. The most accurate statistics concerning the population of Macedonia, gathered on the eve of the Balkan War, distribute the different nationalities as follows:

Bulgarians	1,095,355
Turks	541,615
Greeks	253,366
Albanians	184,336
Vlachs (Romanians)	77,365
Gypsies	43,370
Jews and others	106,360
TOTAL	2,301,767[36]

In that part of Macedonia given to Serbia by the Treaty of Bucharest the population was distributed as follows:

Bulgarians	632,620
Turks	205,885
Greeks	480
Vlachs	33,725
Albanians	161,870
Gypsies	16,175
Jews and others	20,420
TOTAL	1,072,415

In terms of percentage, the Bulgarians comprised 59% of the total population, the Turks 19.3%, the Greeks 0.05%, the Vlachs 3.05%, the Albanians 15.1%, the Gypsies 1.5%, the Jews and others 2%.

In that part of Macedonia that was acquired by Greece as the result of the settlement in Bucharest there were:

Bulgarians	297,735
Turks	299,880
Greeks	249,657
Vlachs	39,470
Albanians	21,770
Gypsies	23,130
Jews and others	84,170
TOTAL	1,015,812

Expressed in terms of percentage, the Bulgarians comprised 29.3%, the Turks 29.5%, the Greeks 24.6%, the Vlachs 3.9%, the Albanians 2.1%, the Gypsies 2.3%, the Jews and others 8.3%. We must bear in mind, however, that in the three southernmost districts—Kassandra in the Chalcidice, Anaselitsch, and Grebena—the Greeks were an absolute majority. It was the Greek population of these districts that raised the general percentage of the Greeks. Without these districts (which are more or less outside the extent of Macedonia) the percentage of the Greeks in that part of Macedonia ruled by them was 17% of the total population.

In the five former Turkish *kazas* or districts in northeastern Macedonia, left to Bulgaria by the Treaty of Neuilly,[37] there were:

Bulgarians	165,000
Turks	34,850
Greeks	3,230
Vlachs	4,270
Albanians	695
Gypsies	4,065
Jews and others	1,430
TOTAL	213,540

Expressed on a percentage basis, the Bulgarians comprised 77.3% of the total population, the Turks 16.3%, the Greeks 1.5%, the Vlachs 2%, the Albanians 0.3% the Gypsies 1.9%, the Jews and others 0.7%.

The fictitious Serbian propaganda referring to the Macedonian Slavs as "Old Serbs" or "South Serbs" proved to be a grand myth. When the Serbian army occupied western Macedonia in 1912, they found the Slavs there to be a compact Bulgarian population. The Serbians as well as the Greeks immediately began to carry out a systematic persecution of the Bulgarian inhabitants in Macedonia. The Serbians, after they invaded Macedonia, even before the war with Turkey was terminated, began to terrorize the Bulgarians with the so-called "black hand" organization in order to compel them to call themselves Serbians and thus gradually acquire the Serbian consciousness. Commenting on this matter, the *Report* of the Carnegie International Commission writes:

For six months, while waiting for the allied armies to take up arms, the Serbians had been carrying on guerrilla warfare in Macedonia, side by side with the regular army. They armed their old bands whose captains and soldiers wore military uniform. At Uskub, a central committee of "national defense" with branches in other Macedonian towns, was formed side by side with the higher command upon the arrival of the troops. The population of Uskub (Skopie) called their station behind the house of Weiss, near the Russian consulate, "the black house" from the name of the league itself, "the black hand." The worst crimes were committed by this secret organization, known to all the world and under powerful protection. It was of distinct advantage for the regular government to have under its hand an irresponsible power which, like this, soon became all powerful and which could always be disowned if necessary. There were so many things which were not crimes but which from the point of view of Serbian assimilation were worse than crimes. Such, for example, as being too influential a citizen, aware enough, while remaining an ardent Bulgarian patriot, not to contravene the orders of the authority and whose past called for vengeance; the Bulgarian flag, a business house, a library, a chemist shop kept by a Bulgarian or a café, not amenable to the prohibition of public meetings, etc. The man was taken, one evening he was led into the "black house" and there beaten; then for whole months he lay ill, if indeed he did not disappear completely. Our records are full of depositions which throw light on the sinister activities of these legalized brigands. Unhappily, *all* the names can not be cited. . . . Each town had its captain who soon acquired fame. At Koumanovo there was a captain, Major Voulovits and his assistant, Captain Rankovits; at Vélés, one Voino Popovits, a Vassa, a Vanguel, etc. When complaints were made to the regular authorities, they pretended to know nothing of the matter or if the person complaining was obscure they punished him. If he were a personage, as for example in the case of the Archbishop of Vélés, his complaint was met by sending the bands from the town of Vélés down to the villages . . . only to replace them immediately afterwards by bands from Uskub.

It was in the villages that the activity of these bands assumed its most fatal form. In the towns the regular authorities kept up appearances and did not concern themselves with the bandits; but lower in the administrative scale, in the villages, the responsible and the irresponsible mingled and were lost in one another. This was the easier that from the end of 1912 on the administrative posts in the villages were filled by men . . . paid representatives of national minorities, Serbo-mans or Graeco-mans,[38] who very often had served as spies with the Turks. . . . These people, while possessing a highly intimate knowledge of affairs, had their own score to wipe off . . . they had only to utter the name of one of their enemies and the bands arrest him, leave him to find a ransom, beat him or even kill him with impunity.[39]

The tyrannical Serbian regime in Macedonia was well exemplified by the official ordinance on "public security" issued on September 21, 1913.[40] By virtue of this document, one can see that Macedonia was not treated by the Serbians as a redeemed "Old Serbia" but was treated as a conquered foreign territory. Although Serbia and Greece were still in alliance with Bulgaria, they were in fact treating the Bulgarians as their enemy. The terror reached its height when the interallied war began. The Bulgarian archbishops, bishops, and priests in Macedonia, all natives of the country, were arrested and sent across the border into Bulgaria. The teachers and the most prominent citizens were also arrested. The Serbian authorities arrested 99 Bulgarian teachers and prominent citizens of Skopie and sent them to prison in the town of Mitrovitza. At Tetovo, 200 Bulgarians were arrested and deported from Krivocherna Palanka, some were murdered on the way to Koumanovo; at Vélés, 200 were arrested, some of whom were killed and their bodies thrown into the Vardar River. At Monastir, 600 persons were arrested and, at Ressen 350 and so on. Meanwhile, the Serbian troops burned eight Bulgarian villages, and more than 6,000 people were killed and maltreated.[41]

During the interallied war, still greater atrocities were committed by the Greeks in that part of Macedonia that they occupied. More than 400 Bulgarians were taken from Salonika, Enidje-Vardar, Voden (Edisa), and Lerin (Florina) and thrown into prison in Salonika. Some were exiled in the Aegean Islands and others thrown into the sea, as was the case of Archmandrite Evlogie, the vicar of Salonika, and his secretary, Christo Balandjieff. Several hundred Bulgarians from the districts of Kostour (Kastoria) and Florina were arrested and exiled. In eastern Macedonia, where military operations were carried on, the Greek troops, by order of general headquarters, on their campaign from Salonika to the Rilo Mountain range, burned 161 Bulgarian villages and destroyed 16,000 houses. In this part of Macedonia, those who were unable to flee were slaughtered. In letters captured after the battle in the Razlog district, from which we have reproduced extracts, the Greek soldiers boast of the cruelties and bestial acts they have committed on the Bulgarian population.[42] About 70,000 Bulgarians—men, women, and children—horrified by the sight of their burning villages, left their homes without shoes or clothing and started for Bulgaria. These barbarities were revealed by the impartial *Report* of the International Commission to Inquire into the Causes and Conduct of the Balkan Wars, published in Washington, D.C., in 1914.

The task of denationalization of the Macedonian Bulgarians by the Serbians and the Greeks was much easier because the Bulgarian nation had been decapitated; Bulgaria itself was defeated and the revolutionaries in the interior of Macedonia were gotten rid of. The Bulgarian peasantry in Macedonia was left at the mercy of the Serbian and Greek terrorists—their assimilation by the Serbian and Greek regimes was to be consummated through all conceivable means. Arrests, tortures, exiles, and killing were but a few of the barbaric methods used by the new masters of Macedonia in their zeal for denationalizing and assimilating the minorities in their respective dominions.

To combat the Bulgarian schools was more difficult. The time was already long past when most of the teachers were members of the IMRO. The Serbians and the Greeks saw things in Macedonia as they had been decades ago. To the Turks the Bulgarian schoolmaster was always the conspirator and a *comitajis*. He was also considered as such by the Serbians and the Greeks. He was a dangerous man who must be gotten rid of, and the school, however professional, was a center from which Bulgarian civilization emanated. This was why the school became the object of a systematic attack on the part of the Serbians and the Greeks. Their first act on arriving in any place whatsoever in Macedonia was to close the schools and use them as quarters for the soldiery. Then the teachers of the villages were called together and told that their services were no longer required if they refused to teach in Greek or Serbian. "Those who continued to declare themselves Bulgarians," states the *Report* of the International Commission of Inquiry, "were exposed to a persecution whose severity varied with the length of their resistance. Even the most determined had to avow themselves beaten in the end; if not, they were sometimes allowed to depart for Bulgaria, but more usually sent to prison in Salonika or Uskub."

The most difficult people to subdue were the priests, and above all the bishops. They were first asked to change the language of divine service. Endeavors were made to subject them to the Serbian or Greek ecclesiastical authorities, and they were compelled to mention their names in the liturgy. If the priest showed the smallest inclination to resist, his exarchist church was taken from him and handed over to the patriarchists; he was forbidden to hold any communication with his flock, and upon the slightest disobedience was accused of political propagandism and treason. At first an open attack on the bishops was not ventured on. When Neophite, bishop of Vélés, refused to separate the name of King Peter from the names of the other kings of the allies in his prayers, Mr. Pashitch advised the military powers at Uskub (January 17) to treat him as equal to the Serbian bishop and with correctness. This ministerial order, however, did not prevent the local administration of Vélés from forbidding Neophite to hold services and assemblies in his bishopric, to see priests outside of the church, or to hold communication with the villages. As the bishop refused to take the veiled hints given to him to depart for Bulgaria, an officer was finally sent to his house, accompanied by soldiers who took over his abode for the army, after beating his secretary. In the same way Cosmas, bishop of Debra, was forced to abandon his seat and leave his town. It was even worse at Uskub, where the holder of the bishopric, the Archimandrite Methodius, was first driven out of his house, taken by force, shut up in a room and belabored by four soldiers until he lost consciousness (April 21). Cast out into the street, Methodius escaped into a neighboring house, in which a Frenchman dwelt who told the story to M. Carlier, French consul at Uskub. Under his protection, Methodius left for Salonika on April 26, whence he was sent to Sofia. The commission has in its possession a deposition signed by the foreign doctors of Salonika who saw and examined Methodius on April 28 and found his story "entirely probable."

The leaders, intellectual and religious, of the revolutionary movement having been removed, the populations of the villages were directly approached and urged to change their nationality and proclaim themselves Serbian or Greek. The ecclesiastical Bulgarian reports written from every part of Macedonia are unanimous on this head. "You know," Bishop Neophite of Vélés said to his persecutor, "in your capacity as a subprefect, what the Serbian priests and schoolmasters are doing in the villages. They are visiting the Bulgarian villages with soldiers and forcing the people to write themselves down as Serbians, drive out their Bulgarian priests, and ask to have a Serbian priest given them. Those who refuse to proclaim themselves Serbians are beaten and tortured."[43]

Under Turkish rule before Macedonia was divided, the Bulgarian population had and enjoyed certain rights that were entirely denied them by the Serbian and the Greek regimes. The Turks were, therefore, far more tolerant than either the Greeks or the Serbians. Until the eve of the Balkan War, the Bulgarian population in Macedonia had 1,373 schools of various grades, 2,266 men and women teachers, and 78,854 students. There were 1,331 churches, 294 chapels, 275 monasteries, and 7 bishoprics.[44]

In that part of Macedonia that was annexed by Greece there were, in 1912, 378 Bulgarian churches, with 300 priests, as well as 340 primary and secondary schools, with 700 teachers and 19,000 enrolled students. In that part of Macedonia that was acquired by Serbia there were in,

1912, 761 Bulgarian churches, with 6 bishops and 833 priests, as well as 641 Bulgarian schools, with 1,013 teachers and 37,000 students. Since the occupation of the country in 1912, however, neither the Greeks nor the Serbians had recognized the ethnic character of the Bulgarians in Macedonia.[45]

SELECT BIBLIOGRAPHY

Anastasoff, C., *The Tragic Peninsula*, St. Louis, Mo., 1938, pp. 155-254.

Ashmead-Bartlett, Ellis, *With the Turks in Thrace*, New York, 1913, pp. 139-242.

Bazhdaroff, G., *The Macedonian Question—Yesterday and Today*, Sofia, 1926, pp. 29-48.

Derjavin, Professor N. C., *Bulgaro-Srbskite Vzaimni Otnoshenia i Makedonskia Vopros* (The Bulgaro-Serbian Mutual Relations and the Macedonian Question), Sofia, 1916, pp. 7-54.

Drvingoff, Colonel Peter, *Balkanskite Voyni* (The Balkan Wars), Sofia, 1941, pp. 3-53. This work of 216 pages is based on telegrams of the Bulgarian Telegraphic Agency from the end of June 1912 to the declaration of the Balkan War on October 4 of the same year, describing the internal situation of Turkey, the agitation among the Balkan peoples, the mobilization of the armies of the Balkan states, and the policy of the Great Powers. It contains 718 diplomatic telegraphic communications among the various concerned European capitals.

Grogan, Lady, *The Life of J. D. Bourchier*, London, 1925, pp. 133-154.

Gueshoff, Ivan E., *The Balkan League*, London, 1915, pp. 1-111; documents, pp. 112-141.

Miletich, Professor Lubomir G., *Documenti za Protivobulgarskite deistvia na Srbskite i na Grkskite vlasti v Makedonia prez 1912-1913 godina* (Documents about the anti-Bulgarian campaign of the Serbian and Greek authorities in Macedonia during 1912-1913), Sofia, 1929, pp. 1-293.

Monroe, Professor Will S., *Bulgaria and Her People*, Boston, 1914, pp. 87-105; 116-134; 373-395.

Panaretoff, Stephan, *Near East Affairs and Conditions*, New York, 1922, pp. 184-210.

Pozzi, Henri, *Black Hand Over Europe*, London, 1935, pp. 107-192.

Radoslavoff, Dr. Vasil, *Bulgaria i Svetovnata Kriza* (Bulgaria and the World Crisis), Sofia, 1923, pp. 24-90; 203-217.

Report of the Carnegie International Commission to Inquire into the Causes and Conduct of the Balkan Wars, Washington, D.C., 1914, pp. 21-69; 109-147; 277-413.

Stephanove, Constantine, *The Bulgarians and Anglo-Saxondom*, Berne, 1919, pp. 213-266.

Tosheff, A., *Balkanskite Voyni* (The Balkan Wars), Sofia, 1929, Vol. I, pp. 235-293; Vol. II (1931) pp. 1-469. *Note:* Volume II contains also the texts of the following treaties (in Bulgarian):

　a Peace treaty concluded between Turkey and the Balkan Alliance in London on April 17, 1913, pp. 483-484;

　b Greco-Serbian treaty of June 1, 1913, pp. 484-487;

c Peace treaty among Bulgaria on the one hand and Greece, Montenegro, Romania, and Serbia on the other, August 10, 1913, in Bucharest, pp. 487-489;

d Peace treaty between Bulgaria and Turkey concluded on September 29, 1913, and ratified on October 9, 1913.

NOTES

1. *Report* of the Carnegie International Commission, *supra*, Chapter IX, n. 1, p. 35.
2. H. A. Gibbons, *The New Map of Europe*, New York, 1914, p. 201.
3. J. A. R. Marriott, *supra*, Chapter X, n. 2, p. 384.
4. Because of the peculiarity of the Islamic Law—according to which the Moslems were not supposed to make treaties with non-Moslems—certain "capitulations" were voluntarily granted by the Sultan to the various Great Powers. The capitulations provided for judicial as well as economic privileges: the former were concerned over "extra-territoriality" rights, that is, the nationals of the signatory foreign power resident in Turkey were to be under the exclusive jurisdiction of their own consuls, in whose courts any case involving them was tried, while the latter provided for special trading rights conferred on nationals of signatory powers. Under these circumstances, some of the powers have had their own post offices in the principal cities of Turkey. Austria-Hungary was one of the several powers that enjoyed such privileges. But new Turkey, under the leadership of Mustapha Kemal Pasha (Atatürk), demanded the abolition of the capitulations, arguing that they destroy Turkish sovereignty. Therefore, under the provisions of the Lausanne Treaty, July 1923, the capitulations were abolished.
5. C. Anastasoff, *supra*, Chapter VII, n. 3, p. 165.
6. J. A. R. Marriott, *supra*, Chapter X, n. 2, p. 391.
7. *Report* of the Carnegie International Commission, *supra*, Chapter IX, n. 1, p. 43.
8. I. E. Gueshoff, *The Balkan League*, London, 1915, p. 7.
9. Quoted by K. Solaroff, *Bulgaria i Makedonskia Vopros-Prichinite na Balkanskite Voyni* (Bulgaria and the Macedonian Question—The Causes of the Balkan Wars), Sofia, 1925, p. 170, footnote.
10. I. E. Gueshoff, *supra*, n. 8, p. 10.
11. *Report* of the Carnegie International Commission, *supra*, Chapter IX, n. 1, p. 42.
12. *Ibid.*, p. 43; I. E. Gueshoff, *supra*, n. 8, pp. 15-16.
13. *Ibid.*, pp. 16-17.
14. Stoyan P. Daneff (1858-1949) was the leader of the progressive liberal party and served as foreign minister of the P. Karaveloff and T. Todoroff cabinets. He became prime minister in 1901-1903 and led the Bulgarian London peace delegation in May 17, 1913.
15. For the English text of the Treaty of Alliance between Bulgaria and Serbia and the secret annex thereto, see Gueshoff, *The Balkan League*, p. 112 and p. 117, respectively; for the Bulgarian text, see Dr. V. Radoslavoff, *Bulgaria i Svetovnata Kriza*, pp. 34-35; for the French text, see W. M. Sloane, *The Balkans: A Laboratory of History* (Appendix).
16. C. Anastasoff, *supra*, Chapter VII, n. 3, p. 185.

17. I. E. Gueshoff, *supra*, n. 8, p. 37.
18. For the provision of Article XXIII of the Treaty of Berlin, see Chapter IX above.
19. I. E. Gueshoff, *supra*, n. 8, p. 39.
20. *Ibid.*, p. 39; *Report* of the Carnegie International Commission, *supra*, Chapter IX, n. 1, p. 43.
21. For the text of the Greco-Bulgarian treaty of defensive alliance, see Gueshoff, *supra*, n. 8, pp. 127-129.
22. Greece mobilized 210,000 men out of 2,632,000 inhabitants; Bulgaria 620,567 out of 4,329,108 inhabitants; and Serbia 467,630 out of 2,945,950 inhabitants. See the *Report* of the Carnegie International Commission, *supra*, Chapter IX, n. 1, p. 259.
23. The text of the Austro-Russian note to Sofia, Belgrade and Athens may be found in Gueshoff, *supra*, n. 8, p. 105; see also the *Report* of the Carnegie International Commission, *supra*, Chapter IX, n. 1, p. 49.
24. The law of 1880 remained a dead letter. For the provisions of this law see Draganof, *supra*, Chapter X, n. 4, p. 85.
25. G. Bazhdaroff, *supra*, Chapter IX, n. 15, pp. 55-56.
26. *Report* of the Carnegie International Commission, *supra*, Chapter IX, n. 1, p. 50.
27. Mr. Tosheff, a former Bulgarian minister-plenipotentiary, in discussing this conference writes: "The premeditated protraction on the part of Greece and Serbia in London aroused the indignation of the imperturable Sir Edward Grey. On May 27, in the name of the ambassadorial conference, he resorted to an unusual diplomatic measure, by notifying the Balkan delegates, that those ones who wish to sign *tels quels* preliminaries of the peace treaty, should do so immediately; those who are not disposed to sign would do well by leaving London, because it is useless for them to stay there and continue discussions, whose only result is an endless postponement.

    "Naturally, by such an attitude on the part of the British foreign minister, dissatisfied were only our allies, who found themselves forced at last to put their signatures under the long awaited for peace treaty. This took place on May 27 in St. James's Court in London." See A. Tosheff, *The Balkan Wars*, Vol. II, pp. 292-293.
28. For the treaty of peace between Bulgaria, Greece, Serbia, and Montenegro on the one part and Turkey on the other part, London, May 30, 1913, see Oakes and Mowat, *The Great European Treaties in the Nineteenth Century*, pp. 361-362.
29. Nikola Pashich became the new head of the Serbian ministry, succeeding Milovanovich upon the latter's sudden death in the early part of 1912.
30. I. E. Gueshoff, *supra*, n. 8, p. 64; For documents, see the *Report* of the Carnegie International Commission of Inquiry, *supra*, Chapter IX, n. 1, pp. 277-284; 368-377. See also Appendix IV.
31. Translated by the author from the Bulgarian text of the secret Serbo-Greek Treaty of June 1, 1913. For the complete text of the treaty, see A. Tosheff, *The Balkan Wars*, Vol. II, pp. 484-487.
32. For General Savoff's orders to the Second and Fourth Bulgarian armies, see the *Report* of the Carnegie International Commission, *supra*, Chapter IX, n. 1, pp. 67-68.
33. A number of documents have been published in the French periodical, *Revue Bleue*, in 1913 by a French general staff officer showing that three days before the Bulgarian offensive the Serbian commander in chief,

General Putnik, had issued operative orders to the Serbian army in Macedonia for a general attack against the Bulgarian front and that these orders were changed because the Greek headquarters at this moment had not given their consent. See also Henri Pozzi, *Black Hand Over Europe*, London, 1935, pp. 109-111.

34. Upon the resignation of I. E. Gueshoff on May 30, 1913, the post of head of the ministry was taken by Dr. S. P. Daneff. The latter in turn was succeeded by Dr. Vasil Radoslavoff.

35. For the text of the treaty of peace signed in Bucharest on August 10, 1913, between Romania, Greece, Montenegro, Serbia, and Bulgaria, see Oakes and Mowat, *supra*, n. 28, pp. 362-366.

36. *Report* of the Carnegie International Commission, *supra*, Chapter IX, n. 1, p. 28; C. Anastasoff, *supra*, Chapter VII, n. 3, pp. 234-235.

  In these figures are not included the 200,000 Macedonian Bulgarians who had emigrated either into Bulgaria or to the United States of America and Canada.

37. The treaty of peace between the allied and associated powers and Bulgaria, signed at Neuilly-sur-Seine, November 27, 1919.

38. Bulgarian Macedonians paid converts either to the Greek or Serbian cause.

39. *Report* of the Carnegie International Commission, *supra*, Chapter IX, n. 1, pp. 169-170; Henri Pozzi, *supra*, n. 33, pp. 43-104.

40. See Appendix V.

41. *Report* of the Carnegie International Commission, *supra*, Chapter IX, n. 1, pp. 171-186.

42. See Appendix VI.

43. *Report* of the Carnegie International Commission, *supra*, Chapter IX, n. 1, pp. 52-53.

44. *Les Macédoniennes dans la Vie Culturo-politique de la Bulgarie* (Enquête du Comité Exécutif Macédonien), Sofia, 1919, p. 23; also the *Memoir* of the National Committee of the Union of the Macedonian Brotherhoods in Bulgaria presented to the League of Nations in Geneva on September 18, 1924.

45. See Appendix VII and Appendix VIII.

CONTESTED REGIONS
according to the map annexed
TO THE TREATY OF ALLIANCE

Scale of 1:1.500.000

10   0   10   20   30   40   50   60 km

S E R V I A

BULGARIA

Diakova

Giliani   Bỳranovici   Vranja

Prešovo   Staponici   M.Kitka   M.Golem
                       Melegovo   Podarjikon
Prizrend   Tirnovec   Nerav   Bastovo   Gaya
                       Gradec   Libenci
Kačanik   Petarlica   Krivareci
Kumanovo   Talsimanci   M.Ostrić Palanka
                  Jumaleno   Drač
Kalkandelen   Uskub   Kašani   Kratovo
(Tetovo)   1050
                  Gradiste
Novoselo   Gradiste   Kočane
                  Loghinci   M.Goriste   Bregalnica
Gostivar   1023   S.Nikola
Vardar   Vetersa   Ivangvce
         Sopot   Štip
Peškopia   2550   Veles   Radovišt
          (Kœprulu)
Zajac
Dibra   Barbares   Petropole   Negotin
Kičevo   Drenovo
Krupka Tepesi Baba   1200   Krapa
         Sela   Jakrenovo
Trebiste   Belica   Carske   Mt Česme
Varbiani   Demirhissar   Prilep
Brejani   1200
1330   Ilinska Pl.
Struga   Gorence   Livoista
S.Gabora   Okhrida
          Resen
Lake   Monastir (Bitolia)
of Okhrida
Podgorec   Lake   Nikolec
          of Prespa
Starovo
Devol   Florina   Ostrovo   Voden
        Banica   Jenidže Var
Korica
        Kastoria   Karaferia

T.Weinreb

210

Regions Occupées par les Belligérants
Fin Avril, 1913

THE BALKAN STATES

With New Frontiers According to Treaties of London, Constantinople, and Bucharest*

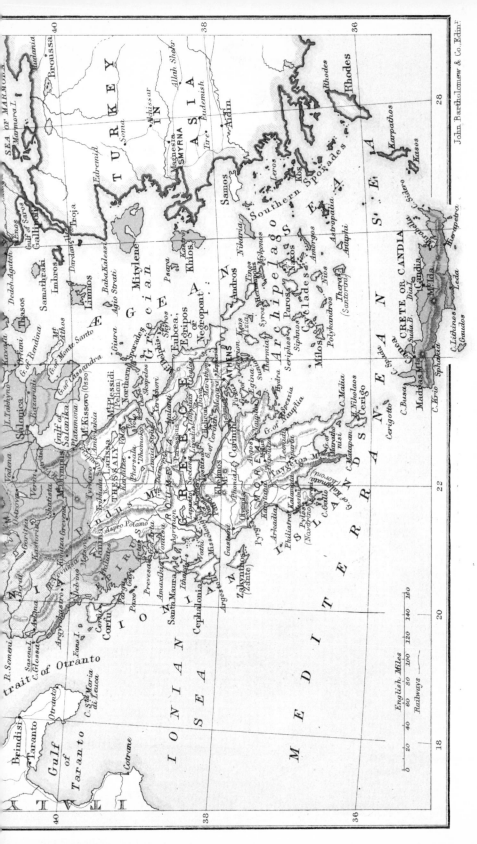

Acquisitions of New Territory shown in darker tints

John Bartholomew & Co. Edinʳ

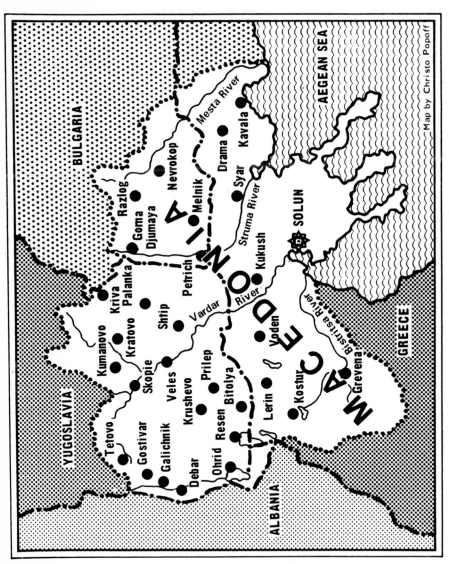

Frontiers of MACEDONIA
and the Divisions of the Treaty of Bucharest (1913)

Map by Christo Popoff

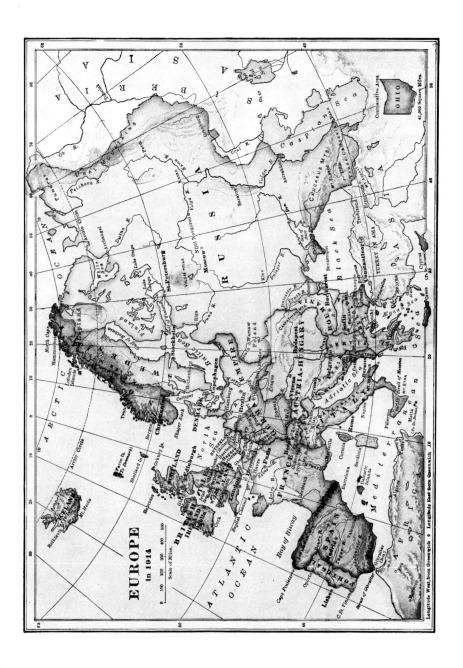

EUROPE
in 1914

Scale of Miles.
0   100 200 300 400 500

Longitude West from Greenwich 0 Longitude East from Greenwich 10

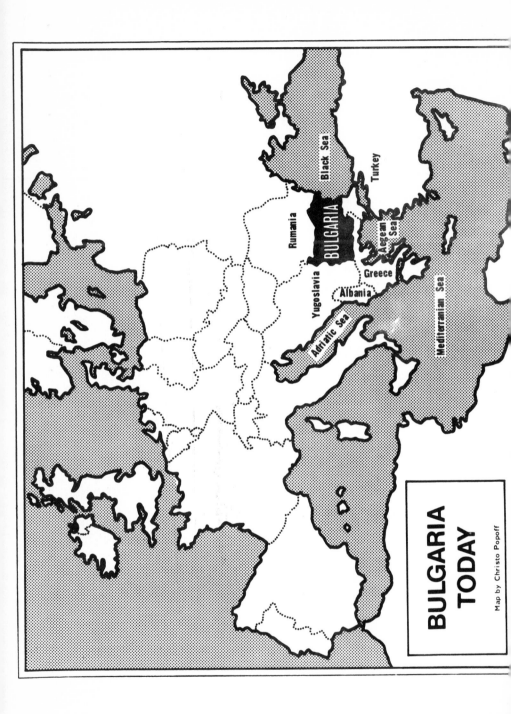

BULGARIA
TODAY

Map by Christo Popoff

216

CHAPTER XII

THE FIRST WORLD WAR (1914-1918) AND BULGARIA

1. TURMOIL ON THE HORIZONS

The two Balkan wars had three far-reaching effects: (1) Turkey was practically ousted from Europe, (2) Bulgaria was eager for revenge against its neighbors who had snatched from it the fruits of victory, and (3) Serbia nearly doubled its territory by acquiring the Sandjak of Novi-Bazar (Old Serbia) and annexing (in violation of her 1912 treaty agreement with Bulgaria) Bulgarian Macedonia. The result was that the Serbians revived their dream of a greater Serbia and thereby Austria felt menaced by Serbian expansion. In fact, Austria was so alarmed that it made ready to attack Serbia in 1913 and was restrained only by her allies Germany and Italy. But one thing was certain—storms lay ahead.

Because of the Great Powers' alliances and counteralliances and the augmenting armament, Europe was a powder keg. It took only a spark to make it explode.

The spark that touched off the explosion was the assassination of the Archduke Francis Ferdinand and his wife. Ferdinand was the nephew of Francis Joseph I, the emperor of Austria-Hungary and heir to the Austrian throne. The crime took place at Sarajevo, the capital of Bosnia, on June 28, 1914. The assassin was Gavrilo Princip, an Austrian citizen. He and other Bosnian revolutionaries acted as agents of the Serbian society Union or Death (The Black Hand), a terrorist organization founded in 1911 for agitation against Austria on behalf of Serbian aspirations.[1] A Serbian officer who belonged to the Black Hand society supplied weapons. The Serbian government was cognizant of the plot but did little to prevent its consummation or to warn the Austrian government.

Nearly a month passed before Vienna acted. Then, on July 23, the

217

Austrian government sent Serbia a harsh ultimatum. The latter demanded that Serbia suppress anti-Austrian publications and societies; dismiss from the army and the government all those having anything to do with the anti-Austrian propaganda; get rid of anti-Austrian teachers and text-books in the public schools; and allow agents of the Austro-Hungarian government to take part in the investigation on Serbian soil of the Sarajevo crime. The Serbian government was given only forty-eight hours to accept or reject the Austrian terms. In making these demands, the Austrian foreign minister, Count Von Berchtold, saw a chance to squelch once and for all the greater Serbian movement that threatened to dismember the Dual Monarchy. If Austria failed to act against Serbia at this time, Berchtold and his advisers feared that the enemies of their country would gain strength. In that case, the submerged nationalities of the Austrian Empire might succeed in breaking the empire into fragments.

Serbia replied to the ultimatum within the given forty-eight hours. The reply agreed to all the Austrian demands except those requiring that Austrian officials enter Serbia to help investigate the Sarajevo crime. Serbia pointed out that such an arrangement would violate its rights as a sovereign state and make it, in fact, an Austrian vassal. Serbia also expressed willingness to submit the entire dispute to arbitration by the Hague Tribunal in Holland or to the mediation of the Great Powers. Austria-Hungary rejected the Serbian reply as unsatisfactory and on July 28 declared war on Serbia. The next day, the Austrians bombarded Belgrade,[2] the Serbian capital, thus firing the first shots of what was to become World War I.

At the outset of the First World War, Europe was divided into two hostile groups: The Triple Entente—England, France, and Russia, and the Triple Alliance—Germany, Austria-Hungary, and Italy. Such being the political scene, the European drama quickly developed.

A. Europe in Flame

It was generally believed that the European nations had abandoned war altogether, save for minor localized struggles at the southeastern fringe of the European continent. The system of rival alliances had originally been intended to keep the peace by preserving a balance of power between the major nations. For more than four decades (1871-1914) a general peace prevailed in Europe, except for the Balkan Wars, which eventually precipitated the First World War.

As discussed elsewhere above, Russia had given in to the Central Powers (Germany and Austria-Hungary) in the Balkan Crisis of 1908 and 1913. This time, however, the situation had changed. Russia could now count without fail upon French support, which had been lacking previously. The then president of France, Raymond Poincaré and his advisers had made it perfectly clear that France would fulfill its obligation under the alliance agreement. And when news came of the bombardment of Belgrade, Russia started a partial mobilization of its armies along the Austrian frontier. Soon a general mobilization along the entire western border of Russia was ordered, thereby serving notice to the Central Powers that it would fight rather than let them take away Serbia's independence and destroy Russia's influence in the Balkans.

Each coalition of powers had attracted smaller countries as satellites; thus, Germany and Austria had Bulgaria and Turkey on their side, while Serbia was tied to Russia. The lineup was partly dictated by two-power rivalries—the struggle between Great Britain and Germany for world trade and naval supremacy, the French desire to get Alsace-Lorraine back from Germany, the ambitions of Russia and Austria in the Balkans and Bulgaria's desire to regain its lost territories by the Bucharest Treaty of 1913. The danger of this situation was that, in any international dispute, no matter how trivial, the opposing governments might call on their allies for support and so bring on a general war.

The general mobilization of Russian troops forced Germany to mobilize its armies at once. The German government, therefore, sent an ultimatum to Russia ordering that country to demobilize within twelve hours or accept the consequences (July 31, 1914). When Russia failed to reply, Germany declared war on Russia (August 1). War with Russia, of course, meant war with its ally, France. The latter had already begun to mobilize. Germany, therefore, declared war on France (August 3). In consequence, the chain of events developed as follows: Germany declared war on Belgium (August 4); England declared war on Germany (August 4); Austria-Hungary declared war on Russia (August 6); the same day, Serbia declared war on Germany; Montenegro declared war on Germany (August 8); France declared war on Austria (August 12); the same day, England declared war on Austria; Japan declared war on Germany (August 23); two days later, Japan declared war on Austria; the latter declared war on Belgium (August 28); Russia declared war on Turkey (November 2); the same day, Serbia declared war on Turkey; England declared war on Turkey (November 5); the same day, France declared war on Turkey.

On May 23, 1915, Italy declared war on Austria and, on August 21, on Turkey;[3] Bulgaria declared war on Serbia (October 14); England declared war on Bulgaria (October 15); France declared war on Bulgaria (October 16); Russia declared war on Bulgaria (October 19); and the same day Italy declared war on Bulgaria.

On August 27, 1916, Romania declared war on Austria;[4] Germany declared war on Romania, and Italy finally declared war on Germany

(August 27); Turkey and Bulgaria declared war on Romania a few days later (August 30, September 1, respectively). The precarious structure of peace, built on the old doctrine of the balance of power, fell like a house of cards. Eventually, of all Europe only the Scandinavian countries and Holland, Spain, and Switzerland remained neutral.

B. *Bulgaria's Crucial Position*

With the break of diplomatic relations between Austria-Hungary and Serbia, Bulgaria had announced its strict neutrality. This declaration on the part of the Bulgarian government made a favorable impression on the Serbian government in Nish. It knew well enough that, with the situation created by the Treaty of Bucharest in 1913, Bulgaria had justifiable grounds for revenge, and, for that reason, Bulgaria's neutrality was a surprise to the Serbians. Austria-Hungary was also pleased by the Bulgarian government's policy of neutrality. She was not sure which side of the warring groups Bulgaria would eventually join. Had Serbia satisfied Bulgaria's pretensions in Macedonia, Bulgaria would most likely have favored the Entente Powers.[5]

But when the war between Austria-Hungary and Serbia implicated Germany, Russia, France, and England, and when soon afterward Turkey joined the Central Powers, Bulgaria, because of her strategic geographic situation, became the most important country to both warring groups. Although Bulgaria had been offended, defeated, and deprived of more territory by the Bucharest Treaty of August 10, 1913, the powers now began to exchange amenities with the Bulgarian government.

The interested Allied powers, which had at first approved Bulgaria's neutrality, now began to force her to renounce her neutrality. To achieve this, they began to work either through the Bulgarian plenipotentiaries accredited to them or through their own representatives in Sofia, or through any other possible means.[6]

In order to secure Bulgarian help, the Entente Powers (Allies) at once offered Bulgaria the Enos-Midia line in eastern Thrace (November 9, 1914) and, after the war, the 1912 uncontested zone of Macedonia as far as the Vardar River, which was in possession of Serbia. It was clear almost from the outset, however, that such an offer would not prove attractive, because the Bulgarians aspired not only to part of Thrace but also to most of Macedonia, the Kavalla-Drama-Seres region of western Thrace, and also that part of Dobrudja lost to Romania in 1913.[7] As the Dardanelles campaign was being decided on, the Allies offered Greece the Turkish city of Smyrna and its hinterland on condition that the Greeks cede the Kavalla region to Bulgaria and join a Balkan bloc in support of Serbia (January 1915). Premier Venizelos of Greece favored this policy strongly, but King Constantine preferred a bird in the hand to two in the bush.

The Allies, more eager than ever before to secure the aid of Bulgaria in view of the failure at the Dardanelles, gave Serbia a conditional guarantee of the eventual acquisition of Bosnia and Herzegovina and "a wide access to the Adriatic," as compensation for the part of Macedonia that was required to bring in Bulgaria. Nearly three months before Bulgaria entered the war, Winston S. Churchill wrote:

The imminent peril in which Serbia stood and the restricted conditions under which the Allies could afford her protection, made it indispensable *that she should cede and, if necessary, be made to surrender the uncontested zone in Macedonia to the Bulgarians to whom it belonged by race, by history, by treaty and—until it was taken from them in the Second Balkan War—by conquest.* Serbia, even when at the last gasp during the Austrian attack upon her in 1914, *had found it necessary to keep large numbers of troops in the Bulgarian districts of Macedonia to hold down the native population. Right, reason, the claims of justice and the most imperious call to necessity alike counseled the Serbians to surrender at least the uncontested zone.* To the ordinary exhortations of diplomacy were added special appeals by the Sovereigns and the Rulers of the allied countries. The Prince Regent of Serbia was besought by the Tsar, by the President of the French Republic and by King George V to make a concession right in itself, necessary in the common cause, vital to the safety of Serbia. But to all these appeals, the Serbian government and parliament proved obdurate. The allied diplomacy, moving ponderously forward— every telegram and measure having to be agreed to by all the other parties to the alliance—had just reached the point of refusing any further supplies of stores of money to Serbia unless she complied with their insistant demand when the final invasion began.

The same sort of thing happened about Kavalla. M. Venizelos, with his almost unerring judgment of great issues, was prepared to imperil his whole personal popularity in Greece and place himself at a deadly disadvantage in his controversies with the king by intimating his readiness to acquiesce in the cession to Bulgaria of Kavalla in certain circumstances. Had the Allies been able to secure for Bulgaria the immediate cession of the uncontested zone in Macedonia and the port of Kavalla, it seems very probable that they might have been induced during the month of July to come to our aid and to march on Adrianople.

It seems certain that, even if this full result has not been obtained, the tangible cession of this territory to Bulgaria at the instance of the Allies would have made it impossible for King Ferdinand to carry his country into the hostile camp. . . .

Serbia, however, though fully conscious of her danger, remained recalcitrant to all appeals to make effective concessions. *Till the last moment she kept her heel on the conquered Bulgarian districts of Macedonia and maintained a stubborn front to overwhelming forces that were gathering against her.* [Italics added.][8]

On May 29, 1915, a more definite offer along these lines was made to Bulgaria. But the Sofia government treated these advances dilatorily; it was already leaning to the Central Powers, which were ready to satisfy Bulgaria's aspirations in Macedonia, western Thrace, and southern Dobrudja. And on July 22, the German government persuaded the Turks to cede to Bulgaria a strip of territory along the Maritza River.

2. BULGARIA JOINS THE CENTRAL POWERS— SUFFERS DEFEAT

After nearly fifteen months of neutrality, Bulgaria concluded an alliance and military convention with Germany and Austria-Hungary (September 6, 1915), providing for mutual aid against attack by a neighboring state; it also provided for a German-Austrian campaign against Serbia within thirty days and for Bulgarian participation five days later.[9] Bulgaria was to receive all of Macedonia and, if Romania joined in the war on the side of the Allies, Dobrudja also; if Greece proved hostile, Bulgaria was to receive the Kavalla region as well. With such assurances given, Bulgaria began to mobilize (September 21). Serbia, being directly threatened, appealed to Greece for aid, under the terms of the treaty of May 1913. Venizelos, the Greek premier, was as eager as ever to intervene but made a condition that the Allies furnish 150,000 troops, which Serbia was required to supply under the treaty terms. The British and French governments gave Greece a promise to this effect and in the early part of October, British and French divisions were landed at Salonika.

But even before Bulgaria actually declared war on Serbia, the latter's troops had already invaded Bulgarian territory around the Vidin regions.[10] On October 11, Bulgarian troops crossed the Serbian frontiers, and on October 14, 1915, Bulgaria and Serbia declared war on each other. England and France declared war on Bulgaria (October 15, 16), and so did Russia and Italy (October 19). At this time, the Allies made a great effort to induce Greece to join their side by offering her the isand of Cyprus (October 16), but this offer, for some reason, was rejected (October 20). The Greek government then declared its "benevolent neutrality" (November 8) and agreed not to interfere with Allied forces at Salonika, in return for a guarantee of the eventual restoration of Greek territory.

On October 6, however, under the command of General August Von Mackensen, the great Austro-German campaign began in Serbia. Belgrade fell on October 9, and Semendria on October 11. The Bulgarian army, under the command of General Jekoff, attacked and rapidly advanced in northwestern Macedonia and the eastern frontiers of Serbia. The city of Skopie and Pirot fell on October 28, and Nish on November 5. An attempt by the British and French from the Salonika front to block the Bulgarian advances on the Strunitsa and on the Cherna was brushed aside (November 12). The Allies were again repulsed on the lower Vardar (December 4-10) and forced to retreat to Greek territory. The British were, by this time, prepared to give up the whole of the Salonika adventure, but the French, under General Sarrail, persisted in staying, without accomplishing much.

By November 16, the Bulgarians took Prilep, then Pristina (November 23), Prizdren (November 29), and Monastir (Bitolia, December 2). The Serbian army was now in full flight into Albania, the Bulgarian army pursuing them and taking Debra and Ohrid (December 8), and ultimately, Elbasan (February 2, 1916). Meanwhile, the Austrian army took Plevije and then Ipek (December 6). Mount Lovechen, guarding Montenegro, was stormed, and Cetinje, the capital, was taken (January 13, 1916). At the same time, the French occupied Corfu as a refuge for the Serbian troops. The Austrians took Scutari and Barat (February 17, 1916). The Albanian provisional government, under Italian protection at Durazzo, left for Naples, and the town was taken by the Austrians from the Italians on February 27. Thus, in less than two months the Austro-German and Bulgarian armies had defeated the Serbians and occupied their country. Bulgaria's occupation was confined within the frontiers of Macedonia and some Bulgarian lands in the Morava area. Macedonia was, therefore, liberated from Serbian oppression, and a Bulgarian regime over the country established. Achieving her objective, Bulgaria was now ready to accept any proposal for peace.

The intervention of Romania on the side of the Allied Powers rendered no effective help. General Von Mackensen's troops crossed the Danube at Sistova and Simnitza and advanced toward Bucharest, while General Erich Von Falkenhayn's troops advanced into Romania from the north. The Austro-German forces continued the advance both in the Dobrudja and Moldavia. Bucharest fell into the hands of the enemy on December 6, and Braila was taken on January 5. By the middle of January most of Romania, with important wheat- and oil-producing areas, was in the hands of the Central Powers.

However, the Balkan situation in 1917 was not really stabilized. The Macedonian front was quiet during the winter of 1916-1917, but operations were resumed in March of 1917. A second battle for Monastir, the Lake Prespa, and Doiran took place. These engagements were inconclusive but they served to convince the Allied powers that success on this front would be impossible so long as the Greek government was unreliable. By forcing the abdication of King Constantine, the Allies made it possible for the Greek government, headed by Venizelos, to break relations with the Central Powers, and Greece definitely entered the war on the Allied side (January 17, 1917).

The Central Powers' campaign against Romania was progressing rapidly. At the same time Count Rubian, the Austrian foreign minister, suggested a proposal for an armistice and an eventual peace among the warring nations. His idea was taken under consideration by Germany, Austria-Hungary, Bulgaria, and Turkey, and, as a result, a joint note for peace was sent to the Allied powers through the mediation of the neutral countries—the United States, Spain, Sweden, and Holland. A copy of the note was also sent to the Pope in Rome.[11]

Meanwhile, President Woodrow Wilson appeared as an ardent champion of world peace. In a speech before the League to Enforce Peace at Washington on May 27, 1916, he said:

> With the causes and the objects of the war we are not concerned. The obscure fountains from which its stupendous flood has burst forth, we are not interested to search or explore. . . . The longer the war lasts, the more deeply do we become concerned that it should be brought to an end and the world permitted to resume its normal life and course again.

In February 1916, the President had sent Colonel Edward M. House to England to confer with Sir Edward Grey on the possibility of getting the Central Powers and the Allies to discuss terms. He even expressed his willingness to go to Europe and sit at the conference himself as mediator and held out hopes to the Allies that the United States would probably enter the war on their side if Germany refused to confer. But it was rather France and England that were cold to the proposition. They had made a number of secret treaties for the division of the spoils of war and did not wish to reveal them or revise them.

The German government appealed to the United States (December 12) to inform the Entente governments that the Central Powers were prepared to negotiate peace. The military situation, after the wiping out of Romania, could hardly have been more favorable, a fact that was not overlooked in the drafting of the German note. Failure of the Germans to mention any specific terms and the fact that all the advantages were on their side made it relatively easy for the Allied governments, especially that of David Lloyd George of England and Aristide Briand of France, to reject the German advances (December 30).

President Wilson transmitted his own proposals to the warring powers. He suggested that the belligerents state their terms for peace and for arrangements to guarantee the world against a renewal of conflicts. The German, Austrian, and Turkish governments replied (December 26) in an appreciative way but reiterated their opinion that the best method would be to call a meeting for exchange of views. No definite terms were mentioned. The Allied powers in their reply on January 10,

1917 named specific terms. These included the restoration of Belgium, Serbia, and Montenegro; the evacuation of French, Russian, and Romanian territory, with just reparations; the reorganization of Europe on the basis of nationalities; the restoration of territory previously taken from the Allies; the liberation of Italians, Slavs, Romanians, and Czechoslovaks from foreign rule; the freeing of subject nationalities under Turkish rule and the expulsion of Turkey from Europe.

The far-reaching nature of the Allied terms at a moment when the military situation was by no means in their favor estranged even President Wilson, who still stuck by the idea of *"peace without victory."*[12] The first step, however, was to elicit Germany's statement of aims. These were confidentially communicated to the president on January 29: restitution of the part of Alsace occupied by the German forces; acquisition of a strategic and economic zone between Germany and Poland on the one hand and Russia on the other; return of colonies and the granting to Germany of colonial territory in accord with her population and economic needs; restoration of occupied France; renunciation of economic obstacles to normal commerce; compensation for German enterprises and civilians damaged by the war; freedom of the seas, and so on.

It was felt that the Allies were rapidly coming to the point where they would be unable to continue the war without American aid and that when that time came they would have to accept American mediation and a compromise peace without victory. But the decision of the highest military and civil officials of Germany to begin unrestricted submarine warfare (January 8, 1917), "the only method by which England could be brought to her knees," was a fatal one. The United States was notified that unrestricted submarine war would begin on February 1, 1917. Two days later, the United States government severed relations with the German government, but President Wilson had decided not to declare war until the Germans committed an overt act. Several American ships were, in fact, sunk during February and March. As a consequence, on April 6, the United States declared war on Germany. The declaration of war on Austria-Hungary was delayed until December 7, 1917.

Meanwhile, between February and June, secret negotiations between the Emperor Charles of Austria and his foreign minister, Count Czernin, and the French and the British governments were taking place. The emperor appeared to have been determined from the accession (November 1916) to make peace, even without Germany. The negotiations were carried on through his brother-in-law, Prince Sixtus of Bourbon, who was serving in the Belgian army. After several secret meetings in Switzerland, Prince Sixtus went to Vienna with the full knowledge and approval of the French foreign office and had a conference with the emperor and Czernin.[13] He returned to Paris with a letter from Emperor

Charles (dated March 24) in which the writer promised to use his influence with his allies to support "the just French claims relative to Alsace-Lorraine." Belgium was to be restored, with compensation for her losses; also Serbia, which was to have access to the Adriatic. The emperor was also not opposed to Russia's acquisition of Constantinople.

Germany succeeded in forcing the Russian Bolshevists Nikolai Lenin and Leon Trotsky to sign an agreement at Brest-Litovsk (March 3, 1918), detaching Russia from the Allies and thereby allowing Germany to transfer her troops from the eastern front to the west. That in itself, however, did not help very much. With the arrival of American troops and supplies in France during 1918, the equation had changed, and Germany's fate was about sealed.

Facing disaster in the east, Germany was no longer able to support its allies on the southeastern front. In the Balkans, a strong offensive by British, Greek, Serbian, French, and Italian troops brought Bulgaria's unconditional surrender (September 29, 1918). This victory cut Turkey off from Germany and Austria-Hungary. On October 30, she signed an armistice that took her out of the war. The collapse of Austria-Hungary was not too far off. General Armando Diaz and his Italian troops pushed the Austrians out of Italy. On November 3, Austria-Hungary signed an armistice that amounted to unconditional surrender. On the western front, the Allied troops defeated Germany, and an armistice was signed on November 11, 1918, ending the First World War.

3. BULGARIA AT THE
PARIS PEACE CONFERENCE

The peace conference opened on January 18, 1919, in the foreign ministry building in Paris. *No representatives from the defeated nations were invited to attend.* It was not, therefore, to be a "peace of equals," for which President Wilson had contended just a year before in a speech to the Senate (January 22, 1917), "but a victor's terms imposed upon the vanquished."[14]

The direction of affairs, the appointment of the fifty-eight special committees, the hearings of the claims that the delegates of the various countries had to present were all taken over by a Supreme Council of ten, consisting of President Wilson and Colonel Edward M. House for the United States and the prime ministers and foreign ministers of Great Britain, France, Italy, and Japan. After more than two months had passed without much progress toward a settlement of the confusing claims and counterclaims, the Council was narrowed down to four men—President Wilson, Lloyd George, Georges Clemenceau, and Vittorio

Orlando. Because the latter spoke no English, the major work of the Council was done by Wilson, Lloyd George, and Clemenceau.

"Open covenants openly arrived at" was the first of President Wilson's Fourteen Points, on which the treaty was supposed to be based. But three men in a secret session took practically the whole responsibility for preparing the most fateful series of treaties in the history of the world. These treaties were: The peace Treaty of Versailles, imposed upon the Germans in the Hall of Mirrors at Versailles on June 28, 1919; the Treaty of St. Germain (September 10, 1919), which registered the breakup of the Hapsburg Monarchy; the Treaty of Neuilly (November 27, 1919), signed by the Bulgarians; the Treaty of Trianon (March 22, 1919), with Hungary; and the Treaty of Sèvres (August 20, 1919), with Turkey.

As pointed out, Bulgaria collapsed under the strain of the war, and the entire Bulgarian race was put at the mercy of the victorious Allies. The Macedonian Bulgarians had every reason to believe that they would be given an opportunity to determine their political status, for peace was to be accomplished on the basis of President Wilson's program, the famous Fourteen Points, announced to the world on January 8, 1918.

Point 11 of President Wilson's basis for peace at the time states: "Freedom, restoration and adjustment according to nationality for the Balkan States." This was in fact the announcement of the principle of "self-determination" of national groups.

The territorial arrangement established by the peace treaties of 1919 changed the former character of central Europe: a new map of Europe was effected. Under the leadership of the French "Tiger"—Clemenceau—the Allied statesmen, in their deliberations during the peace conference, concurred in the amalgamation of the various southwestern Slavic groups ruled by the former Hapsburg dynasty. Little Serbia, of course, was the nucleus around which these groups were to unite and thus develop into a political system. Because Serbia, however, had been allied with the Entente Powers during World War I, she was given an artificial, preponderant position in shaping the destiny of the newly redeemed provinces of Croatia, Slovenia, Bosnia-Herzegovina, Dalmatia, and even the former kingdom of Montenegro.

Macedonia and the Sandjak of Novi-Bazar were, of course, restored to Serbia as by the Treaty of Bucharest of 1913 and, in addition, the Serbians claimed (and were given) a considerable belt of territory along the whole frontier of Bulgaria, on the ground that they needed it to protect their railway communications. Perhaps they were prevented from exerting heavier pressure by being allowed four areas, of which the largest included Strumitza, with a total of about 90,000 inhabitants, practically all of whom were unquestionably Bulgarian. "I had the painful duty," states Professor Albert H. Lybyer, "of tracing the bound-

aries of these amputations."[15] Under the provision of the Treaty of
Neuilly, Bulgaria recognized the independence of Triune Kingdom of
Serbs, Croats, and Slovenes (Kraljevina Serb-Horvata-Slovenca), which
was maintained as such until 1929.[16] Bulgaria agreed also to pay reparations of $445,000,000. Her army was reduced to 20,000 men, and she was
obliged to surrender most of her war materials.

Defeated in the First World War, Bulgaria not only failed to recover
any of the territory lost in the second Balkan War but was also deprived
of an access to the Aegean Sea. But there were many compassionate and
authoritative Americans and Britishers who had raised their voices of
protest against the injustices imposed upon the Bulgarian people by the
Treaty of Neuilly. Leading American missionaries of the American
Board sent, on December 11, 1918, the following telegram to President
Wilson:

To His Excellency The President of the United States.

Excellency,
The missionaries of the American Board residing in Bulgaria follow
with pride and sympathy your work in behalf of a just and permanent
world peace, and on the eve of the conference send you sincere and loyal
greetings.
In fulfillment of your high purpose to apply the principle of nationality alike to conquered and conquering nations, we respectfully urge
that, in the settlement of boundaries in the Balkans, due and full consideration be given to the evidence of unbiased witnesses, that the world
may be spared a repetition of such disastrous wrongs as were perpetrated
against France in 1871 and against the Bulgarian nation in 1878 and 1913.
It is the testimony of our Mission, which has worked without political
purpose among Balkan peoples for sixty years, that in the territory of our
Macedonian field, extending from Skopia and Ochrida to Drama, the great
bulk of the population is Bulgarian in origin, language and customs, and
forms an integral part of the Bulgarian nation. As the result of travel
throughout the Adrianople villages for the distribution of relief we are
convinced also that the non-Moslem population, with the exception of the
littoral, is almost entirely Bulgarian.
Entreating for you Divine guidance and support in the tremendous task
of solving present world problems,

> Respectfully yours,
> Missionaries of the American Board,
> *Signed:*
> LEROY F. OSTRANDER
> LYLE D. WOODRUFF
> H. B. KING

Samokov, Bulgaria, Dec. 11, 1918.

President Wilson was absent from Paris on a visit to Washington from
the middle of February to the middle of March 1919. During this time,
many points of settlement were made. The French point of view pre-

vailed for most of the continent of Europe. A central idea was to count certain countries as victors and give them everything reasonably possible. The defeated countries were to lose everything possible and to be put where they might be repressed by force. Of course, Bulgaria was a defeated power and Serbia and Greece were to be favored.

4. NOTED BRITISHERS
FOR MACEDONIAN AUTONOMY

A. *James David Bourchier (1850-1920)—Memorial to President Wilson*

It was, above all, on the American delegation to the Peace Conference and on President Wilson that Bourchier fixed his hopes for obtaining a just and final solution of the Balkan problem. He drew up a *Memorial to President Wilson* with regard to autonomy for Macedonia, to which were appended the signatures of a number of people who had spent some time in the Balkan Peninsula, and had been able to acquaint themselves directly with the wishes of the people. The list of signatures includes, among many others, the names of Colonel Leon Lamouche, O'Mahoney, Sir Edwin Pears, Dr. H. A. Gibbons, and Miss M. E. Durham, all noted authorities on the Balkan problem. Following is Bourchier's *Memorial* to Wilson:

(1) In the interests of justice and of the future peace of the Balkan Peninsula, it is necessary that the new frontiers of the Balkan States should be made to coincide as far as possible with the limits of nationalities.

(2) If in any instance this system of delimitation cannot be carried out, the principle that no Balkan people should be placed under the rule of another may still be maintained by according self-government to the population concerned.

(3) In the case of Macedonia, the application of this principle is peculiarly desirable in view of the rival claims of neighboring countries, which have been the cause of infinite misery to the population for nearly half a century. Under an autonomous government, the population would be enabled to care for its own interests, and to live and thrive without the molestation to which it has hitherto been subjected.

(4) If we accept the theory advanced by the Serbians and Greeks that the national conscience of the Macedonians is "fluid," and displays no partiality for any foreign propaganda, the natural conclusion is that they should govern themselves, and that the principle, "Macedonia for the Macedonians," should be adopted. If, on the other hand, there exists such a partiality, the bestowal of autonomy would enable this sentiment to declare itself freely in accordance with the principle of self-determination.

(5) The autonomous Macedonian State would extend from the Shar Mountains (the Serbian ethnical boundary) on the north to the Aegean Sea on the south, and from the Bulgarian frontier on the east to the

Albanian on the west. The southern frontier, extending from Lake Castoria
to the mouth of the Vardar, would also retain Nigrita and the Chalcidike
Peninsula.

(6) It would be desirable that the autonomous State would be under
the care of a Mandatory Power, America for preference, during the earlier
years of its existence.

(7) It would not be unreasonable to expect Serbia and Greece to renounce the Macedonian territory they have occupied since 1913 in view
of the great extension which each of these States will now receive.

(8) Salonica, which is commercially inseparable from the interior,
would naturally become the capital of the new State. If this is thought
impossible, a maritime outlet would still exist at Kavala.

(9) The solution thus proposed would satisfy the widely-felt desire
for autonomy which has existed in Macedonia and at Salonica for many
years past, and would be in harmony with the principles laid down by
your statesmanlike wisdom and accepted by the Allied Powers.[17]

B. *Justice and Conciliation in the Balkans*

An indisputable Balkan authority, champion for a just Balkan
settlement, Bourchier was greatly disturbed at the results of the Paris
peace settlement. It not only did not correct the Bucharest settlement of
August 10, 1913, but, in fact, at the end of World War I, Bulgaria
suffered the most severe punishment. Under the above caption, Bourchier
wrote an article on the Balkan situation. It is a masterpiece on the
subject. The article appeared in *The Contemporary Review* of February
1919. Bourchier's statesmanlike counsel and recommendation constituted
a rational and lasting solution of the Balkan problem based on justice
and conciliation. He wrote:

> The arrangement of Bucharest cannot be allowed to stand, not only
> because it is unjust, but because it will inevitably lead to fresh conflicts
> in the Balkans and possibly to another European war. We want a lasting
> peace, says Lord Phillmore, but we want a just peace. We want it because
> no peace but a just peace can be counted upon as lasting but also for
> higher reasons. In what sense do we speak of a just peace? Is it retributive
> justice or distributive justice, the *suum cuique* of the Roman justice? Retri-
> bution there should be, he said, in order to prevent powerful states from
> wantonly engaging in war but it should not take the form of deprivation
> of territory without regard to the wishes of the population of that terri-
> tory. "The justice which should be the principal object in the (future)
> trinity is distributive justice, justice to nations, peoples and races." In this
> sense we must reply to those who tell us that Bulgaria by her treachery
> and ruthlessness has "forfeited" all claims to Macedonia. It is not a ques-
> tion of punishing Bulgaria, even if she is guilty of all the enormities of
> which her foes (of whose misdeeds we never hear) accuse her; with
> regard to the "balance of criminality" some strange surprises may be in
> store for us when another Carnegie Report appears. *It is a question of
> punishing the Macedonian Bulgars by severing them permanently from*

their kith and kin and subjecting them to the merciless processes of compulsory assimilation applied by their bitterest enemies.

"No right anywhere exists," said President Wilson in his message to the Senate in January 1917, "to hand people about from sovereignty to sovereignty as if they were property." That is what has been done by the Treaty of Bucharest. *The greater part of Macedonia has been handed over to the Serbians who, even thirty years ago, never made any ethnic claim to its possessions.* At the time, and for many years later, nothing was heard of a Serbian movement. The Serbians never discovered that they had any interests in Macedonia until 1885, the year of King Milan's unsuccessful attack on Bulgaria; the new propaganda was encouraged by Austria in order to divert popular attention from Bosnia and Herzegovina and was welcomed by Turkey as a counterblast to the more dangerous Bulgarian movement. During the writer's visit to Macedonia in the 90's, little was heard of it beyond amusing stories of the good pair of boots, suits of clothes and even dinners which the poorer class of Bulgarian peasants obtained by sending their children to the Serbian schools; the children learned to read and write Serbian and, after leaving school, found the knowledge they had acquired was more or less useful for reading and writing Bulgarian.

Meanwhile, what has happened in the country itself during these thirty years? In 1878, as soon as the Bulgarian population in the Vardar and Struma Valleys heard of the decision of the Powers of Berlin, it revolted but was induced to lay down arms by an European commission. For the time, under the statesman-like guidance of Stamboloff and the Exarch Joseph, it remained quiet, awaiting the realization of the promised reforms. But the Turkish yoke grew more and more intolerable and the younger generation lost patience. In 1895, came a partial outbreak in the Melnik district and in 1902 revolts in the districts of Monastir and Razlog. Lastly, in 1903, came the great insurrection of Macedonia, repressed like its predecessors with the utmost barbarity by the Turks, who were in many cases aided by a number of Greek bands. More than 100 Bulgarian villages were burned and some 80,000 peasants were homeless in the mountains at the approach of winter. The Powers intervened with ineffective reforms; the Young Turks then tried their hand and their blind and indiscriminate severity brought about a Balkan combination and the extinction of the Ottoman Empire in Europe.

In the sad history of this period, one fact stands out: *all the efforts to shake off the Turkish yoke were made by the Bulgarians, all the sacrifices were theirs.* As Lord Bryce observes, there is no poetic justice in history, yet it seems hard to believe that for those who made those sacrifices there is no better fate than subjection to their deadly foes, no hope of national unity. Some 18,000 young Macedonians fought by the side of their kinsmen at Lule Burgas; when the survivors sought to return to their homes they had to choose between renunciation of their nationality or perpetual exile. It would have been better for them had Lule Burgas been lost, for the victorious Turkish army would have occupied Macedonia and whatever horrors might have ensued the prospect of eventual liberty would not have been destroyed. Most of them might have perished, but "better an end with horrors" says the Bulgarian proverb, "than horrors without end."

Why Macedonia is Bulgarian: To those who know the country it may seem superfluous to insist on this fact which was generally admitted in years past, but since the war the public has undoubtedly been much misled on this point by a voluminous and unrebuked partisan literature. Efforts are even made to deny that the language of the people is Bulgarian; with regard to this, it is enough to quote Weigand, a very high authority: *"all linguistic specialists,"* he says, *"are unanimous that it is Bulgarian and the politicians cannot alter the fact."* The language in the northwest naturally approximates in some respects to Serbian but even here it possesses all the distinctive features of Bulgarian. Language is not a necessary test of nationality; the Albanians in Attica, for instance, may be regarded as politically Greeks though the language of the home betrays their Albanian origin. The best test of a man's nationality is what he believes himself to be. *In Turkish times, the Macedonian Slav peasant when asked as to his nationality, invariably replied, "I am a Bulgarian."* Today, he would be afraid to make such an avowal but his national consciousness remains the same.

Another indication almost equally convincing is to be found *in the reluctance of the Bulgarians to consent to any division of Macedonia.* The Serbians and Greeks have always demanded partition, the Bulgarians have consistently opposed it, *declaring that rather than hand over a partition of their kindred to alien rule they would welcome the creation of a Macedonian autonomous state and renounce all claims to annexation.* The difference of aims more than once prevented an arrangement in the past. In 1897, Greece could have had the aid of Bulgaria against Turkey had she been willing to consent to Macedonian autonomy. *In 1912, Bulgaria only agreed to a delimitation with Serbia in case autonomy should prove impossible;* could she induce the Congress to maintain the integrity of Macedonia and to grant it autonomy, she would now resign all her claims, like the real mother who besought King Solomon to spare her child.

In regard to the geographical distribution of the Bulgarian element in Macedonia, the following official documents possess unquestionable importance:

(1) The *firman* of February 29, 1870, establishing the Exarchate, in accordance with which the *exsequatur* was granted to seven Bulgarian metropolitans whose dioceses covered the greater part of Macedonia. These bishops have all been expelled by the Serbs.

(2) The establishment of the two autonomous "Bulgarian" villayets by the Constantinople Conference in 1876. The southern villayet, with its capital at Sofia, embraced the greater part of Macedonia.

(3) The Treaty of San Stefano which included all Macedonia in the "Big Bulgaria."

(4) The Reform area laid down by all the Murzteg programme in 1904 (after the Bulgarian revolt of the previous year). This excluded "Old Serbia" and the Greek districts in the extreme South.[18]

C. *Lord James Bryce (1838-1924)—Speech in the House of Lords Regarding the Paris Peace Treaties*

The peace treaty with Bulgaria was signed at Neuilly-sur-Seine on November 27, 1919. The treaties with Austria and Bulgaria were laid before the British Parliament in the shape of a single bill, which was introduced in the House of Commons on April 14 and in the House of Lords on April 23, 1920. The debate in the House of Lords occasioned the statesmanlike speech of Lord Bryce, every word of which deserves careful attention. He laid down four principles that ought to have guided those who negotiated the treaties:

1. The principle of nationality and self-determination, to which all the world assented at the time of the Armistice (November 11, 1918) and on the faith of which the armistices were accepted by the enemy powers.
2. No nation or group of nations should be required to guarantee the possessions of territory unjustly assigned to an alien power.
3. The object of the treaties should be to secure peace, which cannot be assured when sections of peoples are placed under alien and hostile rule.
4. Treaties ought not to be concluded in a spirit of revenge or with punishment as their main object.

In this speech, Lord Bryce touched on the question of Macedonia, a country he had visited. He said:

"*The population from Ochrida on the west to Serres on the east is Bulgarian in tradition and in ecclesiastical organization.*" To create a stable set of conditions in the Balkans, Lord Bryce maintained the idea of making "*Macedonia autonomous;* to create it into a separate principality.*"

Following is Lord Bryce's speech in the House of Lords:

My Lords, the noble Viscount (Lord Milner), in moving the Second Reading of this Bill to give effect to these Treaties, stated that we were confronted with an accomplished fact. That is so. These Treaties have been negotiated, and now nothing remains to be done. They are settled. It is beyond the powers of this House to alter them without starting upon a long and very difficult task, perhaps an impossible task. But I must remind your Lordships that no opportunity has been given to the British people or to Parliament to express its opinion at any stage upon these negotiations, although both in your Lordships' House and in the other House there are many persons who have given long and careful attention to these problems, who have visited these countries, who know the difficulty which these problems present. We have never had any inkling whatever of what the Conference at Paris was doing. We have had to trust to mere rumors, and when questions have been asked in another place or here we have been told that it would be dangerous to answer those questions. Therefore, no moral obligation rests in this matter upon the British people, although a legal obligation is now going to be fixed upon them.

It may seem useless in such circumstances to criticize the Treaties. A protest is idle at this stage. Nevertheless, when matters of such importance are presented to Parliament, I do not think that they ought to be passed over in silence. Those who see the errors, the injustices, and the dangers—I dwell particularly upon the dangers—that are likely to arise from these Treaties are bound to state their opinion, and they are bound to say in the face of this House and of the country that they do not believe that these Treaties would ever have been concluded if the British nation had been free and allowed to express its opinion on their provisions.

The few words that I have to say will not be said in criticism of our Foreign Office. I do not know how far the Foreign Office is responsible for these Treaties. We have had an extraordinary condition of affairs in the management of our foreign relations ever since the Armistice; we have never known who particularly was responsible for any word that was said or any act that was done abroad except, of course, that the Government as a whole was responsible. But it is quite possible that the Foreign Office itself regrets these Treaties. Possibly His Majesty's Government regrets them. The noble Viscount admitted with great candour, which I respect, that these Treaties are far from perfect—in fact, his whole tone was much more apologetic than commendatory. He could not recommend these Treaties as being things of which his judgment approved. He said the best that could be said by way of palliation for their faults. It reminds me of the way in which an agent is employed who comes back bringing an extremely unsatisfactory report, and says, "Well, of course, it is not very good, but is the best we could get." I suppose that is the substance of the defense that is made by His Majesty's Government, and it is not very high praise. I am not here, I repeat, to criticize the Foreign Office. Therefore, I hope it will not be taken that in anything I am saying I am reflecting upon our Foreign Office. What I want to speak of is not the workmen but the work that has been done.

Now what Principles ought to have guided the Conference in Paris when they started after the Armistice to deal with the great mass of questions?—I admit far more difficult and far more complicated than any European Conference or Congress was ever confronted with before. I think we may say that there were four principles which ought to have guided them in the negotiations for the Treaty which they conducted. *In the first place, they were bound to fulfill and carry out the purposes which they proclaimed at the time of the Armistice, the purposes that were stated in the famous "Fourteen Points," and which were accepted and made the basis of the Armistice, and upon the faith of which the Armistice was accepted by the enemy Powers. Those principles are briefly known as the principles of nationality and self-determination—the idea that boundaries ought to be drawn by the natural conditions of race, and speech and tradition, and not arbitrarily, and that no people ought to be forced under an alien yoke, and that when there is any doubt as to the wishes of people, they should be given an opportunity of expressing their wishes by having what is called a popular vote, or a Plebiscite, taken in the area where it may be difficult to determine what the race and what the wishes of the people are. That principle was proclaimed and adopted. Everybody assented to it and said, "What an improvement upon all previous times; how unlike we are to the people of the Congress of Vienna; how much superior. Freedom is bearing its appropriate fruits in the proclamation of these principles."*

Secondly, the League of Nations Covenant contains an important provision by which all who enter into the League guarantee the territories as existing and defined in those Treaties to the various Powers and States which are parties thereto, and indeed all over the world to any State holding certain territories at the date of the conclusion of the Treaties. That is a very important provision: it is a guarantee to every Power of its territories, giving the right of that Power, when threatened from abroad, to call upon all the members of the League to support it in defending its guaranteed territory. It was clearly most important that if that obligation was to be undertaken it should be undertaken to guarantee that it was just, and that no Power should be expected to guarantee territory which it knew did not rightfully belong to the State into whose possession it was expected to go. No nation ought to be called upon, where it knows that a territory has been unjustly and unwisely assigned to an alien Power, to guarantee the possession of that territory by that alien Power. I strongly suspect that this has been one of the causes which has done a good deal to prevent the entry of the United States into the League of Nations. Although I do not suppose that the people in the United States realize as fully as we do what have been the mistakes committed at Paris, still they do know that many complaints have been made and many reclamations proclaimed against the decisions which the Powers have made. As your Lordships are aware, that was the Article in the Covenant of the League of Nations to which, perhaps more than any other, objection was taken in the United States, and not unnaturally. They might well say, "If the Paris Conference has sanctioned allotments of territory which are unjust, which ought not in justice to be maintained, how can you ask us to sign our names to a Covenant which guarantees the possession of those territories?" I am afraid that this has a good deal to do with the difficulties which have arisen in the United States with regard to their entry into the League of Nations. I do not say that it would not have been possible in some way or other to have avoided those, but I fear that a certain amount of prejudice has been created by those decisions. To oblige the League of Nations to defend what is unjust would be to run counter to the very object for which the League of Nations was created. It was meant to be the shield of justice and not the defender of injustice.

Thirdly, the aim both of these Treaties and of the League of Nations is to prevent oppression, which is the enemy of peace, and to secure peace in the world at large. Peace can come only by content. *If the result of these Treaties is to make nations discontented, to put sections of peoples under a Power which to them is alien and hostile, you cannot expect that there will be peace. On the contrary, you are preparing for revolts and for wars. It was out of discontents of this kind that the late war largely arose; and if you provide fresh grounds for discontent and insurrection, you are going counter to the very object which you set out to attain, and there will be no prospect of stability.* Last, I would observe that the Paris Conference ought to have thought, we all ought to have thought, through this matter not so much of the past as of the future. *These treaties ought not to have been concluded in the spirit of revenge; they ought not to have been concluded in a way which thought first of punishment.* Resentment against the enemy was very natural, particularly in those who most suffered. One cannot expect that those feelings of resentment could have been entirely laid aside. At the same time we are not here to do abstract justice; *we are not here to be the instruments of the Divine Wrath. We are here to do the best we can for the world in the future, and to give it the peace that it desires.*

I think it is a misfortune that so many provisions have been introduced into these Treaties which obviously come from passion rather than from wisdom, and which are likely, therefore, to bear very unfortunate fruits in the future. The noble Viscount in one part of his speech seemed to me to lapse into the view that we were here to punish people and to deal with nations in accordance with the way in which they had treated us. He complained of Austria for joining in the war, and he complained of Bulgaria for joining in the war. He said, quite justly, that if a nation chooses to leave its fortunes in the hands of unscrupulous or unwise guides; if, like Austria, it was in the hands of a camarilla of people most of whom were not Austrian-Germans at all; or, if like Bulgaria, it falls under the control of Ferdinand and the group of satellites which surround him—then that country must suffer for being in the hands of bad rulers. I cannot deny it. But at the same time it ought a little to mitigate our feelings towards the people if we know that in the case of these two peoples there was no evidence whatever that they were in general sympathy with the purposes of their Governments. I do not speak of Germany—that is a large question which I will not enter—but certainly as regards the German-Austrians and the Bulgarians I do not think that was any public sentiment in favor of the entry of their Governments into the war.

As regards Bulgaria in particular, those of your Lordships who have followed her history must know that no country existed in which there was a warmer friendship towards Britain. Bulgaria was extremely grateful to us for the part we played, in days now comparatively distant, in helping her to secure her independence against the aggressions of Russia as well as against the oppression of Turkey; and I believe that even during the past war the Bulgarian forces were very unwilling to fight against us. I need not remind your Lordships that in Austria and in Hungary and in Bulgaria anyone who was in any of those countries who did not speak well of the treatment given to British prisoners—an extraordinary contrast to the most unspeakable cruelty and brutality with which they were treated in Turkey.

Now all these, I venture to think, are considerations which will commend themselves to your Lordships. All these four principles which it seems to me ought to have guided us were neglected at Paris. The principles were transgressed, and the promises made in the Fourteen Points were broken.

The noble Viscount said that very few holes had been picked in the Treaty with Bulgaria. I should have thought that there were many that could have been picked, though I do not intend to detain your Lordships by referring to more than one of them. There are, as you know, three very important boundary questions raised in regard to Bulgaria. One of them related to the Dobrudja, an intricate question, and one in which I think there is a very strong moral claim that the ill-gotten claims which Rumania made in 1919 ought not to have been allowed to remain with her. There are also the difficult questions of Thrace, where no doubt it is very hard to determine how much territory should be assigned to the Bulgarians, how much to the Greeks, and how much should be left, on the ground of nationality, to the Turks. But I will not enter into that.

I do, however, know something about Southern Macedonia. I have traveled there and have had opportunities of observing what is the character of the population. The population of Southern Macedonia all the way from Ochrida and Monastir on the west as far as Serres on the east— that is to say, all the way from the Lake of Orchrida to the rivers Vardar and Struma—is inhabited by a Bulgarian population. *That is a population Bulgarian in race, Bulgarian in speech, Bulgarian in tradition and in ecclesiastical organization, and the Serbian population ceases a little way south of the town of Uskub, between Uskub and Veles, and from there to a considerable way south, till you approach the Greek-speaking population, it is not Serbian, but mainly Bulgarian.* All this has been left in the hands of Serbians. It was taken by the Serbs from Bulgaria in the second Balkan war of 1913. Technically, of course, it did not come necessarily within the terms of this Treaty because although Bulgaria overran it in the course of the war, still it was then in the hands of Serbia.

But it was very unfortunate, I think, that when the Powers wanted to create a stable set of conditions in the Balkans they did not rectify that injustice and remove Southern Macedonia from the rule of Serbia. I can quite understand the argument that we were not called upon to reward Bulgaria considering that Bulgaria was our enemy in the war. That is an argument the force of which I entirely admit. But there was another course, a course which according to rumor was proposed and discussed at the Conference and which indeed had the support of some Powers at the Conference. *That course was to make Southern Macedonia autonomous; to create it into a separate Principality, one can hardly call it a State, and in that way remove it from the rule of Serbia.* It need not have been united with the Bulgarian kingdom. That would have been a great deal better and would have removed a sense of injustice on the part of the population, and precluded the necessity of having provisions to safeguard the rights of minorities, provisions which, I think it will be found extremely difficult to enforce.

Unfortunately, that course was not taken and it is much to be regretted. We have created not only an Austria Irredenta in the Balkans. I am saying this in no feeling of partisanship. I think it is the duty of Englishmen to have no partnership between these countries, either as regards the Serbians, Macedonians, Greeks, Bulgarians, or Rumans. I would remind your Lordships, with regard to giving Serbia some benefit out of the war, that she has received enormous benefit out of the war. Serbia had a population of little more than 2,000,000, and, in the new State of which Serbia is the centre, with Serbs, Croats, and Slovenes, which included Bosnia, Herzegovina, Dalmatia, Croatia, and Styria, she will now have more than 8,000,000 inhabitants, and her territory will stretch all the way from Klagenfurt nearly to the coast of the Aegean. No one can say she has not come well out of the war, and I am heartily glad she has done so. Under these circumstances, *it would only have been reasonable to ask her to forego whatever claim conquest gave her on Southern Macedonia and have allowed that country to be made a small autonomous State.* Here again a disaffected population will be a weakness to Serbia. She has troubles enough in store for her without creating another trouble in a disaffected population.

If you will look back over the great European Congresses which have settled the relations of the European States since the sixteenth century, I do not think you will find any which left such elements of danger behind as the so-called settlements being made now. There was the Treaty of Westphalia which stored peace for a long time. There was the Treaty of Utrecht; the Treaty of Vienna, which kept peace in Europe for more than forty years—it was a bad settlement in many ways, but there was peace for forty years. There was the Treaty of Berlin, which kept the peace not quite for so long but for twenty years. I fear now that there may be less than twenty years before we have trouble out of this Treaty. We seem to be, in a growing crescendo, making worse settlements every time. After all, at Vienna the diplomatists had some principles. They were bad principles, but at any rate, they acted upon them.

I hope that the League of Nations may be able to rectify some of the errors that have been committed—those I have mentioned, and others which I have spared your Lordships from describing. I hope the League of Nations may be able to remove causes which now threaten future war. It is in the action of the League of Nations that there seems to lie the only hope for the future. Meanwhile, I trust that His Majesty's Government will do their best to mitigate the evils arising from these Treaties, by which, with no knowledge on our part, they have bound us; but it would be foolish to ignore or conceal the dangers which the Treaties have created. This is not the peace which the British people expected, and this is not the peace for which a distracted world is longing.[19]

5. THE BULGARIANS BETWEEN
THE TWO WORLD WARS

A. Political Effects of Bulgaria's Second Defeat

When Alexander Stamboliski (1879-1923) signed the humiliating Treaty of Neuilly in 1919, he was fully aware of the fact that peasant Bulgaria was assessed to pay $445,000,000 in reparations. In addition, Bulgaria was practically disarmed. The Treaty allowed Bulgaria an army of 33,000 men, made up of 20,000 soldiers, 10,000 gendarmes, foresters, and custom guards, and 3,000 frontier guards. This number of armed forces allowed to Bulgaria was less than the total police force of New York City. These men were to be enlisted volunteers—the officers for twenty years, the men for twelve. Bulgaria was not allowed to possess military airplanes, arsenals, arms, or munitions factories, or more than a few dozen machine guns and pieces of light artillery. Thus disarmed, Bulgaria was in no way a threat to any of her neighbors.

Meanwhile, the country was flooded with thousands of refugees from Macedonia and Thrace, whom the government, loaded with debt and with heavy reparation payments, was unable to settle. They formed a huge mobile element, easily converted to the revolutionary program of the Macedonian liberation movement or to Bolshevik agitators. Moreover, the drastic policy of nationalization pursued by the Serbian and Greek governments in Macedonia stimulated the unrest in Bulgaria, which the government was unable to control.

The Treaty of Neuilly not only sanctioned the Bucharest settlement of 1913 but it further aggravated the situation by carving more Bulgarian territory to the advantage of Serbia (henceforth Yugoslavia) and Greece.

Because of this state of affairs, Todor Alexandroff (1881-1924) resolved to revive the then temporarily dormant Internal Macedonian Revolutionary Organization (IMRO), and, as a result, raids of revolutionary bands across the frontiers became the order of the day, creating chaotic tension between Bulgaria and her neighbors.

Born in the Macedonian town of Shtip, Alexandroff completed his elementary and pre-Gymnasia education in his native town. Soon after, he enrolled in the Bulgarian Gymnasia in Skopie, where he graduated in 1897. He chose and prepared himself for the teaching profession. At the same time he was secretly enlisted in the ranks of the IMRO, in which he became a very active member. He soon became secretary for the revolutionary committee of the district of Shtip under the leadership of Mishe Razvigoroff. Not much longer after that, Alexandroff was elected as *rayon voyvoda* (district chief), and in 1911 he became a member of the Central Committee of the IMRO. In this committee, Alexandroff was the leading and dominating figure, but his work was cut short. Unfortunately, on August 31, 1924, Todor Alexandroff was treacherously assassinated. "The Macedonian leader, Todor Alexandroff," states Professor Hans Ueberberger, "belongs to an unusual type of men that live a life not of their own but for the sake of their people. Alexandroff was unassuming, modest and of cool judgment, having always at heart the greatest good of his people. Though ten years have passed since I last saw him and spoke to him, for the first and last time, I still clearly see this exceptional man standing serenely before me. With the exception of Leo Tolstoi, no one has left such an inextinguishable impression upon me as Todor Alexandroff."

Stamboliski's Peasant Party regime inaugurated a domestic policy that antagonized a great segment of the Bulgarian people. It turned the rural population against the urban, and a heavy income tax was levied on all but the peasants. Moved by hatred of the middle class and the intellectuals, he closed the University of Sofia, suspended freedom of the press, and dealt ruthlessly with all opponents of the regime. Because of such a stern policy, Stamboliski was overthrown and murdered in 1923 by a conspiracy of army officers and others affected by his class policies.

He was succeeded by Alexander Tsankoff (1879-1959), and the new government proceeded with great vigor in a policy of revenge. It inaugurated a policy of terror in Bulgaria, especially after the abortive communist insurrection in September of 1923. After the bomb outrage in the Sofia Cathedral, which killed 123 persons, the Communist Party was outlawed in Bulgaria.

Neither of the other succeeding governments—of Andrea Lapeheff (1866-1933) or of Alexander Malinoff (1867-1938), or even that of Nicholas Mushanoff—were able to normalize the political situation in Bulgaria. Until the signing of the Balkan Entente in 1934 (See Appendix

XI), continuous IMRO raids took place on the Yugoslav and Greek frontiers. Naturally, these incidents created tension between Bulgaria and her neighbors. Under the threat of the Balkan Entente, a *coup d'etat* took place in 1934, led by army officers under General Kimon Georgieff, and a dictatorship was set up. As leader of a group called "Zveno," Kimon Georgieff favored rapprochement with Yugoslavia and soon established diplomatic relations with the Soviet Union. All political parties were declared abolished, and vigorous action was taken against the Macedonians (IMRO), who were the chief opponents of the government's Yugoslav policy. As a result, IMRO's fighting units, who were operating from Bulgaria's part of Macedonia—*Pirinska Makedonia,* were disarmed, and thereby the IMRO dissolved: it ceased to function as an armed fighting organization.

In the early part of 1935, Kimon Georgieff was forced out, and his place taken by General Petko Zlateff, who was supported by Tsar Boris III. But a few months later a purely civilian cabinet was formed, headed by Andrea Tosheff, a noted historian and former minister plenipotentiary abroad. The latter was succeeded on November 23 by Georghi Kioseivanoff (1884-1960), whose policy favored Germany.

In the early part of 1936, trials were held and sentences rendered to a number of military men, including Colonel Damyan Velcheff, who was supposed to be the leader of the military party. But for all intents and purposes, Tsar Boris was master of the situation. He announced his intention of restoring a constitutional regime but proceeded very cautiously in that direction. Political parties continued to be forbidden, and steps were taken to keep the Tsankoff group in check; they had National Socialist leanings.

Finally, on January 24, 1937, a pact of friendship was concluded between Yugoslavia and Bulgaria, bringing an end to the long period of hostility and opening the way for closer relations between Bulgaria and the other Balkan states. And in the summer of 1938, an agreement with Greece, acting for the Balkan Entente, recognized Bulgaria's right to rearm. By this time, however, Bulgarian rearmament (in contravention of the treaties) had already made considerable headway, Germany supplying much of the matériel. This did not necessarily imply acceptance of German National Socialism by the Bulgarian government. The latter had already accepted an Anglo-French loan of $10,000,000 to help Bulgaria's rearmament program.

B. *Greece and Yugoslavia Violate the Minority Rights of the Bulgarians*

As soon as Greece took her share of Macedonia in 1913, she began to apply a policy of denationalization, using all kinds of coercive methods in order to assimilate the Bulgarian population of Macedonia. As was pointed out elsewere above (see Chapter XI), all Bulgarian schools and churches were closed, and the use of the Bulgarian language was prohibited. One after another, all Greek governments relentlessly attempted to Grecianize the Bulgarian Slavs under their jurisdiction.

Because of these conditions in Macedonia, the late Roger N. Baldwin, chairman of the International Committee for Political Prisoners, with headquarters in New York City, was impelled, on January 19, 1931, to address to the Greek minister in Washington the following letter:

Mr. Charalambos Simapoulos,
Minister of Greece,
Greek Embassy,
Washington, D. C.

Sir,

We thank you for transmitting our letter of November 8, 1930, to the proper authorities in Greece. We do not feel satisfied with the general statements you made, and would have preferred direct answers to the questions we asked concerning the promise of Mr. Venizelos that Bulgarian schools in Greek Macedonia would be opened if there was a request for them.

Furthermore we do not agree with your statement that "the question of the minority has been handled in Greece in the most liberal way" and "it is a fact universally admitted, that the treatment toward minorities has been for a long time eminently liberal." According to information in our possession, the Macedonian minority under Greek rule receives treatment, which is by no means liberal. Will you please give us an answer to the following charges which we shall otherwise assume to be correct?

1. Since 1918, the year when the Greeks re-occupied Macedonia, all Bulgarian schools, churches, libraries, and other Bulgarian national institutions have been closed and are still closed. Not one single Bulgarian paper or magazine has been allowed to be published. The use of the Bulgarian language at home or on the streets is strictly forbidden.
2. The Bulgarian names of villages and towns which have been in use for centuries, have been changed by a special law and corresponding Greek names substituted.
3. All Macedonians are compelled to adopt Greek endings to their given and surnames.
4. Letters addressed to Macedonians living in Macedonia by their kinsmen in the United States and Canada, are not delivered and are destroyed, or when registered are returned marked unknown, when the Bulgarian ending is used in the name of the addressee. Even the Greek newspapers have condemned their policy.
5. The protocol signed by Mr. Politis of Greece and Mr. Kalfoff of Bulgaria in 1925, which had the support of the League of Nations, was rejected and killed in the Greek Parliament. This protocol aimed at a solution of the minority question but apparently the Greek legislators preferred to disregard it.

6. The mixed claims Commission appointed by the Council of the League of Nations in 1924 to investigate the attack against the 27 inhabitants of Tarlis who had been arrested on July 26 and 27, 1924 (ten of whom were killed),[20] found Greece guilty of mistreating her minorities.[21]

We could enumerate a great many more instances tending to disprove your statement that the "treatment toward minorities has been for a long time eminently fair and liberal" but we believe the above is sufficient and would appreciate your answer.

We also wish to state that the desire of this committee is to help arrive at a favorable solution of the minority question. It does not matter what nationality is concerned, or to what state the minorities belong. We call your attention to the unhappy fate of the Bulgarians in Macedonia because we have what we believe to be uncontestable proof that they are being oppressed. This letter will be given to the press and we trust that you will forward it to the proper authorities in Greece.

Referring to the last paragraph in your letter, we would appreciate information concerning the treatment of Greek minorities outside her frontiers. We are equally interested in them.

Sincerely yours,
(Signed) ROGER N. BALDWIN

Greece has ratified a number of international agreements calling for respect for the rights of man. She has signed the Treaty of Sèvres (August 10, 1920) for the "Protection of Minorities in Greece"; she has also undertaken similar obligations under Article 46 of the Treaty of Neuilly (November 27, 1919). Greece has signed "The European Convention of Human Rights" (March 28, 1952).

Greece has signed all these agreements, but in practice she mocks them. She has also completely ignored the provisions of the Charter of the United Nations, which she has endorsed. The brutal treatment of her Bulgarian minority continues and even becomes ever more incredible. Obviously, she holds that a world consciousness does not exist, or that it has become completely deaf. Notwithstanding Greece's violation of minority rights, the government of Athens and the Greek Holy Synod do not hesitate to launch pitiful appeals and fictitious charges of oppression and "colonialism" when it is a question of defending the Cypriot Greeks, even when the latter enjoy and possess all cultural, civic, linguistic, and national rights.

Nearly fifteen years ago, the Greek authorities resorted to an entirely new and cruel method of forcible assimilation. Here are the facts, such as we find them in Greek newspapers:

The Greek newspaper *Eliniki Phoni* (Greek Voice) of Florina published, on August 8, 1959, the following announcement:

Tomorrow the inhabitants of Atrapos[22] will swear before God and the people in an official ceremony that hence forward they will promise not to speak the Slav dialect, which in the hands of Slav propagandists, has become a weapon pointed at the national consciousness of the Macedonians. The proud people of Atrapos will take an oath to speak Greek only, so that in this way they may stress their Greek origin and their Greek consciousness.

The Athens newspaper *Sphera* (Globe) in the issue of September 1, 1959, published a detailed article about the event, which took place in the village of Atrapos, accompanied also by a photograph of the moment when the villagers, mostly women and children, took "the oath before God." The article states that representatives from a hundred neighboring villages, together with many military and civil authorities, were present at the ceremony. The newspaper published also the oath as follows:

> *I do promise before God, the people, and the official state authorities, that from this day on I shall cease to speak the Slav dialect, which gives ground for misunderstanding to the enemies of our country—the Bulgarians—and that I will speak always and everywhere the official language of our fatherland, the Greek language, in which the Holy Gospel is written.*

(For a photostatic copy of this article, see Appendix XII-B).

Another Greek newspaper, *Phoni tis Kastorias*, in the issue of October 4, 1959, reprints an article from the Salonika newspaper *Makedonia* with the following introduction:

> *During the last two months, the inhabitants of some villages in north Greece (Macedonia) in official mass ceremonies proclaimed that they will cease to use the Slav dialect and that in the future they will speak only Greek. The first ceremony took place in the village of Trebeno, district of Kojani, which has, according to the census of 1952, 692 inhabitants. It was followed by other villages such as Breshcheni, Kostour district (41 inhabitants), Atrapos, Florina district (466 inhabitants), and so forth.*

(See photostatic copy, Appendix XII-C).

The above quotations are sufficient to demonstrate the nature and method of pressure applied by the Greek authorities to hasten the assimilation of the Bulgarian-speaking people in the Greek part of Macedonia.

The situation of the Bulgarian population in that part of Macedonia acquired by Serbia was even worse. Oppressive methods were immediately employed by the Serbian authorities in a grand effort to denationalize the Bulgarian population there. As pointed out elsewhere above, all Bulgarian schools and churches were closed, and a stern policy to alter the character of the Macedonian Slavs was inaugurated by the Belgrade regime. They were referred to as either "Old Serbs" or "South Serbs," meaning that no Bulgarian minority existed in aggrandized

Serbia. Discussing the minority situation there, David Lloyd George wrote:

> Strangely enough, there exists no comprehensive and systematic record, compiled by the League, as the guardian of these minority safeguards, but only scattered minutes and other documents, the bulk of them unpublished, owing to the Hush! Hush! methods of dealing with minority petitions adopted by the League Council after the first few years. Several flagrant instances of violations, whether founded or unfounded, of minority rights have been dealt with, more or less openly, by the Council, but without being definitely settled by the Council in each instance.
>
> By many authorities the most tragic instance of minority oppression in violation of the 1919 Treaty is held to be that of the 600,000 Macedonians now resident within the borders of Yugoslavia. Of this community an overwhelming majority are of Bulgarian stock and language, in other words, Bulgaro-Macedonians. It was because of this fact, at the Peace Conference, the Italian, British and American members of the New States Committee, when drafting the Yugoslav Minority Treaty, endeavored, first to secure a special local regime for this area, and, when their efforts in this direction failed in the face of Franco-Yugoslav opposition, to ensure the appointment of a resident League Commissioner. But, once more, Franco-Yugoslav opposition defeated this proposal, which was raised again, and again, and finally defeated, owing to the same cause, in 1922. Ultimately the League Council would appear to have acquiesced in the Serbian contention that no minority problem really existed in Macedonia, as the Macedonians could be regarded as overwhelmingly Serb in race and language! If any disproof were needed, one could easily turn to the troubles in this area before 1914, when there was riveted on it for years the attention of the then Concert of the Great Powers of Europe.[23]

Because of the unrestrained persecutions, imprisonment, and murders committed by the Serbian authorities in Macedonia, the International Committee for Political Prisoners, of New York City, made the following protest on May 6, 1931, to the Yugoslav minister in Washington:

His Excellency, Dr. Leonide Pitamie
Honorable Minister of Yugoslavia
Yugoslav Legation
Washington, D. C.

Sir:

The undersigned American citizens desire to enter with you their protest against the policies of the Yugoslav government directed against the Croatian and Macedonian minorities.

It is notorious that thousands of Croats and Macedonians are held in Yugoslav prisons under increditable conditions solely for their efforts to obtain national independence. Hundreds, if not thousands, have been killed. All efforts by minorities in Yugoslavia to agitate for cultural or political autonomy are treated as illegal. Complete suppression of all rights of agitation has forced these movements underground, and has led to terrorism by the oppressed as well as by the police.

Trustworthy information coming to us from those who are the victims of persecution in Macedonia, states that only in Bulgaria are the political rights of these people respected. Although they have a highly developed spirit of nationalism and demand autonomy or independence, both the Greek and Yugoslav authorities have met their demands by trying to impose on them their own national cultures.

Since 1918, all Macedonian schools and churches have been closed by the Yugoslav authorities. The use of the Bulgarian language is forbidden and even possession of a Bible printed in Bulgarian is a crime.

The inhabitants of this part of Yugoslavia are subjected to a constant reign of terror because they must support an armed force of Yugoslav soldiers. Macedonia with a population of one million inhabitants must support a police force of 11,000 whereas the rest of Yugoslavia with 12,000,000 inhabitants has only 4,000 policemen. There is also a standing army of 80,000 men in Macedonia. All civil and military offices are filled by Yugoslavs. The Macedonians are dominated by an alien and tyrannical government.

We desire to join our protest to that of Professor Albert Einstein, Heinrich Mann and the French League for the Rights of Man against the unpunished murders said to have been committed by an organization known as "Young Yugoslavia." On behalf of interested American citizens as well as on behalf of the thousands of Croats and Macedonians in the United States, we desire to enter our solemn protest against the violent repression of their nationalist movement.

Very truly yours,

(Signed) ROGER N. BALDWIN
(Signed) ARTHUR GARFIELD HAYS
(Signed) E. C. LINDEMAN

C. *The Role of the American Bulgarian Immigrants*

It was not a poetic license when the great French philosopher François M. A. Voltaire (1694-1778) said that "the more you enjoy liberty the more you like it." He spoke a fundamental truth.

Enjoying the respect and dignity of man, freedom, and democracy in the United States and Canada, the Macedono-Bulgarian citizens of the United States and Canada have been hoping for more than five decades that similar privileges would soon prevail in their country of origin—Macedonia.

In considering the Bulgarian immigration situation, one must bear in mind, however, that the Bulgarian immigrants have originated mainly from two separate Bulgarian regions. About ten percent of these American Bulgarians came from the principality, later the kingdom, of Bulgaria and ninety percent from the unredeemed province of Macedonia. The immediate cause was the Macedonian insurrection of 1903 (see

Chapter IX above) and the extensive massacres that accompanied its suppression in that year. In fact, up to 1910, most of the Bulgarian immigrants came from Macedonia. Before 1913 the Macedonian Bulgarians arrived in the United States with Turkish passports as Turkish citizens, and after the division of Macedonia in 1913, either as Greek, Serbian, or Bulgarian citizens.

The bulk of the Macedono-Bulgarian immigrants, however, came from the Vilayet of Monastir (Bitolia) of southwestern Macedonia, where the fiercest fighting took place in 1903. With the crushing of the insurrection, thousands of refugees fled to Bulgaria, and only a very few, if any, dared to pass through Greece on their way to the United States, because the Greeks had actively assisted the Turks in crushing the Ilinden insurrection.

The continued Macedonian troubles and the unsatisfactory local conditions brought new immigrants. The Balkan Wars of 1912 to 1913 produced another wave. On the other hand, when the war broke out in 1912 in the Balkans, thousands of Macedonian volunteers gathered in New York on their way to Macedonia, where they joined the Macedonian Legion of the Bulgarian army, hoping to liberate their country. But as the Bucharest Treaty did not make Macedonia free, a number of them, who found themselves under Greek and Serbian domination, again crossed the ocean.

In the early part of December 1918, the first Macedonian conference was held in Chicago, Illinois, and resolutions were passed and sent to President Woodrow Wilson while he was in Paris. In January 1919, a Memorandum was sent to the representatives at the Peace Conference in favor of freedom of Macedonia. But it was not until October 1922 that the Union of the Macedonian Patriotic Organization (MPO) was founded in Fort Wayne, Indiana. It set forth as its object to work in behalf of the subjugated and oppressed Macedonian people. At the head of the MPO is a Central Committee, elected at the annual conventions. Its headquarters is in Indianopolis, Indiana. Its official organ is the *Macedonian Tribune*, a weekly publication since 1927.

The unhappy situation that currently prevails in Greek and Yugoslav Macedonia disturbs scores of thousands of American and Canadian citizens who originated in that area. Many of those unfortunate people abroad have close relatives in the United States and Canada. Because they are gagged and cannot raise their voices in protest against their new oppressors, the task of speaking in their behalf has fallen upon the MPO Central Committee.

Articles 1 and 2 of the Constitution and Bylaws of the MPO state:

Article 1—The Macedonian immigrants of the United States and Canada, as well as their descendants, regardless of nationality,[24] religion, sex or conviction, realizing the necessity of joint organized activity for the liberation of Macedonia, formed the Macedonian Patriotic Organization with the slogan "Macedonia for the Macedonians."

Article 2—The aim of the organization is:

a. To work for strengthening the feelings of loyalty and patriotism among the immigrants and their descendants toward the respective countries where they live: the United States and Canada.

b. To strive in a legal manner for the establishment of Macedonia as an independent state unit within her historic and geographic boundaries, which should constitutionally guarantee the ethnical, religious, cultural, and political rights and liberties for all citizens.

Recognition of the MPO work is found in many works of authorities dealing with the Balkan problems. Newspapers in the United States, Canada, and abroad have published in part or in their entirety many resolutions and memoranda sent to the leading statesmen of many governments for the past fifty-three years.

Hoping that the injustices to Macedonia would be corrected after the end of the Second World War, the MPO held a special conference in Akron, Ohio, on April 23, 1944, and sent the following Memorandum to President Roosevelt:

Mr. Franklin Delano Roosevelt
President of the United States
The White House
Washington, D. C.

Mr. President:

We, the undersigned delegates of the Macedonian Patriotic Organization of the United States and Canada, the Macedonian Church Congregations, and the Macedonian Benevolent Societies in the United States, gathered at a special meeting held on April 23, 1944, at Akron, Ohio, after duly considering the current political, social, and economic development of the Balkans and especially that of Macedonia, take the liberty of presenting for your consideration certain plans which we feel will be of material benefit in bringing about a settlement of the Macedonian problem and restoring tranquility to the war-torn Balkan States.

Since we are familiar with the broad democratic principles of our country—the United States of America, and enjoying the rights of citizenship, education, linguistic and religious freedom, we recognize that we must, especially in time of war, stand united under the flag of the United States to defend all those sacred principles of freedom which it symbolizes. Only those who have lived under subjugation of tyrannical regimes can completely appreciate the full value of freedom and democracy.

You may be assured, Mr. President, of our unreserved and all embracing loyalty to our adopted country. You may count on us to do our share in all undertakings which the United States Government may plan, to bring about a quick victory over the darkness of Fascism, Nazism, and Nipponism. We are aware of the fact that your concern at the present and that of your administrative aids, is to win the war against the destructive forces of Fascism. In this fateful time, we realize the tremendous responsibility which rests upon your shoulders, but we think that if we may point out that which touches the Americans of Macedonian descent during these historical events, we shall fulfill a humanitarian duty to our brethren abroad, who were divided and subjugated by the regimes of three neighboring countries—Yugoslavia, Bulgaria and Greece, and now live under Hitler's Nazi rule.

Mr. President, in the heart of the Balkan Peninsula, there is a country which bears its ancient name—Macedonia. There live approximately three million inhabitants who speak several Balkan languages, namely: Bulgarian, Greek, Albanian, Turkish, Jewish, Serbian, and Rumanian. The fact that there are in Macedonia ethnic elements from each of several neighboring countries, has given these neighbors of Macedonia a pretext upon which to base their claims for domination of Macedonia.

In order that we may recall to your mind the fact that the Macedonian Question is not of recent origin but has occupied the minds of European statesmen ever since 1878, we present a brief resume of certain historical crises in the long drawn out turmoil that has characterized the Balkan problems as an "active volcano." Article 23 of the Treaty of Berlin (July 1878) provided for an autonomous status of Macedonia. The Turkish government had ignored the provisions of this Article. No efforts were made by the Great Powers responsible for the Berlin settlements, to compel Turkey to live up to her pledges.

The Turkish maladministration of Macedonia is a historic record. To protect themselves, the Macedonian people organized secretly (1893-1903), and began a desperate struggle against the aggressive regime of the Sultan. The Macedonians rose in arms (August 2, 1903) to fight for freedom against the forces of Abdul Hamid. The "Illinden" Insurrection (as it is historically known) was violently crushed. The Turkish army began a systematic and a well-planned destructive campaign, by burning villages, killing the peasants, and ravaging everything in its path.

The European Powers were now greatly concerned. After the "Illinden" Insurrection, Francis Joseph of Austria and Nicholas II of Russia drew up the "Murzteg Program" (September 30, 1903), and placed Macedonia under European supervision, thus recognizing that area as a geographic unit and political problem. Because of power politics, the "Murzteg" scheme failed to alleviate the economic and political situation of the Macedonian people. In 1908, King Edward VII of England and Nicholas II of Russia met at Reval and proposed a program for Macedonian autonomy. To avoid further European interference in the internal affairs of Turkey, the "Young Turks" overthrew the Sultan (1908) and proclaimed a Constitution. This maneuver thwarted the corrective efforts of the Great Powers. Macedonia was once more intrusted to the Turks . . . now the "Young Turks."

The new Ottoman regime inaugurated a policy of denationalization and suppression of the Christian subject races in Macedonia. The outcome of this Turkish policy was the formation of the Balkan League, and the war upon Turkey (October 18, 1912). The Turks were defeated, but the Treaty of Bucharest (August 10, 1913) that followed the Balkan wars divided Macedonia among Serbia, Greece, and Bulgaria. It became evident that Macedonia only changed rulers while the political, social, and economic conditions of the people became even more desperate. The Report of the *Carnegie International Commission of Inquiry into the Balkan Wars* contains enough evidence to show the extent of Macedonia's tragedy.

For more than three years during World War I, Macedonia became the theatre of war. Some of the most decisive battles, that determined more or less the outcome of the war, were fought there. The Paris Peace Treaties did not change the fate of Macedonia. Nevertheless, the Macedonian people sincerely believed in President Wilson's Fourteen Points, which provided, among other things, self-determination of peoples. Unfortunately, the Wilsonian principles were not applied to Macedonia. Judging from the Diary of the American representative, David Hunter Miller, the Committee on new States—which also drafted the so-called Minority Treaties —for the first time considered the Macedonian question, on July 10, 1919. Italy stood for the autonomy of Macedonia, while England proposed that the League of Nations should appoint its own representative in Macedonia, to see that the rights of the people there were respected. France, on the other hand, was against both of these proposals. The English diplomat, Mr. Tyrell, suggested to Mr. Miller, the American representative, that the United States should become the League of Nations' mandatory power in Macedonia. But according to Miller, the discussion about Macedonia terminated when, on August 1, 1919, the Committee on New States received a letter from Nicola Pashich, the Serbian Prime Minister, stating that the Macedonians are Serbian and that they would be treated as the rest of the Serbians in the then enlarged Serbian State. By granting Pashich's demand, the Paris Peace Conference thus sanctioned the Bucharest Treaty of 1913, and Macedonia remained divided between Serbia, Greece and Bulgaria.

We who enjoy the fruits of American democracy and the American Way of Life, can readily see how some of the European powers instead of Europeanizing the Balkans, in effect Balkanized themselves. This unfortunate situation did not improve or alleviate the conditions in the southeastern part of Europe. Macedonia, which occupied a central geographic position in the Balkans, became an arena of rivalry among the bigger Powers—a situation with tragic consequences.

Unfortunately, the Paris settlement of 1919 did not contribute to the tranquility of the Balkans. The Balkan peoples continued to live under an atmosphere of intrigues, suspicion, and hatred, which destroyed every possible avenue of understanding for their mutual political and economic prosperity. After World War I they remained as an active volcano ready to erupt at any moment, thus endangering the world peace. Such were the conditions there at the end of the last war, because the first World War was won on the battlefield but the peace which was to follow was lost on the diplomatic front. The hope of the world then was in the realization of Wilson's Fourteen Points. But these points as a basis of peace were quickly obliterated under the pressure of the political atmosphere of bargaining and compromises.

Everyone feels now that new and important historical events are to occur which will shape our civilization for many years to come. The political change which is expected to take place in southeastern Europe will definitely concern Macedonia. The Macedonian population is now subjected to dual military regimes—that of Nazi Germany, and the satellite pro-Nazi Bulgaria. It cannot raise its voice either to express its wishes or defend its interests.

Mindful of the recent past as well as the present, we are convinced that the best solution of the Macedonian question would be for it to cease to be a vital political and state problem of every Balkan state. The Macedonian problem must cease to be a football in the politics of the Balkans. Our motto in this case is: *Macedonia for the Macedonians.* We believe the only just and equitable solution of the thorny problem of the Balkans is *the creation of an independent state of Macedonia in which all the ethnic groups will enjoy equal rights and obligations.* Aside from this, an independent Macedonia which will develop economically, politically, and culturally, may join a Balkan Federation or Confederation.

After the Allied Nations' victory, there will be peace. At the coming peace conference, Macedonia will try once more for the right to live under the principles of liberty which the world has learned from America. We believe that the Americans want Macadonia to have the liberties enumerated in the Four Freedoms and the Atlantic Charter. The application of Points Two and Three of the Roosevelt-Churchill declaration of August 14, 1941 (The Atlantic Charter) for the settlement on the Balkans will make it possible for the Macedonians to attain their long cherished geographic and political unity, independence, and self-government. The Macedonians then hope that their sufferings will end when Macedonia is permitted independence and self-government, in consonance with the principles of justice, liberty and humanity.

We have the honor to be,

> Yours very respectfully,
>
> Central Committee of the Macedonian Patriotic Organization of the United States and Canada.[25]

SELECT BIBLIOGRAPHY

Anastasoff, C., *The Tragic Peninsula*, St. Louis, Mo., 1938, pp. 255-310.

Anastasoff, C., *The Case for an Autonomous Macedonia* (A Symposium), St. Louis, Mo., 1945, pp. 11-203.

Cristowe, Stoyan, *Heros and Assassins*, New York, 1935, pp. 121-202.

Dami, Professor Aldo, *Fatalités Bulgares*, Genève, 1945, p. 41-66.

Derjavin, Professor N. C., *Bulgarsko-Srbskite Vzaimni Otnoshenia i Makedonskia Vopros* (The Bulgaro-Serbian Mutual Relations and the Macedonian Question), Sofia, 1916, pp. 55-140.

Documents and Materials on the History of the Bulgarian People, Sofia, 1969, pp. 11-503. *Note:* This volume of more than 500 pages published by the Bulgarian Academy of Sciences contains 347 documents from the Middle Ages to the present time, showing that the Macedonian Slavs are part of the Bulgarian people.

Grogan, Lady, *The Life of J. D. Bourchier*, London, 1925, pp. 106-118; 155-172.

Hosch, Edgar, *The Balkans: A Short History from Greek Times to Present Day*, New York, 1972, pp. 138-167.

Lamouche, Colonel Léon, *Les Bulgares en Macedoine dans les Confins Occidentaux et en Thrace*, Paris, 1931, pp. 11-65.

Lybyer, Professor Albert H., *Macedonia at the Paris Peace Conference*, Indianapolis, Indiana, 1944, pp. 4-24.

Radoslavoff, Dr. Vasil, *Bulgaria i Svetovnata Kriza* (Bulgaria and the World Crisis), Sofia, 1923, pp. 78-130; see also the treaty of alliance of Bulgaria with Germany and Austria-Hungary, of September 6, 1915, and the secret annex to it, pp. 131-134; 142-217.

Roucek, Dr. Joseph S., *The Politics of the Balkans*, New York, 1939, pp. 118-162.

Stephanove, Constantine, *The Bulgarians and Anglo-Saxondom*, Berne, 1919, pp. 267-366.
Sugar, Peter F. and Lederer, Ivo J. (Editors), *Nationalism in Eastern Europe*, University of Washington Press, Seattle and London, 1969, pp. 93-165.

NOTES

1. For a revealing story, see Henri Pozzi, *supra*, Chapter XI, n. 33, pp. 248-267.
2. With the declaration of war on Serbia, the latter moved its government along with the diplomatic corps from Belgrade to Nish, near the Bulgarian border. In a speech delivered by N. Pashich in the Skupshtina (Parliament) on August 12, 1915, he said: "We have chosen the most suitable moment which could have happened for the realization of our ideals by provoking Austro-Hungary to declare war on us." See Radoslavoff, *supra*, Chapter XI, n. 15, p. 89. *Note:* Dr. V. Radoslavoff was the Bulgarian premier during most of World War I. He was succeeded by Alexander Malinoff on June 18, 1918.
3. Before 1914, Italy had been a member of the Triple Alliance. But at the outbreak of World War I, it remained neutral. The Treaty of Alliance, Italy declared, did not bind it to assist the Central Powers in an aggressive war, and Italy regarded them as the aggressors.
4. Romania's sympathy was with the Central Powers, but Ion Bratianu, the premier and foreign minister (January 14, 1914-February 6, 1918), made a better deal with the Allies. Transylvania, part of Bukovina, and Banat were promised to Romania in addition to the retention of Bulgarian Dobrudja.
5. Dr. Radoslavoff, *supra*, Chapter XI, n. 15, p. 91.
6. *Ibid*, p. 92 and pp. 105-107.
7. Years later, Romania was compelled by Adolf Hitler to cede southern Dobrudja to Bulgaria. See William L. Shirer, *The Rise and Fall of the Third Reich*, Greenwich, Connecticut, 1960, p. 1050 footnote.
8. Winston S. Churchill, *The World Crisis*, New York, 1949, pp. 517-518.
9. Dr. Vasil Radoslavoff, *supra*, Chapter XI, n. 15, p. 130. See also the text of the treaty (in Bulgarian) on pp. 131-134.
10. *Ibid.*, p. 134.
11. *Ibid.*, p. 147. See also the text of the note (in Bulgarian), pp. 146-147.
12. On January 22, 1917, President Wilson addressed the Senate in a remarkable speech, stating the conditions on which America would "give its formal and solemn adherence to a league of peace." "The present war must be ended," he said, "but it must be ended by terms that would create a peace worth guaranteeing and preserving, a "peace representing security by organized major force of mankind." "First of all," he said, "*it must be a peace without victory.*"
13. For this secret negotiation and the text of letters and terms for peace agreement, see Dr. Radoslavoff, *supra*, Chapter XI, n. 15, pp. 152-167.
14. In this speech, among other things, Wilson said: "Victory would mean a peace forced upon the loser; a victor's terms imposed upon the vanquished. It would be accepted in humiliation under duress, at an intolerable sacrifice and would leave a sting, a resentment, a bitter memory upon which terms of peace would rest not permanently but only as upon quicksand. Only a peace between equals can last."
15. *Infra*, Appendix X.

16. In 1929, King Alexander suspended the Constitution of June 21, 1921, established a dictatorship, and renamed the country "Yugoslavia."
17. James D. Bourchier was Balkan correspondent for the London *Times* from 1888 to 1920. Four wars were fought on Balkan soil, and many insurrections, which brought with them all the horrors of war, broke out one after the other in Crete, Greece, Albania, and Macedonia, while he was Balkan correspondent. None knew more of the inner history of the Balkan wars than did Bourchier. A great friend of the Greek and Bulgarian people, Bourchier was instrumental in bringing about the Balkan Alliance in 1912 against the Turks. As a great expert on Balkan problems, Bourchier was never able to reconcile himself with the Bucharest settlement (August 1913), which left Macedonia divided between Serbia, Greece, and Bulgaria. In articles to the *Times* as well as to the *Fortnightly, Quarterly, Contemporary,* and other reviews, he constantly pleaded for a just Balkan settlement. During 1919-1920, he sojourned in Paris and made great efforts to win the diplomats and friends on behalf of the Macedonian people.
18. All italics in this quotation are ours. See also C. Anastasoff, *The Case for an Autonomous Macedonia* (a symposium), St. Louis, Missouri, 1945, pp. 64-67.
19. All italics in the above speech are ours. *Note:* The late James Bryce was Professor of Civil Law at Oxford; member of Parliament, 1880; Under Secretary of State for Foreign Affairs, 1886; Chancellor of the Duchy of Lancaster (with seat in Cabinet), 1892; President of the Board of Trade, 1894; chairman of Royal Commission on Secondary Education, 1894; member of the Senate of London University, 1893; one of the British members of the International Tribunal at The Hague; His Majesty's Ambassador Extraordinary and Plenipotentiary at Washington, 1907-1913; one of the British representatives of the Hague Court; author of *The Flora of The Island of Aran,* 1859; *Report on the Condition of Education in Lancashire,* 1867; *The Trade Marks Registration Act, 1877; The American Commonwealth* (2 Vols.), 1888; *Modern Democracies,* 1921; and numerous other works. See also C. Anastasoff, *supra,* n. 18, pp. 171-176.
20. Enquiry into the Tarlis events by Commandant Marcel De Roover and Lieutenant Colonel A. Corfe, members of the Commission appointed by the Council of the League of Nations.
21. See the *Memoir* of the National Commitee of the Union of the Macedonian Brotherhoods in Bulgaria, presented to the League of Nations in Geneva on September 18, 1924.
22. *Atrapos* is the new Greek name of an old Bulgarian village known to the people of the Florina district for centuries as *Krapeshina.* For a photostatic copy of this announcement, see Appendix XII-A.
23. David Lloyd George, *Memoirs of the Peace Conference,* Vol. II, p. 899 and pp. 901-902.
24. Besides the Bulgarians, there are other national groups, such as Romanians, Turks, and Greeks, who were immigrants from Macedonia. If they acquiesce in the MPO Bylaws they too are eligible for membership in the organization.
25. This document was signed by the Central Committee of the MPO of the United States and Canada, representatives from eleven Church Congregations of the United States and Canada, representatives of twenty-eight local MPO Chapters, and by representatives of fifteen Macedonian Benevolent Societies in the United States and Canada. This document may also be found in C. Anastasoff, *supra,* n. 18, pp. 200-203.

CHAPTER XIII

THE BULGARIANS IN THE SECOND WORLD WAR (1941-1944)

Modern nationalism is based on psychosociological factors: feelings or emotions, common traditions and memories of the past, and common ideals and hope for the future; it is a feeling of unity with people of one's own race and language, whether they are fellow citizens or subjects of a foreign state. Like any other national group of people having these characteristics, the Bulgarians have aspired to achieve national unity within their ethnographic limits. For the attainment of this objective, Bulgaria had, since its liberation in 1878, formed and directed its domestic and foreign policy.[1]

1. *FACTORS CONTRIBUTING TO THE SECOND WORLD WAR*

When, in October 1925, the Locarno Pacts were drawn up by representatives of Germany, France, Great Britain, Belgium, and Italy, the world was assured that they would not attack one another and that differences were to be submitted to arbitration through the League of Nations or a special conciliation commission.

In 1927, to strengthen the peace-keeping machinery of the League of Nations, Aristide Briand, the French minister of foreign affairs, suggested to the American secretary of state, Frank B. Kellogg, that their two nations enter an agreement to outlaw war. As a result, the Briand-Kellogg Pact of 1928 was formulated. Article I of the pact states: "The High Contracting Parties . . . condemn recourse to war for the solution of international controversies and renounce it as an instrument of national policy in their relation with one another." Article II of the same pact states: "Settlement of all disputes of whatever nature which may arise among them never to be sought except by pacific means." Article III provides for ratification by the signatory powers and permits all other powers to adhere to the treaty at any time.

By means of such multilateral treaties, war was renounced as an "instrument of national policy" by the Great Powers of Central and Western Europe, the United States, and Japan. Thus, the outlawry of war was universally proclaimed![2]

After World War I, the conditions for general peace were far from favorable. The period from 1919 to 1939 proved to be only a twenty years' truce. The ratification of the Treaty of Versailles by the German Reichstag and by the principal Allied nations and its formal proclamation at Versailles had automatically brought the League of Nations into existence. The latter, however, was greatly handicapped from the start because the United States was not a member. The League had no authority to enforce its decisions. The war, moreover, had left fierce hatreds in its aftermath, and the Paris peace settlement was fully satisfactory to no one. It had not been possible to apply the principle of self-determination to all the nations of Europe, and a number of national minorities had been left under foreign rule. Such was, for example, the case of the 1,250,000 Bulgarian minority incorporated in Bulgaria's neighboring states. As was amply pointed out above, their hardship was real and intolerable.

The great world depression of 1929 to 1940 undermined the foundation of the peace machinery set up after the First World War. Unemployment, heavy reparations, inflation, and unrest strengthened the grip of the dictators of Germany, Italy, and Japan. Each dictator claimed that prosperity would be restored if his nation could expand its territory, that is, gain *Lebensraum* (living space). The depression caused each of the industrial nations to try to advance its own economic interests regardless of what happened to other nations. This policy of economic nationalism made the depression worse.

Divided and weakened, the democratic powers did not take measures to check the aggressive moves of the dictators—Adolf Hitler and Benito Mussolini—until it was too late. Instead, France and England adopted a policy of "appeasement." Believing that the dictators' ambitions could be satisfied, Edouard Daladier, the premier of France, and Neville Chamberlain, the British prime minister, made a pilgrimage to Munich in September 1938 to award Hitler with the Sudetenland and later all of Czechoslovakia, notwithstanding the fact that Hitler had violated the Treaty of Versailles by occupying the Rhineland in 1936 and by effecting the *Anschluss* with Austria in 1938.

The German attack on Poland on September 1, 1939, which started the Second World War, and the subsequent German victories for the first three years of the war, were greatly reflected in Bulgaria's foreign policy. Although neutral, the Bulgarian government in the fall of 1940 allowed German units under the guise of "economic," "tourism," and other types of "commissions" and "groups" to visit the country, thereby preparing the way for German military penetration.

Preparing for war, Hitler's Germany increased its economic and political influence in Bulgaria. Under the regime of Prime Minister Bogdan Filoff, supposedly neutral, Bulgaria fully cooperated with Germany. Although the Germans could not pay for them, Bulgaria continued to make deliveries of foodstuffs and other goods to Germany. Three years prior to the beginning of the war, Bulgaria's exports to Germany increased about one-fifth, and during 1939 they reached nearly 68 percent. At the same time, imports of Bulgaria from Germany reached 65.5 percent.[3]

2. BULGARIA ENTERS THE
SECOND WORLD WAR (1941)

The Bulgarian government joined the Axis Powers under the pressure of Hitler's Germany and, perhaps, under equal pressure from the sentiment of Bulgarian nationalists who felt that this was the opportunity to regain their lost territories by virtue of the Bucharest (1913) and Neuilly (1919) treaties. The German Balkan campaign of the spring of 1941 virtually fulfilled Bulgaria's territorial demands by occupying Macedonia and Thrace, restoring to Bulgaria an access to the Aegean Sea. The Bulgarian government entered into a secret agreement with Germany, and on February 28 German army units crossed the Danube from Romania, and through Bulgaria occupied Greece. The next day, March 1, 1941, Bulgaria joined the so-called Tripartate Pact. Once again, however, Bulgaria made a wrong guess as to which side of the warring groups would really be the victor. Unfortunatey, she lost again.

Bulgaria was neutral in regard to the Soviet Union, but she was at war with Great Britain and the United States.

Air raids on Sofia began in November 1943 and were repeated in December and the first months of 1944. This helped to precipitate a political crisis and stimulate the growth of pro-Russian sentiment, which has always been strong. Public opinion favored abandonment of the Germans and the making of peace, but the government could not bring itself to face a possibility of full-scale German occupation or run the risk of losing the recently occupied Bulgarian lands of Macedonia and Thrace. Meanwhile, the Russians demanded that the Bulgarians reopen the Soviet Union consulate at Varna and permit new ones at Bourgas and Russe so that they could see for themselves what the Germans were doing in those parts. The Germans, on the other hand, demanded that Bulgaria break diplomatic relations with the Soviet Union.[4]

Finding themselves in such a precarious situation, the Bulgarian regimes began to fall one after the other. On May 21, 1944, the Dobri Bozhilov (1884-1945) government succumbed, and a new government was formed by Ivan Bagrianav (1891-1945). The latter was also compelled to resign. Soon afterward, the Bulgarian government sent envoys to negotiate with the allies in Cairo, Egypt, on August 30, 1944. Stoicho Moshanoff, the president of the *Sobranie* (National Assembly), was chosen to head the negotiating delegation. Here they negotiated with the British and American representatives, but not of course with the representatives of the Soviet Union, because Bulgaria was not at war with Russia.[5]

On August 29, 1943, King Boris III of Bulgaria suddenly died and was succeeded by his six-year-old son as Simeon II. A council of regency, including the young King's uncle, Prince Kiril (Cyril), the statesman Bogdan Filoff, and General Nikola Micheff, was established and approved on September 9 by the Bulgarian parliament.

While the terms were under discussion, the Regency, on September 2, replaced the Bagrianav government. Moving definitely in the direction of the Western allies, they now installed a cabinet headed by Kostatin V. Mouraviev (1893-1965), a nephew of Alexander Stamboliski. Mouraviev's government consisted chiefly of democrats and "right wing" Agrarians. The new regime thus represented the "tolerated opposition" and contained no element of the Fatherland Front resistance or left-wingers. It was this that apparently doomed it. The Soviet Union was manifestly unwilling to allow moderates to run Bulgaria, or the Western allies to dictate the peace terms.

On September 5, 1944, the Soviet Union suddenly declared war on Bulgaria. The Mouraviev government at once asked for armistice terms and within three days freed all political prisoners and all Allied prisoners, dissolved the political police, and declared war on Germany. But Russian troops marched into the country on September 8. Under such favorable conditions the final stroke for the overthrow of the Mouraviev government occurred during the night of September 8 and 9, 1944.[6] The next day the Fatherland Front staged a coup, ousted the Mouraviev government, and installed a new cabinet, which in turn installed a new Regency. All ministers who had served since 1941 were arrested.

The new cabinet was headed by Kimon Georgiev (1882-1969), one of the founders of the *Zveno*. One of the unusual circumstances was that after the coup of September 9, along with the National Democratic Party, the Workers Party participated in the first Fatherland Front government with an equal number of representatives—four persons—together with the Agrarian Union and Zveno. Besides these parties, the Social Democratic Party participated, with two representatives and one independent member. Although in the minority, the Workers Party played a leading role in the government.

In the end, however, the Allies all insisted that Bulgaria accede to the original requirement and evacuate the Greek and Yugoslav territory. On this basis, the Bulgarian armistice was finally signed in Moscow on October 28, 1944. It provided for an "Allied Control Commission" to function under the "general direction of the Allied (Soviet) High Command."[7]

"The question of the Bulgarian elections, as required by the Yalta declaration of February 1945," writes Professor Wolff, "now preoccupied the Communists and they stepped up their efforts to establish their own political dominance. They demanded a common Fatherland Front list of candidates for the future assembly with a prearranged ratio of seats to be allotted to the various parties making up the coalition. Needless to say, the Communists were planning to make sure that they themselves would obtain at least half the seats in the new assembly. The Agrarians and Zveno both wanted to have their own separate lists."[8]

Because of the unsettled international situation of Bulgaria and the pending solution of a number of internal problems, the coalition government did not take immediate action after September 9 "of expropriating private property and the means of production."[9]

Soon after the war, the government of the Fatherland Front arranged for a parliamentary election in August 1945. For political reasons the projected election was postponed for about three months. On the eve of the election, Georgi M. Dimitrov returned to Bulgaria. There was no particular reason for one to doubt that the Fatherland Front would emerge victorious. Of the 4,501,035 registered voters for this election, 3,855,097 of whom voted, 3,397,672, or 88.18 percent, cast their ballots for the Fatherland Front.[10] One must bear in mind that at this time Bulgaria was virtually occupied by the army of the Soviet Union.

3. *THE PEOPLE'S REPUBLIC OF BULGARIA—*
END OF THE MONARCHY

During the summer of 1946, the National Assembly approved a law for a referendum to do away with the Monarchy in Bulgaria. After the death of King Boris in 1943, the Regency ruled for Simeon II (born in 1937). And after September 9, 1944, the Regency was retained under new regents. The referendum took place on September 8, 1946, and as a result 92.2 percent of the people voted the proclamation of Bulgaria as a Republic and only 4.2 percent for the retention of the Monarchy. As a result, on September 15, 1946, the National Assembly proclaimed the People's Republic of Bulgaria. The *ad hoc* president of the Republic was Vasil Kolarov, who had returned to Bulgaria after September 9, 1944.[11]

On December 4, 1947, a new constitution was adopted by the Grand National Assembly, modeled after that of the Soviet Union. Confirming the national democratic government, the constitution provided for the national sovereignty of Bulgaria and the building up of a Socialist society.

At the fifth congress of the Workers Party, which was held in December 1948, the Party was renamed the Bulgarian Communist Party. At the same time a law was proclaimed creating a five-year plan patterned after that of the Soviet Union. But to achieve its goal, the National Democratic government (the Communist Party) assumed the "dictatorship of the proletariat."[12]

4. THE SOCIALIST MOVEMENT IN BULGARIA

Of all the Balkan states, the Socialist Democratic movement found the most fertile soil for its growth and development in Bulgaria. This was not because the country had attained a highly industrialized system but simply because there had emerged in the later part of the nineteenth century a number of individuals influenced by the teachings of Karl Marx (1818-1883), Friedrich Engels (1820-1895), Georgi V. Plekhanov (1856-1918), Karl Kautsky (1854-1938), and others.

In Bulgaria, however, there has never existed a mass of proletarians to warrant a social revolution. The country was and in fact is mainly agricultural—a peasant country. With the liberation of the country in 1878, the Turkish feudalism had also vanished. Few in number were the Bulgarians that owned any considerable acreage of land.

The founder of the Socialist revolutionary movement in Bulgaria was Dimiter N. Blagoeff, affectionately referred to as "Dyado" (Grandfather). Along with the names of the Macedonian Bulgarians precursors of Bulgaria's renaissance, such as Father Paissy, the Miladinoff Brothers— Dimiter and Konstantin—Grigor Perlicheff and others, Dimiter Blagoeff made a tremendous contribution to the Socialist revolutionary movement not only in Bulgaria but also in other countries.

Blagoeff was born in the village of Zagonichani, district of Kostour, Macedonia, in that part of the country that since 1913 has been under Greek rule. He received his Bulgarian elementary education in his native village, and at the age of fifteen he enrolled in the Bulgarian school at Constantinople. Later, he went to Bulgaria and studied in the Gabrovo and Stara-Zagora High School (Gymnazia). Influenced by the Bucharest Bulgarian Central Committee, he joined in 1876 the movement for Bulgaria's political liberation and participated in the Gabrovo revolt of 1876. Subsequently, he went to Odessa and enrolled in the seminary and a year later in the local university. In 1880, he went to Petrograd (Leningrad) and in 1884 enrolled in the Petrograd University. While there, he was greatly influenced by the works of Nicholas Chernishevski (1828-1889) and the socialism of Ferdinand Lassalle (1825-1864).

Under the *nom de plume* of "Peter Egrov," he was first to establish a labor newspaper, *Raboche* (Worker), in the capital of the Russian Tsar. In 1885 he was deported to Constantinople and later went to Sofia. There he began to write for the *Makedonski Glas* (The Voice of Macedonia), advocating a Balkan federation. He later founded his own journal, *Svremeny Pokazatel* (Contemporary Index), around which the first Bulgarian socialist group was organized. He advocated broad social revolutionary reforms. In 1887, Blagoeff was appointed to teach at Shumen and the following year (1889) at Vidin, but there as principal of the local Gymnazia (high school).

While in Vidin he founded the first teachers organization and edited *Vestnik na ouchitelskoto drouzhestvo* (Journal of the Teachers Association). Because of his association as co-editor of *Rabotnik*, he was dismissed from his principalship at Vidin in 1892, but later he was again appointed to teach at the Plovdiv Gymnazia (1894-1897). In 1884 he founded and edited the periodical *Dyalo* (Cause) and in 1897 began to publish in its place the well-known periodical *Novo Vreme* (New Time).

Blagoeff was founder and leader of the Bulgarian Democratic Party (part of which later became the Bulgarian Communist Party) and served in the Sobranie for more than two decades. An outstanding Marxist, he popularized the teachings of Socialism in Bulgaria. His most important works are *Economicheskato razvitie na Bulgaria* (The Economic Development of Bulgaria), Varna, 1903; *Sotsialismat i rabotnicheskia vpros* (Socialism and The Workers' Question); *Dialekticheskia materialism i teoriata na poznanieto*, 1903-1904 (The Dialectical Materialism and the Theory of Knowledge); *Prinos kum istoriata na sotsialisma v Bulgaria* (A Contribution to the History of Socialism in Bulgaria), Sofia, 1906; and other works.[13]

In Bulgaria, therefore, Socialism dates back to the last decade of the nineteenth century. Founded in 1891, the Socialist Democratic Party soon found itself split between two factions, the *Tesni* ("narrow") and the *Shiroki* ("broad"). The *Tesni*, whose leader was Blagoeff, were the staunch "anti-reformist" Marxists and opposed any cooperation with non-working class parties, while the *Shiroki* took the opposite position. Their leader was Yanko Ivan Sakazoff (1860-1941), who had attained his higher education in Russia, Germany, England, and France. He was the editor of a number of publications and author of *Tsarism ili demo-kratsia* (Royalty or Democracy), Sofia, 1905; *Bulgaria v svoyata istoria* (Bulgaria in Its History), Sofia, 1917; and other works.

In 1903 however, the *Tesni* split away from the *Shiroki*. After the First World War (1919), they broke with the Second International, joined the Comintern, which was set up in Moscow and, as pointed out above, took the name of Bulgarian Communist Party, but now under the leadership of Georgi M. Dimitrov and Vasil P. Kolarov.

Because of a series of events that took place in 1923 (armed revolts) and 1925 (the bombing of the Sofia Cathedral), the regime of Professor Alexander Tzankoff (1879-1959) banned the Bulgarian Communist Party, which, as a result lost its representatives in the *Sobranie*. Dimitrov and Kolarov both fled to Russia, where they took high office in the Comintern (Communist International). Favorable publicity came to the Communists during the celebrated Reichstag fire trial in Germany in 1933, when G. Dimitrov himself became a kind of a hero of the anti-Nazi world by his courtroom defiance of Hermann Goering, Hitler's right-hand man.

In accordance with the Communist policy, the leadership in Bulgaria sought to rally all those opposed to the Germans into a popular-front organization called *Otechestven Front* (Fatherland Front), formed in 1942, in addition to the Social Democrats and Zveno, all of them legal parties but hopelessly unable to assume leadership. From the first, the Workers Party[14] took the lead of the Fatherland Front, and eventually the other parties approved of their anti-German resistance. The old Democratic Party was strongly anti-German, and its leader, Nikola Mushanoff, led the "tolerated opposition" in the Sobranie.

5. THE RECENT SOFIA-BELGRADE DISPUTE OVER MACEDONIA

With the establishment of the Communist regime in Bulgaria, Sofia's foreign policy has been to maintain peace and good-neighborly relations with its surrounding Balkan states. This policy was particularly followed more for the cause of internationalism than for national interests. Such, however, was not the case with that of the Belgrade regime.

In conformity with Josip Broz Tito's policy for an integral Federal Yugoslavia, the partisan's Sobranie (Assembly) of the National Liberation of Macedonia met for the first time in Ilinden, August 2, 1944, and the formation of a "Macedonian People's Republic" within Federal Yugoslavia was proclaimed. This was a radical departure from the policy of Belgrade's royal regime, as has been pointed out above.

But with the establishment of Tito's regime in Yugoslavia after the Second World War, the Serbo-Communists quickly accepted the advice of the Serbian professor, Stoyan Novakovich, by applying the term "Macedonianism" in regard to the newly proclaimed People's Republic of Macedonia. By using the geographic name of the country rather than the ethnographic, Belgrade, along with their satraps in Skopie, sponsored the idea of artificially creating a "Macedonian nationality" and a "Macedonian language," the latter based on a local Macedono-Bulgarian dialect spoken near the Serbian frontier. The new Macedonian language, however, is filled with Serbian words and Serbisms. It has been designed to hasten the Serbianization of the Macedonian Bulgarian Slavs. To achieve this objective, no Bulgarian books, newspapers, or other publications are permitted to enter the People's Republic of Macedonia. Moreover, the use of the Bulgarian language is strictly forbidden in Yugoslav Macedonia. To create a "Macedonian culture" and "literature," the Skopie academicians are flagrantly falsifying the history of the Bulgarian people by substituting the word *Macedonian* in places where the word *Bulgarian* occurs.

For more than twenty years the Sofia regime and, of course, the Bulgarian people had to swallow the pill. The anti-Bulgarian propaganda from Belgrade and Skopie made its impact in Sofia. As a result, the Institute of History at the Bulgarian Academy of Sciences published in 1968 a brochure exposing the falsifications and false accusations by the Skopie Serbo-Communists.[15] Although the Bulgarian Communist regime projects no territorial claims against Yugoslavia, it nevertheless refuses to acknowledge the existence of a "Macedonian nationality" or of a distinct "Macedonian language." Ethnically and culturally, the Macedonian Slavs are a part and parcel of those in Bulgaria proper.[16] Although it has been claimed by the occupiers of the country that the Macedonian question has been solved, it constantly appears on the Balkan scene, and with greater intensity.

6. BULGARIAN LITERATURE AND
SCIENTIFIC PROGRESS PRIOR TO 1944

Almost ninety percent of the Bulgarian creative writers and poets were well established long before the advent of the Communist regime in 1944. Although there are gifted men of letters in Bulgaria today, they are still overshadowed by the old ones. (See also Chapter VI, section 10.)

During the first half of the last century the new Bulgarian poetry made its appearance. The first gifted poets were Naiden Gerov (1813-1900) and Dobri Chintoulov (1821-1866). In 1845 Naiden Gerov wrote "Stoyan and Rada," the first Bulgarian poem of some artistic value. Dobri Chintoulov wrote rebel songs that became quite popular among Bulgarian youth at the time of the national liberation movement. Georgi Rakovsky (1821-1867), the father of the national revolutionary ideology, also wrote revolutionary poems. His poem "Mountain Traveler," published in 1857, was an appeal to armed struggle against Turkish rule.

The father of Bulgarian belles-lettres was Vassil Droumev (1841-1901), with his short novel *Hapless Family*, published in 1860 and describing the epoch of the Kirdjali unrest. Another fairly well-known writer of that time was Ilia Bluskov (1839-1913), who wrote a number of patriotic narratives, the most popular of which were *Hopeless Stanka* (1866), describing the Tartar cruelties in the Crimean War (1854-1856), and *Ill-fated Krustinka* (1870).

The first Bulgarian dramas also appeared at that time. The outstanding playwright was Vassil Droumev, whose *Ivanko, the Slayer of Assen* (1872) is generally considered to be the best Bulgarian drama written before the country's liberation and even today is successfully staged.

The creator of the new Bulgarian militant and lyrical poetry was Petko R. Slaveikov (1827-1895), who wrote lyrical and satirical social works, epics, and patriotic poems such as "Boika Voyvoda," "Krakra Pernishki," and "The Source of the White-legged," as well as fables. No other Bulgarian writer prior to the liberation of the country has produced such a variety of literary work.

Another prominent writer and poet of that period was Luben Karavelov (1837-1879), still better known as a leading political figure and journalist in the national revolutionary struggle. His was the first to introduce critical realism into Bulgarian literature. His *Bulgarians of Yore* (1867), *Mamma's Boy* (1875), *Is Your Fate to Blame* (1867), and other books give a true description of the life of the Bulgarian people.

Bulgarian poetry attained its as yet unsurpassed apogee as regards ideas, artistic form, and style in the eternally young poems of Hristo Botev (1848-1876), the inspired lord of the national revolution. His poetry bears the stamp of utter originality. Botev's verses, reflecting the most beautiful traditions of the Bulgarian revolutionary lyric and Haiduk epos, are unsurpassed in their natural charm, revolutionary pathos, forcefulness, and music. The ballad "Hadji Dimiter"[17] is a wonderful song of freedom, which might well be considered one of the masterpieces of world literature. While still very young, Botev perished with arms in hand in the revolutionary struggle for the freedom of the Bulgarian people.

Another writer and prominent figure in the national revolutionary struggle for freedom was Zakhari Stoyanov (1851-1889). Stoyanov wrote many articles and pamphlets, as well as biographies and memoirs, the most important of which is *Notes on Bulgarian Uprisings* (1884-1892). It places its author in the front ranks of Bulgarian literature. Zakhari Stoyanov was the first Bulgarian biographer of such great figures in the national revolutionary movement as Hristo Botev, Vasil Levsky, and Luben Karavelov.

The national revolutionary struggle also had a strong impact on the development of the popular writer, Ivan Vazov (1850-1921). Next to Botev, Vazov ranks highest in Bulgarian literature. His collections of poems, *Banner and Fiddle* (1876), *Bulgaria's Woes* (1877), and *Rescue* (1878), express the ideas and aspirations of the Bulgarian emigration in Romania. Ivan Vazov is the patriarch of Bulgarian literature. His works —poetry, prose, drama—reflect the joys and sorrows, the hopes and sufferings of the Bulgarian people, as well as many important events in Bulgaria's medieval and modern history. Vazov's *Under the Yoke*, the first Bulgarian novel, gives a broad picture of the April 20, 1876, uprising, its preparation and actual breaking out. Vazov is the greatest of Bulgarian prose writers, a realist narrator, many of whose works have been translated.[18]

In the nineties, a whole crop of young promising writers came to the fore, including Todor Vlaikov (1865-1943), Mikhailaki Georgiev (1854-1916), Stoyan Mihailovsky (1856-1927), Aleko Konstantinov (1863-1897), Anton Shrashimirov (1872-1937), Tsanko Tserkovsky (1869-1926), and others.[19]

In his classical *Bai Ganyu* and in his feuilletons, Aleko Konstantinov showed himself as one of the outstanding and most typical representatives of critical realism in Bulgarian literature, a stern critic of the social system in the nineties and one of the loftiest figures in Bulgarian public life.

The satirist Georgi Stamatov (1869-1942) was a staunch critic of the shortcomings of city life and intelligentsia from the turn of the century to the First World War.

One of the most prominent Bulgarian representatives of critical realism was Elin Pelin (1878-1949). A classic in Bulgarian literature, the best painter of village life, a truly democratic and humanist writer, Elin Pelin depicts the woes of village life, the peasant's resentment toward the middle social class, had the disintegration of the patriarchal order under the impact capitalism.

The plight of the peasants, however, found a powerful emotional echo in the lyrical work of P. K. Yavorov (1877-1914) during the first period of his literary activity, while he still stood close to the people and contemporary social and political problems. Yavorov is one of the classics of Bulgarian verse. During the second period of his literary activity he embraced individualistic positions. In his collection of poems, *Sleeplessness*, he introduced symbolism into Bulgarian literature. Yavorov also wrote two dramas—*Nestled in the Vitosha* and *When the Thunder Strikes*, the first psychological dramas written by a Bulgarian.

Pencho P. Slaveikoff (1866-1912), the son of Petko Slavaikoff and the Bulgarian who came close to winning the Nobel Prize in literature, produced a good many realist works, imbued with ideas and emotions close to the people. His masterpiece, *The Bloody Song*, portrays folklife and the heroism and revolutionary upsurge of the Bulgarian people in their liberation struggle against Turkish domination.

Poets prominent among the symbolists are Todor Trayanov (1882-1945), Nikolai Liliev (1885-1960), the master of Bulgarian poetic prose, Emanuel Popdimitrov (1887-1943), Geo Milev (1895-1925), Lyudmil Stoyanov (1888-   ), Hristo Yasenov (1889-1925), and Dimiter Boyad-jiev (1880-1911).

Yordan Yovkov (1880-1937) was of the greatest Bulgarian short-story tellers. A humanist and a poet of village life, he depicts with profound sympathy the unremitting toil of the poor peasant and the hopes and sufferings of Bulgarians under Turkish rule. He drew artistic and realistic pictures of the Balkan wars, portraying the heroism of the Bulgarian soldier with forcefulness and enthusiasm. He also wrote *Boryana, Albena*, and other popular sketches on Bulgarian rustic life.

Along with the creative writers and poets, a number of Bulgarian scholars have attained international reputation in their respective disciplines. Some of them are V. N. Zlatarsky (1886-1935), P. Nikov (1884-1938), and P. Moutafchiev (1883-1943) in history; Stefan S. Mladenov (1880-1963), Benyo Tsonev (1863-1937), Lubomir Miletich (1863-1937), and Jordan N. Ivanov (1872-1947) in linguistics and comparative phil-ology; Krusto I. Myatev (1892-   ) in archeology; and Alexander M. Balabanov (1879-1930), Dimiter Dechev (1877-1958), and Konstantin S. Gulbov (1892-   ) and others in classical and modern languages and literature.

In the field of natural sciences, the most significant work is that of the mathematicians Nikola D. Obreshkov (1896-1963), Kiril G. Popov (1870-1927), and Lubomir N. Chakalov (1886-1963); the physicists Peter B. Penchev (1873-1956) and Georgi S. Nadjakov (1896-   ); the chemists Z. Karaangov, D. Balarev, and Assen Zlatarov (1885-1936); the biologists Methody A. Popov (1881-1954) and Hristo S. Daskalov (1903-   ); in medicine, Alexander Mankovsky (1868-1946), Vasil D. Molov (1875-1938), Konstantin N. Chilov (1898-1955), and others.[20]

Bulgarian scientific thought has come into its own and is making remarkable progress. The combination of theory and practice has become the guiding principle of Bulgarian scientists.

7. BULGARIAN CULTURAL, LITERARY, AND SCIENTIFIC DEVELOPMENT SINCE 1944

A. Education

The Bulgarian school system has been reorganized during the past several decades in accordance with the science and practice of Soviet pedagogy.

A unified school system was introduced with one and the same program for all schools, regardless of whether they are urban or rural, Bulgarian, or national minority schools. A complete system of secondary school education, from the first to the eleventh grade was established and placed under the direction of the Ministry of Education. Elementary education is obligatory from seven to fourteen years of age.

The new school programs set aside more hours to Bulgarian, mathematics, foreign languages, biology, and history. The school material has been elaborated with a view to ensuring school children full mastery of the subject learned and a "genuine communist education."[21]

Wherever there existed no school prior to 1944, elementary schools have been opened. As of 1955, there were 6,560 schools for compulsory elementary education. In the past, the Turkish minority had only 404 schools, which it supported out of its own funds; now 712 new schools have been added, and all are supported by the state. Eleven Armenian schools and 28 Gypsy schools have also been opened; these two national minorities had no schools of their own in the past.

Compulsory elementary education has been successfully carried out in practice. Although in the past more than 100,000 school-age children did not go to school, now 99.5 percent of all school-age children are attending school. This figure includes Turkish children as well, only 13.9 percent of whom used to go to school in the past. There is no locality without a school.[22]

Much has been done to stamp out illiteracy among adults. The heritage left from the past included hundreds of thousands of illiterates. "As a result of a systematic campaign on a voluntary basis, by the end of 1953 there was hardly an illiterate person below the age of fifty in Bulgaria."[23]

In every county a forest-climatic school has been opened for children predisposed toward illness. There are also schools for foreign languages—Russian, French, German, and English. Musically and artistically gifted children have their own boarding school and a ballet school. Scores of music schools have been opened throughout the country.

B. *Literature and Science*

Under the newly formed Fatherland Front and after September 9, 1944, a new era began in the development of Bulgarian culture, literature, and science. It may well be characterized as the unfolding of a deeper and all-round bloom of education, science, and literature. The new socialist culture was built on the principle of the proletarian ideology. In quality, it is new—national in form and socialistic in culture. Its aim is to unify the masses of the people in the effort of building a socialistic society in Bulgaria. Although new in quality, the socialist culture is being built and developing along the cultural attainment of the Bulgarian people prior to the advent of the Communist regime.

From the beginning of the Fatherland Front regime, the Communists, through their Permanent Secretary General to the Ministry of Education, made several purges of the teaching personnel of all universities and schools. The campaign was carried out under the plausible pretext of a "de-Nazification" of the educational institutions. Similar purges were made against university students suspected of entertaining "anti-democratic" ideas or simply because their parents were politically unreliable. A number of trials were staged in the "people's tribunals," against some intellectuals, like journalists, authors, scientists, artists, painters, actors, publishers, and professors, for their prewar or wartime authoritarian-like cultural activities.[24]

Along with these persecutions, the newly established Bulgarian regime attempted to win over some of the bourgeois intellectuals whom they have chosen to qualify as "progressive." Offering certain privileges and extremely generous salaries, the Communist regime continued to employ a large number of the former scientists, professors, academicians, doctors, architects, engineers, artists, actors, and so on. "Some of the intellectuals were even admitted as members of the Party, like the rector of the Sofia State University, Professor Georgi Nadzhakow, a former pro-German sympathizer, or the old outstanding dramatic actor, Krustyu Sarafov, brother of the late Macedonian revolutionary, Boris Sarafov."[25]

The Bulgarian Communist Party, however, won over most of the old intelligentsia and technical cadres to the construction of socialism. A great majority of the Bulgarian intelligentsia takes an ever-increasing part in the construction of a new life in the country. At the same time, the Party and government devote much attention to developing a new intelligentsia loyal to the Marxist-Leninist tenets.[26]

The economic backwardness of Bulgaria prior to the advent of the Communist regime did not necessarily require the building of and widespread opening of technical scientific institutes. Under the new regime, however, emphasis was placed on diversified higher education, not only in the social sciences but also in the natural sciences. Along with the University of Sofia and the other higher commercial-economic institutes, a number of higher technical and agricultural institutes have been built in the first two decades of the new regime. Thousands of construction, mining and mechanical engineers, architects, chemists, and agronomists have graduated from these institutes. For the needs of the continuous industrial and agricultural development of the country, scores of research institutes were established to help in the building of reservoirs and factories and in the production of new varieties of agricultural crops.

The research work in the higher institutes of learning has also been placed on a new basis. Here, too, the tie-up between theory and practice has been established. Postgraduate courses have been introduced for the training of young scientists.

The Bulgarian Academy of Science is the supreme scientific institute in Bulgaria. It traces its beginnings to the Bulgarian Literary Society, founded in 1869 in the Romanian city of Braila by Bulgarians living abroad, primarily in Romania and Bessarabia. Even before that attempts had been made by educated Bulgarians within or outside the Turkish Empire to found an institute for the dissemination of knowledge and education among the Bulgarian people. Its founders were the historian Marin Drinov (1838-1906), Vassil Drumev (1838-1901), and the Prague graduate Vassil Stoyanov.[27] After Bulgaria's liberation (1878), this society was transferred to Sofia and in 1911 renamed the Bulgarian Academy of Science.

An important stage in the development of the Bulgarian Academy of Science *(Bulgarskata Akademia na Naoukite)*, or, as it is popularly known by its Bulgarian initials, *BAN*, was the reorganization carried out in 1949. Instead of three departments—historico-philosophical, physico-mathematical, and juridical—there are now seven departments:

1. physico-mathematical and technical sciences
2. geological-geographical and chemical sciences
3. biological and medical sciences
4. juridical and economic sciences
5. historical-archeological and philosophical sciences
6. linguistic, ethnography, and literature
7. fine arts and culture.

Although prior to 1944 only one institute was attached to the *BAN*— the Institute of Bulgarian Vocabulary (now Institute for Bulgarian Language)—now there are 31 scientific institutes, with 935 research scientists. And in 1961, an academy of agricultural sciences was established, comprising 24 research institutes, with a working force of 974 scientists.

Significant scientific research work is being carried on in other higher educational institutions, whose number in 1939 was only five but which had grown to 26 in 1964. The number of students during the same periods increased from 10,200 to 82,300, while the instructional personnel increased from 453 to 5,430.[28]

The scientific workers at the *BAN* institutes and other research institutes are making a distinct contribution in solving or clarifying major problems in industry, farming, transport, the tapping of natural resources, and public health. Bulgarian scientists take part in the building of dams, in the planning and implementing of electric power, in the creation of forest and field shelter belts, in soil and water ameliorations. They work on the creation of new improved crop varieties and farm animals. Through their efforts many commodities formerly imported are now locally produced with local raw materials.

Bulgarian scientists already have some noteworthy achievements to their credit. Findings on the stimulation of life processes by the late Professor Methodi Popov (1881-1954) constitute a remarkable contribution to science in the field of crop yields. His researchers were met with great interest in the world of science.

Bulgarian chemists have worked out a new method for obtaining benzylalcohol, benzylaldehyde, and vanillin.

Professor Dimo Velev (1903-   ) and other technologists have made a valuable contribution to the electrification and hydromelioration of the country.

Particularly valuable are the researches of Bulgarian geologists on subsoil wealth. The geomorphological studies made by Professors Atanas Beshkov (1896-   ) and Z. Gulubov in the Dobrudja and North Bulgaria are hardly less important.

Bulgarian biologists have found a method for reducing the nicotine in tobacco. The botanists have made considerable advances in establishing definite types of meadow and pasture plants, which is most important for solving the country's forage problem.

Professor Yordan Milkovsky (1898-   ) and other plant-breeders have created new cotton plants, while Professors Hristo Daskalov (1903-   ) and Nikola Kolev have created new tomato varieties and other vegetable crops.

The microbiologists have prepared a special vaccine for avoiding abortions in farm animals. They have obtained a special preparation—bistrin—which is widely applied in the canning industry.

Medical workers have investigated trachoma (Professor Dr. K. Peshev), endemic syphilis (Professor Dr. Tsevetan Kristov, 1898-   ), pellagra (Professor Dr. Konstantine Chilov, 1898-1955), illnesses of the lungs and blood vessels, and so on.

There are considerable achievements in Bulgarian linguistics. Professor Vladimir Georgiev (1908-   ), widely known abroad, has succeeded in deciphering Cretan-Mycenaean and Etruscan inscriptions. His works *Problems of the Minoan Language* and *Deciphering Etruscan Inscriptions* have been translated.

The works of a number of prominent young Bulgarian writers, poets, and journalists may well be characterized as anti-war or anti-capitalism. The first and most gifted creator of "socialist realism" in Bulgarian literature was Hristo Smirnensky (1898-1923). He is one of the most gifted representatives of revolutionary socialist poetry. In Smirnensky's poetry and literary works is reflected the turning point in the life of the Bulgarian people after the First World War. He is considered as the "trumpeter of building up of the socialist revolution in Bulgaria."[29] Following the tradition of Smirnensky, an array of poets and writers came to the fore. Most prominent among these are Hristo Radevsky (1903-   ), Mladen Issaev (1907-   ), Kroum Penev (1901-   ), Kamen Zidarov (1902-   ), Nikola Lankov (1902-1965), Angel Todorov (1906-   ), Pantelei Mateev (1898-1957), Georgi Djagarov (1925-   ), and others.

A good representative of this group of Bulgarian poets and writers is Georgi Djagarov, currently president of the Bulgarian Writers Union. Djagarov's poems are concise, passionate, and replete with love for his people and country. He is also a talented and skillful playwright of some standing in Bulgarian literature. His drama *The Public Prosecutor* was the first bold civic voice against the Cult of the Personality period. It has been translated into English and was eventually staged with great success in London. He is also the author of the following books of poetry: *My Poems* (1954), *Lyrics* (1956), and *A Minute of Silence* (1958), and dramas *The Doors Are Closing* (1960) and *Tomorrow is Another Day* (1962).

A large-scale literary work is the historical trilogy *The Iron Candle* (1960), *The Bells of Prespa* (1960), and *Ilinden* (1957), by Dimiter Talev (1898-1966), dealing with the Bulgarian Renaissance and the national liberation of his native Macedonia. Talev is also the author of the three volumes of the *Bulgarian Tsar Samuil* (1968), *I Hear Your Voices* (1969), and other works.[30] Talev's trilogy and many other Bulgarian works are translated into English, French, and German.[31]

C. *Bulgarian Fine Art*

A large number of wood carvings have been preserved from the period of Bulgarian feudalism, the most interesting of which are to be found in St. Nicolas Church in Ohrid (twelfth and thirteenth centuries), the old cloister of Rila Monastery (fourteenth century), Slepchensky Monastery (fifteenth century), and elsewhere. Professional craftsmanship is successfully combined here with creative imagination.

Even after they were overrun by the Turks (1393) the Bulgarian people, drawing on their centuries-old cultural heritage, continued to develop their arts. During these years of foreign domination, the applied arts, connected with various trades such as carpentry, weaving, pottery, goldsmithing, and others went farthest ahead. Fresco painting also received a new impetus. Out of it there gradually emerged secular art—portrait and landscape painting, historic compositions, and so on. Pioneers of the new trend in Bulgarian painting were Dimiter Dobrovich (1816-1905), Stanislav Dospevsky (1823-1878), Hristo Tsokev (1847-1883), and Nicolai Pavlovich (1835-1894).

After the country's liberation from the Turkish yoke, Bulgarian painting began to develop freely and up to the First World War achieved considerable successes. The foremost painters of that period were Ivan Murkvichka (1856-1938), Yaroslav Veshin (1860-1915), Anton Mitov (1862-1930), Hristo Stanchev (1870-1950), Tseno Todorov (1877-1953), and Stefan Ivanov (1875-1951). They all continued the sound realistic traditions of paintings.

After the First World War a number of Bulgarian painters and sculptors adapted their art to the requirements of the time of various formalistic trends. This does not apply, however, to the foremost among them, such as Vladimir Dimitrov—the Master (1882-1960), Boris Angheloushev (1902-1962), Stoyan Venev (1904-1958), Ivan Founev (1900-1961), and Andrei Nikolov (1878-1959).[32]

The twenty-five years following the Second World War were characterized by an unprecedented creative activity and the appearance of new tendencies and aspects in the cultural history of Bulgaria.

The new Union of the Bulgarian Artists was founded in 1944. The main line in the art of that time was determined by the masters belonging to the generation of the 1930s: Vladimir Dimitrov—the Master, Iliya Petrov (1903-   ), Dechko Ouzounov (1899-   ), Nenko Balkansky (1907-   ), Tsanko Lavrenov (1896-1963), Vassil Stoilov (1904-   ), Zlatyu Boyadjiev (1903-   ), and Stoyan Sotirov (1903-   ) in painting; Andrei Nikolov, Ivan Lazarov, Marko Markov (1889-1962), Ivan Founev, and Nikolai Shmirgela (1911-   ), in sculpture; Vassil Zahariev (1895-   ) and Vesselin Staykov (1906-   ), in graphic art; and Alexander Zhendov (1901-1953), Boris Angeloushev, Iliya Beshkov and Stoyan Venev, in the cartoons.

Giving new meaning to Bulgaria's rich artistic heritage and its blending with the modern outlook has been the task of several artistic generations. All this had led to a remarkable diversity of artistic output of new and original talents.

An important phenomenon of the last decade is the revival of folk arts and crafts.

Contemporary Bulgarian imitative arts have been represented at many exhibitions abroad. Among them were the retrospective exhibitions in Athens and Ankara in 1965, the exhibition at Galérie Charpentier in Paris in 1963, and the exhibition at Villa Hugel in Essen in the same year.[33]

D. *The Bulgarian Theater*

In the years following Bulgaria's liberation from Ottoman domination in 1878, the classical works of Russian and West European dramatists were staged in Bulgarian theaters. Bulgarian plays by Ivan Vazov, P. K. Yavorov, Anton Shrashimirov, and S. L. Kostov began to appear at the turn of the twentieth century. Their works treated some of the most crucial problems of their period, recalling Bulgaria's glorious past, the forgotten ideals of the National Revival, and the public's responsibility for the future of the nation.

The Bulgarian theater emerged and grew to maturity under the beneficial influence of the Russian realistic school. The rich experience and traditions of the Moscow and Petersburg theaters were introduced in Bulgaria through the work of Bulgaria's outstanding actors—Krustu Sarafov, Adriana Boudevska, and Atanas Kirchev.

Prior to the Second World War, Bulgaria had several state-run professional theaters, one opera company, and a few touring theatrical companies. Today, there are thirty-two drama theaters, eight puppet theaters, and five opera houses. Nine of the theaters are in Sofia. Modern theaters housed in beautiful buildings now exist in Blagoevgrad, Pazardjik, Pernik, Shoumen, Gabrovo, Stara Zagora, and Ruse.

The Krustyu Sarafov Higher Institute of Theatrical Art in Sofia, the only one of its kind in the Balkan Peninsula, trains actors, producers, and drama critics.

For outstanding artistic achievements of lasting importance, Bulgarian actors are granted national recognition in the form of two distinctions: the titles of People's Artist and Honored Artist. Those distinctions have been awarded to 188 actors in the past twenty-five years.[34]

The group of the older and most renowned masters of the stage, include the internationally famous operatic bassos Boris Christoof and Nikola Ghiaurov, as well as Vladimir Trendafilov, Olga Kircheva, Zorka Yordanova, Marta Popova, Rouzha Delcheva, Irina Tasseva, Hristo Brumbarov, and Nikola Nikolov. These have been joined by a host of

talented actors of the middle and younger generations: Georgi Kaloyan-
chev, Stefan Getsov, Apostol Karamitev, Ivan Kondov, Professor K.
Mirski, Lyubomir Kabakchiev, Rachko Yabandjiev, Kiril Yanev, Nikolai
Lyutskanov, Hristo Hristov, Raina Kabaivanska (internationally famous
soprano), Lilyan Bareva, Margarita Lilova, Julia Wiener, Dimiter
Petkov, and many others.[35]

E. *Music*

Bulgarian folk music literature is exceedingly rich and diversified.
Through the centuries, the people have produced their own music,
which has distinctive features of its own. Bulgarian folk music is characterized chiefly by its singsong elements and a rich melodic line, the
rhythmic metric structure, and the fact that it is predominantly in the
minor key. The folk dance music *Horo* and *Rachenitsa* is original and
vivacious and frequently irregular in beat.

In their songs through the ages, the Bulgarian people have expressed
their joys and sorrows, hopes and struggles for a better life. This explains
the unusual thematic variety of the Bulgarian folk song: harvesting,
sowing, shepherd's songs, and other songs connected with everyday work;
wedding, mourning, and other songs connected with everyday life;
Haiduk, epic, recitative, and other songs connected with the fight for
freedom.

Bulgarian folk songs are sung primarily without accompaniment.
Instrumental performances are usually a separate show—without songs.
The best-known popular instruments are the *gaida* (bagpipe), the
gadoulka (rebec), the *kaval* (wooden flute), and the *tamboura* (lute).

After Bulgaria's liberation, the first Bulgarian composers came forward, their works much influenced by folk music. Among the first generation of composers stand out the names of Emanuel Manolov
(1860-1902), one of the musical pioneers; Angel Boukoreshtliev (1870-
1950), a collector of folk songs; Dobri Hristov (1875-1941), the most
gifted of that generation; Panayot Pipkov (1871-1942); and George
Atanasov (1882-1941), the first composer of serious Bulgarian operas.[36]

After the First World War, a new generation of composers sprang
up who refashioned all major musical styles. The most prominent among
them is Pancho Vladigerov (1899-   ), a talented musician and composer with rich orchestral technique and a profound knowledge of the
Bulgarian folk song, from which he draws his motifs. His best known
works are: *Bulgarian Vardar Rhapsody, Jewish Rhapsody, Bulgarian
Suite, May Symphony,* four piano concertos, and a violin concerto, as
well as many symphonic, chamber music, and solo compositions.
Vladigerov is the first and foremost Bulgarian symphonic composer, and
his fame has long since spread beyond the confines of his country. The

Bulgarian folk song, as reincarnated in his compositions, has been interpreted by world-famous artists in the concert halls of Moscow, Paris, Vienna, New York, Berlin, Prague, Warsaw, and other international music centers.

The composer Petko Stainov (1896-   ) belongs to the same generation. Without making direct use of folk motifs, Stainov's works are deeply inspired by the folk song, stamping him as a realist close to the people. He has chiefly produced symphonies—the suite *Thracian Dances*, the symphonic poem *Thrace, A Legend*, the suite *A Tale*, two symphonies, and other, minor compositions.

Among the composers who came to the fore in the thirties and forties the names of Lyndomir Pipkov (1904-   ), Philip Koutev (1903-   ), Vesselin Stoyanov (1902-   ), Assen Karastoyanov (1893-   ), Marin Goleminov (1908-   ), Parashkev Hadjiev (1912-   ), and Alexander Raichev (1922-   ) stand out.

A proud accomplishment of the Bulgarian musical world has been the creation of the State Folk Song and Folk Dance Ensemble under Philip Koutev. Its visit in 1955 to London, Paris, Belgium, and Holland was a resounding success.

Bulgarians have a penchant for the opera. The first attempt to open an opera house was made in 1891 in Sofia. Today, in addition to the Sofia Opera, there are operas in Plovdiv, Varna, Ruse, and Stara Zagora, as well as three amateur opera ensembles.

Symphonic orchestras have also made considerable progress. In addition to the State Philharmonic Orchestra in Sofia, there is a state radio symphonic orchestra and symphonic orchestras in Plovdiv, Varna, Ruse, Bourgas, Dimitrovo, Pleven, Razgrad, Vidin, and Shumen. This large number of symphonic orchestras has made it possible to popularize symphonic music throughout the country.[37]

F. *Resources, Industries, and Government*

Bulgaria is located on the Black Sea and has an area of 42,729 square miles, with a population of 8,370,000 (1970), or approximately the size of the state of Ohio. It is bounded by Romania, Turkey, Greece, and Yugoslavia. The Balkan Mountains stretch across the center of the country, with the Danubian Plain in the north and the Rhodope Mountains and Thracian Plain in the south.

The principal crops are wheat, fruit, rye, barley, oats, corn, potatoes, and tobacco. Fruit is exported. Agriculture claims a large percentage of the population, but the country is being industrialized under the national planned economy, which emphasizes electric power, coal, chemicals, machinery, metals, textiles, building materials, fur, leather goods, and oil. A socialized economy embraces 98 percent of industry,

95 percent of agriculture, and 99 percent of retail trade. Rich oil and gas fields were discovered near Pleven in 1964.

New economic reforms were launched in January 1966 to decentralize planning and management. Industrial output rose 12.2 percent in 1966. Exports were also up. About 80 percent of trade is with nations of the Communist bloc. Exports include maize, wheat, vegetables, chemicals, silver, textiles, hides, tobacco, rose attar, lead, zinc, cement, and machinery. About 2,000,000 tourists now visit Bulgaria each year.

The religion of the country is Eastern Orthodox. The National Church is disestablished and may not have schools or hospitals. In Bulgaria today there are about 750,000 Moslems.

The constitution of May 1971, modeled after that of the Soviet Union, provides that the unicameral National Assembly shall be the supreme organ of government. The National Assembly is elected for a four-year term and chooses a premier and a state council, whose president is the head of the state.

On June 27, 1971, an election was held under the new constitution adopted at the Communist Party congress in May. The present premier is Todor Zhivkov, also the first secretary of the Communist Party. The election has confirmed the present foreign policy of the present leadership under Secretary General Todor Zhivkov.

Bulgaria, however, strives to maintain friendly relations with her neighboring countries.

In addition to that with the Soviet Union, currently Bulgaria has trade agreements with the following countries: Italy, Norway, the German Democratic Republic, Czechoslovakia, Romania, Hungary, Yugoslavia, Albania, the United Arab Republic, the People's Republic of the Congo, and Sri Lanka.[38]

SELECT BIBLIOGRAPHY

Andriotes, Nic. P., *The Confederate State of Skopje and Its Language*, Athens, 1957, pp. 4-57.
Barker, Elizabeth, *Macedonia: Its Place in Balkan Power Politics*, London, 1950, pp. 78-129.
Kofos, Evangelos, *Nationalism and Communism in Macedonia*, Salonika, 1964, pp. 212-222.
Kosev, D., Hristov, Hr., Angelov, D., *Kratka Istoria na Bulgaria* (A Brief History of Bulgaria), Sofia, 1969, pp. 264-273; 286-292; 299-363.
Makedonskia Vupros, Istorico-Politicheska Spravka (The Macedonian Question, A Historical-Political Verification), published by the Institute of History at the Bulgarian Academy of Sciences, Sofia, 1968, pp. 3-39.
People's Republic of Bulgaria, Sofia, 1955, pp. 75-80.
Shirer, William L., *The Rise and Fall of the Third Reich*, Greenwich, Connecticut, 1960, pp. 1040-1060.

Taylor, A. J. P., *A History of the First World War (1914-1919)*, New York, 1966, pp. 9-182.
Wolff, Robert Lee, *The Balkans in Our Time*, New York, 1967, pp. 191-497.

NOTES

1. C. Anastasoff, "Bulgaria's National Struggles." *The Annals of The American Academy of Political and Social Science*, March 1944, p. 101.
2. C. Anastasoff, *The Revisionist*, Vol. I, No. 2, February 1934, p. 2. *Note: The Revisionist* was published in St. Louis, Missouri, on behalf of the European minorities, and its editor in chief was Christ Anastasoff.
3. D. Kosev, et al., *supra*, Chapter IV, n. 6, p. 265.
4. R. L. Wolff, *The Balkans in Our Time*, New York, 1967, p. 245.
5. Dr. Christo Ognjanoff, *Bulgarien*, Nuremberg, 1967, pp. 163-166.
6. D. Kosev, *et al.*, *supra*, Chapter IV, n. 6, pp. 282-284.
7. R. L. Wolff, *supra*, n. 4, p. 248.
8. *Ibid.*, p. 295.
9. *Ibid.*
10. D. Kosev, *et al.*, *supra*, Chapter IV, n. 6, p. 295.
11. *Ibid.*, p. 296.
12. *Ibid.*, p. 302.
13. Christ Anastasoff, "Dimiter Blagoeff" in the *Encyclopaedia Slavonic*, edited by Dr. Joseph S. Rouchek, New York, 1949, p. 102; Professors Hristo Hristov and K. Vasilev, *Dimitar Blagoev* (Biographical Sketch), Sofia, 1956.
14. After 1927 the banned Bulgarian Communist Party began to function under the name of Workers Party.
15. *Makedonskia Vupros, Istorico-Politicheska Spravka* (The Macedonian Question, A Historical-Political Verification), Sofia, 1968, pp. 3-39. *Note:* This brochure was published by the Bulgarian Academy of Sciences.
16. See the article "Ne Hvurlyate Boumeranga, Toy se Vurshta" (Do Not Throw the Boomerang, It Returns to the Thrower), published in the official organ of the Bulgarian Communist Party, *Rabotnichesko Delo*, No. 234, August 21, 1968; See also the article "Koii Izopichava Istinata?" (Who Falsifies the Truth?), published in *Pirinsko Delo*, No. 93, August 10, 1968.
17. For an English translation of this ballad, see *Balkania* quarterly magazine Vol. IV, No. 4, October 1970, pp. 21-22. For the Bulgarian text and also accompanied by an English translation, see *Slaviani*, Vol. XXV, No. 1, January 1969, p. 12.
18. Professor Assen Nicoloff, *Bulgarian Folklore and Fine Literature—A Selected Bio-Bibliography*, Cleveland, 1971, pp. 28-29.
19. *People's Republic of Bulgaria*, Sofia, 1955, pp. 75-80. This booklet of 114 pages is published by the Committee for Friendship and Cultural Relations with Foreign Countries. It gives, among other things, information on every aspect of Bulgaria's cultural development.
20. D. Kosev, *et al.*, *supra*, Chapter IV, n. 6, pp. 353-361.
21. *People's Republic of Bulgaria*, *supra*, n. 18, p. 69.
22. *Ibid.*, p. 70.
23. *Ibid.*, p. 71.

24. See Professor Nicola Dolapchiev's *Bulgaria: The Making of a Satellite* (1944-1953), *Foyer Bulgare* Bulgarian Historical Institute (abroad), 1971, pp. 192-201.
25. *Ibid.*, pp. 192-193.
26. D. Kosev, *et al.*, *supra*, Chapter IV, n. 6, pp. 353-354.
27. *People's Republic of Bulgaria, supra*, n. 18, p. 72.
28. D. Kosev, *et al.*, *supra*, Chapter IV, n. 6, p. 354.
29. *Ibid.*, p. 289.
30. *Ibid.*, pp. 286-292; 353-361.
31. *People's Republic of Bulgaria, supra*, n. 18, pp. 69-87; Assen Nicoloff, *Bulgarian Folklore and Fine Literature—A Selected Bio-Bibliography*, Cleveland, 1971, p. 77.
32. *People's Republic of Bulgaria, supra*, n. 18, pp. 92-93.
33. *Slaviani*, Vol. XXVI, No. 2, February 1970, p. 20; *Ibid.*, Vol. XXVII, No. 1, January 1971, p. 14; D. Kosev, *et al.*, *supra*, Chapter IV, n. 6, pp. 291-292.
34. *Slaviani*, Vol. XXVI, No. 10, October 1970, p. 21.
35. *Ibid.*, p. 21; *People's Republic of Bulgaria, supra*, n. 18, pp. 96-98.
36. *Ibid.*, p. 94.
37. *Ibid.*, pp. 94-95.
38. *Economic News of Bulgaria*, Sofia, February 1971, No. 2 (published by the Bulgarian Chamber of Commerce).

APPENDICES

THE RUSSIAN SCHEME OF REFORMS FOR MACEDONIA OF MARCH 26, 1908

Projet russe de reformes en Macedoine du 26 mars 1908
Saint-Pétersbourg le 13 (26) mars 1908.

Le gouvernement impérial, ayant reçu une communication du Cabinet de Londres en date du 3 mars courant (n. s.) au sujet des réformes à introduire dans les trois vilayets macédoniens, croit devoir y répondre de la manière suivante:

La question des améliorations à apporter à l'administration des vilayets de Salonique, de Monastir et d'Uskub, qui fait l'objet de la communication susmentionnée, continue à préoccuper vivement le gouvernement impérial.

Nous nous associons entièrement aux considérations exposées par sir E. Grey quant à la responsabilité morale qui incombe aux grandes puissances dans leurs efforts pour alléger les souffrances des populations qui habitent ces provinces de l'Empire ottoman, pour y rétablir l'ordre, pour y assurer la sécurité de la vie et de la propriété, et pour éviter ainsi un danger pour la paix.

On ne saurait non plus nier que la situation actuelle dans les provinces susnommées exige d'urgence, ainsi que le constate sir Edward Grey, l'application de mesures énergiques.

En vue de cette circonstance et après avoir soumis à une étude détaillée chacune des questions que traite la communication britannique, nous estimons que les suggestions y contenues peuvent dès à présent servir de base à une discussion entre les Cabinets intéressés.

Le premier point auquel touche la communication de sir Edward Grey est celui de la gendarmerie.

A notre regret, nous ne saurions reconnaitre que les considérations formulées par Son Excellence puissent écarter les objections exposées dans notre aide-mémoire du 15 (28) janvier 1908, concernant cette question.

Toutefois le gouvernement impérial est pret à admettre que des améliorations doivent être introduites dans l'organisation et dans les attributions actuelles de la force publique des trois vilayets. Ces améliorations devraient porter en premier lieu sur la situation du général réorganisateur de la gendarmerie.

Ce général devrait avoir la faculté d'assister aux séances de la Commission financière touchant aux questions administratives, avec voix consultative. Dans cette situation il serait mieux à même de coordonner l'activité de la gendarmerie avec celle des autres organes administratifs locaux.

De plus, les puissances pourraient consentir à ce que les officiers supérieurs adjoints au général réorganisateur de la gendarmerie dans les trois vilayets entrassent, suivant la suggestion du gouvernement britannique, au service ottoman, sans que rien fût changé dans le mode de leur nomination.

Quant à la gendarmerie elle-même, le gouvernement impérial est prêt à admettre que les cadres et effectifs de la gendarmerie soient augmentés dans la mesure du possible. Ce soin incomberait à la Commission financière, qui se chargerait également, d'accord avec le général réorganisateur, d'élaborer un règlement pour la gendarmerie, approprié aux nouvelles conditions de l'activité de cette dernière. Ces nouvelles conditions ne devraient pas, de l'avis du gouvernement impérial, consister dans l'emploi d'une gendarmerie beaucoup plus nombreuse et plus mobile en remplacement des troupes turques pour la répression des bandes. La question d'une diminution des dites troupes dans les trois vilayets ne nous semble non plus pouvoir être utilement examinée dans les circonstances actuelles. Il va de soi que, dans ce cas, il n'y aurait pas lieu de soulever la question d'une garantie de la part des grandes puissances se rapportant aux trois vilayets et mentionnée dans la circulaire britannique.

Mais nous voudrions attirer l'attention particulière des puissances sur le voeu émis par la Commission des adjoints militaires a l'unanimité des voix, dans sa première séance du mois d'octobre 1907, voeu qui porte, entre autres, que dans chaque village un certain nombre d'habitants, désignés par les autorités sur la proposition de la gendarmerie, soient armés de manière a constituer une sorte de garde communale, fonctionnant sous la surveillance des postes de gendarmerie ayant jurisdiction sur le village.

Cette institution serait celle dite des «gardes champêtres», qui a déjà fait l'objet des instructions supplémentaires au sujet des provinces de la Roumélie en 1903. Le gouvernement ottoman lui-même l'a reconnue comme étant d'une grande utilité, et on a ordonné l'introduction par le mémoire remis par le ministre ottoman des Affaires étrangères à l'ambassadeur de Russie à Constantinople, le 10 (23) février 1903.

Effectivement, si l'activité de la gendarmerie était développée dans le sens du voeu précité, tous les villages des trois vilayets obtiendraient un minimum de garanties matérielles pour la sécurité de leurs habitants contre des actes de pillage, d'incendie et de violence de la part de bandes peu nombreuses.

Celles qui seraient plus considérables seraient aussitôt signalées à la gendarmerie, leur circulation à travers le pays serait rendue moins facile et l'action, soit de la gendarmerie elle-même, soit de la force militaire ottomane requise, serait rendue plus prompte pour la suppression de ces bandes.

Le développement de l'institution des gardes champêtres offrirait encore un important avantage, c'est celui de ne point grever de nouvelles dépenses le budget des trois vilayets. En effet, l'entretien des gardes champêtres incomberait aux communes elles-mêmes qu'ils seraient appelées à servir et à protéger.

L'affermissement de l'ordre et la sécurité qui résulterait de l'application pratique des mesures ci-dessus exposées rendraient on ne peut plus opportune l'introduction de la réforme judiciaire et d'une amélioration de l'organisation actuelle de la Commission financière.

La communication britannique en se référant à l'article 23 du Traite de Berlin mentionne la nomination d'un gouverneur pour la Macédoine, comme une mesure pouvant le mieux y assurer l'oeuvre des réformes et la pacification de cette province. Tout en étant favorables en principe a ce plan, nous sommes obligés de reconnaître qu'il n'a aucune chance d'être adopté par l'unanimité des puissances, ni accepté par le sultan. Nous sommes d'avis que le même but pourrait être atteint dans une mesure suffisante en créant pour l'exercice des fonctions dévolues actuellement à l'inspecteur général des trois vilayets des conditions plus favorable que celles existantes aujourd'hui.

Dans cet ordre d'idées, le gouvernement impérial estime que le poste d'inspecteur général ayant rang de vizir et dont les attributions sont définies dans les instructions concernant les vilayets de la Turquie d'Europe en 1902, ainsi que dans les instructions supplementaires au sujet des provinces de la Roumélie de 1903, soit maintenu pour un terme à fixer entre les puissances et la Porte et qui ne sera pas moindre que celui convenu pour le prélèvement de la surtaxe douanière de 3%. Le titulaire de ce poste ne sera pas révoqué avant l'expiration du dit terme sans que les puissances soient préalablement consultées à ce sujet.

De plus, la réforme projetée de l'administration de la justice et de la Commission financière contribuerait puissamment à donner plus d'efficacité à l'action combinée de l'inspecteur général et des autres organes de l'administration réformée locale.

Pour ce qui est de la Commission financière, nous serions disposés a nous ranger à la manière de voir du gouvernement britannique quant à la proposition relative à l'admission éventuelle au service ottoman des agents civils et des membres de la Commission financière.

Cette mesure serait destinée à sauvegarder expressément le principe de la souveraineté du sultan et faciliterait par la, sans doute, une meilleure et plus large organisation de la Commission financière susmentionnée, ainsi que de l'administration de la justice dans les trois villayets.

Pour arriver à ce résultat, il nous paraîtrait nécessaire d'adopter les mesures suivantes: Les membres de la Commission financière et les agents civils, en qualité de membres de cette Commission, étant admis au service du gouvernement ottoman, sans que rien soit changé dans le mode de leur nomination, cette Commission exercerait dorénavant le contrôle de l'activité des Tribunaux locaux dans les conditions et avec le concours des organes établis par le projet de réformes judiciaires russo-autrichien qui vient de faire l'objet des délibérations des ambassadeurs à Constantinople et qui serait, dès lors, accepté par la Porte dans tout son ensemble.

En même temps, le principe de l'égalité des droits pour les six puissances représentées au sein de la Commission financière pourrait servir à mieux assurer l'institution d'un controle efficace de l'administration générale dans les trois vilayets.

En effet, ce principe a déjà trouvé une application pratique dans l'organisation de la gendarmerie confiée à des instructeurs choisis par toutes les puissances susindiquées.

Dans cet ordre d'idées, il s'agirait d'obtenir de la Porte en faveur des délégués de l'Allemagne, de la France, de la Grande-Bretagne et de l'Italie au sein de la Commission financière, la reconnaissance des mêmes droits dont jouissent les agents civils russes et austro-hongrois.

Dès lors, tous les membres de la Commission financière pourraient exercer dans la même mesure un contrôle sur l'action des organes de la police locale, en obtenant des renseignements précis sur la marche des affaires par l'intermédiaire des officiers-instructeurs de leur nationalité et notamment dans les districts où ces derniers résident. Cette mesure procurerait aux officiers de chaque nationalité la possibilité présenter des rapports directs à l'instance nationale préposée.

De plus, la Commission financière pourrait étudier avec approbation de la Sublime-Porte la question si importante d'une meilleure coopération des troupes ottomanes avec les autorités civiles, pour la répression de désordres.

La Commission financière élaborera aussi d'autres règlements qui seraient reconnus nécessaires pour le bon fonctionnement de l'administration locale. L'institution des gardes champêtres ayant déjà donné des résultats satisfaisants dans les quelques cas où elle a été appliquée, la Commission financière aurait a s'occuper également de l'élaboration d'une organisation plus parfaite de cette institution et, en même temps, plus conforme à la tâche sérieuse qui lui serait dévolue en vue de la pacification des contrées en question.

Vu le sincère désir des puissances de voir l'ordre, la sécurité et la prospérité fermement établis parmi les populations des trois vilayets et vu l'urgence qu'il y a d'adopter des mesures pratiques propres à assurer ce résultat, le gouvernement impérial se plaît à espérer qu'une décision unanime des puissances viendra sans retard mettre fin à une situation dont les inconvénients et les dangers sont signalés dans la communication du gouvernement britannique.[1]

NOTE

1. Turkey, n. 2 (1908): Further correspondence respecting proposals by His Majesty's Government for reforms in Macedonia, London 1908, docum, n. 1. See also Dr. A. I. Krainikwsky, *La Question de Macédoine et la Diplomatie Européenne*, pp. 310-314.

NIAZI BEY, THE HERO OF THE YOUNG TURKS REVOLUTION AND IMRO'S FREEDOM FIGHTERS

In 1906, a band of the IMRO of more than 150 men, made up of the various revolutionary *chetas* of the Vilayet, was gathered for a conference near the Babouna Mountains, district of Monastir. As usual with the tactics of the IMRO, the various units of the *chetas* were scattered over strategic points while their leaders were in conference. The *asker* of more than 3,500 men under the command of Niazi Bey took up the trail of the band. Noticing the overwhelming hordes of Turkish troops approaching, the chiefs sent an order to the various *chetas* to retreat. It was considered impractical and unwise to combat such an enormous number of the enemy. One *cheta* made up of fifty young men refused to abide with the order of the chiefs, exclaiming, "We came here to fight—not to retreat!" Unfortunately, the chief of this particular band, being away in conference, was in no position at the time to approach his band and lead it out of the dangerous situation. The cordon of the Turkish troops was getting closer and closer to the besieged "revolutionists of fifty." On approaching the band the Turks asked them to surrender. The answer was unhesitating and quick—a volley at the *asker*. The struggle began—it was short but sharp! Because of the topography of the place of battle and the advantageous positions held by the troops, it was impossible for the other *chetas* who were in the vicinity at the time to come to the assistance of their comrades-in-arms. Nevertheless, the struggle was carried on until the last cartridge was fired by the revolutionists. Those of them who first finished their ammunition began to destroy their rifles and other equipment in their possession. The majority of them were killed by the Turks. But seven of them after destroying whatever they could, reserved two bombs for themselves.

They got together in a ring, fired the bombs, and into the air their bodies were hurled!

The *asker* arrived at the spot to find everything "quiet on Babouna." The Turkish casualties were heavy—but that did not matter. Niazi Bey called for a formation of his troops and after delivering a brief speech he exclaimed: "Look at these heroes! That's how they fight for their rights and liberty!" He then ordered the firing of three volleys in honor of the "dead heroes." With their hands stretched toward the sky, all the troops began to murmur, "Allah, Allah!"

This incident was reported by Louci, the Italian officer and instructor of the gendarmerie in Monastir. He immediately rushed to the scene in order to investigate and make a report of the episode. He took a number of photographs of the bodies of the killed revolutionists.[1]

NOTE

1. See *Illustratsia Ilinden*, Sofia, October 1927, I, book 5, 2-6.

APPENDIX III

GREEK BISHOPS AID
THE TURKS AGAINST
THE MACEDONIAN
BULGARIANS

The Bulgarian Ilinden insurrection of 1903[1] and its impact on the Ottoman rule in Macedonia aroused for the first time the national interest of the Greek government. Prior to this event, Greece had never shown any significant interest in Macedonia, because her nationals there were about ten percent of Macedonia's total population. All through the insurrectionary period, the Greeks in Macedonia leaned heavily toward the Turks. The latter were assisted in every possible way in the persecution of the Bulgarian inhabitants of the country. The Turks, in need of a Christian ally to crush the Bulgarian Christians in Macedonia, readily found such an ally in Greece. The latter cheerfully rendered the necessary assistance to the Turks in order to crush the Bulgarian liberation movement. This was an open secret to the people in Macedonia. For a more convincing clarification, however, we are adding as a part of Appendix III the following quotation from a recently published work, which also discusses the role of the Greek clergy and Greek army officers in Macedonia:

> The Bulgarian insurrection had significant repercussions, disproportionate to its achievement in the field. The measures adopted by the Ottomans against the native population created a stormy indignation in public opinion abroad. More important, however, was the fact that the events finally awakened the Greek nation. Mass demonstrations in Athens followed the announcement of the destruction of Krusovo and the murder of many Greeks who refused to become instruments of Bulgarian aspirations.[2] The Greek government clearly realized that Macedonia was in danger of being lost by default to the Bulgarians and that neither the

285

Great Powers nor the Ottoman could be trusted to safeguard the rights of the Greeks in the region. The moment had ripened for the Greek counter-offensive to take a concrete form.

Thus, the crushing of the "Ilinden" uprising ushered in the "Macedonian Struggle," which in turn prepared the way for the liberation of Macedonia ten years later.[3]

Prior to the launching of the Greek offensive, there were only a few discerning minds in the Greek Kingdom and in Macedonia who had been able to grasp the significance of Bulgarian activities for Hellenism in Macedonia. The first encouraging sign for the Greek cause came at the turn of the century with the appointment to many Macedonian dioceses of younger, more energetic religious leaders determined to protect the faithful—the "Greek Patriarchist"—against the terror of the "Bulgarian Exarchists." The most capable of them all was Germanos Karavangelis, who was appointed bishop of Kastoria in 1900 at the age of 34. One of his first successful undertakings was the formation of Slavophone Greek bands[4] to protect the villages of his diocese against the *comitadjis*.[5]

The prelates in Monastir, Kastoria, Serres, Nevrokop and elsewhere tried to encourage the submissive peasants to resist Bulgarian pressure. At the same time, they flooded the Patriarchate at Constantinople with reports of the weak position of Hellenism in Macedonia. Meanwhile, Greek consuls in Macedonian cities sent similar reports to the government at Athens. Among the most dedicated was the then young secretary of the consulate at Monastir, Ion Dragomis . . . whose brilliant mind and noble idealism aroused the interest of influential Greeks of Athens in the fate of Macedonia.

The "Ilinden" uprising, however, succeeded where the reports of the bishops and the consuls had failed. Early in 1904, four young Greek officers, including Pavlos Melas . . . secretly visited Macedonia and reported back to Athens that time was rapidly running short for the Greek cause. The only solution was to detail armed bands from Greece and to arm the natives.

A Macedonian Committee was formed in Athens under Dimitrios Kalapothakis, publisher of the newspaper *Ethnos*, which undertook to organize and direct the struggle. Ostensibly a private society, the Macedonian Committee was invested with the moral and material support of the Greek government. In Thessaloniki, the Greek consulate under the new Consul-General Lambros Koromilas . . . became the headquarters of the armed struggle against the Bulgarian *comitadjis* and later against Romanian and Albanian propaganda and subversion.

The first Greek band led by Melas entered Macedonia in September 1904. Already bands of native Greek and Slav-speaking Macedonians were in the field. Melas was ambushed and killed by the Turkish army before he could even reach Kastoria.[6] His death caused a sensation in Athens, which reacted in anger sending numerous bands to Macedonia to combat the Bulgarians.[7]

After the downfall of the insurrection of 1903 the Turks undertook an unspeakable method of repression. The Sultan, assisted by the Greek bishops, assumed a systematic vengeance against the Bulgarian inhabitants of Macedonia. Regular troops and *bashi-bazouks* were let loose on the countryside and threw themselves on the villages, while the police of the towns proceeded to make wholesale arrests. On August 10, 1903, the Bulgarian government issued a Memorandum to the Great Powers[8] primarily responsible for the administration of Macedonia under Turkey, calling their attention to the reign of terror in Macedonia. Among the other things the Memorandum contains the following occurrences:

> Turkish gendarmes, accompanied by Greek emissaries, march through the villages, inciting the Bulgarian population to recognize the Patriarchate and menacing the villagers with massacre and exile if they do not abandon the Exarchate. . . .[9]
>
> Encouraged and assisted by the Ottoman authorities, the Greek bishops and archimandrites overrun the country, force their way into the Bulgarian churches, trample on or burn the Slav books, use promises and threats in order to force the Bulgarian population to recognize the Patriarchate. The Greek Archimadrite of Salonika, preaching to the inhabitants of the villages of Gradobor, Negovan, Garovo, Novo-Selo, etc., used language to the effect that "the Sultan no longer wishes to have exarchist Bulgarians in his empire, and that if any remained they would be exterminated." These sermons were delivered in the presence of the Ottoman functionaries. . . .
>
> The Ottoman authorities obliged sixteen families of the village of Tashly-Muslim to write a declaration that they had gone over to the Patriarchate; the Greek bishop went to Tashly-Muslim and officiated in the Bulgarian Church, in spite of the protests of the great majority of Bulgarian families, who refused to abandon the Exarchate. The same bishop caused the notables of neighboring Bulgarian villages to be forcibly brought to Ortakey by gendarmes and told them in his sermon that "if they did not wish to be exposed to the persecution of the Turkish government, they must recognize the Patriarchate."

To what extent the Greeks fraternized with the Turks against the Bulgarian movement in Macedonia may be seen from the following experience of Dr. H. N. Brailsford. We are quoting the latter's observation as testimony on the character and behavior of the high Greek dignitaries. Being in the city of Kostour in 1904, Dr. Brailsford visited the Greek archbishop's mansion. Writes Dr. Brailsford:

> I remember well our first meeting. We began our conversation in Greek, but in a few minutes we discovered that we had been at a German university together and the man I had taken for a Byzantian assumed the guise of a Berliner. Education is rare among the Greek bishops and I had never met a man among them who spoke a western tongue. His Beatitude seemed a modern of the moderns. Could this be the fanatic who persecuted Bulgarian peasants to force them into his church? Could this be the raging partisan who massed his people to drive the schismatic Bul-

garian bishop from the town? In five minutes he had professed himself
a philosopher. In ten minutes he had avowed himself a free-thinker. . . .
But there, above my head, on the wall, in a conspicuous place hung the
photograph of a gastly head, severed at the neck, with a bullet through
the jaw, dripping blood. And then I remember the tale. That head belonged to a Bulgarian chief.[10] A band of bravoes in the archbishop's pay
had murdered him as he lay wounded in hiding. And the tale went on
to tell how the murderers carried the bleeding trophy to the Palace and
how the archbishop had had it photographed and paid its price of fifty
pieces of gold. And there, over my head, hung the photograph. Somehow,
we stopped talking moral philosophy.

We met once again, and this time in the Konak of the Turkish *Kaimakam* and once more a photograph caught my eye. It showed the Turkish
authorities standing in full-dress round a Turkish cannon and in their
midst, handsome and conspicuous with an air of mastery and command,
was the archbishop himself. And then I remembered another tale which
told how his Grace had sent his bravoes to guide the Turkish troops in
their work of massacre and blessed the cannon that was to batter the Bulgarian villages to dust. And then, under the very ears of the *Kaimakam*
and the local commandant, his Beatitude began to talk treason—in German. He assured me that his alliance with the Turks was only temporary.
A great day was coming, when Hellenism would claim her own. It was
necessary to crush the Bulgarians first. A smile played over the handsome
face as he assured me that he had brought up Cretans, trained mountaineers, redoubtable fighters, to spy out the land and study the passes,
against the day when he would unfurl the flag of revolt. Nor had he
forgotten to collect his store of rifles.[11]

LAZAR POP TRAYKOFF

The photographed head of which Dr. Brailsford refers to above was
that of Lazar Pop Traykoff, a well-known leader and organizer of the
revolutionary movement in the Kostour district.

Pop Traykoff was born in 1877 in the village of Dembeny, district of
Kostour. He received his elementary education in his home town and
later in the Bulgarian Gymnazia of Salonika. While still a junior in the
Gymnazia, Traykoff was "baptized" in the secrets of the IMRO. Upon
his graduation in 1898, Pop Traykoff was appointed teacher in his home
village. He began to work among the peasants in the district of Kostour
and was successful in extending the revolutionary network of the IMRO.
During his school vacation, Traykoff roamed from village to village and
preached the gospel of revolt against the Sultan. He terrorized the
Christian spies and traitors, eliminated a number of tyrannical Turkish
officials and openly defied the *Spahi*-Turkish tax collectors. As consequence, Traykoff became the most feared and one of the most popular
insurgents in the Kostour district. Being suspected by the authorities of

Lazar Pop Traykoff (1877-1904)
Leader of the revolutionary movement in the Kostour District

The severed head of Lazar Pop Traykoff

The Greek Bishop of Kostour, Kara Vangelis, gracing a Turkish review. Next to the Bishop stands the Turkish civil governor of the Kostour district, and further to the right, the

The picture with which the Greek Minister of Education has decorated the classroom walls in the schools of Macedonia now under Greek rule. It represents a Greek soldier who bestially strangles and devours a living Bulgarian soldier. At the top of the picture the inscription "Vulgarophagos" written in Greek means "Bulgar-eater."

*A popular Greek poster showing a Greek soldier gouging out the
eyes of a living Bulgarian.*

his conspiratorial work, Pop Traykoff was arrested in 1899 and sent to the Korcha prison, where he was kept for over more than three years. In the early part of 1903, Traykoff was released from prison. He immediately rejoined the revolutionary bands. Subsequently, he, together with Pando Klasheff, Manol Rozoff, and Misheff, became a member of the rayon Central Committee, and Traykoff became its chairman. At the head of a large *cheta* during the insurrection of 1903, Pop Traykoff was engaged in a number of battles with the troops of the Sultan. During the latter part of the insurrection, when the Kostour district became infested by hordes of Turkish troops and *bashi-bozouks,* Traykoff, at the head of a *cheta* of 485, and assisted by his subordinates, Ivan Popoff, Vassil Konomladsky, Peter Pogouncheff, Lazar Palcheff, and others, departed for the Morovo district in western Macedonia. There they were engaged several times with the Turks. After the *cheta* was dispersed, Traykoff, with a detachment of 108 men, entered the village of Tchanista.

"Upon the arrival in Tchanista," states the late Mr. Palcheff, a veteran of the insurrection of 1903 who lived in Madison, Illinois, "Pop Traykoff, myself, and several others were quartered in the village priest's house. To our surprise, the priest, who happened to be a convert to the Greek Patriarchate, had already betrayed us to the Turks, and as a result a battle ensued early in the morning, the ninth of September." It was in this skirmish that Traykoff received a bullet wound through his jaw.

Soon he returned to his district to treat his wound. Unfortunately, he was promised medical attention by one of his subordinates in the district —the Voyvoda Kote Christoff of Rula. The latter had been a brigand before he joined the IMRO. As a member of the latter, he became very active in the Kostour district. When the insurgents began to lose ground, Kote, possessing the instinct of a brigand, became a renegade by selling his services to Kara Vangelis, the Greek bishop of Kostour. Kote notified the Greek bishop that the most hated Bulgarian chief, Lazar Pop Traykoff, was under his care. The bishop immeditely ordered that at any cost Traykoff's head be delivered to him. For the consideration of fifty gold pieces, Kote murdered Traykoff, severed the head and sent it to Kara Vangelis, the bishop. The latter delivered it to the *Kaimakam* and Traykoff's head was exhibited before the rejoicing Greek and Turkish crowds. Such was the tragic end of Lazar Pop Traykoff. He was not killed by the Turks with whom he battled in numerous skirmishes, but by a renegade at a time when he was in an utterly helpless physical condition. This tragedy occurred early in 1904. So was the youthful revolutionist, at the age of twenty-seven, treacherously slain at the instigation of the Phanariote "soldier," the Greek Bishop of Kostour.

NOTES

1. See Chapter IX, Section 6, above.
2. The town of Krusovo (Krushevo) is in the district of Prilep, now Yugoslav Macedonia. Its inhabitants were Vlachs or Romanians and some of them Grecianized. During the uprising of 1903 the town was captured by a revolutionary band led by Pito Guli, native of Krushevo, and proclaimed the "Krushevo Republic," which lasted only three weeks. Surrounded by a Turkish army of 15,000 with heavy artillery, the insurgents took position and battled with the Turkish troops, but it was a hopeless case. Some of them were killed when the town was destroyed by Turkish artillery. See Bajdaroff, G., *Douhat na Makedonia* (The Spirit of Macedonia), pp. 89-91.
3. *Note:* The "liberation of Macedonia" is an euphemism for the division of Macedonia at Bucharest in 1913.
4. The so-called "Slavophone Greeks" were Bulgarian peasants who could not speak a word of Greek but who received either monthly or annual payment from the Greek bishops in Macedonia to work for the cause of Hellenism.
5. The Turks as well as the Greeks called the Bulgarian insurgents *comitadjis*.
6. Had the Turkish commander of the garrison stationed in the village of Konomladi known that Pavlos Milas was quartered in a Slavophone "Greek" home in the village of Statitsa, which is less than one hour's walking distance from Konomladi, the Turkish troops would not have gone to "ambush" Milas. The latter was tricked by Mitre Vlaho, a Romanian, but chief of a Bulgarian band that roamed in the district of Kastoria. He was the most wanted and most hated chief in the district because he was not only fighting the Turks but also trailing the Greek bands.
   When Mitre Vlaho found out that Pavlos Milas had arrived in the village of Statitsa, he sent a letter to the commanding officer of the Konomladi garrison challenging him to come to Statitsa; he even indicated the house in which he was lodging. At dawn, the village was surrounded and guns aimed at the house. Surprised and bewildered, Pavlos Milas emerged on the balcony trying to identify himself. But the Turkish soldiers cared less because they were firing at the hated *giauor*, Mitre Vlaho. Such was the tragic end of Milas, the "Byron of the Greek struggle." The few members of Milas's band that managed to escape were captured by another Bulgarian band stationed at the time in the village of Turie, who disarmed them and took them to the Greek border, where they were turned loose. This is an eyewitness episode well remembered by the author of this work.
7. Evangelos Kofos, *Nationalism and Communism in Macedonia*, Salonika, 1964, pp. 33-35. *Note:* This work was published by the Institute for Balkan Studies at Salonika.
8. *Sofia,* July 28 (August 10), 1903.
9. That is the head of the "schismatic" Bulgarian Church.
10. See discussion below.
11. Brailsford, *Macedonia,* pp. 193-194.

DOCUMENTS RELATING TO THE SERBO-GREEK ANTI-BULGARIAN CONSPIRACY

NOTE: *The following diplomatic documents were published for the first time by Mr. Gueshoff, the Bulgarian prime minister (1911-1913), in his book* The Balkan League, *pp. 199-205.*

Petrograd, December 16, 1912.

1. The Russian Minister of Foreign Affairs to the Russian Minister in Belgrade.

In his conversation with our Ambassador in Paris, M. Movakovitch said that in some event of non-compliance with the Serbian demand for sovereign ownership of an Adriatic port, Serbia would be forced to look for compensation beyond the frontiers fixed by the Serbo-Bulgarian treaty. On the other hand, our latest information speaks of a considerable change in the tone of the Turkish plenipotentiaries, thus indicating the danger which might result from disagreement among the allies. . . . It is equally important that complete unity should continue to reign between Bulgaria and Serbia. A violation of the territorial understanding between the two countries . . . can find in us neither sympathy nor support.

We consider that it is in the interest of the allies not to raise the subject of the delimination so long as the principal question with reference to the negotiations in London remains unsettled.

Petrograd, March 10, 1913.

2. The Russian Minister of Foreign Affairs to the Russian Minister in Belgrade.

. . . We cannot help regretting that, without waiting for the conclusion of peace, the Serbian government should raise a question with which we can have no sympathy, because it is in contradiction to the obligations assumed by the Serbian government.

SAZANOFF.

Petrograd, April 17, 1913.

The Russian Minister of Foreign Affairs to the Russian Minister in Belgrade.

. . . The Greek and Serbian armies are being reinforced against the Bulgarian troops. Besides, it appears that special negotiations have been opened between Serbia and Greece, it being seriously rumored that an alliance between those two countries has been concluded. Please point out to the Foreign Minister how serious and regrettable are all these measures, which can only lead to a disruption of the Balkan Alliance.

SAZANOFF.

Petrograd, April 30, 1913.

The Russian Minister of Foreign Affairs to the Russian Ministers in Belgrade and Sofia.

. . . We deem it our duty to remind them of a stipulation in the Serbo-Bulgarian treaty which cannot lose its force, whatever system of interpretation be adopted; viz., that every dispute concerning the interpretation or the application of the treaty and the military convention must be submitted to the arbitration of Russia, as soon as one of the sides declares that it is impossible to attain agreement by direct negotiation. . . . That all disagreements will be settled in the way indicated in the treaty and not by armed force.

We instruct you to make a declaration in the above sense to the government to which you are accredited.

SAZANOFF.

May 2, 1913.

3. From the Russian Minister in Sofia.

. . . Bulgaria is in sympathy with your proposal that all disputes between Bulgaria and Serbia should be settled in the way indicated by the Serbo-Bulgarian treaty. Mr. Gueshoff is wiring to the Bulgarian Minister in Petrograd to repeat this to you and to express in advance the confidence of Bulgaria in the equity and impartiality of the arbitration verdict of the Russian government.

NEKLUDOFF.

May 4, 1913.

From the Russian Minister in Belgrade.

. . . M. Pashich . . . said that Serbia continued to be in favor of the alliance with Bulgaria and did not intend to destroy it, but only maintained that in view of what has happened the treaty of alliance must undergo an amicable revision. He still hopes that the two countries will arrive at a friendly understanding. Should this, however, prove impossible, the Serbian government is always ready, in accordance with the treaty, to submit its claims and interpretation to the arbitrament of the Imperial Government.

HARTWIG.

Petrograd, May 27, 1913.

The Russian Minister of Foreign Affairs to the Russian Ministers in Belgrade and Athens.

It looks as if the Serbian and Greek governments are playing a dilatory and dangerous game professing to us their peaceful intentions, but at the same time avoiding clear and definite replies to our proposals and getting ready for common war against Bulgaria. We must warn the two governments against the ruinous consequences of such a policy, and therefore instruct you to make the most serious representations to that effect to the Foreign Secretary.

SAZANOFF.

Petrograd, June 26, 1913.

4. The Russian Minister of Foreign Affairs to the Russian Minister in Sofia.

. . . We blame Serbia for not having given us a definite answer whether she will submit to the arbitration of the Imperial Government.

SAZANOFF.

Belgrade, March 8, 1913.

The Romanian Minister in Belgrade to the Minister of Foreign Affairs in Bucharest.

I have learned from several places that Serbia is negotiating with the Greeks for the purpose of concluding a defensive alliance against Bulgaria. Both the Serbian government and the Greek Minister here are impenetrable. The latter spends daily several hours in the Ministry of Foreign Affairs.

FILALITY.

The Romanian Minister in Belgrade to the Minister of Foreign Affairs in Bucharest.

. . . General Radko Dimitrieff has been sent to Petrograd in connection with the fixing of the boundaries between the allies, who evidently are no longer able to agree among themselves. All those with whom I have spoken tell me that, from the general to the last soldier, the Serbians under arms refuse to abandon Monastir and the other towns claimed by the Bulgarians in virtue of the treaty of alliance, and would rather be killed by Savoff than give up what they have conquered.

FILALITY.

Bucharest, April 19, 1913.

5. Report to His Majesty the Romanian King by the Romanian Minister of Foreign Affairs.

This morning at 9 o'clock I was visited by M. Rustich, the Serbian Minister, who spoke to me about a disagreement between Serbia and

Bulgaria. He told me that the Bulgarians have not fulfilled the treaty obligations towards Serbia, etc. During these preliminary remarks, in the course of which I was informed of the mutual engagements of the allies, M. Rustich told me that M. Pashich was still in favor of a friendly understanding with the Bulgarian government, he has instructed him to ask what our conduct would be and whether we are inclined to conclude with Serbia a purely defensive alliance against Bulgaria. . . .

Bearing in mind that the King of Greece, in the course of the audience given to our Minister towards the end of March, also spoke of an alliance between Greece and Romania against the Bulgarian pretentions, it is possible that the Greek government will, in its turn, make us proposals similar to those of Serbia. Given the firm attitude of H. M. the King, it is only natural that I should reply to the Greek government in the same evasive manner. There is always a danger that before matters come to a head between the allies and Bulgaria and war breaks out, all negotiations for an alliance with us might only serve to render the Bulgarians more conciliatory towards the claims of the Greeks and Serbians and help to consolidate their alliance, to the detriment of Romania.

We cannot intervene except when war breaks out between the Greeks, Serbians and Bulgarians. At that moment our hands must be free, so that we shall be able to impose peace.

T. MAIORESCO.

Bucharest, May 15, 1913.

6. Report to His Majesty the Romanian King by the Romanian Minister of Foreign Affairs.

At 11 o'clóck this morning the Greek Minister, M. Papadiamantopoulos, visited the Ministry of Foreign Affairs and acting on instruction from his government, made to me the following oral communication:

1. The Greek government will grant to all the Macedonian-Romanian churches and schools, in the territory annexed by Greece, full liberty to carry on their work and to use the Macedonian-Romanian language.

   I replied that we expected that much after the declaration made by M. Venizelos to M. Take Ionesco in London, and requested him to give me the same declaration in writing and to add that Romania will be allowed to subsidize these churches and schools, as under the Turkish rule, and that in accordance with the Eastern Orthodox canons the said Macedono-Romanian churches will be entitled to have its own episcopate.

M. Papadiamantopoulos added that:

2. The Greek government wished to know whether we are prepared to conclude an alliance with Greece in view of the fact that the demands of Bulgaria are becoming more threatening.

I replied to him that I could not answer such a question before reporting the matter to H. M. the King and to the other Ministers, and that in my view Parliament must first finish with the question of the intervention in Petrograd, after which we could decide what conduct Romania must folow in the event of a Balkan crisis.

T. MAIORESCO.

Bucharest, Sunday, June 9, 1913.

7. Report to His Majesty the Romanian King by the Romanian Minister of Foreign Affairs.

At 10 o'clock this morning the Greek Minister, M. Papadiamantopoulos, again called on me to speak about an alliance with Greece against an excessive expansion of Bulgaria, adding that Turkey also might participate in such an alliance. I replied to him that as far as Turkey was concerned it would be wiser to wait until the internal conditions had been consolidated. With respect to a rapprochement with Greece, I postponed my reply until a later moment, when the friction between the allies should be greater.

T. MAIORESCO.

THE SERBIANS IN MACEDONIA (1913)— DECREE ON PUBLIC SECURITY

We have pointed out above how the Serbians in the nineteenth and the early part of the twentieth century began to lay claim upon Macedonia. The Serbians were aware that their movement in Macedonia was an artificial creation. They had no ethnic or other valid claim upon Macedonia. By virtue of the Bulgaro-Serbian treaty of alliance of March 13, 1912, the Serbians gave Macedonia to Bulgaria. Does this not mean that the Serbians, by this act, acknowledged the fact that the Macedonian Slavs are Bulgarians? With the occupation of northwestern Macedonia, however, the Serbian authorities established a military dictatorship. Considering the country as their conquered colony, the Serbian government on September 21, 1913, issued the following decree on public security:

Article I.

The police authorities are authorized, in case of a deficiency in the regular organization for securing the liberty and security of persons and property, to ask the military commander for the troops necessary for the maintenance of order and tranquility. The military commander is bound to comply immediately with these demands, and the police is bound to inform the Minister of the Interior of them.

Article II.

Any attempt at rebellion against the public powers is punishable by five years' penal servitude.

The decision of the police authorities, published in the respective communes, is sufficient proof of the commission of crime.

If the rebel refuses to give himself up as prisoner within ten days from such publication, he may be put to death by any public or military officer.

Article III.

Any person accused of rebellion in terms of the police decision and who commits any crime shall be punished with death.

If the accused person himself gives himself up as a prisoner into the hands of the authorities, the death penalty shall be commuted to penal servitude for ten or twenty years, always provided that the commutation is approved by the tribunal.

Article IV.

Where several cases of rebellion occur in a commune and the rebels do not return to their homes within ten days from the police notice, *the authorities have the right of deporting their families whithersoever they may find convenient.*

Likewise the inhabitants of the houses in which armed persons or criminals in general are found concealed, shall be deported.

The heads of the police shall transmit to the Prefecture a report on the deportation procedure, which is to be put in force immediately.

The Minister of the Interior shall, if he thinks desirable, rescind deportation measures.

Article V.

Any person deported by an order of the Prefecture who shall return to his original domicile without the authorization of the Minister of the Interior shall be punished by three years' imprisonment.

Article VI.

If in any commune or any canton the maintenance of security demands *the sending of troops, the maintenance of the latter shall be charged to the commune or the canton.* In such a case the Prefect is to be notified.

If order is restored after a brief interval and the culprits taken, the Minister of the Interior may refund such expenses to the canton or the commune.

The Minister may act in this way as often as he may think desirable.

Article VII.

Any person found carrying arms who has not in his possession a permit from the police or from the Prefect, or who shall hide arms in his house or elsewhere, shall be condemned to a penalty varying from three months' imprisonment to five years' penal servitude.

Anyone selling arms or ammunition without a police permit shall be liable to the same penalty.

Article VIII.

Any person using any kind of explosives, knowing that such use is dangerous to the life and goods of others, shall be punished with twenty years' penal servitude.

Article IX.

Anyone who shall prepare explosives or direct their preparation or who knows of the existence of explosives intended for the commission of a crime shall, subject to Article VIII, be punished by ten years' penal servitude.

Article X.

Any person receiving, keeping or transporting explosives intended for a criminal purpose shall be punished by five years' penal servitude, except where he does so with the intention of preventing the commission of a crime.

Article XI.

Any person who uses an explosive *without any evil intention,* shall be punished by five years' penal servitude.

Article XII.

(1) Anyone deliberately harming the roads, streets or squares in such a way as to endanger life or public health, shall be punished by fifteen years' penal servitude.

If the delinquency be *unintentional* the penalty shall be five years.

(2) If the author of the crime cited above causes danger to the life or health of numerous persons, or if his action results in the death of several individuals (and this could be foreseen), he shall be punished by death or twenty years' penal servitude. If the crime be unpremeditated the punishment shall be ten years.

Article XIII.

Any attempt at damaging the railway lines or navigation, shall be punished by twenty years' penal servitude. If the attempt is not premeditated the punishment shall be for ten years.

If the author of such attempt has endangered the life of several individuals, or if his action results in death or wounds to several persons, he shall be punished by death or twenty years' penal servitude.

Article XIV.

Any person injuring the means of telegraphic or telephonic communication shall be punished by fifteen years' penal servitude. If the act is not premeditated the penalty shall be five years.

Article XV.

Generally speaking the concealment of armed or guilty persons shall be punished by ten years' penal servitude.

Article XVI.

Anyone who knows a malefactor and does not denounce him to the authorities shall be punished by five years' penal servitude.

Article XVII.

Those instigating to disobedience against the established powers, the laws and the regulations with the force of law; rebels against the authorities or public or communal officers; shall be punished by twenty-one months' imprisonment up to ten years' penal servitude.

If such acts produce no effects, the penalty may be reduced to three months.

Article XVIII.

Any act of aggression and any resistance either *by word* or force offered to a public or communal officer charged with putting in force a decision of the tribunal, or an order of the communal or police public authority, during the exercise of his duties, may be punished by *ten years' penal servitude* or at least six months' imprisonment, *however insignificant be the magnitude of the crime.*

Any aggression against those helping the public officer, or experts specially called in, may be punished by the same penalty.

If the aggression offered to the public officer takes place outside the exercise of his official duties the penalty shall be two years' imprisonment.

Article XIX.

Where the crimes here enumerated are perpetrated by an associated group of persons, the penalty shall be fifteen years' penal servitude. The accomplices of those who committed the above-mentioned misdeeds against public officials shall be punished by the maximum penalty, and, if this is thought insufficient, they may be condemned to penal servitude for a period amounting to twenty years.

Article XX.

Those who recruit bands against the State, or with a view to offering resistance to public authorities shall be liable to a penalty of twenty years' penal servitude.

Article XXI.

Accomplices of rebels or of bands offering armed resistance to Serbian troops or the public or communal officers, shall be punished by death or by at least ten years' penal servitude.

Article XXII.

Persons taking part in seditious meetings which do not disperse when ordered to do so by the administrative or communal authorities are liable to terms of imprisonment up to two years.

Article XXIII.

In the case of the construction of roads or, generally speaking, of public works of all kinds, agitators who incite workmen to strike or who are unwilling to work or who seek to work elsewhere or in another manner from that in which they are told and who persist in such insubordination, after notification by the authorities shall be punished by imprisonment from three months up to two years.

Article XXIV.

Any soldier or citizen called to the colors who does not follow the call, or who refuses in the army to obey his superiors shall be condemned to a penalty varying from three months' imprisonment to five years' penal servitude.

Soldiers who assist anyone to desert from the army or who desert themselves, and those who make endeavors to attract Serbian subjects to serve with foreign troops, shall be punished by ten years' penal servitude.

In time of mobilization or war the penalty for this delinquency is death.

Article XXV.

Anybody releasing an individual under surveillance or under the guard of officials or public employees for surveillance, guard or escort, or setting such person at liberty, shall be condemned to penal servitude for a maximum period of five years.

Where such delinquency is the work of an organized group of individuals, each accomplice shall be liable to a penalty of between three and five years' penal servitude.

Article XXVI.

The Prefects have the right to prescribe in their name police measures to safeguard the life and property of those subjects to their administration. They shall fix penalties applicable to those who refuse to submit to such measures.

The penalty shall consist of a maximum period of three years' imprisonment or of a pecuniary fine up to a thousand dinars.

The edicts of the Prefects shall come into force immediately, but the Prefects are bound to communicate them at once to the Minister of the Interior.

Article XXVII.

The crimes set forth in the present regulations are to have precedence of all other suits before the judicial tribunals and judgment upon them is to be executed with the briefest possible delay.

Persons indicted for such offenses shall be subject to preventive detention until final judgment is passed on their cases. Within a three days' delay the tribunal shall send its findings to the High Court, and the latter shall proceed immediately to the examination of this decision.

Article XXVIII.

The law of July 12, 1895, as to the pursuit and destruction of brigands, which came into force on August 18, 1913, is applicable to the annexed territories, insofar as it is not modified by the present regulations.

Article XXIX.

Paragraphs 92, 93, 95, 96, 97, 98, 302b, 302d (so far as concerns paragraphs *b* and *c*), 304, 306, and 360 and Section III of the penal code which do not agree with the present regulation, are null and void.

Article XXX.

The present regulation does not abolish the provisions of paragraph 34 of the penal military code, in connection with paragraph 4 of the same code, paragraphs 52 and 69 of the penal military code and paragraph 4 of the same, which are not applicable to civil persons.

Article XXXI.

The present regulation is in force from the day of its signature by the King, and its publication in the Serbian press.

We order our Council of Ministers to make the present regulation public and to see that it is carried into effect: we order the public authorities to act in conformity with it, and we order each and all to submit to it.

Executed at Belgrade,
September 21, 1913.
PETER.

Commenting upon the above decree, the Carnegie International Commission, among other things, quotes from the Socialist Serbian paper *Radnitchke Novine:* "If the liberation of these territories is a fact, why then is this exceptional regime established there? If the inhabitants are Serbians, why are they not made the equals of all the Serbians; why is the constitutional rule not put in operation according to which 'all Serbians are equal before the law'? If the object of the war was *unification,* why is not this unification effectively recognized and why are these exceptional ordinances created, such as can only be imposed upon conquered countries by conquerors? Moreover, our constitution does not admit of rules of this nature!" The document is so characteristic and so important we are herewith incorporating it *in extenso.*[1]

NOTE

1. See the *Report of the Carnegie International Commission of Inquiry into the Causes and Conduct of the Balkan Wars,* pp. 160-162.

GREEK ATROCITIES IN MACEDONIA (1913)

Bulgaria, being blockaded during the duration of the Second Balkan War, and for that matter during the entire period of the World War I, was unable to disprove the charges brought against her by the Greeks and the Serbians. Unlike the Bulgarians, the Greeks welcomed war correspondents, and every resource of publicity was at their disposal, while Bulgaria itself was isolated and its telegraphic communications cut. The Greeks, as well as the Serbians, charged the Bulgarians with massacres and destruction and appealed to the civilized world to brand the "criminal conduct of the Bulgarians." But these accusations were soon after unmasked by the impartial and neutral Carnegie International Commission of Inquiry. In the *Report* of the said Commission one finds the following statement of fact, which might almost literally be applied to a good many of the charges brought against Bulgaria. "The charges brought by the Greeks against Bulgaria," states the Commission, "are already painfully familiar to every newspaper reader. That some of these accusations were grossly exaggerated is now apparent. Thus: *Le Temps* for example, reported the murder of the Greek Bishop of Doiran. We saw him vigorous and apparently alive some two months afterwards. A requiem mass was sung for the Bishop of Kavalla; his flock welcomed him back to them while we were in Salonika. The correspondent of the same newspaper stated that he personally assisted at the burial of the Archbishop of Serres, who was savagely mutilated before he was killed (letter dated Livonovo, 23rd of July). This distressing experience in no way caused the said prelate to interrupt his duties, which he still performs."[1]

308

The city of Serres, whose population was mostly Greek, was under Bulgarian occupation from October 1912 to June 1913, and as the second war drew near, the relations of the garrison and the citizens became increasingly hostile. The Bulgarian authorities believed that the Greeks were arming secretly, that Greek insurgents were concealed in the town, and that a revolt was in preparation. Five Greek notables of the city were arrested, with the intention of intimidating the population. But the defeat of the Bulgarian forces to the south of Serres rendered the position untenable, and arrangements were made for the evacuation of the city. As a result of this situation, the arrested notables were released by the Bulgarians. But what did the Greeks make of this case? Immediately they set themselves to falsify facts in order to damn the character of the Bulgarians. These notables, according to the false Greek allegations, "were found" killed by bayonet thrusts.

Referring to this particular case, the Carnegie International Commission makes the following observation: "We find, on the other hand, in the semiofficial Greek pamphlet *Atrosités Bulgars*, the statement (p. 85) that the bodies of four Greek notables killed by bayonet thrusts were found outside the town; among them was the corpse of the director of the Orient Bank. For this assertion the authority of the Italian and Austrian Consuls-General of Salonika is claimed.[2] The member of our Commission who visited Serres had the pleasure of meeting this gentleman, Mr. Ghene, alive, well and unharmed and enjoyed his hospitality. Such discoveries as this are a warning that even official statements regarding these events must be subjected to careful scrutiny."[3]

From the above quotations one would be able to see the nature and extent of the false accusations brought against Bulgaria by the Greeks. The Serbian accusations were no less false and unscrupulous. Thus, for example, it has been charged by the Serbians that from 30,000 to 40,000 Serbians had been deported by the Bulgarians to Asia Minor to perish there from starvation. It was also asserted that from 6,000 to 16,000 Serbian girls of the age of fourteen and above had been carried off by the Bulgarians to Constantinople and there distributed or sold into the Turkish harems. These episodes were supposed to have taken place during the World War when Bulgaria was occupying Serbian territory. Is there any truth in these charges? The downright falsehood of both of these accusations has been proven by the fact that after the capitulation of Turkey during the World War, she was for more than a year under the control of the Allied forces and no efforts were made by the Serbian government to discover and recover either the Serbians from the deserts of Asia Minor or the Serbian maidens from the harems.[4]

Another ridiculous accusation was that the Bulgarians were forcing upon the Serbians their heretical religion. There is not an iota or a tittle of difference between the religion of the two peoples, and the accusation is just as silly and baseless as it would be to say that the Italians were forcing upon the Spaniards their heretical religion.[5] The accusers' prejudices against Bulgaria created convictions by distorting reality. To the Greeks and Serbians, truth was a matter of secondary importance; their aim was to fix the character and reputation of the Bulgarians as barbarians animated by low instincts, incapable of controlling and governing themselves and for whom there should be no place in the Society of Nations.

Why should Bulgaria attempt the destruction of Macedonian towns and villages and the massacre of its population? Why should Bulgaria exterminate the inhabitants of Macedonia, of whom the vast majority are Bulgarians? It is true that the Bulgarian army did commit "massacres" in the towns of Doxato, Serres, and Demir-Hissar, but these "atrocities" were deliberately provoked by the armed Greek inhabitants of these towns attacking the retreating Bulgarian army from ambush. These, however, were cases of a self-defense and, of course, punishment was inflicted upon the intruders.[6]

The conception of civilization by the Greeks, that is, those of King Constantine and Venizelos, is well exemplified by a number of well-painted posters, printed and sold in the various cities of Macedonia and Greece. These posters, "which were eagerly bought by the Greek soldiers returning to their homes," states the Carnegie Commission, "reveal the depth of the brutality to which this race hatred had sunk them. It shows a Greek *evzone* (highlander) holding a living Bulgarian soldier with both hands, while he gnaws the face of his victim with his teeth like some beast of prey. It is entitled the *Bulgarophagos* (Bulgar-eater) and is adorned with the following verses:

'The sea of fire which boils in my breast and calls
For vengeance with the savage waves of my soul
Will be quenched when the monsters of Sofia are still
And thy life blood extinguishes my hate.'[7]

Another popular battle picture shows a Greek soldier gouging out the eyes of a living Bulgarian. Commenting on the significance of these war pictures, the Carnegie International Commission of Inquiry makes the following statement: "As an evidence of the feeling which animated the Greek army, these things have their significance. They mean, in plain words, that soldiers wished to believe that they and their comrades perpetrated bestial cruelties. A print seller who issued such pictures in a western country would be held guilty of a gross libel on its army."[8]

The results of such spiritual corruption in the Greek army, however, were widely and unrestrictedly demonstrated. No army of a state, however low and imperfect its discipline might have been, would have fallen to such a state of savagery as did the Greek army. The brutalities inflicted by the Greek army upon the noncombatant population in Macedonia is well shown by a number of letters written by these agents of devastation, the soldiers of the Nineteenth Greek Infantry Regiment, whose postbags were captured by the Bulgarians at Dobrimichte, district of Razlog. Some of these soldiers boast that they everywhere burned the Bulgarian villages. Others boast of the massacres of prisoners of war. One remarks that all the girls they met with were violated. The following extracts, each from a separate letter, may suffice to convey their general tenor:

"Of the 1,200 prisoners we took at Nigrita, only forty-one remain in the prisons and everywhere we have been we have not left a single root of this race."

"We picked out their eyes (five Bulgarian prisoners) while they were still alive."

"And from Serres to the frontier, we have burned all the Bulgarian villages. . . ."

"We enraged them by burning the villages . . . we kill them like sparrows."

"They fled into Bulgaria and we massacred those who remained . . . we have burned the villages. Not a single Bulgarian has been left."

"We burn all the Bulgarian villages that we occupy, and kill all the Bulgarians that fall into our hands."

"The Greek army sets fire to all the villages where there are Bulgarians and massacres all it meets. . . . God knows where this will end."

"I was given sixteen prisoners to take to the division and I only arrived with two. The others were killed in the darkness, massacred by me."

"By order of the King we are setting fire to all the Bulgarian villages, because the Bulgarians burned the beautiful towns of Serres, Nigrita, and several Greek villages. . . ."

"Here we are burning the villages and killing the Bulgarians, both women and children. . . ."

"Wherever there was a Bulgarian village we set fire to it and burned it so that this dirty race of Bulgars couldn't spring up again."

"We have to burn the villages such is the order—slaughter the young people and spare only the old people and the children. . . ."

"What we did to the Bulgarians is indescribable; also to the Bulgarian peasants. It is a butchery. There is not a Bulgarian town or village but is burned."[9]

Such were the shocking horrors inflicted upon the Macedonian Bulgars by the army of Greece, the country "where such brave beginnings in the art of peace, in the development of humane sentiment, and in the foundation of an enduring civilization have been made." The authenticity of the above letters was carefully scrutinized and attested to by the impartial Carnegie Commission of Inquiry. There is not the slightest doubt as to the real authenticity of these letters.

The above letters were only a fraction of what the Commission had in its possession. "Many of these letters," states the Commission in its *Report*, "still await examination. We studied with particular care a series of twenty-five letters, which contained definite avowals by these Greek soldiers of brutality which they had practiced. Two members of the Commission have some knowledge of modern Greek. We satisfied ourselves, (1) that the letters (mostly illiterate and ill-written) had been carefully deciphered and honestly translated; (2) that the interesting portions of the letters were in the same handwriting (bore the official stamp) as the portion which related personal news; (3) that no tampering with the manuscript had been practiced. Such minor errors and inaccuracies are interesting as an evidence of authenticity. . . . The letters have been published in facsimile. The addresses and the signatures are those of real people."[10] Of course, as anyone would suspect, these letters have been stigmatized by the Greeks, as, to quote Professor Sloane, "awkward forgeries."[11] But, states the Commission, "If they had been wronged by some incredibly ingenious forger, the Greek government would long ago have brought these soldiers before some impartial tribunal to prove by specimens of their handwriting that they did not write these letters. The Commission, in short, is satisfied that the letters are genuine.[12]

Notwithstanding its impartiality, certain charges were made against the integrity of the Carnegie Commission of Inquiry. Some of its members were denounced as being anti-Serbian, pro-Bulgarian, or anti-Greek. The plain fact, however, is that the Commission found no quarter in Serbia and was given a cold reception by Greece. The members of the Commission, who were accused of partialities and prejudices, were Professor Milyukoff and Dr. Brailsford. The former was charged with anti-Serbian and the latter with anti-Greek attitudes. Writes Professor Sloane, "We cannot think that the choice of Professor Milyukoff to head the Commission was entirely wise. It is true, indeed, that he is a man of high quality, thoroughly familiar with the Slavic conditions and a genuine liberal. But he is nevertheless a Russian and, therefore, subject to the suspicion, however unmerited, of sympathy with Bulgaria."[13] The Serbians openly denounced Professor Milyukoff as being pro-Bulgarian— as if he were in the service of the Bulgarian State. Yet this objection to

Professor Milyukoff was at a time when the Russian government gave "body and soul" to the building up of a powerful Serbian State!

Who can tell us better about the quality, character, and position of the constituent members of the Commission than its President? Let us quote from the man who was greatly responsible for the organization of the Commission and who was its President, the Honorable Baron d'Estournelles de Constant, French Senator and member of the Commission. He states as follows:

> All our Russian friends were of the same opinion as ourselves in considering that the man best able to represent them was Professor Paul Milyukoff, member of the Duma, who gladly responded to their pressing invitation, as he did to ours. Professor Milyukoff adds to his political authority, the distinction of being a scholar who not only knows the Balkan nations thoroughly but their languages as well. He has been reproached for this and so has Mr. Brailsford. Professor Milyukoff was at once denounced as being violently hostile to the Serbians, Brailsford as not less hostile to the Greeks. It is true that by way of balance I was represented as an impenitent Philhellene. . . . Milyukoff was perfectly just to the Bulgarians when we in Europe were all unanimous in praising and upholding them. Later on he blamed them as we all did. He censured the Serbians when censure was unanimous and he denounced the offenses of the Turks and the Greeks. But he also paid sincere tribute to their merits, as he did to those of the Greeks and the Turks. His only sin, in the eyes of each, was his perfect impartiality. He was nobody's man, precisely what we were looking for. . . . Milyukoff was not the whole Commission. They had the right to decline his testimony. That of the other members of the Commission then became of more value; it constituted a recourse. Brailsford, on the other hand, had been frankly partisan, but for whom? For the Greeks. He took up arms for them and fought in their ranks, the true disciple of Lord Byron and of Gladstone; and in spite of this fact, today Brailsford is held to be an enemy of Greece. Why? Because passionately loving and admiring the Greeks, he has denounced the errors that bid fair to injure them with all the heat and vigor of a friend and of a companion in arms.[14]

Such is the evaluation of the "objectionable" members of the Commission by its President, who frankly propounds his *credo*, as regards Greece, when he says, "I love Greece. The breath of her war of independence inspired my youth. I am steeped in the heroic memories that live in the hearts of her children, in her folk songs, in her language, which I used to speak, in the divine air of her plains and mountains. Along her coasts every port, every olive wood, or group of laurels, evokes the sacred origin of our civilization. Greece was the starting point of my active life and labor.[15] She is for the European and the American more than a cradle, a temple or a hearth, which each of us dreams of visiting one day in pilgrimage. I do not confine myself to respecting and cherishing her past. I believe in her future, in her eager, almost excessive, intelligence. But the more I love Greece, the more do I feel it my duty in the crisis of militarism which is menacing her now in her turn, to tell the truth and serve her by this, as I serve my own country, while so many others injure her by flattery."[16]

With Baron d'Estournelles at the head of the Commission, therefore, there were associated men of the highest standing, representing different nationalities,[17] who were able to bring to this important task large experience and broad sympathy. The result of the work of the International Commission of Inquiry is shown in its *Report*, "which has been written," in the words of Dr. Nicholas Murray Butler, then President of Columbia University, and acting director of the Division of Intercourse and Education of the Carnegie Endowment for International Peace, "without prejudice and without partisanship." Hence the Commission's work and adjudication on the various phases of the Balkan Wars of 1912 and 1913 is the highest and most authoritative investigation of its kind on the Balkans.

1. *Report* of the Carnegie International Commission, p. 78, Appendix 5, n. 1.
2. *Ibid.*, Appendix B, n. 17, p. 290.
3. *Ibid.*, pp. 84-85.
4. See "The Official Document presented to the Peace Conference in Paris by the Bulgarian Delegation," p. 3.
5. *Ibid.*, p. 4.
6. For the events that took place in these towns and the provocation of the same, see the *Report* of the Carnegie International Commission of Inquiry, pp. 79-95.
7. *Ibid.*, p. 97.
8. *Ibid.*, p. 97.
9. *Ibid.*, p. 105, and Appendix C, n. 51, p. 307. The above extracts are from letters Numbers 1, 3, 5, 7, 8, 9, 10, 13, 15, 17, 21, 25, respectively.
10. *Report* of the Carnegie International Commission, p. 104.
11. Sloane, *The Balkans*, p. 222.
12. *Report* of the Carnegie International Commission, p. 105.
13. Sloane, *The Balkans*, p. 225.
14. *Report* of the Carnegie International Commission, p. 7.
15. H. P. Constant has written several works and studies on Greece. *Ibid.*, see footnote, p. 3.
16. *Ibid.*, p. 2.
17. See also Chapter IX, *supra*, n. 1.

APPENDIX VII

AMERICANS IN BULGARIAN HISTORY— TESTIMONY ON THE ETHNIC CHARACTER OF THE MACEDONIAN SLAVS

1. DR. RIGGS'S SERVICE FOR THE BULGARIAN LANGUAGE

Arriving in Smyrna, Asia Minor, in 1839, the Reverend Elias Riggs became interested in spreading missionary work among the Bulgarian population in the Ottoman Empire. About the same time, Constantine Photinoff was in Smyrna to supervise the printing of the New Testament, translated into Bulgarian by Neophite Rilski. Intrigued by the Bulgarian language, Dr. Riggs soon composed the first elementary grammar for the study of the same by the English and Americans.

In a recently published article by Dr. Christo Ognjanoff, "American Missioner Reveals the Bulgarian Language to the Western World," which appeared in the *Macedonian Tribune*, Indianapolis, Indiana, (Vol. 49, No. 2482), issue of May 8, 1975, there appeared also a facsimile, which reads:

NOTES
On the Grammar of the Bulgarian Language*

1. The Bulgarian (like the Russian, Serbian, Bohemian, Polish, etc.) is a dialect of the ancient Slavic. It is spoken throughout the region lying

---

*As there does not exist, so far as I am aware, any grammar of the Bulgarian either in English or in any European tongue, I have thought that the following notes ought not to be lost. Especially, should I hope they might be useful in case any of our Protestant churches should feel called in Divine Providence to make efforts for the spiritual good of the Bulgarian people. E.R., Smyrna, May 1, 1844.

south of the Danube as far as Mt. Haemus and beyond and from Widdin to the Black Sea. In the large cities, however, Turkish is also spoken. Its literature is very slender, consisting almost entirely of a few elementary books printed in Bucharest, Belgrade, Buda, Cracow, Constantinople and Smyrna. At the latter place the New Testament was printed in 1840 and, in April of the present year (1844), the first number of a monthly magazine entitled *Luboslovie* (Philology) was issued from the same press.
2. The alphabet consists of 40 letters exclusive of the obsolete S.

2. MEMORIAL SERVICE FOR DR. RIGGS

The following is an excerpt from a paper—Memorial Service for the late Rev. Elias Riggs, D.D., LL.D.—read by the Reverend Robert Thomson at Constantinople, 1901. Among other things, Dr. Thomson states:

Closely connected with this must be mentioned Dr. Riggs' share in exercising a powerful influence on the Bulgarian language itself. This influence has repeatedly and generously been acknowledged by competent authorities. In the first instance, he had to decide, when he began work on the Bulgarian Bible, whether the Macedonian or Thracian dialect should be employed—the two being at that time about equally prevalent. With astonishing intuition, he decided in favor of the Thracian; and there can be little doubt that this fact did much—perhaps everything—to turn the tide in the direction in which it has flowed so strongly ever since. Then, there had to be laid down the principles, which presently became the traditions, by which the work of the Bulgarian Publication Department was to be guided. These were strongly conservative. The Department refused to give way in the slightest before the on-rush of foreign words, phrases and terms of expression. Always when possible it fell back upon the Slavic and Russian rather than adopt a European word. It aimed at the purest Bulgarian; and it adhered to the most classic orthography till finally compelled to yield some points. (*Annual Review for 1897-1898*, p. 20.)

3. CONCERNING THE WORK OF THE MISSIONARIES

Reverend Robert Thomson, in a letter written in Samokov, Bulgaria, on May 12, 1906, dealing with the "Seventy-fifth Anniversary of the American Mission at Constantinople, 1906" and published in *Almanac of Missions, American Board*, 1915, writes:

Reasons will doubtless easily suggest themselves to you that largely explain the much readier acceptance which Asia Minor has given to the evangelical message than this Peninsula has; but it is not so easy to find an explanation of why Bulgaria alone, of all this group of little nations, should have opened its heart to that message. Greece, which received so much sympathy and aid from Europe, but especially from Britain and the United States, during the period of its emergence as a sovereign people, very soon practically expelled the missionaries that came to her from these very lands, and has ever since remained all but inaccessible to evangelistic effort. Serbia, Romania and Montenegro have from the first maintained rigidly closed doors; while the Albanians, though more perforce than by choice, have made no response to the modest effort that for a dozen or more years past has been put forth among them. Can it be that the providence of God so timed events as designedly to delay Bulgaria's achievement of independence until the Gospel had gained such a place on her soil that she—and she alone of all these nationalities—could hardly have banished it even had she been inclined? If that is so, then it would seem that Bulgaria has been marked out by God to play a vastly higher and more important role in the history of southeastern Europe than even has been predicted for her on other considerations.

Be that as it may, how interesting it is, in the light of the progress that has been made, to read of those earliest inquiries about the Bulgarians, instituted by Constantinople missionaries some twenty or more years after Dr. Goodell's first arrival in the Golden Horn. Dr. Riggs' contact with Photinoff of Smyrna—the pioneer of modern Bulgarian literature, and the first translator of the Scriptures into that vernacular—his visit to America and fellowship with the Methodist Episcopal Church there just when its mission to Northern Bulgaria was about to be opened, his tour of exploration with Dr. Byington from Salonika to Stara Zagora, passing through all the four towns that are at present the stations of our Mission, those singular though abortive negotiations carried on through him between the Bulgarian and Greek hierarchy with the final triumph of the former, these things seem clearly now to have been the drawing of God's Spirit and the guiding of His providence to lead us to occupy the one field which in this region was to prove fruitful and the field which seems to hold in promise mighty results for the whole Peninsula and beyond. So also the leading that guided Dr. Riggs to select the Thracian and not the Macedonian dialect for the language of the Bulgarian Scriptures has fitted wonderfully into the plan.

And now, on the verge of the jubilee of the starting of evangelical work in Bulgaria both north and south of the Balkans and in Macedonia, we have nothing but words of good cheer and confidence to send you. God has not permitted us the wide extension and strong growth that He had given you at this stage in your history; but He has given us enough to assure us that He is with us. (p. 89)

4. MEMORIES FROM ROBERT COLLEGE

One of the greatest authorities on the Balkans and the Near East has been the distinguished Dr. G. B. Washburn, former Professor and President of Robert College in Constantinople. Living for decades in the Turkish capital, Dr. Washburn has made an excellent study of the races and nationalities—their struggles and aspirations—in European Turkey. Witnessing the formation of the Bulgarian state, Dr. Washburn discusses the San Stefano Treaty, the Berlin Treaty, the Macedonian Insurrection of 1903, and England's role in the affairs of Turkey. The quotations and page references below, bearing on the Bulgarian people, are from Dr. Washburn's book *Fifty Years in Constantinople*, published in Boston, Massachusetts, in 1909. Speaking about the students at Robert College, Dr. Washburn writes:

Most of the boarders at this time were Bulgarians and for twenty years the great majority of the graduates were of this nationality. During the previous decade, the Bulgarians had awakened from the sleep of centuries. They had thrown off the yoke of the Greek patriarch of Constantinople and began to dream of escaping from that of the Turk. It was a nation of peasants, held in ignorance by a double bondage. When they began to seek for enlightenment their attention was first directed to Robert College by Dr. Long, then an American missionary in Bulgaria and later a professor in the College. Although Dr. Hamlin had interested himself in the Bulgarians in 1856 and used his influence to have missions established in Bulgaria, it does not appear from their correspondence that either he or Mr. Robert had ever thought of them as possible students in the college and Mr. Robert died without knowing that he had played an important part in founding a new state in Europe. (p. 39)

We were brought into somewhat intimate relations with it (The Constantinople Conference of 1876) by the fact that England had been leader in the plan of the conference and that we know more of the people and the situation in Bulgaria than anyone else in Constantinople. Lord Salisbury and Sir Henry Elliott were the English delegates and two of the men who came with Lord Salisbury were in later years ambassadors here, Lord Curry and Sir William White. (p. 116)

The anticipated antagonism between Lord Salisbury and General Ignatieff, the Russian delegate, did not appear. They worked together all through the conference and reached a plan which, if it had been accepted by the Turks, would have brought peace and prosperity to the empire. Unhappily, Sir Henry Elliott did not agree with Lord Salisbury, as he told me himself, and perhaps unconsciously, he encouraged the Turks to resist. (p. 117)

March 3, 1878, a treaty of peace was signed between Russia and Turkey at San Stefano which would have been final but for the attitude of England and Austria. (p. 131)

The Treaty of San Stefano was of course a hard one for Turkey but it would have been better for England and for all the people of European Turkey if it had been allowed to stand and far better for the Armenians in Asia. (p. 132)

The Treaty of Berlin which was signed July 13, 1878, was one most important event of the nineteenth century in European history but it was not made in the interest of any one in the Turkish Empire. I do not know that it professed to be, although Lord Beaconsfield congratulated himself on having "consolidated" the empire, an euphemism for having reduced the size of it. Each power sought only to further its own interests and ambitions; and for the people chiefly concerned, the result has been a succession of wars, revolutions and massacres down to the present day. This is not the place to discuss this treaty but we may take a single illustration from the people in whom Robert College was most interested at that time, the Bulgarians. The treaty of San Stefano had created a Bulgaria essentially on the lines agreed to by the Powers at the Conference of Constantinople. The Treaty of Berlin divided the Bulgarians into five sections, going one part to Serbia, one to Romania, one to an autonomous province called Eastern Roumelia, one to Turkey and one to constitute the Principality of Bulgaria under the suzerainty of the Sultan; and it was England especially that insisted upon this and also upon the right of Turkey to occupy and fortify the range of the Balkan; all with the object of making it impossible for the Bulgarians to form a viable state, which might be friendly to Russia. The Englishmen who know Bulgaria, all our friends, understood the folly and wickedness of this at the time. All England has learned it since. Thus far, the results have been the revolution of 1885, which resulted in the union of Bulgaria and Eastern Roumelia, the war with Serbia, the insurrection in Macedonia and the Province of Adrianople, and all the massacres and unspeakable horrors of the last thirty-nine years in Macedonia, to say nothing of what Bulgaria has suffered from the intrigues of foreign powers ever since the Treaty of Berlin. The awful massacres and persecutions from which the Armenians have suffered since 1886, have been equally the result of this treaty. (p. 133)

The year 1903 was marked by the outbreak of the revolution planned by the Macedonian committee, not only in Macedonia but in the province of Adrianople. The insurgents were Macedonian Bulgarians but were not supported by the government of free Bulgaria or by any European Power and they failed, although they demanded nothing more than the execution of the Treaty of Berlin. Russia and Austria intervened but neither of the powers wished to have the Macedonian question settled until they could settle it in their own interest. (p. 286)

The college is best known in Europe for the influence that it had in building up a free state in the Balkan Peninsula. Fifty years ago, except to a few students of history, the Bulgarians were a forgotten race in America and western Europe. We did not exactly discover them but we played an important part in making them known to the Western world at the time when they most needed help. Years before this they had discovered us and through the young men who studied in the college they had come to have faith in our wisdom and good will. The most important thing that we ever did for them was the educating of their young men to become leaders of their people at a time when there were few Bulgarians who knew anything of civil government in the free state.

This was our legitimate work and naturally and inevitably led to our doing what we could for them after they left the college, to give them the advice which they sought in their own work and to defend their interests where we had influence in Europe. That, in this way, we had an important part in the building up of this new state is a fact known to all the world and best of all by the Bulgarians themselves, who have never failed to recognize their obligation to the college and to manifest their affection for us as individuals. (p. 298)

5. BULGARIAN BISHOPS IN MACEDONIA

The spiritual development of the Bulgarian people was greatly hindered by the Greek ecclesiastical hierarchy. Even after the Sultan had recognized the independent Bulgarian national church, the Greek bishops did not cease to provoke anti-Bulgarian incidents in Macedonia. In *The Missionary News from Bulgaria*, No. 50, issue of February 26, 1895, occurs the following item:

> In their unceasing opposition to Greek efforts in Bulgarian communities in Macedonia, Bulgarians have long sought for the appointment through their Exarch in Constantinople, of their own Bishops in different parts of Macedonia. The coming of Bishop Ilarion to Nevrokop, is one of the results of those endeavors. . . .
>
> His coming means the emancipation of Bulgarians from Greek ecclesiastical oppression and the use of the Bulgarian language in their schools and churches. In a talk of an hour at his residence in Nevrokop, he gave, among others, his experiences in the village of Zurnovo, which place I visited a few years before, and where the Greek teacher, on being asked, why he taught in the Greek language children who were all from Bulgarian homes, replied, "To open their eyes."
>
> By the imperial *firman* the bishop has right to hold religious services in any place to which a Bulgarian community invites him to come. He was so invited by the people of Zurnovo and went and held an Easter service there, to the gratification of the inhabitants and without any disturbance. The Greek bishop in Nevrokop endeavored to stir up opposition. He induced the old *caimacam* of the city to send a *zaptie* to prevent the visit to Zurnovo but an intelligent Turk had convinced the *caimacam* that he had no right to hinder such an authorized visit and a second *zaptie* was sent to turn back the first. . . .
>
> . . . Similar changes are taking place in quite a number of other villages and in nearly every case the Greeks are the losers. . . .
>
> It is well known and appreciated that we sincerely desire the development of the Bulgarian language among Bulgarians and we have repeatedly heard grateful mention made of the circulation through Evangelical colporters, of spiritual books in the Bulgarian language, under circumstances in which no other Bulgarian books were obtainable. (p. 6)

6. THE EARLY WORK IN MACEDONIA

The Reverend G. F. Morse of St. Johnsbury, Vermont, reporting in *The Missionary Herald*, Vol. 91, No. 4, issue of April 1895, describes the missionary work among the Bulgarian people. It is interesting to note that Reverend Morse was assigned to Sofia, Bulgaria, in 1862, sixteen years before Bulgaria attained her independence from Turkey. The Bulgarian people were not then, and are not now, confined within the political boundaries of Bulgaria. The ethnic extent of the Bulgarian people is beyond Bulgaria's present frontiers. Discussing the missionary work and the growth of the Bulgarian schools, Rev. Morse writes:

As the work in Macedonia is the outgrowth of the general Bulgarian work and in the beginning was superintended from Sofia, it becomes necessary to take a wide range in order to trace its development. The writer was assigned to Sofia in the fall of 1862 . . . because it was central and the best place from which to superintend the general work. . . .

The greatness of the field was appalling, extending from the Balkan on the north to Thessalonica on the south and from Nish on the west to Ichtiman on the east. It was undeveloped. Colporters had not traversed it. . . . It was the wildest part of Bulgaria.

Bulgarian Schools

Previous to the coming of the missionaries, the Bulgarians in the larger towns woke up to the necessity of education if they were to become a nation. Young men of promise were selected and sent to Europe to be educated as teachers. Our mission was commenced about this time. These teachers returned but had nothing to work with, not a single school book. They had to translate from the French and German the lessons for their pupils. In the same manner, the missionaries had to make translations from the excellent American school books. A Bulgarian publishing house was opened about this time in Vienna and took our manuscript school books and published them beautifully. In ten years' time, the Bulgarians had as good school books as we had in America. The combined influence of these books and of our two schools, one for boys and one for girls, awoke a general interest in education through all Bulgaria. Schools opened up everywhere. Macedonia felt the impulse. Up to that time Greek was almost universally used in the schools and in the churches. Now the Bulgarian took the place of the Greek. Schools were multiplied. In this way, the people were prepared to read the Bulgarian books and literature circulated by the missionaries. But for this change it would not have been practical even now to have established a successful mission in southern Macedonia. The impulse given by missionaries to Bulgarian education and its influence upon the Bulgarian nation is enough to repay all the sacrifices of the missionaries and of the contributions of the patrons of the Board. (p. 138)[1]

7. AMERICAN MISSIONARY LETTER

Finding their work blocked by the new masters of Macedonia, the members of the American Balkan Mission finally were compelled, on August 5, 1913, to send the following note of protest to Sir Edward Grey, as well as to the prime ministers of the other Great Powers.

Sir:

It is a well-known fact that for more than fifty years American Protestant missionaries have carried on religious and educational work in various parts of the Balkan Peninsula. In this work they have been without political purposes or political alliances and, on principle, have consistently avoided all interference in political affairs. In view of these facts, a brief statement as to the places where this work has been conducted, the people among whom it has been conducted, and the manner of conducting it may be of value at this time when the fate of large portions of the Balkan Peninsula is about to be decided.

About the middle of last century the attention of American missionaries in Constantinople was attracted to the Bulgarian peasants in and about that city and the impression made by them was so favorable that it was decided to investigate the region from which they came. This investigation was made in the late fifties and its result was that religious societies in Great Britain and the United States of America decided to inaugurate missionary work in the Balkan Peninsula, mainly among the Bulgarians. The Methodist Episcopal Church of North America took as its field the region between the Danube and the Balkan Mountains, and began its work in 1857; while the region south of the Balkans was assigned to the Missionary Society of the Congregational Churches of America, which society sent out its first missionaries in 1858.

These missionaries located at Adrianople. Others followed them and, in turn, Stara Zacora, Philippopolis, Sofia and Samokov were occupied before 1870. The work was extended to the Razlog district and, in 1871, the first Bulgarian Protestant church was organized in Bansko.

In 1878, after a tour of investigation, the city of Monastir was selected as the most favorable centre for work in Macedonia, and in the fall of that year, two missionary families were located there. From this centre the work was extended all through Macedonia and churches or preaching stations were established in Monastir, Ressen, Prilep, Vodena, Vardar-Enije, Kafadartsi, Velles, Skopie, Prishtina, Redovish, Raklish, Strumitsa and its villages, Velusa and Monospitovo. In 1894, after the opening up of the railway lines which converge upon Salonika, that city was made a new centre of work with supervision over the outlying districts, from Mitorvitsa on the northwest and Mehomia on the north, to Drama on the east. New preaching stations were established in Kileshnitsa, Doiran, Koukoush with its villages Todorak and Mazhdurek, Gurmen (Nevrokop district), Drama, Tetovo and Mitrovitsa.

Although it was originally the plan of the Mission to work among the Mohammedans of European Turkey as well as among the Bulgarians, as a matter of fact, the work has been confined, with the exception of the recently established Albanian branch, almost exclusively to the Bulgarians. The Bible was translated into modern colloquial Bulgarian and has been circulated all through Bulgaria, Macedonia and Thrace. Over six hundred hymns and sacred songs have been prepared in Bulgarian for the use of the religious communities connected with the Mission in Bulgaria and Macedonia. The language of preaching in all the places of assembly, except Prishtina and Mitrovitsa, where Serbian is used, is Bulgarian. Schools of Gymnasium rank have been established in Samokov and Monastir and an Agricultural and Industrial Institute in Salonika. Primary schools have long been maintained by the Mission in many cities and villages in Bulgaria and in the following places in Macedonia: Monastir, Todorak and Mezhdurek (Koukoush district), Vardar-Enije, Koleshino, Monospitovo and Strumitsa, Drama, Bansko, Banya, Mehomia and Eleshnitsa in the Razlog district. In all these places the language of instruction has been and is Bulgarian, although English has also been introduced of late years in the Girls' Boarding School of Monastir.

After years of acquaintance with Macedonia, either through residence or travel or both, mingling with the people and living in their homes, we are fully convinced that the great bulk of population in the region which we have indicated as the Macedonian field of our work, is Bulgarian in origin, language and customs, and forms an integral part of the Bulgarian nation.

We desire to call your Excellency's attention to this simple statement of facts with the hope that it may be of some assistance in securing a just and righteous solution of the momentous problem of Macedonia's future; and we also hope that, whatever the solution may be, the necessary measures will be taken to guarantee full religious liberty for all under the new administration of the country and to insure the same freedom to carry on religious and educational work which has been enjoyed in the past.

A statement identical with this has been sent to the Ministers of Foreign Affairs of all the Great Powers.

Signed :
J. F. CLARKE, D. D.
Missionary in European
Turkey for 54 years.

J. W. BAIRD, D. D.
Missionary in European
Turkey for 40 years.

ROBERT THOMSON OF EDINBURGH
Missionary for 30 years
in Constantinople
& European Turkey.[2]

NOTES

1. See Chapter VII above, Part 9.
2. In 1964 the Central Committee of the Macedonian Patriotic Organization of the United States and Canada published a brochure, *The Truth About Macedonia*. It was a compilation by Dr. Christo Ognjanoff from a number of Protestant missionary publications in the U.S. and abroad, dealing with the ethnic character of the Macedonian Slavs. Some of the above excerpts are from the above-mentioned brochure.

STATISTICAL DATA CONCERNING THE POPULATION OF MACEDONIA

Statistical Data Concerning The Population of Macedonia

STATISTICS AND PUBLICATIONS	Nationality of Statistician	YEAR	Total Number of Population	BUL-GARIANS	GREEKS	SERBS	VLACHS	TURKS	ALBAN-IANS	GYPSIES	JEWS	MISC-LANEOUS
V. Teploff-Statistical data concerning Bulgaria, Thrace and Macedonia (in Russian). Petersburg, 1877.	Russian	1877	1,479,417	1,172,136	190,047	(1) 41,284	63,895		12,055			
St. Verkovitch-The Ethnography and Topography of Macedonia (in Russian). Petersburg, 1889.	Serbian	1889	1,949,043	(2) 1,317,211	222,740		74,375	240,261	78,790	10,558	(3) 1,612	3,483
Prof. G. Weigand-The National Struggles of the Balkan People. Leipzig, 1898.	German	1898	2,275,000	1,200,000	220,000		70,000	695,000			9,000	
Dr. Cleantis Nickolaidis-Macedonia. Berlin, 1899.	Greek	1899	1,820,500	454,700	656,300		41,200	576,600				91,700
Nue Constantine-The Rumanians-Koutzovlachs (Arumanians), Bucharest, 1913.	Rumanian	1913	2,200,527	512,000	193,000	21,700	(4) 350,000	1,030,420		25,000	65,600	2,817
Robert Pelletier-The Truth of Bulgaria. Paris, 1913.	French	1913	1,437,000	1,172,000	190,000		63,000		12,000			
Richard von Mach-Der Machtbereich der Bulgarischen Exarchat in der Turkei. Leipzig, 1906.	German	1906	1,334,827	1 166,070	95,005		56,118		6,026	8,550		3,048
Vladimir Sis-Macedonia. Zurich, 1918	Czech	1918	2,173,849	(5) 1,047,012	204,367		67,865	520,845	184,300	43,100	106,360	
Official Turkish Statistics- Published in the Salonica newspaper "ASR", No. 2, January, 1905.	Turkish	1905	2,903,920	(6) 1,203,696		(7) 199,717		1,500,507				
Prof. Yordan Ivanoff-The Macedonian Question, historically, ethnographically, and statistically. Paris, 1920.	Bulgarian	1912	2,342,524	1,103,111	267,862		79,401	548,225	194,195	43,370		106,360
Leon Dominian-The Frontiers of Language and Nationality of Europe (Published by the American Geographical Society of New York; 1917.	American	1917	(8) 1,433,031	1,172,136	190,047		63,895		12,006			

REMARKS:
(1) These Serbs are of the Vilayet of Kossovo, north of Shar Mountain.
(2) In this number are included also the Bulgarian Pomaks (Bulgarian Mohammedans).
(3) The author has omitted to mention in this number the Jews of Salonica, Kavalla, Veria, Bitolia and Kastner.
(4) The author being an Arumanian has considerably increased the number of compatriots at the expense of the Bulgarians.
(5) In this number are included also the Bulgarian Pomaks.
(6) In this number are included also the Bulgarian Patriarchists.
(7) The Serbs included in this number are of the Kossovo Province which is north of Shar Mountain.
(8) L. Dominian gives statistical data only about the Christian population of Macedonia.

NOTE: From these statistical data on the ethnic character of the Macedonian population, one can derive the following conclusion:
First: Not one of the foreign statistics, including the Turkish, the Greek, and the Serbians, acknowledge the existence of the Serbian element in Macedonia.
Second: The number of Greek elements in Macedonia as shown by the Greek statistics is only as large as is indicated by the foreign statistics, and
Third: All the foreign statistics approach approximately the data given in the Bulgarian statistics concerning the Bulgarian population in Macedonia.

APPENDIX IX

ETHNOGRAPHIC MAP OF MACEDONIA

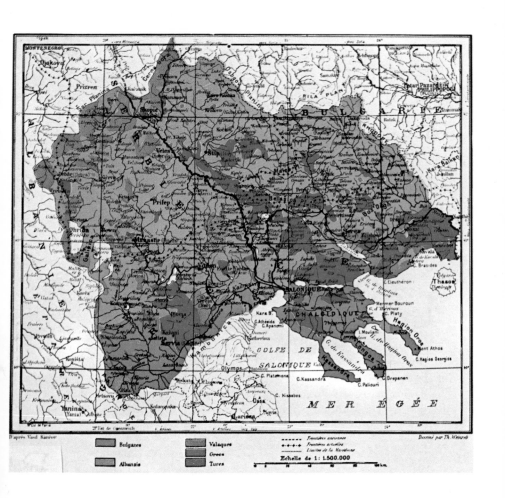

THE BALKAN POLICY OF THE PEACE CONFERENCE (1919)

Three questions suggest themselves at once in considering the subject of the Balkan policy of the Peace Conference: (1) What is this policy at present; (2) is it what it should be; and (3) if not, what should it become. Summary answers to these questions may be made as follows: (1) The Balkan policy of the Peace Conference at present is one of accepting the territorial settlements of 1913 and modifying them in the direction of rewarding and strengthening Serbia and Greece, punishing and weakening Bulgaria and assigning Albania, reduced in territory, more or less according to the provisions of the Pact of London, to the control of Italy. (2) This policy is not what it should be because it revises the settlements of 1913 on a punitive and military, instead of on an equitable and ethnic basis and therefore revises them in the wrong direction, that is to say in a direction contrary to the trend of recent decades, to the rights of small peoples and to the whole body of liberal ideas for which America stands; and because it forms part of a larger scheme, in which the permanent and individual interests of the Balkan peoples are subordinated to the immediate and selfish designs of the great European powers. (3) This policy should be reversed: in order to free the Conference from the charge of abandoning the high principles for which the war was fought, especially as these have been formulated by President Wilson; to make possible the ultimate contentment and prosperity of all the peoples in the Balkan Peninsula; to reduce the likelihood of revolts, brigandage and wars, which grow naturally out of ethnic subjection and economic and political repression; and to lighten the burdens of the League of Nations (which will be heavy enough at the best) by avoiding causes of just complaints and creating as nearly as possible a situation that will take care of itself.

If the influence of the United States is not at present strong enough to revise thoroughly and satisfactorily the very European type of settlement proposed, then in the interest of Europe itself a strong effort should be made to avoid hasty and shortsighted changes and to postpone deliberately the serious alteration of frontiers until tempers have cooled down, all parties have been heard, all evidence has been received and tested, and a genuinely impartial and scientific judgment can be formed.

1. *What is the Balkan policy of the Peace Conference at present?*
The last considerable Balkan settlement was in 1913. The four Balkan states, Bulgaria, Greece, Montenegro and Serbia, had formed an alliance in 1912, had broken the power of Turkey and had obtained by the Treaty of London of April 30, 1913, the cession to themselves jointly of nearly all territory that remained to Turkey in Europe. Had they been free enough from external influence and internal selfishness to be able to divide this cession fairly, much subsequent trouble and perhaps even the Great War itself would have been avoided. The Balkan problems of today are nearly all connected with the distribution of that irregular mass of land, the Turkey-in-Europe of 1912 west of a line from Enos to Midia. To be more specific, the questions of southern Albania and northern Albania, of Greek, Serbian and Bulgarian Macedonia, of Western and Eastern Thrace, and of the Dobrudja are all concerned with revising the treaties of 1913, while only the claims of Serbia on the west go back to the treaties of 1878.

The settlements of 1913 left three of the five principal Christian Balkan peoples, the Serbians, Greeks and Romanians, in a position of unfair superiority over the other two, the Albanians and the Bulgarians. About one million Albanians and a like number of Bulgarians were brought under the rule of the three victors. This was due, looking at the matter in a large way, to the fact that the unredeemed lands of Serbia, Romania and Greece lay still in the hands of Austria, Russia and Turkey and could not be annexed while the entire claims of the Albanians and Bulgarians had been set free from Turkish rule and made subject to acquisition. The decision of the Powers to set aside an Albanian area while entirely right and proper reduced further the territory at the disposal of the four Allies. The principle of a Balkan balance of power was introduced and Macedonia, inhabited very largely by Christian Slavs who preferred either autonomy or Bulgarian rule, was assigned only in small part to Bulgaria and mainly to Serbia and Greece. Thus Serbia and Greece acquired perhaps 600,000 to 800,000 Slavic subjects who preferred rather to be Bulgarian, while Bulgaria received no Serbs and perhaps 60,000 to 80,000 Greek patriarchists, about half of whom spoke Bulgarian.

As regards Albania, a compromise was reached between the

extreme pretentions of the Albanians and the claims of the Serbs and Montenegrins at the north and the Greeks at the south. About one-half of the Albanians were left under neighbors unfriendly to their national existence and the line was drawn so close at the north as to separate kindred tribes and to cut off mountaineers from their market towns.

At the northeast of the peninsula, the Romanians demanded and obtained from defeated Bulgaria an area which contained only three percent of Romanians. The Turks at the southeast recovered a considerable area, which, while containing a proportion of less than one-third of Bulgarians in its population, offered territory in which Bulgarians might be settled in the readjustment of population which began at once to be effected. There was a considerable movement of Albanians out of the Serbian and Greek acquisitions, of Bulgarians and Turks out of Serbian and Greek Macedonia and of Turks and Greeks out of New Bulgaria. About 110,000 Greeks, mostly from Turkish Thrace and Asia Minor, were settled in Greek Macedonia and perhaps 70,000 Bulgarians in Western Thrace before the Great War.

It is now proposed to move the Balkan boundaries further in the direction taken in 1913 by giving a section of southern Albania to Greece and portions of northern Albania to Jugo-Slavia by transferring Bulgarian territory at the west and southwest to Serbia and by withdrawing Western Thrace from Bulgaria and giving it to Greece. Romania may be advised to recede a portion of her Dobrudjan acquisition of 1913 to Bulgaria, though not the whole.

In other words, the method of considering in commissions the claims of Greece and Serbia has resulted in the reopening of certain portions of the settlements of 1913. Such portions are those which are to the disadvantage of the Albanians and the Bulgarians, the peoples who had the worst end of the settlement in 1913. The regions which were then occupied by Greece, Serbia and Montenegro, in violation of the principle of self-determination, are not by this method brought into view.

2. *Is the Balkan Policy of the Conference what it should be?*

This policy is most strongly supported by the French. The British acquiesce in much of it and the Americans in a part of it, while the Italians in some measure oppose all of it. The motives behind these attitudes are perhaps as follows: The French have suffered terribly throughout the war and they feel keenly the desire to punish those who have opposed them and to secure themselves and their allies strategically against further fighting. They have also reached a state of great financial anxiety an dare desirous of making every possible provision for the future. They feel that since Serbia fought most bravely and held out unflinchingly to the end, she should be rewarded. The reason for the French support of Greece is not so clear from the course of Greece in the war. But for some years before the war, from about the time when M. Venizelos came to power, France was in close relations with Greece. Perhaps an important reason for enlarging both Serbia and Greece is that French finance may establish there a sort of commercial protectorate, under which Serbian agriculture and Greek commerce may be managed profitably. As regards Albania, the French have perhaps no special hostile feeling but they think of the little country as a probable protectorate of the rival Italian power and therefore to be made as small as possible. Toward Bulgaria there is something of the same feeling which is held toward Germany, which desires both financial and territorial punishment without much thought of the possibility of future reconciliation and resumption of trade.

The British attitude seems to be as usual eminently practical. They feel for Albania and do not hate Bulgaria. But they signed the Pact of London which secures advantages to them as well as to France and Italy, and they prefer to keep on good terms with France. They (and the French, too) believe it good policy to support M. Venizelos in his none too secure position as prime minister of Greece. They seem not to be greatly inclined to favor Serbia, but here also would follow France to a certain extent. Therefore, albeit with some pity and regret, they join in the proposals to reduce Albania and Bulgaria.

Italy's course favors in general an ethnic adjustment in the Balkans. Probably there is in this a desire to act justly but there is clearly also a particularist motive in desiring to build up an Italian influence in the Balkans which will replace that of Austria and Germany. If Italy should have the protectorate of Albania and favorable economic and political relations with Bulgaria and perhaps with Romania (not to speak of Hungary, German Austria and Germany itself), her position would contain elements of considerable strength. This reflection reveals also a rivalry with France who, besides continuing her support of Greece, becomes through befriending Serbia the successor of Russian influence in the peninsula.

The United States is, in accordance with our history and traditions, the champion of liberty and fair opportunity for all peoples, and therefore for each of the national groups in the Balkan Peninsula. We have been in alliance with none of them and at war with none of them. We sympathize with the desire of all to be free from foreign control or interference and the desire of each to have a sufficient territory for its own population and entire freedom from political or economic subjection to any of its small neighbors. We wish to assure a healthy internal and international life to all the Balkan States so that they can labor tranquilly within their own borders and cease to enter upon conflicts which might readily spread to Europe and even to America. This American attitude is so far from being wholly sentimental that it is eminently practical. Should the Balkan situation be left so unstable as to require later our active participation in a great European conflict, we might, besides losing thousands of our young men, spend as much money as would buy all salable property in the entire peninsula.

It is therefore in the interest of the United States and conformable to its tradition of desiring for the peoples of all the world the full recognition of the right to "life, liberty and the pursuit of happiness," that we should work with all our power toward a free and equitable solution of the difficult Balkan problem, without regard to European secret treaties or the friendships and enmities of the moment or of the interlocking selfish policies and the ambitions and rivalries of the great European states. Such an aim and the results it may attain look also in the truest and largest sense to the practical interest of the European powers. In the midst of their torubled situation, they are unable to see far ahead. They cannot understand their own advantage. It is generally admitted by their statesmen that they have committed great follies in the past in their handling of the Balkan questions. They seem now to be in danger of making as bad a blunder as they have ever made. No one but ourselves can save them from wasting an opportunity such as cannot recur soon, of settling the Balkan questions on a sound and durable basis and thus securing not only for the populations there but for themselves, peace, order and genuine security.

3. *What should be the Balkan Policy of the Peace Conference?*

If a proper Balkan settlement is to be had, one of two courses should be followed comprehensively and thoroughly. (1) The present situation, ethnographic, economic and political, might be taken as a basis with all due reference to the history which has led up to it. Or (2) the entire settlement of 1913 might be reopened and carefully studied in every part, taking some account of legitimate changes since. In either case, the establishment at the nearest possible future date of every Balkan people in a state of prosperity and contentment, within territorial limits which make such a state possible, should be the aim of the settlement. Military and strategic considerations should be given only a subordinate place, because a weak frontier, with contentment on each side, is a much better security against war than a strong one which does violence to one of the peoples concerned.

Compare, for instance, the frontier between the United States and Canada with that between France and Germany after 1871. The results by the two courses would not be greatly different. The first would probably be on the whole the more satisfactory, because of the considerable readjustments of population which took place after 1913 and which were as regards some areas reciprocal; families which found new homes five or six years ago have become adjusted to their surroundings.

The changes which are called for with a view to permanency are in a contrary direction to those desired by France, Serbia and Greece. At the present time the Austrian, Russian and Turkish Empires are in a state of dissolution and Serbia, Romania and Greece can be given all of the "unredeemed" areas to which they are entitled. Without regard to the passions of the recent conflict, ethnic justice should be rendered to Albania and Bulgaria also and thus all can be established on a nationalistic basis and after a comparatively short period of confusion can be left to keep the peace without much supervision.

The most important elements of a relatively permanent solution appear to be as follows:

1. Albania should have a sufficient area and an administration which would aid her toward complete self-government.

    a. The southern boundary as established in 1913 should not be changed to the disadvantage of Albania without the production of more satisfactory evidence of the wishes of the people than has yet been seen.

    b. The northern boundary should be modified to the advantage of Albania so as to allow the people access to markets and the possession of sufficient cultivable land. This could be done and still the limit of the ethnic rights of the Albanians would not be reached.

    c. It is undesirable that Italy should become the protector of Albania. Italy is so near as to be under temptation in the direction of exploitation. Her political ambitions also make probable a provocative interference in all Balkan affairs.

    d. The United States ought to take a mandate for Albania. We are friendly to the other neighbors, we have no political ambitions and we would exert an alleviating influence throughout the entire peninsula. The representatives of the Albanians urge us to aid them and the alternative possibilities are unsatisfactory. We might very probably have to go to far more trouble later under more unfavorable conditions.

    e. In case it seems wholly impossible for the United States to take a mandate for Albania, it is worth considering whether Switzerland might not be given such a mandate. There is reason to believe that in order to secure a proper position in the League of Nations the Swiss would consent to depart from their isolation and accept a mandate proportioned to their powers and resources. Albania is not too great for them politically or financially and the common mountaineer life of the two regions constitutes an initial bond of great strength.

2. It is imperative that Macedonia receive careful consideration, if healthy conditions are to be established in the Balkans. That territory has been a bloody battleground for twenty-five years; the arrangements of 1913 did not give it peace; a resumption of its treatment as a conquered territory cannot be expected to ensure tranquility.

   a. The Serbians and Greeks might be assisted through the supervision of a western power to establish better conditions. What is needed is not repression, heavy taxation, economic exploitation and interference with churches and schools but freedom, assistance and liberty of worship and education. It is doubtful, however, whether external supervision with maintenance of the present sovereignty could possibly attain the end desired. This would merely repeat the unsuccessful experiments of the Powers in attempting to reform Macedonia while maintaining Turkish sovereignty contrary to ethnic justice.

   b. Macedonia from the Shar Mountains to the present Greco-Serbian frontier with the addition of Eastern Macedonia, including the Struma Valley, Serres and Kavala, might be assigned to Bulgaria. Serbia would retain the indisputably Serbian areas north of the Shar Mountains and Greece would keep Salonika and adjacent territories which were Slavic before 1913 but which by exchange of populations have become more Greek. This would be by all odds the fairest and most stable solution. It would be so nearly ethnic that the exchange of populations need be small. It would give western Bulgaria a satisfactory outlet to the Aegean Sea with which also the new Bulgarian Macedonia could easily be connected. Serbia with a proper outlet on the Adriatic does not need the Vardar Valley, possession of which moreover does not bring her to the Aegean. She would really be strengthened by relief from the burden of administering an unwilling population.

   c. Another solution which would not meet with so much resistance growing out of present feeling would be the establishment of a separate or "autonomous" Macedonia under a disinterested mandatory power. Portions of the 1913 acquisitions of Bulgaria, Serbia and Greece should be included with the declared and firm object of building up an independent Macedonian state which would never become incorporated with any of its neighbors. There has been much local sentiment which would support such a solution strongly. The population would be mixed and this would necessitate, on the one hand, full provision for educational and religious tolerance, so that Albanians, Bulgarians, Greeks, Gypsies, Jews, Serbians, Turks and Vlachs could all lead their own lives; and on the other hand, strict regulation against interference on the part of the neighboring states by brigand bands or religious and educational propaganda.

3. Bulgaria should retain or have restored to her all the territory assigned in 1878 and be allowed something more on the basis of her possessing a sufficient area for the settlement of her population.

   a. The only argument in favor of taking territory from her at the west is strategic; but any change there would be so serious a violation of self-determination as to outweigh greatly in the permanent hostility created the advantage Serbia might receive from a more advanced frontier.

   b. Likewise, the only valid reason for the retention by Romania of any part of the acquisition of 1913 is strategic and precisely the same consideration holds against such a procedure. In both cases also, it is of importance to remember that Bulgaria will be less than half as large as either Jugo-Slavia or Romania, and it seems unnecessary to do her the compliment of taking special precautions against her. If on the other hand she is left the boundaries of 1878 at both the west and the northeast and if the Macedonian problem is solved, Bulgaria will have no reason for a lasting grudge against either of the two neighbors.

   c. The adjustment in Thrace has a relation to the settlement of Macedonia. Both Western and Eastern Thrace were predominantly Turkish before 1912. In 1915 as a result of change of populations, Western Thrace was largely Bulgarian and Eastern Thrace was much more Turkish than before; there has probably been little change since. If the boundaries in Macedonia be left as now, Bulgaria should by all means retain Western Thrace; she has already settled there a large number of refugees from Macedonia and others are now crossing her borders from both Serbian and Greek Macedonia.

But if Macedonia could be made secure and free for the former Bulgarian population—if either the second or the third solution indicated above for Macedonia were adopted—then a large part of the Bulgarians lately settled in Western Thrace would wish to return. If Bulgaria should be given the Struma Valley outlet to the Aegean, she would not need that by the Maritza.

In such a case, however, Western Thrace would not become Greek but would return to being predominantly Turkish. If it should be withdrawn from Bulgaria, it should be added to the charge of the mandatory power which rules at Constantinople. The question arises whether even so slight a measure of encouragement should be given in the direction of a restoration of Turkish power in Europe. Accordingly, it seems better in any circumstances to leave Western Thrace to Bulgaria.

As regards Eastern Thrace, there are two good reasons for assigning it to Bulgaria as far as an adjusted Enos-Midia line: Bulgaria needs territory upon which to settle refugees from Macedonia; and the control of the navigation and drainage of the Maritza basin can best be attained under unified ownership. If proper care should be taken of Macedonia, the first reason would disappear. As regards the second, while Bulgaria and Turkey or Bulgaria and Greece could hardly be expected to undertake a large joint enterprise, Bulgaria and a mandatory power at Constantinople might be able to do so to the profit of both. Therefore, substantially the present remnant of Turkey-in-Europe might be left with Constantinople. Minor adjustments might well be made, such as to run the frontier up the thalweg of the Maritza and the Tunja to where the present line turns eastward and to follow this line and the waterparting between the Black Sea and the Aegean as far as Boyuk Maghiada and then to pass eastward to the Black Sea near Sandal Point.

CONCLUSIONS

1. The present Balkan policy of the Peace Conference does not make for an enduring peace.

   a. It is unfair to two of the Balkan peoples, the Albanians and the Bulgarians, and would therefore leave them with a well-founded sentiment of irredentism, which would at every opportunity lead to action, by agitation, revolution, brigandage or war.

   b. It would oblige Serbia or Yugoslavia and Greece, and to a less extent Romania, to keep on foot a disproportionate military establishment and to become more and more, instead of a commercial and an agricultural state, two small military empires.

   c. Each of these states will have difficult and dangerous international relations with neighbors outside the Balkan Peninsula; Yugoslavia, Hungary and the Ukraine; Greece with Italy and Turkey. To leave two neighbors within the Balkan Peninsula possessed of well-founded grievances would invite combination, intrigue, offensive alliances and war.

2. This policy tends to weaken rather than to strengthen the states it apparently favors.

   a. The government of Yugoslavia will have very difficult problems in organizing and administering the indisputably Serbo-Croatian areas. To continue to hold several hundred thousand unwilling Albanians and Bulgarians would require a considerable diversion of energy that is greatly needed elsewhere.

   b. The problem for Greece is very similar. The Greek administration is now hardly able to take good care of the Greek population. To add hundreds of thousands of subject Albanians, Bulgarians and Turks would increase existing difficulties out of proportion to advantages received.

   c. Romania has serious internal questions in regard especially to improving the status of Jews and peasants and to unifying the old and new areas. Continual friction with Bulgaria would hinder internal adjustments.

3. This policy tends to increase financial difficulties which will be at the best, well-nigh intolerable.

   a. Yugoslavia, Greece and Romania would of course receive a larger amount of taxes from a larger area and population. But the yield of revenue from northern and southern Albania and from Macedonia will be limited in the immediate future since many years of revolution and war have destroyed much property and greatly impoverished the population, which moreover has been reduced by emigration and death. On the other hand, the expense of military occupation and of provision against renewal of war would be much greater under an unfair settlement than under an equitable one. The balance of expense cannot but be decidedly against a situation which wil not permit the contented settling down of the different states.

   b. Albania has at present few active resources and very limited tax-paying capacity. It has need of the comparatively few fertile plains and rich valleys which lie adjacent to its bare mountains in order to provide the means or a pledge for the means to build roads and schools.

   c. Bulgaria is burdened already to the verge of bankruptcy with debts of peace and war. Large claims for reparation and damage, many of them legitimate, have been presented against her. If the Conference should adopt a financial policy toward her comparable to the proposed territorial policy, she could hardly escape ruin. A more moderate financial policy would involve her in well-nigh hopeless difficulties, if her territories were reduced as proposed, and she were to receive a large number of destitute refugees, with no empty lands upon which to settle them. Not sentiment but common sense demands that a small thrifty industrious nation should not be reduced to hopeless indigence and become for the world a liability instead of an asset.

4. The present Balkan policy of the Peace Conference prepares an unnecessary and embarrassing burden for the League of Nations.

   a. The League of Nations would be obliged to guarantee territories to which the ethnic and moral title is, to say the least, doubtful, and would on this account be open to continual attack and opposition from many persons whose natural inclination is to support it.

   b. Well-founded complaints would come up continually to the court of the League of Nations, based on inevitable troubles between the governments and the subject populations in the Albanian, Macedonian and Thracian regions.

   c. It is not unlikely that armed intervention would be necessary at different junctures: as for instance *against* the subject populations in establishing Serbian rule in North Albania and Greek rule in Thrace; and at a later time when the situation is more thoroughly understood, *on behalf* of the subject populations in Macedonia and Thrace.

5. It is desirable, then, that the Balkan policy of the Peace Conference should be altered radically.

   a. If possible, the whole Balkan situation should be opened up and settled in a manner comformable to ethnic justice and the hope of durable peace.

   b. If this cannot now be done, no further injustice should be carried through and adequate means should be provided for a thorough review and adjustment in the near future of the Balkan situation on an equitable basis.

   Paris, March 22, 1919.

                                              ALBERT HOWE LYBYER.[1]

NOTE

1. The late Dr. Albert H. Lybyer was an outstanding scholar and authority on Balkan problems. From 1900 to 1907 he was professor at Robert College at Constantinople, Turkey. This in itself gave him an opportunity to study the Balkan problems by being in actual contact with the people and political conditions there. From 1913, Dr. Lybyer was connected with the Department of History of the University of Illinois. In 1918, he was a member of Colonel House's Commission of Inquiry into the terms of peace. In 1919, he was assistant to Dr. Clive Day in the Balkan Division

of the section on territorial, economic, and political information for the American Commission to Negotiate Peace.

Since 1922, the Macedonian Patriotic Organization of the United States and Canada (MPO) has had its annual convention in the early part of September. It became a tradition to have a specially invited guest speaker, one who is familiar with the Balkan situation, to address the convention. As vice president of the MPO Central Committee, the author of this work had the honor of inviting Dr. Lybyer to be the guest speaker. He graciously accepted the invitation. In the course of his address on "Macedonia at the Paris Peace Conference"° at the twenty-third MPO annual convention held in Cleveland, Ohio, on September 3, 1944, Dr. Lybyer said: "I ceased to work in the Balkan Division at the end of March and became technical adviser for the King-Crane Commission on Mandates in Turkey. Before leaving, however, I spent some hours in writing an opinion on 'The Balkan Policy of the Peace Conference,' of which I sent a copy to President Wilson and left one with Dr. Day. I do not know that this memorandum had any effect whatever; decisions had pretty much all been made."

The writer of this note asked Dr. Lybyer where this memorandum could be found. Unfortunately, he was informed that "the document has never been published." Asked whether he would furnish a copy of it so that the MPO Central Committee could publish it, Dr. Lybyer cheerfully consented. And in October 1945, the document was published in Indianapolis, Indiana, under the title: *The Balkan Policy of the Paris Peace Conference as Seen in 1919 and 1945.*

POSTSCRIPT

Dr. Lybyer sent from the Hotel Crillon in Paris to President Woodrow Wilson at 11 Place des Etats-Unis, on March 22, 1919, a copy of the foregoing memorandum on the Balkan policy of the Peace Conference. He received on April 16 by courier an acknowledgment, composed and signed by the President himself. President Wilson at the same time sent his thanks to Dr. Victor Berard for a copy of the latter's book *The French Peace*, which had been transmitted by Dr. Lybyer. Dr. Berard, professor in the college of naval studies, became a senator of France in 1920. He wrote much on Balkan problems, including very sympathetic studies on Macedonia.

A facsimile of President Wilson's letter to Dr. Lybyer is presented herewith.

°Dr. Lybyer's speech was published in Indianapolis, Indiana, in November 1944 by the MPO Central Committee.

THE PRESIDENT
OF THE UNITED STATES
OF AMERICA

Paris, 15 April, 1919.

My dear Mr. Lybyer:

I am very much obliged to you for
sending me a memorandum about the Balkan policy
of the Peace Conference.   I am going to make a
point of reading it and I am sure I shall be
very much helped by it.

Will you not also be kind enough to
thank Mr. Victor Berard for his kindness in sending me a copy of his new book La Paix Franoaise?

In haste,

Cordially and sincerely yours,

Woodrow Wilson

Mr. Albert Howe Lybyer
4 Place de la Concorde,
Paris.

THE BALKAN ENTENTE

A. *THE PACT OF BALKAN ENTENTE*[1]
[Between Greece, Romania, Turkey, and Yugoslavia, signed at Athens, February 9, 1934.]

The President of the Hellenic Republic, His Majesty the King of Romania, the President of the Turkish Republic and His Majesty the King of Yugoslavia, being desirous of contributing to the consolidation of peace in the Balkans;

Animated by the spirit of understanding and conciliation which inspired the drawing up of the Briand-Kellogg Pact and the decisions of the Assembly of the League of Nations in relation thereto;

Firmly resolved to ensure the observance of the contractual obligations already in existence and the maintenance of the territorial situation in the Balkans as at present established;

Have resolved to conclude a

"Pact of Balkan Entente"

And for that end have designated their Plenipotentiaries, to wit:

The President of the Hellenic Republic, His Excellency Mr. Demetre Maximos, Minister for Foreign Affairs;

His Majesty the King of Romania, His Excellency Mr. Nicholas Titulescu, Miinster for Foreign Affairs;

The President of the Turkish Republic, His Excellency Mr. Tevfik Rüstü Bey, Minister for Foreign Affairs;

His Majesty the King of Yugoslavia, His Excellence Mr. Bogolioub Jevtich, Minister for Foreign Affairs.

Who, having exchanged their full powers, found in good and due form, have agreed upon the following provisions:

339

Article 1

Greece, Romania, Turkey and Yugoslavia mutually guarantee the security of each and all their Balkan frontiers.

Article 2

The High Contracting Parties undertake to concert together in regard to the measures to be taken in contingencies liable to affect their interests as defined by the present Agreement. They undertake not to embark upon any political action in relation to any other Balkan country not a signatory of the present agreement without previous mutual consultation nor to incur any political obligation to any other Balkan country without the consent of the other Contracting Parties.

Article 3

The present agreement shall come into force on the date of its signature by all the Contracting Parties and shall be ratified as rapidly as possible. It shall be open to any Balkan country whose accession thereto is favorably regarded by the Contracting Parties and such accession shall take effect as soon as the other signatory countries have notified their agreement.

In the faith whereof the said Plenipotentiaries have signed the present Pact.

Done at Athens, this ninth day of February, nineteen hundred and thirty-four, in four copies, one of each having been delivered to each of the High Contracting Parties.

D. MAXIMOS, DR. T. RUSTU
N. TITULESCU, B. JEVTICH

B. *THE PROTOCOL-ANNEX*

In proceeding to sign the Pact of Balkan Entente, the four Ministers for Foreign Affairs of Greece, Romania, Yugoslavia and Turkey have seen fit to define as follows the nature of the understandings assumed by their respective countries and to stipulate explicitly that the said definitions form an integral part of the Pact.

1. Any country committing one of the acts of aggression to which Article 2 of the London Conventions of July 3rd and July 4th, 1933, shall be treated as an aggressor.[2]
2. The Pact of Balkan Entente is not directed against any Power. Its

object is to guarantee the security of the several Balkan frontiers against any aggression on the part of any Balkan State.

3. Nevertheless, if one of the High Contracting Parties is the victim of aggression on the part of any other non-Balkan Power and a Balkan State associates itself with such aggression, whether at the time or subsequently, the Pact of Balkan Entente shall be applicable in its entirety in relation to such Balkan State.

4. The High Contracting Parties undertake to conclude appropriate Conventions for the furtherance of the objects pursued by the Pact of Balkan Entente. The negotiation of such Conventions shall begin within six months.

5. As the Pact of Balkan Entente does not conflict with previous undertakings, all previous undertakings and all Conventions based on previous Treaties shall be applicable in their integrity, the said undertakings and the said Treaties having all been published.

6. The words "Firmly resolved to ensure the observance of the contractual obligations already in existence," in the Preamble of the Pact, shall cover the observance by the High Contracting Parties of existing Treaties between Balkan States to which one or more of the High Contracting Parties is a signatory party.

7. The Pact of Balkan Entente is a defensive instrument; accordingly, the obligations on the High Contracting Parties which arise out of the said Pact shall cease to exist in relation to a High Contracting Party becoming aggressor against any other country within the meaning of Article II of the London Conventions.

8. The maintenance of the territorial situation in the Balkans as at present established is binding definitely on the High Contracting Parties. The duration of the obligations under the Pact shall be fixed by the High Contracting Parties in the course of the two years following the signature of the Pact or afterwards. During the two years in question, the Pact cannot be denounced. The duration of the Pact shall be fixed at not less than five years and may be longer. If, two years after the signature of the same, no duration has been fixed, the Pact of Balkan Entente shall *ipso facto* remain in force for five years after the signature thereof. On the expiry of the said five years or of the period on which the High Contracting Parties agreed for its duration, the Pact of Balkan Entente shall be renewed automatically by tacit agreement for the period for which it was previously in force, failing denunciation by any one of the High Contracting Parties, one year before the date of its expiry; provided always that no denunciation or notice of denunciation shall be admissible, whether in the first period of the Pact's validity (namely seven or more than seven years) or in any subsequent period fixed automatically by tacit agree-

ment, before the year preceding the date on which the Pact expires.
9. The High Contracting Parties shall inform each other as soon as the
   Pact of Balkan Entente is ratified in accordance with their respective
   laws.

Athens, this ninth day of February, nineteen hundred and thirty-four.

D. Maximos, Dr. T. Rustu
N. Titulescu, B. Jevtich

NOTES

1. *League of Nations Treaty Series,* Vol. CLIII, pp. 153-159; Henri Pozzi,
   Black Hand Over Europe, pp. 233-241.
2. The definition of aggression as stated here greatly concerned Bulgaria
   because the latter was being accused of aiding or abetting armed bands
   of Macedonian *comitajis* (members of the IMRO) to invade the territories of her neighbors. In July 1933, a series of non-aggression conventions were signed in London. Point 5 of Article II of these conventions,
   among other things, states: "Provision of support to armed bands formed
   in its territory which have invaded the territory of another State or refusal,
   notwithstanding the request of the invading State, to take in its own
   territory all the measures in its power to deprive those bands of all
   assistance and protection."
   The Bulgarian semiofficial press ironically suggested that the definition
   of aggression as stipulated in the London conventions was inadequate. It
   made the proposal that a State should also be considered an aggressor
   (1) if it disregards its international obligations and deprives, for instance,
   its minorities of their rights and liberties thereby forcing them to emigrate
   from their country to the great prejudice of a neighboring country or
   forcibly denationalizing them; (2) if it organizes subversive propaganda
   in foreign states with the aim of undermining their foundation and modifying the order of things established therein; (3) if it furnishes financial
   means for such propaganda; (4) if it practices toward a feeble state,
   without any reason, the policy of the wolf towards the lamb, constantly
   accusing it of troubling the waters. See *League of Nations Treaty Series,
   Near East,* Vol. XLII (1933), p. 649.

THE GREEK METHOD OF ASSIMILATING ITS BULGARIAN MINORITY

Ἑλληνικὴ Φωνή

ΣΑΒΒΑΤΟΝ
8
Αὐγούστου 1959

ΕΤΟΣ 45 ΠΕΡΙΟΔΟΙ Δι

ΑΡΙΘ. ΦΥΛΛΟΥ 1396

ΤΙΜΗ ΦΥΛΛΟΥ ΔΡΑΧ. 1,50

| ΙΔΙΟΚΤΗΤΗΣ : ΔΙΕΥΘΥΝΤΗΣ ΔΗΜ. ΤΣΩΓΚΟΣ | ΕΒΔΟΜΑΔΙΑΙΑ ΕΦΗΜΕΡΙΣ ΕΝ ΦΛΩΡΙΝΗ | ΓΡΑΦΕΙΑ—ΤΥΠΟΓΡΑΦΕΙΑ ΜΕΓΑΛΟΥ ΑΛΕΞΑΝΔΡΟΥ 26 | ΔΙΕΥΘΥΝ. ΣΥΝΤΑΞΕΩΣ ΘΕΟΔ. ΒΟΣΔΟΥ |

Εἰς τὸν ἡρωϊκὸν Ἀτραπὸν

ΟΙ ΚΑΤΟΙΚΟΙ ΤΟΥ ΘΑ ΟΡΚΙΣΘΟΥΝ ΝΑ ΟΜΙΛΟΥΝ ΜΟΝΟΝ ΕΛΛΗΝΙΚΑ

Αὔριον οἱ κάτοικοι τοῦ χωρίου Ἀτραπὸς ἐν ἐπισήμῳ τελετῇ θὰ ὁρκισθοῦν ἐνώπιον Θεοῦ καὶ ἀνθρώπων νὰ μὴν ὁμιλήσουν εἰς τὸ ἑξῆς τὸ σλαβοφανὲς γλωσσικὸν ἰδίωμα, τὸ ὁποῖον εἰς τὰς χεῖρας τῶν σλάβων προπαγανδιστῶν, ἔχει καταστῆ ὅπλον, στρεφόμενον κατὰ τῆς ἐθνικῆς συνειδήσεως τῶν Μακεδόνων.

Οἱ ὑπερήφανοι κάτοικοι Ἀτραποῦ θὰ ὁρκισθοῦν νὰ ὁμιλοῦν μόνον τὴν Ἑλληνικὴν γλῶσσαν, δ:ατρανώνοντες καὶ οὕτω τὴν Ἑλληνικήν των καταγωγὴν καὶ τὴν Ἑλληνικήν των ἐθνικὴν συνείδησιν.

Εἰς τὴν ὡραίαν αὐτὴν τελετὴν προσεχλήθησαν αἱ ἀρχαὶ καὶ οἱ κάτοικοι τῆς περιοχῆς.

A reproduction of the Greek newspaper "Eliniki Phoni" of August 8, 1959 published in Florina (Greek Macedonia) which printed the following announcement:

"Tomorrow the inhabitants of Atrapos (Atrapos in the new Greek name of an old Bulgarian village known to the people of the Florina district for centuries as Krapeshina) will swear before God and the people in an official ceremony that hence forward they will promise not to speak the Slav dialect, which in the hands of Slav propagandists, has become a weapon pointed at the national consciousness of the Macedonians. The proud people of Atrapos will take an oath to speak Greek only, so that in this way they may stress their Greek origin and their Greek consciousness."

ΚΟΝΤΑ ΣΤΗ ΦΛΩΡΙΝΑ

ΤΡΙΑ ΧΩΡΙΑ ΩΡΚΙΣΤΗΚΑΝ...

Μιὰ πολὺ παράξενη τελετὴ ἔλαβε χώραν σ' ἕνα γραφικὸ χωριουδάκι τῆς Μακεδονίας. Οἱ ἁπλοϊκοὶ κάτοικοι τοῦ χωριοῦ αὐτοῦ, ἐνώπιον Θεοῦ καὶ ἀνθρώπων ὡρκίστηκαν, ὅτι στὸ ἐξῆς θὰ πάψουν νὰ χρησιμοποιοῦν τὸ σλαυικὸ ἰδίωμα στὴν ὁμιλία τους καὶ ὅτι θὰ μιλοῦν μόνον τὴν ἑλληνικὴ γλῶσσα...

.∙.

Ὁ Ἀτραπὸς εἶναι ἕνα μικρὸ ἱστορικὸ χωριουδάκι κοντὰ στὴ Φλώρινα, στοὺς πρόποδες τοῦ ου. Εἶναι σὰν ὅλα τὰ γρα α ἑλληνικὰ χωριά, πνιγμένο τὸ πράσινο μὲ τὰ ὁλόασπρα καθαρά του σπιτάκια, ποὺ κρύβονται κάτω ἀπὸ τοὺς ἴσκιους τῶν πλατανιῶν.

Οἱ κάτοικοι τοῦ χωριοῦ αὐτοῦ, ὅπως καὶ πολλῶν ἄλλων ἀπομέρων χωριῶν τῆς Μακεδονίας, ἐπηρεασμένοι ἀπὸ τὶς ἀλλεπάλληλες ἐπιδρομὲς τῶν Σλαύων, πῆραν κάτι ἀπὸ τὴν γλώσσα τῶν ἐπιδρομέων καὶ δημιούργησαν μιὰ

Στὴν ἀπόφασι αὐτὴ λίγες μέρες νωρίτερα, προηγήθηκαν δυὸ ἄλλα ἱστορικὰ χωριὰ τοῦ Βιτσίου: Ἡ Καρδιὰ καὶ τὰ Κρύα Νερά. Ἐμεῖς βρεθήκαμε στὴν τελετὴ τῆς ὁρκωμοσίας τοῦ Ἀτραποῦ. Αὐτὴ θὰ περιγράψουμε.

.∙.

Ξημέρωνε Κυριακή. Τὸ ὁλόασπρο χωριουδάκι ξύπνησε προτοῦ βγῆ ὁ ἥλιος. Μιὰ ἀσυνήθιστη κίνησι παρατηροῦσε κανεὶς στοὺς καλοσκουπισμένους δρόμους του. Οἱ νοικοκυρὲς καὶ οἱ κοπελλοῦδες, συμπλήρωναν τὶς τελευταῖες προετοιμασίες. Ὁ ἀφέντης ἔδινε μιὰ ξεκουραστικὴ ἀσπράδα καὶ πάστρα στὰ μικρά του σπιτάκια. Μὲ τὴν αὐγὴ ὅλα ἦταν ἕτοιμα. Κι' οἱ δρόμοι γέμισαν ἀπὸ γραφικὲς ἀρχοντικὲς μακεδονίτικες ἐνδυμασίες. Ὅλοι κατευθύνονταν πρὸς τὴν ἐκκλησία. Ἱστορικὴ μέρα γιὰ τὸν Ἀτραπό. Ἡ δοξολογία τελείωσε καὶ ὁ αὔλόγυρος τοῦ σχολείου γέμισε.

ἔπειτα μίλησε ὁ πρόεδρος τοῦ χωριοῦ κ. Ἰωάν. Κάλλης. Ἀφοῦ εὐχαρίστησε τοὺς ἐπισήμους, ποὺ εἶχαν τὴν καλωσύνη νὰ τιμήσουν τὴν τελετή, κάλεσε τοὺς συγχωριανούς του νὰ δώσουν τὴν μεγάλη ὑπόσχεσι.

Ἐπακολούθησε λίγη σιγὴ κι' ἔπειτα οἱ χωρικοὶ μὲ σηκωμένο τὸ δεξί τους χέρι ἐπανελάμβαναν ὅσα ὁ πρόεδρος ἔλεγε καὶ γέμισαν τὸν ἀέρα μὲ μιὰ αἰώνια ὑπόσχεσι:

«Ὑπόσχομαι ἐνώπιον τοῦ Θεοῦ, τῶν ἀνθρώπων καὶ τῶν ἐπισήμων Ἀρχῶν τοῦ Κράτους μας, ὅτι ἀπὸ σήμερον θὰ παύσω νὰ ὁμιλῶ τὸ σλαυικὸν ἰδίωμα, ποὺ μόνον ἀφορμὴν πρὸς παρεξήγησιν δίδει εἰς τοὺς ἐχθροὺς τῆς χώρας μας, τοὺς Βουλγάρους, καὶ ὅτι θὰ μιλῶ, παντοῦ καὶ πάντοτε, τὴν ἐπίσημον γλῶσσαν τῆς πατρίδος μου, τὴν Ἑλληνικήν, εἰς τὴν ὁποίαν εἶναι γραμμένο καὶ τὸ Ἱερὸν Εὐαγγέλιον τοῦ Χριστοῦ μας».

A photograph of villagers taking "the oath before God" not to speak the Slav dialect

δική τους γλώσσα μὲ ἔντονο τὸ σλαυικὸ ἰδίωμα.

Μολονότι ἡ ἑλληνικότης τῶν χωριῶν αὐτῶν εἶναι ἐπισήμως, ὄχι μόνον ἀναμφισβήτητος, ἀλλὰ καὶ θεωροῦνται σὰν προμαχῶνες κάθε ἀπὸ βορρᾶν ἐπιδρομῆς, συχνὰ δημιουργοῦνται παρεξηγήσεις, ποὺ ἔχουν σὰν ἀποτέλεσμα ν' ἀμφισβητῆται ἡ ἑλληνικωτάτη προέλευσις τῶν κατοίκων τους.

Οἱ ἁπλοϊκοὶ Ἀτραπιῶτες, λοιπόν, δὲν μποροῦσαν νὰ ἀνεχθοῦν τὸ ἄγχος αὐτῶν τῶν παρεξηγήσεων ποὺ καταρράκωνε τὸ ἐθνικό τους γόητρο. Καὶ πῆραν τὴν ἡρωϊκὴ ἀπόφασι νὰ ἀποβάλουν ἀπὸ τὴν ὁμιλία τους κάθε γλωσσικὸ σλαυικὸ ἰδίωμα καὶ στὸ ἑξῆς νὰ μιλοῦν τὴν καθαρή, σὰν τὰ κρυσταλλένια νερὰ τοῦ χωριοῦ τους ἑλληνικὴ γλώσσα.

Ἀπὸ τὸ ἕνα μέρος οἱ Ἀτραπιῶτες κι' ἀπὸ τὸ ἄλλο οἱ ἀντιπρόσωποι 100 χωριῶν τῆς περιοχῆς, οἱ στρατιωτικὲς καὶ πολιτικὲς Ἀρχὲς τῆς Φλωρίνης καὶ οἱ ἐκπρόσωποι ὅλων τῶν παραγωγικῶν καὶ ἐθνικῶν ὀργανώσεων.

Στὰ πρόσωπα τῶν ἀκριτῶν μας ἦταν ζωγραφισμένη ἡ συγκίνησις καὶ ἡ θέλησις νὰ τηρήσουν τὴν ὑπόσχεσι ποὺ σὲ λίγο θὰ ἔδιναν.

Περήφανη ἀνέβηκε ἡ γαλανόλευκη, ἐνῶ ἡ στρατιωτικὴ μουσικὴ παιάνιζε τὸν Ἐθνικό μας Ὕμνο. Οἱ γεροντότεροι — παλαιοὶ μακεδονομάχοι — δὲν μπόρεσαν νὰ κρατήσουν τὴν συγκίνησί τους καὶ μερικὰ δάκρυα κύλησαν στὰ ρυτιδωμένα τους πρόσωπα. Ἔ-τὴν Ἑλλάδα

Ὁ ὅρκος τελείωσε. Ἡ συγκίνησις ἦταν φανερὴ πλέον στὰ πρόσωπα ὅλων τῶν Ἀτραπιωτῶν. Μιὰ εἰλικρινὴς συναίσθησις τῆς ὑποσχέσεως τοὺς κατείχε. Κι' ἡ καρδιά τους ἔπαλλε ἀπὸ ἐθνικὴν ἔξαρσιν.

Ὕστερα ἦλθε ἡ σειρὰ τῶν ὁμιλητῶν. Πρῶτος ὁ δάσκαλος τοῦ χωριοῦ κ. Κωνστ. Βακαλης. Κατόπιν ἄλλος συγχωριανός, ὁ κ. Ἰωάννης Δήμου, ἔδωσε τὴν ἔννοια τῆς ὑποσχέσεως. Ἀκολούθησαν ἀπαγγελίες ἀπὸ μικροὺς μαθητὰς καὶ ἡ ὡραία τελετὴ ἔληξε μὲ ἑλληνικοὺς χοροὺς καὶ πανηγύρια στὸ ἀκριτικὸ χωριό.

Οἱ ἡρωικοὶ ἀγωνιστὲς τοῦ Βιτσίου ἔδιναν ἕνα ἀκόμα δεῖγμα τῆς ἀκλόνητης πίστης τους πρὸς ΔΡΙΖΟ

A reproduction of the Athens' newspaper "Sphera" of September 1, 1959, which published a detailed story of the ceremony which took place in the village of Atrapos (Krapeshina), accompanied by a photograph of the moment when the villagers --mostly women and children-- took "the oath before God" to cease speaking Bulgarian. The uniformed man in front is the field-guard. The oath, marked on the side, reads as follows:

"I do promise before God, the people, and the official state authorities, that from this day on I shall cease to speak the Slav dialect which gives ground for misunderstandings to the enemies of our country -- the Bulgarians-- and that I will speak always and everywhere the official language of our fatherland, the Greek language, in which the Holy Gospel is written "

345

ΦΩΝΗΤΗΣΚΑΣΤΟΡΙΑΣ

| Ιγρηη - Ιδιοχτήτης - Διευθυντής· | ΕΒΔΟΜΑΔΙΑΙΑ ΕΘΝΙΚΗ ΠΟΛΙΤΙΚΗ ΑΝΕΞΑΡΤΗΤΟΣ ΕΦΗΜΕΡΙΣ | ΕΤΟΣ 15ον | ΚΑΣΤΟΡΙΑ |
| ΕΡ. Χ. ΗΛΙΑΔΗΣ | ΓΡΑΦΕΙΑ ΕΝ ΚΑΣΤΟΡΙΑ | Αρ.Φ. φύλ. 696 | Κυριακή 4-10-1 |

Κατά τοὺς δύο τελευταίους
μῆνας οἱ κάτοικοι μερικῶν
χωρίων τῆς βορείου Ἑλλάδος
προέβησαν εἰς ὁμαδικήν, ἐν
ἐπισήμῳ τελετῇ, δήλωσιν ὅτι
θά παύσουν πλέον νά χρησι
μοποιοῦν τὸ σλαβικὸν ἰδίωμα
καὶ ὅτι θά ὁμιλοῦν ἐφεξῆς
ἀποκλειστικῶς τὴν ἑλληνικὴν
γλῶσσαν. Ἡ ἀρχή ἔγινεν εἰς
τὸ χωρίον Καρδιά τῇ ἐπαρ
χίας Ἑορδαίας· τοῦ νομοῦ Κο
ζάνης, τὸ ὁποῖον ἔχει 692 κα·
τοίκους, συμφώνως πρὸς τὴν
ἀπογραφὴν τοῦ 1951. Ἠκο-
λούθησαν ἔπειτα καὶ ἄλλα χω
ρία, ὅπως τά Κρύα Νερά τῆς
κοινότητος Λακκωμάτων· τοῦ
νομοῦ Καστορίας (κατ. 41), ὁ
Ἀτραπὸς τοῦ νομοῦ Φλωρί
νης (κατ. 466) κ λ.π.

A reproduction of the Greek newspaper ''Phoni tis Kastorias'' of October 4,
1959, which reprints an article from the Salonica newspaper ''Makedonia''
with the following introduction:

''During the last two months the inhabitants of some villages in northern
Greece (Macedonia) in official mass ceremonies proclaimed that they will
cease to use the Slav dialect and that in the future they will speak only
Greek. The first ceremony took place in the village of Trebeno, district
of Kojani, which has, according to the census of 1952, 692 inhabitants.
It was followed by other villages such as Breshcheni, Kostour district,
(41 inhabitants), Atropos (Krapeshina), Florina district, (466 inhabitants)
and so forth. ''

CHRONOLOGY
OF THE HISTORY
OF BULGARIA

480   The first invasion of the Proto-Bulgarians in the Balkan lands.

5th Century (end)   The beginning of the Slav settlement in the Balkans.

6th Century (second half)   The further Slav advancement in the Balkan lands.

6th Century (end)   The rise of the Proto-Bulgarian tribal league "Great Bulgaria" headed by *Khan Kubrat.*

7th Century (middle)   The conquest of almost the entire Balkan Peninsula by the Slavs. About 650, the death of *Khan Kubrat.*

660 (approx.)   The fall of "Great Bulgaria" under the pressure of the Avars and Khazars. During the second half of the seventh century (670) the unification of the seven Slavic tribes takes place in Moesia; part of the Proto-Bulgarians at the head of their tribal leader *Khan Asparuh* (644-701) settle in southern Bessarabia, and from here they begin their attacks against Byzantium; an alliance is formed between the Slavs and the Proto-Bulgarians.

679   The penetration of the Proto-Bulgarians in the present northeastern part of Bulgaria and the formation of the Slavo-Bulgarian state with Pliska as its capital.

681   The recognition of the new Slavo-Bulgarian state by Byzantium.

701-718   Khan Tervel. After Tervel's reign two groups struggle for supremacy in the Slavo-Bulgarian state. While this turmoil is taking place, a number of Khans from either faction occupy the throne. It is not until the reign of *Kardam* that peace among the warring factions is restored.

718-773   There are a number of rulers of no special significance.

773-777   Telerig, whose family is unknown. Bulgaria is subjugated by the Greeks.

777-791   Ruler unknown.

791-797 *Kardam,* whose reign marks the turning of the tide. During the disorders and confusion in the empire, he defeats the Greeks (792) and restores the Bulgarian state.

808-814 *Krum,* one of the greatest Bulgarian rulers. For five years (808-813) he carries on war with Byzantium. *Krum* is defeated and killed the emperor in a battle in 811.

814-831 *Omortag,* the son of *Krum,* founds the new capital, Great Preslav (821).

831-836 *Malamar,* the son of *Omortag,* who expands his possessions in upper Macedonia and Serbia.

836-852 *Presian.*

852-889 Boris I. Boris's reign is important chiefly for his conversion to Christianity (865). In 885, the Slavic liturgy is introduced among the Slavs of Bulgaria by the successors of Sts. Cyril and Methodius (Kiril and Methodi).

889-893 *Vladimir,* the son of Boris I.

893-927 *Simeon* (Symeon) the Great, another son of *Boris,* the first Bulgarian ruler to assume the title *Tsar.* Simeon is educated at Constantinople, as a monk. He encourages translations from the Greek. In addition to the splendor of Preslav, he causes the development of a second cultural center at Ohrid, southwestern Macedonia, under St. Clement and St. Naum. In 925, Simeon proclaims himself emperor of the Romans and the Bulgarians. The Pope recognizes the title.

927-969 *Peter I,* the son of *Simeon,* a pious but weak ruler. His reign is characterized as one of unrest and religious ferment. One of the many monasteries founded is St. Ivan (John) of Rila.

969-972 *Boris II.* The reign is filled with the second invasion of Sviatoslav, who takes Preslav and captures Boris and his family (969). In 972, the Emperor John Zimisces attacks the Russians by land and sea. He takes Preslav and destroys it, besieges Sviatoslav at Dristra on the Danube, and finally forces him to evacuate Bulgaria. Boris is obliged to abdicate, the patriarchate is abolished, and Bulgaria comes to an end as a separate state.

972-980 Bolyar *Nikola* and his four sons, David, Moisey, Aron, and Samuel (or Samuil).

980-1014 *Samuel,* son of Nikola, who was a governor of one of the western districts, which had been unaffected by the Russian invasion, sets himself up as ruler. He soon expands his domain to Sofia and reestablishes the patriarchate in Ohrid, which is the capital of the new state. The campaign of Basil II (*Bulgaroktonos* —Slayer of the Bulgarians) lasts from 996-1014. The defeat of the Bulgarians at Balasitsa (1014) and the sight of his 15,000 blinded warriors brings on Samuel's death.

1014-1016 Gavrail Radomir, the son of Samuel. As he tries to make peace, he is murdered by his cousin.

1016-1018 Ivan Vladislav continues the war but is killed in battle. Bulgaria is incorporated into the Byzantine Empire; the Bulgarian Patriarchate is abolished, but the Archbishopric of Ohrid remains practically autonomous until it is abolished by a decree of the Constantinople Greek Patriarchate in 1767.

1018-1187 Bulgaria is for 168 years an integral part of the Byzantine Empire.

SECOND BULGARIAN KINGDOM (1187-1393)

1187-1196 Assen I. The rise of Ivan and Peter Assen I (1185), two Bulgarian lords from the vicinity of Tarnovo (or Turnovo). Defeated by the Emperor Isaac Angelus (1186), they flee to the Cumans and return with an army of the latter. After raiding into Thrace, they accept a truce that leaves them in possession of Bulgaria north of the Balkan Mountains.

1196-1197 Peter II. Peter Assen succeeds to leadership of the movement after the murder of Ivan by a boyar (lord) conspirator. Peter himself falls a victim (1197) to his boyar rivals.

1197-1207 Kaloyan (Joannista), the younger brother of Ivan and Peter. He makes peace with the Greeks (1201) and then engages (1202) in campaigns against the Serbs (taking Nish) and the Hungarians, whom he drives back over the Danube. The collapse of the Eastern Empire (1204) gives *Kaloyan* an excellent opportunity to reaffirm his dominion. At the same time he takes over the whole of western Macedonia.

1207-1218 Boril, the nephew of *Kaloyan,* whose position is not recognized by all other leaders, some of whom attempt to set up independent principalities. *Boril* is completely defeated by the Frankish crusaders under Henry I at the battle of Philippopolis (Plovdiv) in 1213 and is compelled to make peace. *Ivan Assen,* son of Kaloyan, supported by the Russians, begins to rebel in northern Bulgaria. He besieges and takes Tarnovo and deposes Boril (1218).

1218-1241 Ivan Assen II. His reign marks the zenith of the Second Bulgarian Empire. Ivan is a mild and generous ruler, much beloved even by the Greek population. In 1230, *Ivan Assen* defeats Theodore of Epirus at Klokotnitsa on the Maritza River and captures him. He then occupies all of western Macedonia and even northern Albania.

1241-1246 Kaliman I, the son of Assen II. His reign is distinguished chiefly by the great incursion of the Mongols, returning from the expedition into central Europe (1241).

1246-1257 Michael Assen, the youngest son of Assen II, is a mere child. The Nicaean emperor, Ivan Vatatzes, takes advantage of the situation to conquer all southern Thrace and Macedonia.

1257-1258 Kaliman II, with the support of the boyars (lords), drives out Michael Assen, only to be deposed and expelled in his turn. He is the last ruler of the Assen dynasty.

1258-1277 Constantine Assen.

1277-1280 Ivalo.

1280-1292 Gheorgi Terter I.

1292-1298 Smiletz.

1298-1300 Tchaka.

1300-1322 Todor Svetoslav.

1322-1330 Mihail Shishman.

1330-1371 Ivan Alexander.

1371-1393 Ivan Shishman. He is the last ruler of the Second Bulgarian State.

1393-1878 Bulgaria is part of European Turkey.

THE THIRD BULGARIAN KINGDOM (1878-1946)

1879-1886 Prince Alexander of Battenberg, a relative of the Russian Empress. He is only twenty-two years old and well received by the Bulgarian people. For political reasons, he is dethroned in 1886.

1887-1908 Prince Ferdinand I, of Saxe-Coburg-Gotha, is elected prince.

1909-1918 Tsar Ferdinand I. Taking advantage of the Young Turks revolt against Abdul Hamid II in 1908, Bulgaria declares its independence from Turkish suzerainty, and Prince Ferdinand becomes *Tsar Ferdinand,* thus assuming the traditional Bulgarian royal title of Simeon the Great (893-927).

1918-1943 Tsar Boris III, son of Ferdinand I. Under the influence of Tsar Boris III, Bulgaria joins the Axis Powers in World War II, occupying the western Bulgarian lands given to Serbia in 1919 and most of Macedonia. Tsar Boris dies in 1943.

1943-1946 Simeon II, son of Tsar Boris, is born in 1937. A regency rules for Simeon II until the establishment of the People's Republic of Bulgaria.

ESTABLISHMENT OF THE PEOPLE'S
REPUBLIC OF BULGARIA (1946)

1946-1949 Gheorgi Dimitroff, Communist Party secretary, becomes the first premier of Bulgaria. In connection with the German Reichstag fire of February 27, 1933, he is falsely accused by the Nazis, especially Hermann Goering. Acting as his own defense lawyer at the Supreme Court in Leipzig, Dimitroff is acquitted.

1949-1950 Vasil P. Kolaroff. After the death of Gheorgi Dimitroff in 1949, Kolaroff becomes his successor as head of state until his death in January 1950.

1950-1956 Velko V. Tchervenkoff becomes president of the Council of Ministers. Because of the "personality cult" he is ousted (1961) from the party and later on reinstated (1969).

1956- Todor Zhivkoff is elected first secretary of the Central Committee of the Bulgarian Communist Party in 1954 and president of the Council of Ministers in 1962. In the Sixth National Assembly of July 7-9, 1971, and under the new Constitution of the same year, a State Council is formed for the first time in the People's Republic of Bulgaria. Todor Zhivkoff is currently the president of the State Council of Ministers of the Republic.

NOMINAL PRESIDENTS OF THE PRESIDIUM
OF THE NATIONAL ASSEMBLY

1947-1950 Mintcho K. Neycheff, President of the Presidium.
1950-1958 Gheorgi P. Damyanoff, President of the Presidium.
1958-1964 Dimiter V. Ganeff, President of the Presidium.
1964-1971 Gheorgi Traikoff, President of the Presidium.
1971- (July 7)—Stanko Todorov, President of the Presidium.

BULGARIAN EXARCHS AND PATRIARCHS SINCE 1870

1870 Establishment of the Bulgarian Independent National Church—the Bulgarian Exarchate.

1872 Ilarion Makariopolski (1812-1875), Metropolitan of Târnovo (Turnovo), an *ad hoc* member of the Bulgarian Synod and acting Exarch for a very brief period of time.

1872 Antim I (1816-1888), Metropolitan of Vidin, first elected Bulgarian Exarch (1872-1877).

1877 Yosif I (1840-1915), Metropolitan of Lovetch (1876) and Exarch from 1877-1915. In November 1913, Exarch Yosif moves his residence from Constantinople (now Istambul) to Sofia. After his death in 1915, the election of his successor is delayed because of procrastination on the part of Bulgaria's governing factors.

1945 Stephan (1878-1957), Metropolitan of Sofia (1922) and, from 1945 to 1948, Bulgarian Exarch. He brings about the lifting of the schism imposed on the Bulgarian Church by the Greek Constantinople Patriarch in 1870.

1953 Kyril or Kiril (1901-1971), Metropolitan of Plovdiv (1938) and of Sofia in 1953. The National Church Council restores the Patriarchate of the Bulgarian Orthodox Church, and the first Bulgarian Patriarch elected is Kyril (1953-1971).

1971 Maksim (1914-   ), Metropolitan of Lovetch, is elected in 1971 as the second Bulgarian Patriarch.

IMPORTANT DATES IN THE HISTORY OF MODERN BULGARIA (1762-1971)

1762   The monk Father Paissy writes his *History of the Bulgarian People*—beginning of the Bulgarian national renaissance.

1767   Abolition of the autonomous Bulgarian Archbishopric of Ohrid.

1833   The Bulgarians of Skopie, dissatisfied with the Greek bishop, demand that the Patriarchate send to Skopie a bishop of Bulgarian nationality. They are therefore the first to raise the Church question.

1836   The first Bulgarian school is opened in Skopie, funded by the local church parish.

1839   The Hatt-i-sherif of Gulhane, a reform decree, is issued by the Sultan under the influence of Reshid Pasha, who favors reforms on Western lines and hopes to increase the popularity of the Turks in England.

1840   Translation of the Bible into Bulgarian by the monk Neophite, aided by the American missionary Dr. Elias Riggs.

1846   The first Bulgarian church, St. Stephan, is built in Constantinople.

1848   A Bulgarian publishing house is established in Constantinople.

1852   The second Bulgarian publishing house is established in Salonika.

1856   The *Hatti-Humayun,* the most important Turkish reform edict of the nineteenth century, guaranteeing Christian subjects security of life, honor, and property.

1858   Rapid growth of the Bulgarian national movement, with revolutionary committees at Bucharest and Odessa. Connection of the revolutionary leaders (Rakovsky and Boteff) with Prince Michael of Serbia.

1860   During the Solemn Easter Service at the St. Stephan Church in

Constantinople, the Bulgarian prelate, Ilarion Makariopolski, repudiates the authority of the Constantinople Greek Ecumenical Patriarchate.

1861 Opening of the first American mission in Bulgaria. Founding of the Samokov Seminary by Dr. J. F. Clarke.

1864 In Bitolia, southwestern part of Macedonia, the struggle begins for a Bulgarian national church.

1865 The first Bulgarian school for girls is founded in Salonika.

1866 The first Bulgarian *chitalishte* (reading room) is founded in Constantinople, and in 1870 it begins to publish the periodical *Chitalishte.*

1869 In Prilep, Macedonia, the Bulgarian *chitalishte* "Nadezhda" (Hope) is established.

1870 Establishment of the Bulgarian Exarchate. The Exarch is given jurisdiction over a large part of Macedonia and Thrace as well as Bulgaria.

1872 (March 17), Antim I, Bulgarian Exarch, arrives in Constantinople.

1875 (July). Insurrection in Bosnia-Herzegovina—war on Turkey by Serbia and Montenegro.

1875 (September). Abortive rising of the Bulgarians against Turkish rule.

1876 (April-August). Great insurrection in Bulgaria, subdued by Turkish irregulars. William E. Gladstone's brochure *Bulgarian Horrors.*

1877 (April 24). Russia declares war on Turkey.

1878 (March 3). The liberation of Bulgaria. Treaty of San Stefano, with provision for a large state to include most of Macedonia.

1878 (June 13). Representatives of the Great Powers assemble at the Congress of Berlin.

1878 (July 13). The Treaty of Berlin establishes a small Bulgarian principality north of the Balkan Mountains, and an Eastern Rumelia south of the mountains. Macedonia is left under Turkish rule, with promises (Article XXIII) for reforms.

1879 (February 22). A constitution is framed for the new Bulgarian state, under Russian auspices.

1879 (April 29). Alexander of Battenberg is elected Prince. Alexander I, Prince of Bulgaria (1879-1886).

1880 In Bitolia, southwestern Macedonia, the first Bulgarian Pro-Gymnasium (junior high school) is founded.

1881 In Salonika, the first Bulgarian Gymnasium (high school) for boys is opened for class work.

1884 A Bulgarian seminary is opened in Prilep, Macedonia.

1885 Union of Eastern Rumelia with the Principality of Bulgaria.

1885 (November 13). Serbia declares war on Bulgaria. Serbia is defeated at the battle of Slivnitsa.

1887-1918 Prince Ferdinand I.

1893 Formation of the Internal Macedonian Revolutionary Organization (IMRO) to fight for an autonomous Macedonia.

1903 (August 2). The Ilinden insurrection in Macedonia.

1908 (October 5). Declaration of Bulgaria's independence by Ferdinand, who assumes the title *Tsar*.

1912 (March 13). Conclusion of the alliance with Serbia.

1912 (March 29). Treaty of Alliance with Greece.

1912 (October 17). Outbreak of the First Balkan War between Bulgaria, Serbia, and Greece on the one hand, and Turkey on the other.

1912 (May 30). Treaty of London, ending the First Balkan War.

1913 (June 29). Second Balkan War. Bulgaria is defeated by the combined forces of Serbia, Greece, Romania, and Turkey.

1913 (August 10). The Treaty of Bucharest, end of the Second Balkan War.

1915 (October 14). Bulgaria enters the First World War.

1918 (October 4). Abdication of Tsar Ferdinand.

1918 Boris III, son of Ferdinand, Tsar.

1919 (November 17). Peace Treaty of Neuilly.

1923 (October 6). Alexander Stamboliski, leader of the Peasant Party, becomes premier. On June 6, Stamboliski is overthrown.

1924 The IMRO is reorganized by Todor Alexandorff. The latter is killed on August 31.

1925 (April 16). Bomb outrage in Sofia Cathedral, killing 123 persons.

1926 (January 4). A cabinet by Andrea Lapcheff follows a more conciliatory policy.

1928 (July 7). Assassination of General Alexander Protogeroff.

1932 (February 8). Bulgaria denounces further reparations payments.

1934 (February 8). Conclusion of the Balkan Entente, without Bulgaria. The latter refuses to recognize the *status quo* established by the peace treaties.

1935 (January 22). Kimon Georgieff is forced out, and his place is taken by General Petko Zlateff, who is supported by the Tsar.

1936 The Military League is dissolved. Tsar Boris is in command of the situation.

1937 (January 24). Conclusion of the Pact of Friendship with Yugoslavia.

1938 (July 31). Agreement with Greece (acting for the Balkan Entente), recognizing Bulgaria's right to rearm.

1941 Bulgaria joins Hitler's Germany.

1944   The Soviet Union is in a state of war with Bulgaria.

1944   (September 8). The Soviet army crosses the Bulgaro-Romanian border and rapidly advances to the interior of Bulgaria. The latter's army concentrates in northeastern Bulgaria, does not resist the Soviet army.

1944   (September 8-9). Sofia is invaded by partisan units, who occupy the most important ministries and arrest the Council of Regency. A new government of the Fatherland Front is formed, with Kimon Georgieff as leader. Beginning of the "dictatorship of the proletariat."

1944   (October 28). Negotiations in Moscow between Bulgaria and the Soviet Union with representatives of the United States and England. By virtue of this agreement, Bulgaria is compelled to withdraw from occupied Yugoslav and Greek territories. The Bulgarian army is placed under the Soviet high command and participates in the war against Hitler's Germany on the Ukrainian front.

1946   (September 9). The establishment of the People's Republic of Bulgaria.

1947   Peace treaties are signed between the Big Four and the defeated Axis—Italy, Hungary, Romania, Bulgaria, and Finland. Of the five defeated nations, only Bulgaria is reasonably satisfied with the peace terms.

1955   Bulgaria is admitted to the United Nations.

1971   (May). A new constitution is adopted. It provides that the National Assembly, elected for four years, is the supreme organ of the government. The Assembly chooses a premier and a State Council, whose president is the head of the state.

BIBLIOGRAPHY

SOURCES

Treaties, Secret Conferences, Agreements, and Alliances over the Balkans

"Resume of The Secret Conference of Reichstadt of July 8, 1876," in Alfred F. Pribram, *The Secret Treaties of Austria-Hungary, 1879-1914,* II, 188-190.

"The Protocols of Conferences between the Plenipotentiaries of Great Britain, Austria-Hungary, France, Germany, Italy, Russia and Turkey for the re-establishment of peace between Turkey, Serbia and Montenegro and for the amelioration of the general situation in the East, Constantinople, December 23, 1876 to January 20, 1877," in Edward Herstlet (Editor), *The Map of Europe by Treaty,* IV, 2541-2545; 2563-2567.

"Preliminary Treaty of Peace between Russia and Turkey, signed at San Stefano, February 19 to March 3, 1878," in E. Herstlet, *The Map of Europe by Treaty,* IV, 2672-2696.

"Treaty between Great Britain, Austria-Hungary, France, Germany, Italy, Russia and Turkey for the settlement of the affairs of the East, signed at Berlin, July 13, 1878," in E. Herstlet, *The Map of Europe by Treaty,* IV, 2759-2799; 2697-2756.

"Treaty of Alliance between Austria-Hungary and Serbia, Belgrade, June 16-28, 1881," and "Personal Declaration of Prince Milan that he would carry out the Treaty without restriction," in A. F. Pribram, *The Secret Treaties of Austria-Hungary, 1879-1914,* I, 50-56.

"Treaty between Austria-Hungary and Serbia prolonging the Treaty of 1881, Belgrade, January 28 to February 9, 1889," and "Declaration of the Serbian Regents recognizing the Treaties of 1881 and 1889, Belgrade, March 7-9, 1889," in A. F. Pribram, *The Secret Treaties of Austria-Hungary,* I, 134-138.

"Dispatch from the Austrian government to the ambassador in St. Petersburg containing the Agreement reached between Austria-Hungary
and Russia in regard to the Balkan Agreement, St. Petersburg, May
5-17, 1897," in A. F. Pribram, *The Secret Treaties of Austria-Hungary*,
I, 184-190.

"A definite Treaty of Alliance and Friendship between Bulgaria and
Serbia, March 13, 1912," and "The secret annex attached to this
treaty," in I. E. Gueshoff, *The Balkan League*, p. 112, 117. The Bulgarian text is in Dr. V. Radoslavoff, *Bulgaria i Svetovnata Kriza*, 34-
35; the French text is W. M. Sloane, *The Balkans: A Laboratory of
History*, Appendix.

"Treaty of Peace between Greece, Bulgaria, Montenegro and Serbia on
the one part and Turkey on the other part, London, May 30, 1913,"
in Sir A. Oakes and R. B. Mowat, *The Great European Treaties of
the Nineteenth Century*, 361-362.

"Treaty of Peace between Romania, Greece, Montenegro, Serbia and
Bulgaria, Bucharest, August 10, 1913," in Oakes and Mowat, *The
Great European Treaties of the Nineteenth Century*, 362-366.

"Treaty of Peace between the allied and associated powers and Bulgaria,
signed at Neuilly-sur-Seine, November 27, 1919," in the British Insti-
tute of International Affairs, *The History of the Peace Conference in
Paris*, V, 39-57 for an analysis and 327-330 for the text. See also the
Convention between Greece and Bulgaria in *League of Nations
Treaty Series*, I, No. 1, p. 68.

Other Documents

British Documents on the Origin of the War, 1898-1914, 7 Vols., London,
1928 (G. P. Gooch and Harold Temperley, Editors). See particularly
The Macedonian Problem and the Annexation of Bosnia, 1903-1909,
V and I, Chapter VIII, Part II.

*Documents Diplomatic Affairs d'Orient, Congre de Berlin, 1878; Affairs
de Macédoine, 1903-1905*, Paris, 1905.

Makedonia i Odrinsko (1893-1903)—Memoar na Votreshnata Organizatsia
(Macedonia and the Adrianople Region—Memoirs of the Internal
Macedonian Revolutionary Organization—IMRO), Sofia, 1904.

*Report of The International Commission to Inquire into the Causes and
Conduct of the Balkan Wars*. Carnegie Endowment for International
Peace, Washington, D.C., 1914.

*The Accusation Against Bulgaria—Official Documents Presented to the
Peace Conference in 1919* by the Bulgarian delegation.

The English Blue Book for the years 1876, 1877, and 1878.

OTHER PRIMARY MATERIALS

Beltcheff, G., *La Bulgarie et ses Voisins: Faits et Documents, 1870-1915,* Sofia, 1919.

Chertcheff, C. H., *Aveux Serbes sur la Macedoine,* Sofia, 1919.

Derjavin, N. S., *Les Rapports Bulgaro-Serbes et la Question Macedonienne,* Lausanne, 1918.

Disraeli, Benjamin (Lord Beaconsfield), "Peace With Honour," in *Modern Eloquence,* I, 21-29.

Documents and Materials on the History of the Bulgarian People (Published by the Bulgarian Academy of Sciences), Sofia, 1969.

Draganoff, M., *Macedonia and the Reforms,* London, 1908.

Gabrys, J., *Carte Ethnographique de l'Europe,* Lausanne, 1918.

Gansolphe, M., *La Crise Macédoine, Enquête dans les Vilayets Insurges,* Paris, 1904.

Gueshoff, I. E., *The Balkan League,* London, 1915.

Ivanoff, Iordan, *Bulgarite v Makedonia, so dokoumenti po potekloto, ezika i narodnosta na Makedonskite Slaviani, so ethnographicheska karta i statistiki* (The Bulgarians in Macedonia, Documents on the Origin, Language and Nationality of the Macedonian Slavs—An Ethnographic Map and Statistics), Sofia, 1925.

Mishew, D. (Pseudonym—D. M. Brancoff), *La Macédoine et sa population Chretienne* (avec deux cartes ethnographique), Paris, 1905.

Miletich, Professor L., *Makedonia i Makedonskite Bulgari; Koultouro-Istoricheski Pogled* (Macedonia and the Macedonian Bulgarians; A Cultural-Historical Study), Sofia, 1925.

Miletich, Professor L., *Dokoumenti iz 1912-1913 godina za Deystviata na Serbski i Gertski Vlasti v Makedonia* (Documents from 1912-1913 About the Activity of the Serbian and Greek Authorities in Macedonia), Sofia, 1914.

WORKS IN ENGLISH

Abbott, G. F., *The Tale of a Tour in Macedonia,* London, 1903.

————, *Turkey in Transition,* London, 1909.

Anastasoff, Christ, *The Tragic Peninsula,* St. Louis, Missouri, 1938.

————, *The Case for an Autonomous Macedonia* (Editor), St. Louis, Missouri, 1945.

Ashmead-Bartlett, Ellis, *With the Turks in Thrace,* New York, 1913.

Bailey, William F., *The Slavs of the War Zone,* London, 1917.

Baker, Bernard G., *The Passing of the Turkish Empire in Europe*, London, 1913.

Barker, Elisabeth, *Macedonia: Its Place in Balkan Power Politics*, London, 1950.

Barkley, H. C., *Between the Danube and Black Sea: Or Years in Bulgaria*, London, 1876.

Bell, H. T. M. (Editor), *Near East Year Book*, London, 1931.

Berard, V., *Pro-Macedonia*, Paris, 1904.

Black, Professor E. E., *The Establishment of Constitutional Government in Bulgaria* (Princeton University Press), Princeton, New Jersey, 1943.

Brailsford, N. H., *Macedonia: Its Races and Their Future*, London, 1906.

Bury, Professor J. M., *The History of the Eastern Roman Empire*, London, 1912.

Buxton, C. R., *Turkey in Revolution*, London, 1909.

Buxton, Noel E., *With the Balkan Staff*, London, 1913.

_____, *The War and the Balkans*, London, 1915.

_____ and Leonard, L. C., *Balkan Problems and European Peace*, New York, 1919.

Campbell, Cyril, *The Balkan War Drama*, New York, 1913.

Cernovodeanu, Paul, *England's Trade Policy in the Levant 1660-1714*, Bucharest, 1972.

Chekrezi, C., *Albania Past and Present*, New York, 1919.

Cheradame, André, *The Pangerman Plot Unmasked*, New York, 1917.

Christowe, Stoyan, *Heros and Assassins*, New York, 1935.

Clark, E. L., *Turkey*, New York, 1900.

Dolapchiev, Professor Nicola, *Bulgaria: The Making of a Satellite* (Analysis of the historical developments 1944-1953), Foyer Bulgare, 1971.

Dominican, Leon, *The Frontier of Language and Nationality in Europe*, New York, 1917.

Doolard, A. D., *Express to the East*, New York, 1935.

Durham, Mary Edith, *The Burden of the Balkans*, London, 1905.

Eliot, Sir Charles, *Turkey in Europe*, London, 1908.

Eversley, Lord, *The Turkish Empire—Its Growth and Decay*, New York, 1917.

Evtimoff, Simeon, *An Open Wound in the Heart of the Balkans: Macedonia and Her Claims*, Geneva, 1928.

Flanders, W. Howard, *Balkania: A Short History of the Balkan States*, London, 1909.

Forbes, N., *The Balkans—A History of Bulgaria, Serbia, Greece, Romania and Turkey*, New York, 1919.

Fox, Frank, *Bulgaria*, London, 1917.

Freeman, Edward A., *Historical Geography of Europe, 1881*, Edited by E. B. Bury, London, 1903.

Fyffe, C. F., *History of Modern Europe*, New York, 1887.

Gallenga, A., *Two Years of the Eastern Question*, 2 Vols., London, 1877.

Gawenda, Dr. J. A. B., *The Soviet Domination of Eastern Europe in the Light of International Law*, London, 1974.

Georgiev, Professor Emil, *et al.*, *Bulgaria's Share in Human Culture*, Sofia Press, 1968.

Geshkoff, Theodore Iv., *Balkan Union: A Road to Peace in Southeastern Europe* (Columbia University Press), New York, 1940.

Gibbons, H. A., *The New Map of Europe*, New York, 1914.

————, *The Foundation of the Ottoman Empire*, New York, 1916.

Gibbs, Philip and Bernard, Grant, *The Balkan War: Adventures of War with Cross and Crescent*, Boston, 1913.

Gladstone, W. E., *Bulgarian Horrors and the Question of the East*, London 1876.

————, *Lessons in Massacre*, London, 1878.

Gooch, G. P., *History of Our Time*, London, 1911.

Green, Francis V., *The Campaign in Bulgaria, 1877-1878*, London, 1903.

Grogan, Lady, *The Life of J. D. Bourchier*, London, 1927.

Halpen, Joel M., and Halpen, Barbara K., *A Serbian Village in Historical Perspective*, New York, 1972.

Harris, David, *Britain and the Bulgarian Horrors of 1876* (University of Chicago Press), Chicago, 1939.

Hogarth, D. G., *The Near East*, London, 1905.

Holland, T. E., *The European Concert and the Eastern Question*, Oxford, 1885.

Keppel, Major F. S. A., *A Journey Across the Balkans*, London, 1833.

Knight, E. F., *The Awakening of Turkey*, London, 1909.

Laveleye, E. L. V. de, *The Balkan Peninsula* (with a letter from W. E. Gladstone), New York, 1887.

Lybyer, Professor Albert H., *Macedonia at the Peace Conference, 1919* (Published by the Central Committee of the Macedonian Patriotic Organization of the United States and Canada), Indianapolis, 1944.

MacDermott, Mercia, *A History of Bulgaria 1393-1885*, London, 1962.

————, *The Apostle of Freedom* (A portrait of Vasil Levsky against a background of nineteenth-century Bulgaria), London, 1967.

Macdonald, John, *Czar Ferdinand and His People*, New York, 1913.

————, *Turkey and the Eastern Question*, London, 1912.

MacGahan, J. R., *The Turkish Atrocities in Bulgaria, Letters of the Special Commissioner of the "Daily News," J. A. MacGahan, Esq., with an Introduction and Mr. Schuyler's Preliminary Report*, London, 1876.

Mach, R. Von, *The Bulgarian Exarchate: Its History and the Extent of its Authority in Turkey*, London, 1907.

Mackenzie and Irby, *Travels in the Slavonic Province of Turkey in Europe*, 2 Vols., London, 1877.

Markham, R. H., *Meet Bulgaria*, Sofia, 1931.

Marriott, J. A. R., *The Eastern Question: A Historical Study of European Diplomacy*, Oxford, 1917.

Mason, D. M., *Macedonia and Great Britain's Responsibility*, London, 1903.

Miller, Marshall Lee, *Bulgaria During the Second World War*, Stanford University Press, 1975.

Miller, William, *The Balkans: Romania, Bulgaria, Serbia and Montenegro*, New York, 1907.

———, *The Ottoman Empire (1801-1913)*, Cambridge, 1913.

Monroe, W. S., *Bulgaria and Her People: With an Account of the Balkan Wars, Macedonia and the Macedonian Bulgars*, Boston, 1914.

Mowrer, Paul S., *Balkanized Europe*, London, 1921.

Muir, Edwin and Willa, *Night Over the East*, New York, 1936.

Newbigin, Marion I., *Geographical Aspect of Balkan Problems*, New York, 1919.

Nicoloff, Professor Assen, *Bulgarian Folklore and Fine Literature* (A Selected Bio-Bibliography), Cleveland, Ohio, 1971.

———, *Bulgarian Folklore—Folk Beliefs, Customs, Folksongs, Personal Names*, Cleveland, Ohio, 1974.

———, *Samuel's Bulgaria* (Published by the author), Cleveland, Ohio, 1969.

Oakes, Sir A. and Mowat, R. B., *The Great European Treaties of the Nineteenth Century*, Oxford, 1918.

Padev, Michael, *Escape from the Balkans*, New York, 1943.

Panaretoff, Stephan, *Near Eastern Affairs and Conditions*, New York, 1922.

Pears, Sir Edwin, *Destruction of the Greek Empire*, London, 1903.

———, *Fifty Years in Constantinople*, New York, 1916.

———, *Turkey and Its People*, London, 1911.

Pozzi, Henri, *Black Hand Over Europe*, London, 1935.

Pribichevich, Stoyan, *World Without End*, New York, 1939.

Pribram, Alfred F., *The Secret Treaties of Austria-Hungary, 1879-1914*, 2 Vols., Cambridge, 1926.

Rothschild, J., *The Communist Party of Bulgaria—Origin and Development (1883-1936)*, New York, 1959.

Runciman, S., *A History of the First Bulgarian Empire*, London, 1930.

Savič, Vladislav R., *Southeastern Europe*, New York, 1918.

Schevill, F., *The History of the Balkan Peninsula—From the Earliest Times to the Present Day*, New York, 1922.

———, *The Balkan Problem: Its Difficulties and Their Solution*, Chicago, 1931.

Seton-Watson, R. W., *The Rise of Nationality in the Balkans*, London, 1917.

———, *Disraeli, Gladstone and the Eastern Question: A Study in Diplomacy and Party Politics*, London, 1935.

Shaoulov, L., *The Bulgarian Theatre*, Sofia, 1964.
Singleton, E., *Turkey and the Balkan States*, New York, 1908.
Sipkov, Dr. Ivan, *Legal Sources and Bibliography of Bulgaria*, New York, 1956.
Sloane, W. M., *The Balkans: A Laboratory of History*, New York, 1914.
Smith, A. D. H., *Fighting the Turks in the Balkans*, New York, 1906.
Sonnichsen, Albert, *Confession of a Macedonian Bandit*, New York, 1909.
Stavrianos, L. S., *The Balkans Since 1453*, New York, 1958.
————, *The Balkans 1815-1914*, New York, 1963.
————, *Balkan Federation—A History of the Movement Toward Balkan Unity in Modern Times*, Hamden, Connecticut, 1964.
Stephanove, Constantine, *The Bulgarians and Anglo-Saxondom*, Berne, 1919.
Strangford, Lord, *The Eastern Shores of the Adriatic*, London, 1864.
Talev, Dimiter, *The Iron Candlestick*, Sofia, 1964.
————, *Ilinden* (A Novel of the Macedonian Uprising of 1903), Sofia, 1966.
————, *The Bells of Prespa*, Sofia, 1966.
Taylor, A. J. P., *A History of the First World War*, New York, 1966.
Toynbee, Arnold, *Nationality and the War*, London, 1917.
Tsanoff, Professor Radoslav and Corrine Radoslav, *Pawns of Liberty—A Balkan Tale of Yesterday*, New York, 1914.
Urqhart, David, *The Spirit of the East*, London, 1838.
Vallari, L. (Editor), *The Balkan Question: The Present Conditions of the Balkans*, London, 1904.
————, *The Balkan Question*, London, 1905.
Vazov, Ivan, *Under the Yoke*, Sofia, 1960.
Wagner, Hermenegild, *With the Victorious Bulgarians*, Boston, 1913.
Walker, M. A., *Through Macedonia*, London, 1864.
Walsh, Robert, *Travels in Turkey and Constantinople*, Paris, 1882.
Walpole, R. *Travels in Turkey*, London, 1820.
Washburn G., *Fifty Years in Constantinople*, Boston, 1909.
Wilkinson, Professor H. R., *Map and Politics—A Review of the Ethnographic Cartography of Macedonia*, Liverpool, 1951.
Wyon, R., *The Balkans from Within*, London, 1904.
Young, George, *Nationalism and War in the Near East*, London, 1915.

WORKS IN BULGARIAN

Angelov, Professor Dimiter, *Obrazouvane na Bulgarskata Narodnost* (The Formation of the Bulgarian Nationality), Sofia, 1971.
Arnaoudov, Professor Mihail, *Dela i Zaveti na Belezhiti Bulgari* (Deeds and Bequests of Notable Bulgarians), Sofia, 1969.

364   Bibliography

————, *Ochertsi po Bulgarskia Folklor* (Sketches from Bulgarian Folklore), 2 Vols., Sofia, 1968.

————, *Verkovich i Veda Slovena—Prinos kum istoriata na Bulgarskia
folklor i na Bulgarskoto vuzrazhdane v Makedonia—1855-1893* (Contribution to the History of the Bulgarian Folklore and the Bulgarian
Renaissance in Macedonia—1855-1893), Publication of the Bulgarian
Academy of Sciences, Sofia, 1968.

Baltev, Dimiter, *Georgi Kolarov—Monographichen Ocherk* (Georgi
Kolarov—A Monographic Sketch), Sofia, 1973.

Blagoeff, Dimiter, *Ikonomicheskoto Razvitie na Bulgaria* (The Economic
Development of Bulgaria), Varna, 1903.

Bogdanov, Ivan, *Kliment Ohridski* (Clement of Ohrid), Sofia, 1967.

Boteff, Hristo, *Sochineniata na Hristo Boteff* (The Works of Hristo
Boteff), Sofia, 1907.

Brzitsov, Hristo, *Vo Prilepa Grada* (In the City of Prilep), Varna, 1969.

Derjavin, N. S., *Bulgaro-Serbskite Vzaimni Otnoshenia i Makedonskia
Vopros* (Bulgaro-Serbian Mutual Relations and the Macedonian
Question), Sofia, 1916.

Djeroff, N., *Na Youg* (On to the South), Sofia, 1928.

Donchev, Anton, *Vreme Razdelno—Istoricheski Roman* (Parting Time—
A Historical Novel), Plovdiv, 1968.

Georghoff, Iv. A., *Dneshnoto Polojenie vo Makedonia pod Serbska i
Grtska Vlast i Obshtestvoto no Narodite* (The Present Situation in
Macedonia Under Serbian and Greek Rule and the League Of
Nations), Sofia, 1925.

Haitov, Nikola, *Haiduti* (Outlaws), Sofia, 1968.

————, *Kapitan Petko Voyvoda* (Chief Captain Petko), Varna, 1974.

Hristov, Professor Hristo, *Osvobojdenieto na Bulgaria i Politicata na
Zapadnite Drzhavi, 1876-1878* (The Liberation of Bulgaria and the
Policy of the Western European Powers, 1876-1878), Sofia, 1968.

Ilinden, 1903-1926, Sbornik vo Pamet na Golemoto Makedonsko Bostanie
(Miscellany in Memory of the Great Macedonian Insurrection),
Sofia, 1926.

Ilindenskoto-Preobrazhensko Vostanie 1903 (The Ilinden-Preobrazhensko
Uprising of 1903), Sofia, 1968.

Istoria na Serbsko-Bulgarskata Voyna 1885 (History of the Serbo-Bulgarian War of 1885), published by the Ministry of National Defence,
Sofia, 1971.

Ivanov, Yordan N., *Bulgarski Dialecten Atlas—Bulgarski Govori ot
Egeiska Makedonia* (Bulgarian Dialectical Atlas—Bulgarian Dialects
in Aegean Macedonia), published by the Bulgarian Academy of
Sciences, Vol. I, Sofia, 1972.

Izvori za Bulgarskata Istoria (Sources for the History of Bulgaria), published by the Bulgarian Academy of Sciences, Vol. XVI, Sofia, 1971.

Karalichev, Angel, *Prikazen Sviat* (Fabulous World), 2 Vols., Sofia, 1974.

Karanphilov, Ephrem, *Bulgari* (Bulgarians), Sofia, 1968.

Karavelov, Luben, *Raskazi, Povesti, Memoari* (Short Stories, Narratives, and Memoirs), Sofia, 1973.

Katsaroff, Dr. Gavril, *Tsar Philip II Makedonski—Istoria na Makedonia do 336 godini pr. Hrista* (King Philip II of Macedonia—History of Macedonia Until 336 B.C.), Sofia, 1922.

Kaufman, Nikolai, *Bulgarski Gradski Pesni* (Bulgarian Urban Songs), Sofia, 1968.

Klement of Ohrid, *Sobrani Suchinenia* (Collected Works), Vol. I, Sofia, 1970.

Klincharov, I. G., *Diado Blagoeff—Biographia* (Biography of Grandpa Blagoeff), Sofia, 1926.

Konstantinov Aleko, *Suchinenia v Dva Toma* (Select Works in 2 Vols.), Sofia, 1974.

Konstantinov, Evgeni, *Han Asparouh* (Khan Asparouh), Sofia Press, 1965.

Kosev, D., *et al., Kratka Istoria na Bulgaria* (A Brief History of Bulgaria), Sofia, 1969.

Kunchev, Vasil, *Izbrani Proizvedenia* (Select Works), 2 Vols., Sofia, 1970.

Kyril, Bulgarian Patriarch (1953-1971), *Bulgarskata Exarhia v Odrinsko i Makedonia Sled Osvoboditelnata Voyna (1877-1878)* (The Bulgarian Exarchate in Thrace And Macedonia After the War of Liberation—1877-1878), 2 Vols., Sofia, 1970.

Mitev, Simeon, *et al.* (Editors), *Belezhiti Bulgari,* 1396-1878 (Notable Bulgarians), 7 Vols., Sofia, 1969.

Patnev, Andrey, *Anglia Streshtou Russia na Balkanite, 1879-1894* (England Versus Russia in the Balkans, 1879-1894), Sofia, 1972.

Pastouhoff, Iv. and Stoyan, Iv., *Istoria na Bulgarskia Narod* (History of the Bulgarian People), Plovdiv, 1925.

Popoff, Iv. S., *Bulgarska Istoria* (Bulgarian History), Sofia, 1920.

Radeff, Simeon, *Stroitelite na Suvremena Bulgaria* (The Builders of Contemporary Bulgaria), 2 Vols., Sofia, 1911.

————, *Ranni Spomeni* (Early Memoirs), Sofia, 1969.

————, *Makedonia i Bulgarskoto Vozrajdane vo XIX vek* (Macedonia and the Bulgarian Renaissance in the Nineteenth Century), Sofia, 1927.

Radoslavoff, Dr. Vasil, *Bulgaria i Svetovnata Kriza* (Bulgaria and the World Crisis), Sofia, 1923.

Sakuzoff, Yanko, *Bulgarite vo Svoyata Istoria* (The Bulgarians in their History), Sofia, 1922.

Shatev, Pavel, *V Makedonia Pod Robstvo—Solounskoto Suzaklatie (1903) Podgotovka i Izpulnenie* (In Macedonia Under Bondage—The

Salonika Conspiracy of 1903, Its Preparation and Execution), Sofia, 1968.

Silianoff, Hristo, *Osvoboditelnite Borbi na Makedonia* (The Liberation Struggles of Macedonia), Vol. I, Sofia, 1933.

————, *Pisma i Ispovedi na Edin Chetnik* (Letters and Confessions of a Revolutionist), Sofia, 1967.

Slaveykov, Pencho, *Stihotvorenia* (Poems), Sofia, 1966.

Solaroff, K., *Bulgaria i Makedonskia Vopros—Prichinite na Balkanskite Voyni* (Bulgaria and the Macedonian Question—The causes of the Balkan Wars), Sofia, 1925.

————, *Balkanskiat Soyouz i Osvoboditelnite Voyni Pres 1912-1913 g.* (The Balkan Alliance and the Wars Of Liberation During 1912-1913), Sofia, 1926.

Stoyanoff, Zahari, *Zapiski po Bulgarskite Vostania* (Notes About the Bulgarian Revolts), Sofia, 1962.

Talev, Dimiter, *Samuel—Tsar Bulgarski* (Samuel, King of the Bulgarians), a historical novel dealing with the First Bulgarian State, in 3 Vols., Sofia, 1968.

————, *Glasovete vi Chouvam* (I Hear Your Voices), a novel, Sofia, 1969.

————, *Khilinderskia Monah—Suchinenia Tom Deseti* (The Monk of Khilinder Monastery, Vol. X), Sofia, 1975.

Tatarcheff, Dr. Hristo, *Purvia Tsentralen Comitet na IMRO* (The First Central Committee of the Internal Macedonian Revolutionary Organization), Sofia, 1925.

Tomalevski, Georgi, *Doushata na Makedonia* (The Spirit of Macedonia), Sofia, 1924.

————, *Ognena Zemia* (The Land of Flames), Sofia, 1928.

————, *Kroushovskata Repoublika 1903* (The Kroushevo Republic of 1903), Sofia, 1968.

Tosheff, A., *Balkanskite Voyni* (The Balkan Wars), Vol. I, 1929; Vol. II, 1931, Sofia, 1931.

Toshev, Dr. Svetozar, *Po Kurvavia Put* (By the Bloody Way), Plovdiv, 1969.

Traikov, N., *Bratia Miladinovi* (The Miladinoff Brothers), published by the Bulgarian Academy of Sciences, Sofia, 1964.

Uzounov, Gavril, *Potomtsi—Houdozhestvena Letopis* (Descendants—Annals of the Work of Art), Sofia, 1969.

Vazov, Ivan, *Rodna Literatoura, XXII And XXIII, Pod Igoto* (Native Literature, Under the Yoke), Sofia 1925.

————, *Nemili Nedragi* (The Outcast), Sofia, 1965.

————, *Izbavlenie Otbrani Tvorbi* (Deliverance—Select Works), Sofia, 1968.

Verkovich, Stefan I., *Narodni Pesni na Makedonskite Bulgari* (National Songs of the Macedonian Bulgarians), Sofia, 1966.

Zagorchinov, Stoyan, *Izbrani Proizvedenia Vol. II—Ivaylo* (Select Works —Ivaylo), Sofia, 1969.

Zaimov, Jordan and Zaimova, Vasilka, *Bitolski Nadpis na Ivan Vladislav Samodrzhets Bulgarski—Starobulgarski Pametnik ot 1015-1016 godina* (The Bitolia Inscription of Ivan Vladislav, the Bulgarian Autocrat— An Old Bulgarian Monument 1015-1016), Sofia, 1970.

Zhinziphov, Rayko, *Poublisistika* (Political Journalism), 2 Vols., Sofia, 1964.

Zlatarski, Professor Vasil N., *Istoria na Bulgarskata Durzhava Prez Srednite Vekove* (History of the Bulgarian State in the Middle Ages), Sofia, 1971.

WORKS IN FRENCH

Avril, A., *St. Cyrille et Méthode*, Paris, 1885.

————, *En Macédoine*, Paris, 1897.

————, *Tableau Comparatif des Ecoles Hellénique et Bulgares*, Constantinople, 1902.

Berard, V., *La Macédoine, le pays et les races*, Paris, 1897.

————, *La Turquie et L'Hellénisme Contemporain, La Macédoine: la lutte des races*, Paris, 1897.

————, *La Révolution Turque*, Paris, 1909.

Boue, A., *Recueil d'intinéraires dans la Turquie d'Europe*, Vienna, 1854.

Bousquet, Georges, *Histoire du Peuple Bulgare depuis les origines jusqu à nos jours*, Paris, 1909.

Brailsford, N. H., *La Population de la Macédoine*, Sofia, 1919.

Cazot, E. *Régéneration d'un peuple, la Macédoine Catholique*, Paris, 1901.

Cheradame, A., *La Question d'Orient*, Paris, 1903.

Consinery, E. V., *Voyage dans la Macédoine*, Paris, 1831.

Dami, Professor Aldo, *Fatalités Bulgares*, Genève, 1944.

de Balogh, Arthur, *La Protection des Minorités*, Paris, 1930.

de Gerando, F., *L'Incident Gréc-Bulgare, 1925*, Sofia, 1926.

————, *La Macédoine, Problème Européen*, Paris, 1927.

de Launey, L., *La Bulgarie d'hier et de demain*, Paris, 1922.

Delvigne, Auguste, *La Problème Macédonienne*, Berne, 1919.

Desbons, G., *La Bulgarie après le traité de Neuilly*, Paris, 1930.

Driauet, E., *La Question d'Orient*, Paris, 1918.

Engelhardt, E., *La Question Macédonienne*, Paris, 1906.

Espagnat, Pierre, *Avant le Massacre*, Paris, 1902.

Eveldipi, C., *Les Etats Balkanique* (Etude comparée politique, sociale, économique et financière, Paris, 1930.

Filoff, B., *L'ancien art en Bulgarie*, Berne, 1919.

Florinski, T. D., *Les Slavs du Sud*, Petrograd (Leningrad), 1882.

Guerin, Longeron, R. P., *Histoire de la Bulgarie depuis les Origines jusqu à nos jours, 1485-1913*, Paris, 1914.

Hybl, F., *Histoire du Peuple Bulgare*, Prague, 1930.

Iorga, N., *Histoire des Etats Balkanique*, Paris, 1925.

Ischirkoff, A., *Les confins occidentaux des Terres Bulgares*, Lausanne, 1916.

————, *La Macédoine et la constitution de l'Exarchat Bulgare, 1830-1897*, Lausanne, 1918.

Ivanoff, Iordan, *Bulgars et Grecs*, Berne, 1918.

————, *Les Bulgares devant le Congrès de la paix*, Paris, 1919.

————, *La Question Macédonienne*, Paris, 1920.

Kanitz, F., *La Bulgarie danubienne et les Balkans*, Paris, 1882.

Karadjitch, Vouk, *Chansons populaires bulgares de la Macédoine, 1815-1822*.

Krainikowsky, Dr. Assen I., *La Question de Macédoine et la Diplomatic Européenne*, Paris, 1938.

Kristich, D., *Les Minorités, l'Etat et la communanté Internationale*, Paris, 1924.

Kupfer, Professor E., *La Macédoine et les Bulgares*, Lausanne, 1918.

Lamouche, Colonel L., *La Bulgarie dans le passé et le présent*, Paris, 1892.

————, *La Péninsule Balkanique*, Paris, 1899.

————, *La Bulgarie*, Paris, 1923.

————, *Quinze Ans d'Histoire Balkanique, 1904-1918*, Paris, 1928.

————, *Les Bulgares en Macédoine, dans les confins occidentaux et en Thrace*, Paris, 1931.

Lavelaye, E., *La Péninsule des Balkans*, Bruxelles, 1888.

Leger, L., *Le Paléoslave*, Paris, 1868.

————, *La Monde Slave*, Paris, 1882.

————, *Les Revendications des Bulgares de Macédoine*, Lausanne, 1885.

————, *Turcs et Grecs contre Bulgares en Macédoine*, Paris, 1904.

Leger, Louis, *Serbs, Croats et Bulgares: études historiques, politique et litteraires*, Paris, 1913.

Lepide, Ghele, *La Macédoine Indivisible*, Lausanne, 1918.

Mazon, A., *Contes Slaves*, Strassbourg, 1923.

Micheff, D., et Petkoff, B., *La Fédération Balkanique*, Sofia, 1930.

Michoff, N. V., *La population de la Bulgarie et de la Turquie aux XVIIIe et XIXe siècles*, Sofia, 1915.

Miletich, L., *Atrocites Greques en Macédoine Pendant la Guerre Greco-Bulgare*, Sofia, 1913.

Mintschew, I. M., *La Serbie et le Mouvement National Bulgare*, Berne, 1917.

Mishew (Misheff), D., *Peuples opprimés et oppresseurs. A propos d'un discours de M. Louis Barton*, Sofia, 1915.

————, *La Serbie et la Bulgarie devant l'Opinion Publique*, Berne, 1918.

Monasteres Bulgares (published by the Committee for Tourism at the Council of Ministers of the People's Republic of Bulgaria), Sofia, 1965.

Moulin, Rene, *Une année de politique extérieure*, Paris, 1905.

Muzet, A., *La Monde Balkanique*, Paris, 1917.

Niederle, L., *La Race Slave*, Paris, 1911.

Non-diplomate, *La Question des reformes dans la Turquie d'Europe*, Paris, 1903.

Papahagi, N., *Les Roumains de Turquie*, Bucharest, 1905.

Parlitcheff, C., *La Régime Serbe et la Lutte Révolutionair en Macédoine*, Sofia, 1917.

————, *Les Atrocités en Macédoine, 1912-1915*, Sofia, 1919.

Peneff, Meryan, *Le Chauvinisme Serbe*, Berne, 1916.

Pernot, M., *Balkans Nouveaux*, Paris, 1929.

Pinon, R., *La Question de Macédoine*, Paris, 1917.

Pittard, E., *Les Peuples des Balkans*, Genève, 1920.

Radeff, S., *La Macédoine et la Renaissance Bulgare au XIXᵉ siècle*, Sofia, 1918.

Rappaport, Alfred, *Au Pays des Martyrs en Macédoine*, Paris, 1927.

Rindoff, C. H., *Les Etats-Unis des Balkans*, Paris, 1930.

Rizel, P., *La ville convoitée Salonique*, Paris, 1917.

Rolley, P., et Visme, *La Macédoine et l'Epire*, Paris, 1919.

Routier, G., *La Macédoine et les Puissance*, Paris, 1904.

Safařik, P. G., *Ethnographie slave*, Prague, 1849.

Schlumberger, G., *L'Europe Byzantine à la fin du Xᵉ siècle*, Paris, 1900.

Skopiansky, M., *La Macédoine telle qu'elle est*, Berne, 1918.

Solaroff, K., *La Bulgarie et la Question Macédonienne*, Sofia, 1919.

Songeon, G., *Historie des Bulgares*, Paris, 1913.

Tibal, A., *Le Problème de minorités*, Paris, 1929.

Verkovitch, S., *Recueil de chansons populaires des Bulgares Macédoniens*, Belgrade, 1860.

Verdene, G., *La Verité sur la Question Macédonienne*, Paris, 1905.

Warfbain, A., *L'Echange greco-bulgare des Minorités ethnique*, Paris, 1930.

Yaranoff, D., *La Macédoine Economique*, Sofia, 1930.

Yossouf, Fehmi, *Historie de la Turquie*, Paris 1909.

WORKS IN GERMAN

Baschadaroff, G., *Die Makedonische Frage*, Wien, 1925.

Clumecky, Leopold F. V., *Osterreich-Ungarn und Italien, das Westbalkanische Problem*, Wien, 1902.

Derjavin, N. S., *Makedonien*, Leipzig, 1918.

Gersin, K., *Makedonien und das Turkische Problem*, Wien, 1903.

Hahn, J. G., *Reise von Belgrad nach Salonik*, Wien, 1861.

Horn, K., *Das Volkstum der Slawen Makedoniens*, Wien, 1890.

Hubka, G., *Die Osterreichisch-Ungarische Offiziersmission in Makedonien 1903-1909*, Wien, 1910.

Jireček, C., *Geschichte der Bulgaren*, Prague, 1878.

Kosev, D., Hristov, Hr., and Angelov, D. *Bulgarische Geschichte*, Sofia, 1963.

Mach, R. V., *Die Makedonische Frage*, Wien, 1895.

————, *Beitrage zur Ethnographie der Balkanhalbinsel* (Petermanns Milleilungen), Wien, 1899.

————, *Der Machtbereich der Bulgarischen Exarchat in der Turkei*, Leipzig, 1906.

Milyukoff, Professor P. N., *Uber Makedonien*, Leipzig, 1918.

Ognjanoff, Dr. Christo, *Bulgarien*, Nürnberg, 1967.

Rappaport, Alfred, *Mazedonien und die Komitadsche*, Berlin 1930.

Schacher G., *Der Balkan und seine Wirtschaftlichen Krafte*, Stuttgart, 1930.

Schacht, Phil, H. H., *Die Makedonische Frage um die Jahrhundertwende*, Halle, 1930.

Sis, V., *Mazendonien*, Zurich, 1918.

Weingand, G., *Die Nationalen Bestrebungen der Balkanvolker*, Leipzig, 1898.

————, *Uber Mazedonien*, Leipzig, 1918.

————, *Ethnographie von Makedonien*, Leipzig, 1924.

WORKS IN RUSSIAN

Derjavin, Professor N. S., *Bogarsko-Serbskia Vzaimnootnoshenia i Makedonskii Vopros*, Petrograd, 1914.

Florinski, T., *Lektsi po Slavianskomou Iazikoznaniou*, Petrograd, 1895.

Gilferding, A., *Sobranie Sochinenii*, Petrograd, 1873.

Kondakoff, Professor N. P., *Makedonia*, Petrograd, 1909.

Koulbakin, S. M., *Drevnetserkovno Slavianski Iazik*, Kracow, 1912.

Lavrob, Professor P. A., *Obzor zvoukovih i formalniah osobennostii bolgarskago iazik*, Moscow, 1893.

Selishtev, A. M., *Vovedenie vo Stravnitelnoi Grammatike Slavianskih Iazikov*, Kazan, 1914.

Verkovitch, S. I., *Opisanio biata Makedonskih bolgar*, Moscow, 1868.

———, *Topographicheski-Ethnographicheski Otcherk Makedonii*, Petrograd, 1889.

WORKS IN BOHEMIAN

Niederle, L., *Slovanske Starozitnosti*, v Praze, 1906.

———, *Makedonska Otazka*, Praha, 1909.

Safařik, P. G., *Sebrane Spisy*, Praha, 1863.

Sis, V., *Makedonio*, Praha, 1914.

———, *Spor o Makedonii*, v Praze, 1916.

———, *Novy Balkan*, Praha, 1924.

PERIODICALS

Balkania Quarterly Magazine, St. Louis, Missouri, Vols. I to VII (1967-1973)—Published and Edited by Christ Anastasoff.

Fortnightly Review, London, April 1891.

Fortnightly Review, London, October 1893.

Fortnightly Review, London, October 1917.

London Geographical Magazine, Vol. III, 1876.

McClure's Magazine, Vol. XIX, May to October 1902 issues.

The Quarterly Review, London, Vol. 220, April 1914.

Westminster Review, London, Vol. CXLVI, 481-490.

INDEX